UNDERSTANDING SCHOLASTIC THOUGHT WITH FOUCAULT

THE NEW MIDDLE AGES

BONNIE WHEELER
Series Editor

The New Middle Ages presents transdisciplinary studies of medieval cultures. It includes both scholarly monographs and essay collections.

PUBLISHED BY ST. MARTIN'S PRESS:

Women in the Medieval Islamic World: Power, Patronage, and Piety
edited by Gavin R. G. Hambly

The Ethics of Nature in the Middle Ages: On Boccaccio's Poetaphysics
by Gregory B. Stone

Presence and Presentation: Women in the Chinese Literati Tradition
by Sherry J. Mou

The Lost Love Letters of Heloise and Abelard:
Perceptions of Dialogue in Twelfth-Century France
by Constant J. Mews

Understanding Scholastic Thought with Foucault
by Philipp W. Rosemann

For Her Good Estate: The Life of Elizabeth de Burgh
by Frances A. Underhill

Constructions of Widowhood and Virginity in the Middle Ages
edited by Cindy L. Carlson and Angela Jane Weisl

UNDERSTANDING SCHOLASTIC THOUGHT WITH FOUCAULT

Philipp W. Rosemann

St. Martin's Press
New York

ISBN 0-312-21713-7

Library of Congress Cataloging-in-Publication Data
Rosemann, Philipp.
   Understanding scholastic thought with Foucault / Philipp W.
Rosemann.
     p. cm.—(The New Middle Ages)
   Includes bibliographical references and index.
   ISBN 0-312-21713-7
   1. Philosophy, Medieval.   2. Foucault, Michel.   I. Title.
II. Series.
B712.R75   1999
189'.4—DC21   99–23062
                                           CIP

Design by Letra Libre, Inc.

First edition: December, 1999
10 9 8 7 6 5 4 3 2 1

CONTENTS

List of Figures and List of Plates		vi
Series Editor's Foreword		vii
Preface		viii

Introduction.   A Change of Paradigm in the Study of
Medieval Thought: From Rationalism to
Postmodernism   1

Study 1.   Michel Foucault's Philosophy of History   19

Study 2.   Defining the Scholastic Tradition   45

Study 3.   Scholastic Intellectual Practices   59

Study 4.   The Prose of the World—The Greek Circle and
the Christian Line   103

Study 5.   Aquinas: The Open Circle   133

Study 6.   The Scholastic Episteme and Its Others   159

Conclusion   183

Appendix. The Library of the Medievalist Philosopher   189
Notes   207
Indexes   257

LIST OF FIGURES

Figure 1.1: The Dialectics of History according to Foucault   26
Figure 1.2: The History of Madness according to Foucault   34
Figure 2.1: Scholastic Thought in the Dialectics of the Western
             Tradition   55
Figure 3.1: A simple stemma illustrating the steps followed in
             textual criticism   75
Figure 4.1: "How the center of a circle can be found by means
             of a cross."   132
Figure 5.1: Aquinas's "Open Circle"   143

LIST OF PLATES

Plate 1: The Gospel of St. Matthew with glosses
Plate 2: Ecclesiastes with glosses
Plate 3: A Gothic Bible
Plate 4: Rose window in the west façade of the abbey
          church of St.-Nicaise, Reims
Plate 5: Robert Grosseteste's *Tabula* (list of indexing symbols)
Plate 6: Robert Grosseteste's *Tabula* (page with index entries)

The plates appear together following page 102.

SERIES EDITOR'S FOREWORD

The New Middle Ages contributes to lively transdisciplinary conversations in medieval cultural studies through its scholarly monographs and essay collections. This series provides focused research in a contemporary idiom about specific but diverse practices, expressions, and ideologies in the Middle Ages. *Understanding Scholastic Thought with Foucault* is the tenth book in the series. Philipp W. Rosemann's brilliant new study of Scholastic philosophical thought challenges us to historicize our understanding of Scholasticism—to understand, that is, that not only we but also medieval writers are historically situated. Rosemann is alert to the richly allusive culture of the Scholastics; he grounds his work in studies of major intellectual practices of the thirteenth century. Equally, however, Rosemann usefully considers Scholasticism through the provacative lenses of postmodernism, deploying Michel Foucault's insights about intellectual history to discern a new vision of the problematics of Scholastic thought. This engagement in Scholastic problematics, termed the "Scholastic episteme" by Rosemann, comes to life in the final chapter, a vivid study of the witch-hunt.

Bonnie Wheeler
Southern Methodist University

PREFACE

A while ago, a medievalist colleague of mine asked me about the series in which I intended to publish my new book. "What does that title mean, The New Middle Ages?" he was wondering. "What is so 'new' about this series?" Well, I replied that most likely the editor had called her series The New Middle Ages in order to associate it with the methodological turn that has occurred in the study of the Middle Ages during the past decade or so—a turn toward an increased use of postmodern, or post-structuralist, theory in medievalist research. "Oh," my colleague remarked, "oh, so it is ideology-driven."

This annoying reaction to post-structuralism and its use as a method-ological backdrop for historical research is, of course, not untypical these days. Only recently, a group of North American historians decided to bolt the American Historical Association and other professional organi-zations, in order to form a new "Historical Society." The reason these scholars advanced for the split was their conviction that contemporary historical research has become far too politicized. Its emphasis upon is-sues such as diversity or minorities has led, these historians argue, to an increasing personalization, trivialization, and relativization of historical studies. To their mind, we need to return to the historian's traditional commitment to facts, empirical evidence, and the primacy of reality over ideology.[1]

This book is intended as a defense of the application of post-struc-turalist theory to the study of history—more precisely, to the study of in-tellectual history. However, the book is more than a mere defense. Insofar as the specific area of intellectual history to which it is devoted—namely, the Middle Ages—has not yet profited from an explicit application of post-structuralist methods, it is also an attempt to show those embarking on the study of the intellectual culture of the medieval period what sys-tematic form a postmodern approach to medieval philosophy and theol-ogy could take.[2]

The New Medievalism: Theory and Material Detail

The postmodern historical methodology of the "new medievalism"[3] is characterized by two trends that, on the face of it, might seem diametrically opposed, but that in fact are closely linked.

The first trend can be summed up in the conviction that naive realism is untenable. As R. Howard Bloch and Stephen G. Nichols have provocatively put it, we must tear ourselves away from the "the prejudice called 'objectivity.'"[4] This does not mean that there is no reality out there for the historian to investigate; that there are no criteria left which we could use to evaluate whether an historical claim is valid or not; or that every quest for historical truth is condemned from the outset to be utterly vain and illusory. It does mean, however, that we must leave behind the unexamined positivism that pretends no factor external to the object of study itself has, or should have, any bearing whatsoever upon the interpretation of the object itself.[5] In its methodological naivety, its lack of self-distance and self-critique, such positivism often turns out to be much more "subjective" in its results than a more "relativist" and, indeed, more humble methodology-conscious approach, which is aware of the limitations circumscribing its own particular perspective upon the subject matter. The philosopher Louis Dupré summarizes this humility very aptly when he writes: "If all truth has an historical dimension, then the truth about history is itself historical, and we must be prepared to accept that further reflection may judge the past differently from the way we do."[6]

The second trend arises from the situation that, despite its characteristic emphasis upon methodology and theory, the postmodern approach does not at all neglect the "facts." Its "reliance on theory" is not at the expense of the "evidence."[7] Quite the contrary; in the field of medieval intellectual history, for instance, we have witnessed in recent years a fascinating resurgence of interest in the material details of medieval intellectual life: in forms of teaching and genres of writing, in reading techniques, in the layout and production of manuscripts, and so forth. As Bloch and Nichols rightly point out, today's graduate students "recognize that material artifacts, such as manuscripts, are the new frontier for a theoretically oriented philology."[8]

Why this combination of theory consciousness with meticulous attention to historical detail? The answer is this: if our perspective upon the Middle Ages is an historically situated one, then this is equally true of the medievals themselves. They, like us, were not free-floating spirits, but human beings rooted in the historical (political, social, institutional, and so on) conditions of their time. Lest we misunderstand them fundamentally, we must therefore endeavor to define the *difference* between these historical conditions and those prevailing in our own day.

About this Book

It is along these two principal axes of the postmodern historical methodology that the present book is organized. On the one hand, it attempts to lay sound theoretical bases for an interpretation of medieval thought from a postmodern perspective. This task requires that we throw the theoretical presuppositions which accompany the application of post-structuralism to history into clear relief, rather than leaving them in half-dimness as mere "tools."

Hence, I have decided to devote the first study to a concise summary and interpretation of Michel Foucault's philosophy of history. Of course, Foucault's thought represents only one dimension in the very complex postmodern philosophical movement; moreover, Foucault himself experimented with a number of different styles of historical analysis. Nonetheless, Foucault is the postmodern thinker who has given the greatest attention to the problem of history, not only developing an explicit methodology of historical research in his *Archaeology of Knowledge,* but also applying it to subjects as diverse as the history of reason and madness, the origins of the modern penitentiary, and the history of sexuality.

In study 2, I shall employ the insights of the *Archaeology of Knowledge* and some other works, especially *Madness and Civilization,* first to situate the Scholastic tradition in the intellectual history of the West, and then to define the most characteristic traits of that tradition—to define, that is, what Foucault might have termed the "Scholastic episteme." As we shall see, an "episteme" is the ensemble of factors—historical, social, institutional, intellectual, and so on—that render a certain form of thought possible; it is not the "essence" of that thought. In attempting to identify the most important elements of the Scholastic episteme, I shall concentrate upon the thirteenth century when, for historical reasons that will be explained in study 2, Scholastic thought came into full bloom.

Among the conditions in which the flourishing of the Scholastic tradition in the thirteenth century occurred, we shall analyze, in study 3, such topics as the handwriting of the Scholastics, their techniques of textual transmission, the curricula of the new universities, methods of teaching and literary forms, and the Scholastic attitude toward textuality. In the course of studying these "intellectual practices," certain structures will emerge that a closer look at the "content" of Scholastic thought in studies 4 and 5 will serve to confirm.

These chapters do not attempt to provide an history of Scholastic thought in the thirteenth century. To furnish such an history is not the goal of the present book. Rather, study 4 will try to define the central *problematic* faced by Scholastic thought—namely, the conflict between Greek "circular" and Christian "linear" thought, which came to a head in the thirteenth century. Study 5 will then outline one (albeit a very powerful one) of the solutions offered to this problem—namely, Thomas Aquinas's. This procedure does not entail the reductionist belief, shared by much of traditional Neoscholasticism, that the whole of medieval thought is nothing but a preparation of the Thomistic synthesis, and should ultimately be studied in its light.

A brief look at the famous Condemnation of 1277 and the intellectual foundations of the witch-hunt will conclude the book in study 6. This chapter will enable us to define the Scholastic episteme not only with regard to what it *was,* but also with regard to what it *was not,* that is to say, what it explicitly excluded from its ambit (Condemnation of 1277), and what it was to become through a subtle but momentous transformation of its episteme (the witch-hunt). Study 6 will suggest that we can interpret modernity as a reaction against this transformation.

Two Predecessors: Père Chenu and Fernand Van Steenberghen

There is nothing new under the sun. The approach of the new medievalism has predecessors amongst some of the most eminent medievalist philosophers and theologians of our century. In 1950, Père Marie-Dominique Chenu published his brilliant *Introduction à l'étude de saint Thomas d'Aquin,*[9] a book that still remains one of the best introductions to St. Thomas. In his *Introduction,* Père Chenu shows that the effort to understand Aquinas cannot succeed without a systematic and detailed consideration of the historical context to which he belonged, and of the historical conditions under which he worked: the university, the Dominican order, the Aristotelian tradition, the Neoplatonic tradition, the literary genres, the Latin language and Scholastic vocabulary, the role of authority and dialectics, and so forth.[10] "A commentary on Aristotle, a commentary on the Bible, a *quodlibet,* a *summa* are not amorphous receptacles which can be used indifferently by some pure thought," writes Chenu in his preface, "they have, together with their laws, their own spiritual comportment."[11]

What Chenu formulates here is the crucial insight that there is no exteriority between form and content, between history and thought, between history and truth. It is not indifferent, for instance, that Aquinas
wrote his *Summa* in the classical form of the Scholastic *quaestio;* to neglect
this historical fact is not simply to overlook an insignificant accident of the
substance of Aquinas's thought, it is to distort that very thought itself.[12]
However, it is only in the last decade or so that medievalist philosophers
and theologians have started taking Chenu's approach seriously, by genuinely attempting to integrate the study of medieval thought and its historical conditions. There is no truth that is not historical; which, by the
way, is not the same as saying there is no truth. "The truth is no less true
for being inscribed in time."[13]

Chenu's *Introduction* impressively draws attention to the historical conditions of the development of medieval thought; it does not contain any
reflection upon the historical nature of the medievalist enterprise itself—
the fact that contemporary medievalist scholarship is itself inscribed in
time, and therefore subject to certain historical, social, intellectual, institutional, and other such conditions. To fill this lacuna, and therefore to become another example of new medievalism *avant la lettre,* was to be the
achievement of Fernand Van Steenberghen's *Introduction à l'étude de la
philosophie médiévale,* published in 1974.[14] The reader will find in this book
no conventional introduction to the great lines of medieval thought, or to
the authors, dates, great works, currents, sources, and influences. Rather, he
or she will discover that the Neoscholasticism in which Van Steenberghen
so enthusiastically situates himself has to be seen as the result of historical
developments beginning at the end of the eighteenth century, and that
these historical developments finally culminated in Pope Leo XIII's celebrated encyclical *Aeterni Patris.* The reader of Van Steenberghen's *Introduction* will be confronted with methodological reflections concerning the
role of the Christian faith in the constitution of medieval thought. He or
she will learn that there are institutions, such as the Société internationale
pour l'étude de la philosophie médiévale (SIEPM), which coordinate the
study of medieval thought worldwide, facilitating the collaboration of the
different centers for medieval studies at universities in Europe and North
America. He or she will find in Van Steenberghen's volume short intellectual biographies of our century's great experts on medieval thought, people such as Clemens Baeumker, Maurice De Wulf, Martin Grabmann,
Auguste Pelzer, Dom Odon Lottin, and Bruno Nardi.[15] Van Steenberghen
does not draw any radical "postmodern" conclusions from his way of presenting the study of medieval thought. His *Introduction* just makes it very

clear, clearer than any other book of the older Neoscholastic tradition, that the study of medieval thought is an "incarnated" enterprise.

With the present book, I wanted to create an introduction to the study of medieval thought in the spirit of Chenu and Van Steenberghen, for our own time. It is a very different book from Chenu's and Van Steenberghen's, but they were my models—together, of course, with Foucault.

This book does not presuppose any knowledge of medieval thought, of postmodernism, or of Foucault. Nevertheless, I should not wish to label it as a book for "beginners," as its reading requires a certain facility with philosophical reflection, especially in the dialectical tradition. It is no conventional textbook, but I hope it will prove useful to advanced undergraduate and graduate students as a methodology-conscious introduction to the study of medieval thought from a postmodern perspective. While I have attempted to argue a coherent thesis about the nature of Scholastic thought, most of the individual studies can be read independently, as introductions to certain aspects of the study of Scholastic thought. One can read *Understanding Scholastic Thought with Foucault* without knowledge of any languages other than English, as long as the reader will forgive me the occasional quotation of a foreign word or title in the body of the text. I have tried to make sure the meaning of foreign terms can always be gathered easily from the context. On the other hand, in my notes I have freely quoted, and made reference to, texts in languages other than English. The serious study of medieval thought requires a good reading knowledge of Latin. Moreover, medieval studies is, more so than many other fields of scholarly work, an international discipline. In a book meant to introduce its readers to the present state of research in the intellectual history of the Middle Ages, the attempt to avoid mentioning works written in French and German, above all, would not be feasible.

Finally, I wish to thank my students at the University of Dallas, where I taught courses on the Scholastic tradition and medieval philosophy in 1997–98. Their interest in my classes encouraged me to summarize my approach to Scholastic thought in this book. Thanks also to my colleagues Robert Kugelmann, John Stephen Maddux, and Angelica Tratter, with whom I cotaught a seminar on Foucault's philosophy of history at the same time. The Provost of the University of Dallas, Dr. Glen Thurow, has been generous in allowing me to take time off to complete my manuscript. Dr. Steve Lofts, of Heidelberg, and an anonymous reader from The New Middle Ages have seen the book in manuscript form and contributed innumerable corrections and suggestions for which I am grateful. The

William A. Blakley Library of the University of Dallas and its efficient interlibrary loans department have been of the greatest help in my research, as has been the Bridwell Library of Southern Methodist University. I am especially grateful to Dr. Eric White, Curator of Special Collections at Bridwell, for his assistance in finding appropriate illustrations. My colleague from Southern Methodist University, Professor Bonnie Wheeler, the editor of this series, received me most graciously upon my arrival in the Dallas area, and offered me the opportunity to have this book published in The New Middle Ages series. To her especially, my warmest thanks are returned.

INTRODUCTION

A CHANGE OF PARADIGM IN THE
STUDY OF MEDIEVAL THOUGHT:
FROM RATIONALISM TO POSTMODERNISM[1]

As we have seen in the preface, one of the central elements of the new medievalism consists in the insight that one can obtain no absolute objectivity in the study of history. This does not imply a tyranny of ideology or personal taste over "fact," as detractors of the post-structuralist historical methodology would have it, but simply means that the historian's own historical standpoint furnishes him or her with the indispensable framework in which to read the "evidence." Rather than a deplorable limitation, this framework constitutes a positive *condition for the possibility* of historical research.

Evidently, this position ultimately represents nothing but the application of Kant's transcendental idealism to the domain of history. Just as Kant rules out the possibility of apprehending objects as they are "in themselves" *(Dinge an sich)*—that is to say, irrespective of their relationship with the subject's forms of cognition—so the new medievalism excludes the possibility of knowing historical facts outside of any theoretical framework. Long before the rise of the new medievalism, the Neo-Kantian philosopher Ernst Cassirer formulated the Kantian position on historical research in the following terms:

> To define historical truth as "concordance with the facts"—*adaequatio rei et intellectus*—is . . . no satisfactory solution of the problem. It begs the question instead of solving it. That history has to begin with facts and that, in a sense, these facts are not only the beginning but the end, the alpha and omega, of our historical knowledge, is undeniable. But what is a historical fact? All factual truth implies theoretical truth.[2]

The History of History

If what Cassirer says here is correct, then it must be possible—no, neces-sary—not only to write histories, but to write the history of these histo-ries: to show that, and why, certain historical epochs have privileged certain kinds of approaches to history. And indeed, this history-writing to the second power has been done. In philosophy, for example, there is the well-known book by Lucien Braun, *Histoire de l'histoire de la philosophie.*[3] For my part, what I intend to do in this introduction is to sketch out a minihistory of the study of medieval thought up to the present day, be-ginning with the renaissance of interest in the Schools that started in the last century. In order to illustrate and substantiate the new medievalism's claim that history is itself historical, I shall thus endeavor to demonstrate that there is no such thing as "the history" of medieval philosophy, but rather a "history of the histories" of medieval philosophy—a history of the different ways of interpreting the evolution of ideas in the medieval pe-riod, with each of these different ways being to a considerable extent a function of the interpreter's own presuppositions. I submit that the recent change of paradigm—a shift from an ultimately rationalist Neoscholastic reading of medieval thought to a postmodern approach—constitutes an advance in our knowledge of medieval philosophy and theology, as it al-lows us to see facets in the intellectual movement of the Middle Ages that had been eclipsed by the Neoscholastic perspective. Nevertheless, it is clear that even the current postmodern approach has its own historical limita-tions, and will eventually have to give way to a new interpretation.

The Interpretation of the History of Medieval Thought: Yesterday . . .

Serious scholarly interest in medieval philosophy and theology dates back to the last century. It is now common to distinguish two kinds of motives for the rise of the modern study of medieval thought, namely, secular and ecclesiastical ones.[4] However, if it is true that, in the nineteenth century, attempts were made to conceive medieval studies along nationalistic lines,[5] nationalism was not to be the dominant force in the development of the subject. Rather, the decisive impetus came from ecclesiastical motives; Catholic circles hoped to find in the thought of the Scholastics the intel-lectual means to combat the perceived dangers of modernity. This move-ment received a considerable boost when, in 1879, Pope Leo XIII defined Scholasticism and, more precisely, Thomism, as the official Catholic phi-

losophy. His encyclical letter, *Aeterni Patris,* is considered to be the found-
ing document of the Neoscholastic movement.[6]

For the study of medieval philosophy and theology, Pope Leo's initiative
turned out to be a mixed blessing. It was a positive step, insofar as it lent massive institutional support to the nascent interest in medieval thought. Catholic
universities started training young researchers in that domain, funds became
available, and there was a clear goal that could orient researchers in their studies—the idea of a renewal of Catholic thought through a return to its medieval sources. Nevertheless, when we consider, from hindsight, the impact of
Aeterni Patris upon the medievalist "scene," we also see some of the more
detrimental effects it produced: above all, its emphasis on Thomas Aquinas was
to generate a one-dimensional reading of medieval thought. This one-
dimensionality is in evidence in most of the literature of a Neoscholastic inspiration. Consider, for example, Fernand Van Steenberghen's classic study of
thirteenth-century philosophy, *La philosophie au XIIIe siècle.*[7] Van Steenberghen, the most outstanding representative of the Louvain school of
Neoscholasticism, systematically reads the whole of medieval philosophy, and
even its ancient and Arabic sources, as a preparation of Aquinas's thought, in
whose system he assumes Western philosophy to culminate. Every other author, work, or current is reduced to a mere step, either leading ultimately to
the Thomistic synthesis, or detracting from it. It is therefore not surprising that
in other publications, such as his *Ontology,*[8] Van Steenberghen has little time
for developments in philosophy after Aquinas. From this Neoscholastic perspective, he comes to regard later medieval philosophy (and theology) as a
gradual decline, eventually leading to the catastrophe of modernity, which—
it must be said—the Neoscholastics often judged more through prejudice
than through any real knowledge. Indeed, even such an eminent philosopher
as Étienne Gilson, who, for his part, did have a thorough acquaintance with
modern thought, failed to see any progress in post-Thomistic metaphysics.
After examining the ideas of, among others, Descartes, Spinoza, Hume, Kant,
Hegel, and Kierkegaard, he concludes in *Being and Some Philosophers:*

> It may seem strange, and almost preposterous, to look back to the thirteenth
> century for a complete metaphysical interpretation of being . . . Yet, such a
> return is unavoidable, since all other philosophies have advocated either a
> metaphysics of being minus existence, or a phenomenology of existence
> minus being.[9]

The irony of Neoscholasticism is that it was itself deeply entangled in
the philosophical presuppositions of the same modern thought it set out

to attack.[10] For its approach was, like every history of philosophy, a product of the intellectual climate of its time. Indeed, we can read Neoscholasticism as a kind of "reverse discourse" with respect to modernity, as Foucault would have said. By *discours "en retour,"* Foucault understands a strategy whereby a marginal group tries to reinscribe itself into the center, or mainstream, of a culture by adopting the center's categories in its own attempts to justify itself.[11]

Thus, Neoscholasticism typically has little time for the medieval mystics, rather concentrating on the most "rational" thinkers of the Middle Ages. Of course, it is difficult to find a medieval philosopher in whose thought there is not also an element of mysticism or negative theology, but these elements are suppressed in the history books. For example, the import of Aquinas's mystical vision at the end of his life—an experience by comparison with which he declared his intellectual production to be "like straw"—is downplayed; for who would want to study the ideas of a thinker who admitted, and in such strong terms, to the limitations of his "system"? The literary form employed by the philosophers and theologians of High Scholasticism—mostly that of the *quaestio,* which is a kind of written dialogue—is jettisoned in favor of systematic expositions, sometimes even presented in the form of series of logical deductions. The clarity (or pseudoclarity) of a totalizing rationality triumphs everywhere over the opacity of the fragments that we have of medieval philosophy, fragments that are for the most part to be found in theological works (such as the *Summa theologiae*). What is more, an unrealistically clear-cut distinction between philosophy and theology is read into medieval thinkers as early as Augustine, lest the "rationality" of their ideas be compromised.[12]

But there is no point in flogging a dead horse, as they say. For Neoscholasticism is dead; mainly, I think, because it lost the institutional support of the Catholic Church after the Second Vatican Council, which emphasized the necessity for theology to enter into a dialogue with the contemporary world and, hence, with contemporary philosophy. In the 1970s, the study of medieval thought faced a crisis; Neoscholasticism lost its impact, and no other paradigm was available to provide a horizon within which to read medieval philosophy and theology. The analytic approach could have become dominant at that time; the historical conditions were right. That it did not become the leading paradigm for the study of medieval thought[13] may be due to the fact that it was seen as being even more limited than Neoscholasticism, affording most of its attention to medieval logic and semiotics. The famous *Cambridge History of Later Medieval Philosophy*[14] exemplifies this tendency, as it reduces the history of medieval philosophy essentially to a history of medieval logic. All theological issues, which are so often inextricably connected with philosophical ones in medieval thought, are carefully avoided by the authors of the *Cambridge History*.[15]

. . . and Today

These days, research in the area of medieval philosophy has turned "postmodern"—less resolutely, and certainly less consciously than other fields of medieval studies, such as Old French, yet undeniably.[16] The "Thomocentrism" and rationalism of the Neoscholastic movement, which tended to reduce the rich diversity of medieval thought to a rational philosophy culminating in the "system" of Thomas Aquinas, has been replaced by an approach that endeavors to highlight all those aspects of the medieval intellectual life which, for the Neoscholastics, were peripheral and unimportant.

One of the most influential representatives of the new ways of reading medieval thought is Alain de Libera, professor at the École pratique des hautes études in Paris. His book, *Penser au Moyen Âge,* which appeared in 1991, has come to be regarded as a sort of manifesto of the new approach.[17] One of the most striking features of *Penser au Moyen Âge* is the very deliberate way its author situates the study of medieval thought in the political landscape of contemporary France. In fact, the title, *Penser au Moyen Âge,* contains a play on words; it can be translated either as "Thinking *in* the Middle Ages," or as "Thinking *of* the Middle Ages." Now de Libera urges his French readers to think *of* the Middle Ages in considering the role of the Muslim minority in their own country. More particularly, de Libera points to the crucial influence that Arabic thought exercised in thirteenth-century European culture, a culture to which Christianity remains fundamentally indebted even today (only think of the role that Thomas Aquinas's *Summa theologiae* was to play in the formation of Catholic theology). From this, de Libera concludes that xenophobic politicians who insist on the irreducible "otherness" of Islam, and its incompatibilty with the Christian values of contemporary France, ignore one fundamental fact— namely, that the presumed "other" has already, for centuries, been at the very heart of the "same."

Not all de Libera's books exhibit such explicitly political intentions. In a volume on Albert the Great, the author provocatively declares in the preface: "il faut oublier Thomas d'Aquin"—"we must forget Thomas Aquinas."[18] We need to forget Aquinas, de Libera argues, in order to be able to appreciate Albert the Great as a thinker in his own right, with his own originality, a thinker not to be read just as "St. Thomas's teacher." De Libera's *Philosophie médiévale*[19] continues the project of "forgetting" the old Neoscholastic presuppositions, constituting in fact the first history of medieval philosophy that gives equal weight to the Latin, Arabic, Jewish, and Byzantine traditions. Neoscholasticism had always favored the thinkers of Latin Europe.

The same trend to subvert the one-dimensionality of the Neoscholastic picture of the Middle Ages, and to "decenter" the history of medieval philosophy, is verified in Loris Sturlese's book, *Die deutsche Philosophie im Mittelalter.*[20] Sturlese (of the University of Lecce, Italy) criticizes the idea that, intellectually, everything pivoted on Paris in the Middle Ages, and he throws into relief the interest and originality of thinkers working in the "provinces." Together with his colleague Kurt Flasch from the University of Bochum in Germany, Sturlese is the editor of a Corpus philosophorum teutonicorum medii aevi, a series devoted to publishing the "Teutonic" philosophical heritage of the Middle Ages.[21] As for the Neoscholastic assumption that early medieval philosophy is to be regarded as a prelude to the thirteenth century, recent research has shown that, as early as the ninth century, the medievals produced fascinating metaphysical speculations of great contemporary interest. I am alluding to the dialectics of John Scottus Eriugena. In Dermot Moran's book, *The Philosophy of John Scottus Eriugena. A Study of Idealism in the Middle Ages,*[22] the author presents Eriugena's negative ontology as a form of metaphysical thought that escapes Heidegger's critique of occidental metaphysics as being "onto-theo-logical." For the Neoscholastics, Eriugena was always slightly suspect, given that his main work, the *Periphyseon,* used to be placed on the Index of Forbidden Books.

At Louvain, formerly one of the centers of Neothomism, a project was started to edit the works of Robert Grosseteste, a thinker long regarded as "minor."[23] Today, he is acknowledged to have been "greater, broader of vision, more versatile and, in the last part of his life, more thorough-going in scholarship than any figure in the Schools of Europe during the two centuries following his death"—this judgment, cited from James McEvoy's study of Grosseteste, is intended to include Aquinas.[24] Another scholar from Louvain, Jos Decorte, has published a remarkable study entitled *The Madness of the Intellect (De waanzin van het intellect*[25]), in which he shows, inspired by Foucault's theses on the dialectics of reason and unreason, that the medieval witch-hunt must be regarded as an intrinsic possibility of medieval rationality itself—as its internal "other," not just its extrinsic opposite. Whether medieval or modern, rationality driven to its ultimate limits turns into madness. (The example of a modern "rational madness" that Decorte cites in his book, written in the 1980s, is the arms race.)

The Fribourg School, too, has turned "postmodern." Ruedi Imbach, who holds the chair of medieval philosophy there, and his collaborators have in the past few years published numerous books that highlight marginal or hitherto neglected aspects of medieval thought. Imbach himself, who began his career with a doctorate on Aquinas and Meister Eckhart,[26] has recently been interested in the role played by lay people in medieval philosophy.[27] His colleague François-Xavier Putallaz is the author of, amongst other titles, a study on controversies and condemnations in the thirteenth century.[28]

Another important consequence of new medievalism is the increased attention scholars now afford to the material conditions of intellectual life in the Middle Ages. More precisely, what is new in recent research is its attempt to show that these material conditions are not something apart from, or accidental to, the "ideas" of the Middle Ages, but rather possess their own "spiritual comportment," to use Chenu's previously cited expression. There is an interdependence of "form" and "substance" in the history of thought that has been neglected in more traditional research. Today, medievalists are in the process of describing this interdependence in a more detailed fashion than has ever been attempted for any other period of thought. Thus, in his book entitled *In the Vineyard of the Text*,[29] Ivan Illich carefully demonstrates the role played by techniques of reading in the constitution of the medieval subject. To summarize Illich's thesis in a few words, the way we read determines the kind of people we are. It is fascinating to note, with Illich, that the great flourishing of Scholastic thought which occurred in the thirteenth century was accompanied by a momentous change in reading techniques. We shall discuss this interesting issue at greater length later.

In the same vein, Olga Weijers (Constantijn Huygens Instituut, The Hague) and her collaborator Louis Holtz (Institut d'histoire des textes, Paris) have founded a new series entitled Studia Artistarum, which is devoted to the study of the institutional conditions prevailing at the arts faculties of the early universities.[30] Weijers's recent book, *Le maniement du savoir*, presents the first comprehensive summary of research upon what the author calls the "intellectual practices" of the medievals—ranging from methods of teaching to the layout of manuscript pages—together with the role these practices played in the intellectual development of medieval culture.[31] Independently of Weijers, John Marenbon, an analytic medievalist from Trinity College in Cambridge, England, some ten years ago published an introduction to medieval philosophy the first half of which is entirely devoted to "the organization of studies in medieval universities, the forms of writing and techniques of thought, the presuppositions and aims of thirteenth- and fourteenth-century scholars."[32]

The Other Thomas Aquinas

The new way of reading medieval philosophy from the perspective of its margins and material conditions has not failed to affect the contemporary interpretation of Thomas Aquinas himself. He is just too big to be "forgotten"; even the former anti-Thomist de Libera has now devoted a long study to one of Aquinas's writings, the *De unitate intellectus contra Averroistas*.[33] However, Aquinas's work is currently being reread in such a fashion as to bring out aspects of his thought that contribute to changing his image as the father of a certain kind of boring textbook Scholasticism. In Canada, Martin Blais, of the Université Laval, has published a little book entitled *L'autre Thomas d'Aquin*,[34] which contains chapters such as, "The Body also exists" *("Il y a le corps aussi"),* "Obeying no one but oneself" *("N'obéir qu'à soi"),* and "Power comes from God; so does Sexuality" *("Le pouvoir vient de Dieu; le sexe aussi").* Blais's intent is to revive interest in Aquinas by challenging, inter alia, the idea that the rigid and legalistic ethics which used to be taught in Québec's schools as "Thomism" corresponds to any historical reality.

Another very interesting example of a revisionist reading of Aquinas is furnished by Father John I. Jenkins's study, *Knowledge and Faith in Thomas Aquinas*.[35] Despite its conventional and somewhat insipid-sounding title, this volume—written by an analytic philosopher from Notre Dame who is equally at home with more historically-oriented approaches to medieval thought—breaks new ground in challenging the idea that there is an account of "knowledge" to be found in Aquinas. Aristotelico-Thomistic *scientia,* Jenkins establishes, was something fundamentally different from the modern concept of "knowledge"; consequently, to seek an explanation of the latter in St. Thomas cannot but seriously distort his thought.

Géry Prouvost, who teaches in Kinshasa, has recently devoted a fine volume to *Thomas d'Aquin et les thomismes*.[36] Note the plural; in this "essay on the history of Thomisms," as the subtitle identifies the book, Prouvost discusses how the different, and often all but warring, historical interpretations of Aquinas can be shown to be rooted in Thomas himself. For his thought was not a monolith allowing of only one interpretation; rather, it evolved and changed so that, depending on the reader's perspective, it could give rise to different "Thomisms." In a somewhat similar way, my own recent study, *Omne ens est aliquid,* deconstructs the conception of Aquinas's thought as a rigorous, rationalistic "system." Rather, I argue, Aquinas's thought has deep affinities with our postmodern philosophies of finitude, which emphasize the ultimate openness of the human quest for knowledge and happiness.[37]

The bottom line of these and other studies on "the other Aquinas" is that we no longer have to "forget" Aquinas in order to engage in a thoroughly contemporary reading of medieval thought. On the contrary, his very centrality to the Neoscholastic project calls for a thorough reevaluation of his thought in the new post-structuralist perspective. For history can never be simply rejected and repressed; it needs to be continually rethought.

Thinking the Other

The foregoing examples are meant to show that, for some years now, medievalists have endeavored to "let the rebellious diversity come to the fore" in the field of the philosophy of the Middle Ages, thus realizing a project already envisaged by Paul Vignaux, Gilson's successor at the Sorbonne.[38] We have come to understand that medieval thought is misconstrued as a homogeneous, rationalist project, teleologically leading to the Thomistic synthesis; no, there are other thinkers than Aquinas, other traditions than the Latin one, other places than Paris, other centuries than the thirteenth. There is even an "other" Aquinas . . . And even the madness of the witch-hunt is not totally extraneous to medieval reason.

But why this new trend to "let the rebellious diversity come to the fore"? The answer is not too difficult to provide; it is because that is what our "post-modern" times are all about—culturally, intellectually, philosophically—and these trends, quite naturally, do not leave historians of medieval thought unaffected. Tolerance with regard to "difference" and openness to the "other" are the watchwords of our contemporary culture. In our Western societies, the "other," the "margin" of the past, demands its reinscription into the center: women, ethnic minorities, religious minorities, linguistic minorities, sexual minorities, and so forth.[39]

This social and political revaluation of "difference" is paralleled in the philosophy of our time, which can be understood, at least in its "Continental" branch, as an extended response to, and critique of, Hegel's quest for absolute knowledge.[40] In the constitution of Absolute Spirit, the opacity of difference is sublated in the transparency of a rationality that has become total. When Hegel identifies the Absolute with the "identity of identity and difference,"[41] it is "sameness" that has the last word over "otherness"—at least according to the most common interpretation.[42] Against these totalizing tendencies of the Hegelian system, contemporary philosophy affirms the necessity of "thinking the Other" *("penser l'Autre"),* according to a particularly felicitous expression Foucault uses in the *Archaeology of Knowledge.*[43] Heidegger's project of understanding the "event" as the differentiation between λήθη and ἀλήθεια, "concealment" and "unconcealment," is as much an effort to "think the Other" as Lacan's theory of psychoanalysis, where listening to the voice of the Other (i.e., the unconscious) between the lines of imaginary discourse becomes the analyst's central task. Is not Levinas's idea of a "totally other" God a search for an otherness lost on the road to absolute knowledge, as much as Bataille's "heterology"? Not to speak of Foucault himself, whose work on the history of reason and madness opens up the possibility of envisaging a rationality not yet differentiated from its "other," that is to say, unreason.[44]

But what about the Letter?

Even if we admit that the interpretation of the history of medieval thought, and of intellectual history in general, may to a considerable extent be determined by the interpreter's own philosophical standpoint, will the diversity of possible interpretations not be limited by the material letter of the texts themselves? In other words, while the "spirit" of any philosophy may not be a category fixed once and for all, does not its "letter" remain unaffected by the changing presuppositions? This is, at least, what one would think. However, the history of editorial techniques[45] and their evolution rather suggests the contrary; at least for ancient and medieval thought, where we have no printed texts approved by the authors themselves, there is no total objectivity even in the textual basis of our interpretations.

The most striking example of the situation prevailing before the invention of the printing press is perhaps the case of Aristotle's *Metaphysics,* one of the most fundamental texts upon which the Western intellectual tradition is based. The *Metaphysics,* as it is printed in our contemporary editions, has little to do with the text as Aristotle conceived it. Indeed, Aristotle did not conceive the *Metaphysics* as a coherent "text" at all. According to Christian Rutten, the *Metaphysics* is a compilation of lecture notes that Aristotle's successors arranged so differently from their original chronological order that one has to break the text up into 154 fragments in order to re-constitute it in the sequence in which it was originally created.[46]

Admittedly, the results of Rutten's research are somewhat extreme, as is the "stylometric" method he employed to reach them. Most classical philologists would not be prepared to go along with his conclusions. Nonetheless, since the publication of Werner Jaeger's *Studien zur Entste-hungsgeschichte der Metaphysik des Aristoteles* in 1912,[47] the basic idea that the text of the *Metaphysics* as it has been handed down to us does not ade-quately reflect the stages of its development has become ineluctable. What Rutten's theses illustrate well, because of their very exaggeration, is the conviction that the scholarly study of a text requires a reconstruction of its original, "authentic" form, that is to say, the form in which the author him-self wrote or dictated it. This conviction has been at the heart of modern editorial scholarship as it was conceived at the beginning of the last cen-tury. In all disputes, for instance over the exact degree of corruption to be found in Aristotle's *Metaphysics,* this conviction itself was never challenged.

The editorial technique that has determined the form of ancient and medieval texts as we know them in today's editions has been a method called after the German philologist Karl Lachmann. Its goal is to eliminate all the mistakes that are inevitable in the transmission of handwritten texts as copies are made from the original, and then from these copies further copies, and so on. What the Lachmannians are trying to do is establish fam-ilies of shared mistakes in the manuscript tradition and thus, by identifying the genealogical order in this tradition of copies, return to the source. We shall enter into some of the philological details and problems of this method later on, in study 3. In the present context, I note only its basic philosoph-ical presupposition, namely that what counts in the history of a text is just the original in its pure identity; the differentiation this textual identity nec-essarily undergoes is an history of errors that should be overcome.

For the change of paradigm on which we are focusing in this intro-duction, it is worth noting that contemporary editors have modified the Lachmannian method, for reasons both practical and, more importantly, theoretical.[48] From a practical point of view, research into the complexi-ties of medieval manuscript transmission has shown the extreme difficul-ties of establishing clear-cut "families" of different traditions of mistakes, as these families very often tend to "contaminate" each other. From a theo-retical point of view, the Lachmannian method is founded upon a quest for lost origins, a quest that contemporary philosophy would denounce as being vain and imaginary. Why attempt to surmount the historical multi-plicity of different readings of an original text, different readings that, after

all, testify to the historical life of the original? What are the advantages of
re-establishing the flawless identity of a text that, in its authentic form, may
have remained totally insignificant? Thus, the German editor Horst
Fuhrmann writes:

> It is important to make quite clear the goal of the Lachmannian method. In
> the final analysis, it aims to reconstruct the original, that is to say, a state of
> the text which, from an historical point of view, might have been without
> influence or of substantially less influence than that of the derived and, in
> the eyes of Lachmann, corrupted versions.[49]

Is it perhaps due to similar doubts that even the most radical advocates
of textual emendation never attempted to actually produce an edition of
Aristotle's *Metaphysics* radically diverging from the traditional order of
books? In any case, in keeping with the sentiments formulated by
Fuhrmann, contemporary editors now aim to produce editions that can at
once give us an idea of the original text *and* reflect this text's transmission
and historical evolution; in other words, they attempt at once to reconstruct the original identity of the text, and to preserve the difference of its
historical expressions. This latter goal is in continuity with what I have described as the tendency to "let the rebellious diversity come to the fore"
in current research on medieval thought. This goal is markedly different
from the purpose of the Lachmannian method applied in its traditional purity—which illustrates my thesis that even the textual bases of our research
into medieval studies do not remain unaffected by paradigm changes.

The best example of a "postmodern" edition attempting to balance the
exigencies of identity (the author's "own words") and of difference (the
form these words took in the historical process of their transmission) is
Édouard Jeauneau's text of Eriugena's *Periphyseon*.[50] Jeauneau, it should be
said, is not at all a rebellious post-structuralist, but rather a well-established
scholar associated with the Pontifical Institute for Mediaeval Studies in
Toronto, which Gilson founded in the 1950s. As Jeauneau remarks in his
introduction to volume 1, the *Periphyseon* is, like so many other medieval
works, a "text in perpetual becoming."[51] There being no "final" edition of
the *Periphyseon* authorized by Eriugena himself and then fixed in print, the
manuscripts containing this work underwent continuous additions during
the author's own lifetime. While we can attribute some of these additions
with reasonable certainty to Eriugena himself, others are more than likely
the work of a disciple. As a consequence, the *Periphyseon* does not correspond to the static concept of a "text" to which we post-Gutenbergs are

used, but bears greater resemblance to a "film." And, as Jeauneau points out, the present state of editorial technology does not yet allow us to produce the "film" adequately reflecting the writing of the *Periphyseon*.[52] Therefore, Jeauneau opts for the printing of five different versions of the text, side by side, preceded by a "main" text—that is to say, a more conventional edition of version V, which is most likely to represent Eriugena's own contribution to the work. And why not limit the edition to this one principal version? For a couple of reasons: one, it is not totally certain that some of the other versions do not also contain contributions written by Eriugena, or at least faithfully reflecting his thought; two, it is the most "complete" version that has historically come to be regarded as the "real" *Periphyseon*. It would be artificial to try to undo this historical fact now.

The Present-Day Interest of the Study of Medieval Thought

After analyzing, in the preceding sections, the ways in which the contemporary "postmodern" philosophical climate has influenced the study of medieval thought, and influenced it right down to the level of editorial technique, I should like to conclude this introduction by inverting perspectives, offering some reflections on the contribution that the study of medieval philosophy can make to contemporary philosophical discussions. This is obviously a pressing question for anyone, student or scholar, who decides to devote him- or herself to this field of study. It is also a burning issue for institutions traditionally devoted to the study of medieval philosophy or theology, which after the demise of Neoscholasticism have become uncertain of their raison d'être. This is mostly the case with Catholic institutions founded in the wake of *Aeterni Patris,* and of the enthusiasm for the Neoscholastic movement that the encyclical helped fashion. It is sad to see such institutions as the Pontifical Institute of Mediaeval Studies in Toronto, the Institut d'études médiévales in Montreal, the Institut supérieur de philosophie at Louvain-la-Neuve, or even the Department of Scholastic Philosophy in Belfast, disappear or lose their sense of direction.

As I pointed out earlier, postmodernity can be understood as a philosophical movement concerned with "difference." Present-day thought, like present-day culture, is suspicious of any attempt to reduce cultural, ethnic, religious, linguistic, and intellectual diversity to the unity of one all-embracing system. This option for diversity and difference does, however, lead to serious problems of a both philosophical and sociopolitical nature. For, it is not enough to critique and "deconstruct" the totalizing systems of the past, if this critique does not at the same time produce a viable model capable of affording the newly discovered differences some kind of unity. Socially and politically, we want the various groups that form our society to enjoy the greatest degree of freedom and autonomy; yet all our difference and diversity notwithstanding, we also need to live together in one society. The challenge is to *vivre ensemble différents* (live together as different people), as the title of a book published in Québec put it.[53] Philosophically, it is not enough to underline the multiplicity of coherent universes of discourse, analyzing each in and for itself, as this must inevitably lead to relativism. Relativism is logically untenable and self-destructive. Hence, we cannot content ourselves with parts, but rather need to move on to the whole, in which each of the parts finds its logical place. In other words, Hegel's quest for the Absolute, largely rejected by contemporary philosophy, remains a philosophically necessary task; Hegel was right in declaring, in the preface of the *Phenomenology of Spirit,* that "the truth is the whole" *(das Wahre ist das Ganze)*.[54] Where he went wrong was not in pursuing the knowledge of the Whole and of the Absolute; but he erred in assuming it was possible to attain this knowledge and, above all, in claiming he had attained it. In other words, we need to search for the Absolute, while acknowledging at the same time that the Absolute irreducibly transcends our capacities.

A paradoxical project, one might object. Yes, but it is precisely this project that the medieval philosophers themselves pursued. Thomas Aquinas would have agreed with the Hegelian phrase that "the truth is the whole"; for his aim as a philosopher and theologian was precisely to synthesize the Christian ideas he inherited from his predecessors with the new Greek, Jewish, and Arabic sources that became available in the thirteenth century. For Aquinas, and for the Scholastics in general, the quest for the truth was a "collective" task, and this in the most literal and etymological sense of the word—a task of "collecting" together the partial truths that individual thinkers managed to attain throughout the course of history, into a more comprehensive synthesis. Thus, in his *Commentary on the Metaphysics,* Aquinas writes:

> . . . in spite of the fact that what one human being is able to contribute to the understanding of the truth, by means of his own study and talent, is something small by comparison to the whole consideration *(totam considerationem)* of the truth, nevertheless what comes together from all the collected partial views *(quod aggregatur ex omnibus "coarticulatis," idest exquisitis et collectis)* becomes something big. This can be seen in the individual branches of

knowledge: through the study and talent of various individuals, the latter have reached an admirable growth . . . while each of the predecessors has discovered something of the truth, the product of all these discoveries brought together into one *(simul in unum collectum)* leads posterity to a great knowledge of the truth . . . And thus, it is just that we should give thanks to those by whom we have been helped with regard to such a great good, which is the knowledge of the truth.[55]

What distinguishes the structure of Aquinas's philosophical and theological synthesis from a system of the Hegelian type is the acknowledgment that, although the knowledge of the whole is a goal to be striven for, the ultimate synthesis is something beyond the grasp of the human mind; for, "no human being can reach a perfect knowledge of the truth" *(nullus homo veritatis perfectam cognitionem adipisci [potest]),* as Aquinas writes in the *Commentary on the Metaphysics.*[56] Thomistic thought is a system in which there is no final word, a system which admits that the final reduction of difference to identity remains an impossible dream—and yet a necessary dream.

We can verify what I have said about Scholastic philosophy as a quest for the whole by means of a "collective" effort—note the etymological meaning of the word—in almost every page of the texts of medieval thought. We can verify it in the structure of these texts, in their very literary form. The Scholastics developed a sophisticated method to reconcile doctrinal oppositions through discussion, and this method, which was used in the public disputations held regularly at the universities, is reflected in the literary form of their writings—at least of those writings following the structure of the *quaestio*. In a *quaestio,* the Scholastic author starts out by availing himself of the tradition of texts accessible to him, in order to determine the extreme poles of possible opinion on the subject matter he is investigating. What guides him in the selection of these extremes is no doubt the conviction that the greater the distance is between the views presented as a starting point for the discussion, the larger is the field of which the eye of the mind must take the measure in view of a solution.

The extreme poles are summed up in the first two parts of the *quaestio*—the *videtur* and the *sed contra*. The contradiction resulting from the juxtaposition of irreconcilable views leaves the author in a momentary impasse. In order to overcome it, he returns to the original question, which he now discusses again in the light of several distinctions, meant to render the question more internally differentiated, and therefore more precise. This discussion makes up the so-called "body" *(corpus)* of the text. Its goal is to show, not that the opposing views of the *videtur* and the *sed contra* are utterly absurd and need to be discarded, but rather that, and from what point of view, each of the positions is derived from a particular perspective upon reality itself. Typically, then, the discussion concludes, as Aquinas once writes, that "both ways of reasoning come to a conclusion which is true from one point of view, and false from another" *(utraeque rationes verum concludunt aliquo modo, et aliquo modo falsum).*[57]

As the truth itself is so "infinitely many-sided" that it "cannot be exhausted by any (human) knowledge,"[58] it is only by combining diametrically opposed poles of opinion—*utrumque coniungentes,* as Aquinas puts it in another context[59]—that we can hope to come closer to an adequate perspective upon the whole of reality. For each of the in-themselves false and inadequate partial points of view sheds light upon a different aspect of the whole of the truth. If one wanted to sum up the Scholastic method in a provocative paradox, one could say it transforms doctrines that are severally wrong into a unified system in which these same doctrines become "collectively" true. We shall have an occasion to examine the functioning of this method, which is crucial for understanding Scholastic thought, in greater detail in study 3.

What finally distinguishes this truly dialectical method of the Scholastics from the Hegelian approach is what one could call the deliberately fragmentary character of the Scholastic syntheses. As it is difficult to speak here in totally abstract terms, I should like to use the concrete example of Aquinas's refusal to finish the great system that he elaborated in the *Summa theologiae.* Whereas the *Phenomenology of Spirit* ends with a chapter rather haughtily entitled "Absolute Knowledge," the *Summa* does not reach its end; it breaks off.

> . . . it is rarely noticed that St. Thomas's *Summa theologica* has remained a fragment.[60] The normal explanation offered is the extrinsic fact that its author died too early. "Snatched away by death" he had to leave his work incomplete: this or similar notes appear in the editions of the *Summa theologica.* In actual fact, St. Thomas explicitly refused to conclude his work because of inner experiences.[61]

After a mystical vision, Thomas declared: *Omnia que scripsi videntur michi palee respectu eorum que vidi et revelata sunt michi*[62] ("Everything I have written seems like straw to me by comparison with what I have seen and has been revealed to me"). Everything he had produced, all the admirable human knowledge that he had collected together and synthesized in his works, appeared to him "like straw" by comparison with the Truth he had seen. Aquinas's philosophical and theological synthesis is of such a nature that it culminates in a denial of the ultimate validity of human knowledge.

Medieval thought, therefore, teaches us how it is possible to live with the realization that no human theory or practice can ever arrive at a final synthesis or integration of all our differences into a flawless unity. We can learn from the medievals that we must live with the radical finitude of the human condition, and yet not fall into a complete relativism according to which "anything goes." In other words, we must continue to search for what we know we cannot find—at least not in this life.

STUDY 1

MICHEL FOUCAULT'S PHILOSOPHY OF HISTORY

In order to understand what is implied in bringing a post-structuralist methodology to bear upon the study of medieval thought, my next step is an exposition and interpretation of an historical methodology developed by one of the most influential post-structuralist thinkers—namely, Michel Foucault.[1] This choice is not difficult to justify; Foucault is, beyond doubt, the post-structuralist philosopher who has devoted the most careful and detailed attention to historical research. As a recent commentator put it: "All of Foucault's major works are histories of a sort, which is enough to make him a historian of a sort."[2]

Understanding Foucault's methodology of historical research, especially as presented in his earlier works, from *Madness and Civilization* to *The Archaeology of Knowledge,* necessitates another preliminary step—an exposition and interpretation of Nietzsche's *The Birth of Tragedy out of the Spirit of Music.* This, too, is not difficult to justify. Foucault himself writes in the preface to his first major work, *Madness and Civilization:*

> At the center of these limit-experiences of the Western world, that of the tragic itself obviously stands out—Nietzsche having shown that the tragic structure from which the history of the Western world develops is nothing but the refusal, the oblivion, and the silent spin-off of tragedy. Around this limit-experience, which is central because it binds the tragic to the dialectics of history in the very refusal of tragedy by history, numerous other experiences gravitate . . . The study which you will read should be but the first one, and perhaps the easiest one, of [a] long inquiry which, under the guidance of the great Nietzschean project, would like to confront the dialectics of history with the immobile structures of the tragic.[3]

Foucault thus explicitly places his entire enterprise under the auspices of Nietzsche. That, in this context, he also mentions the "dialectics of history" in its connection with "the tragic" and with "the refusal of tragedy by history" unambiguously directs our attention toward Nietzsche's first book, *The Birth of Tragedy out of the Spirit of Music*.[4]

Nietzsche: The Birth and Decline of Greek Tragedy and the Tragic Dialectics of History

Nietzsche began his philosophical career with a book that almost instantaneously rendered him an object of fierce debate. *Die Geburt der Tragödie aus dem Geiste der Musik*,[5] published in 1872 when its author was teaching classical philology in Basel, advances the daring thesis that the history of Western civilization has been doomed to a tragic course since its very beginnings in ancient Greece. This tragic course, Nietzsche argues, is a result of the disappearance of the musical element from Greek tragedy, and the subsequent birth of . . . Socratic philosophy.

The criticism following the publication of the *Birth of Tragedy out of the Spirit of Music* was pungent. The influential classicist Ulrich von Wilamowitz-Möllendorff wrote a pamphlet ironically entitled *Philology of the Future! (Zukunftsphilologie!)*, in which he accused Nietzsche of dilettantism. As would be the case with his disciple Foucault later on,[6] Nietzsche, having formulated a fundamentally *philosophical* insight by means of an *historical* thesis, found himself in a situation in which he had to defend himself before a tribunal of colleagues who, predictably, considered his approach overspeculative and insufficiently scholarly. "Not a full nor an adjunct professor, but rather a philologist without a name . . . an undistinguished doctor of philology," wrote the aristocratic Wilamowitz-Möllendorff disdainfully, had dared challenge the very foundations of classical philology.[7]

But what exactly is Nietzsche's claim in *The Birth of Tragedy?*[8] Chapter 1 begins with the idea that there are two basic forces at work in all art. Nietzsche calls them the "Apollonian" *(das Apollonische)* and the "Dionysian" *(das Dionysische)*, terminology derived from the Greek Gods Apollo and Dionysius, in whom he believes Greek culture epitomized the two forces. While the Apollonian gives itself form in plastic art, the Dionysian is the power expressing itself in music. In order to render the difference between the two forces clearer, Nietzsche introduces a psychological element into his explanation. If the Apollonian corresponds to the world of dreams, the Dionysian is connected with rapture and trance. The dream is a pleasant play of appearances; according to Nietzsche, even during the most horrific nightmares, we are never totally unaware that our dreams remain at a distance from reality.[9] "It is a dream," we console ourselves in such situations.

The distancing and, as it were, centrifugal nature of the dream is reflected in the subjectivity of the Apollonian artist—that is to say, the sculptor. While the dream itself is a mere eruption of the Apollonian in the human being, the sculptor "imitates" this natural force on the artistic plane.[10] In his plastic creations, he contemplates the world through "the mirror of appearance,"[11] placing himself over against it. By contrast, the lyric artist and the musician (whom Nietzsche considers to be fundamentally identical), as the "imitators" of rapture and trance, do not contemplate reality as an "object" of their own subjectivity, but become one with it—the centripetal force of the Dionysian draws them into its center. The musician is, therefore, in essence a mystic.[12] For the "magic" of the Dionysian breaks down all divisions between man and man, or man and nature.[13]

Nietzsche allows no doubts about the fact that, by comparison with the Apollonian, the Dionysian is the more primordial force. What is more, he locates the originality and, indeed, superiority of ancient Greece over against the "barbaric" cultures surrounding it, in the specifically Greek attitude toward the Dionysian. Ancient cultures from Rome to Babylon, Nietzsche writes, knew the phenomenon of Dionysian feasts, which usually took the form (if one can speak of form in this context) of unchecked promiscuity, lust, and cruelty. In them, human beings regressed to the "natural" state of wild beasts.[14] The Greeks, on the other hand, while being fully aware of the horrible attraction of the Dionysian, transformed it into a cultural force by keeping it in counterpoise with the Apollonian. For Nietzsche, the whole universe of the Greek gods is nothing but a device that Greek culture fashioned in order to redeem the "primordial One" *(das Ur-Eine)* of Dionysian ecstasy through the world of appearance[15]—in order to soothe the reality of horror and suffering by means of beauty and measure. This interplay between the Dionysian and the Apollonian reached its final reconciliation in the Attic tragedy of Aischylos and Sophocles.

Originally, Nietzsche contends, Greek tragedy was limited to the chorus[16]—hence the title of his work, *The Birth of Tragedy out of the Spirit of Music.* For the audience of the earliest tragedies, the entrancing melodies of the chorus—a chorus of satyrs, beings half human, half beast—would momentarily break down the "usual barriers and limits of existence,"[17] causing an "overwhelming feeling of unity."[18] The audience would have seen itself in the chorus, and, indeed, would have identified with it, as its songs worshipped the god Dionysius. This original "chorus-tragedy" became "drama" only when an attempt was made to represent the audience's mystic vision of the god Dionysius on the stage. Thus, according to Nietzsche, the action of the Attic tragedies must be understood as the result of a process in which the original objectification of Dionysius on the stage gradually unfolded into more numerous characters, involved in more and more elaborate stories. Originally, however, the action was nothing but the "Apollonian" crystallization of the ecstatic visions triggered by the Dionysian chorus.[19] "All the famous figures of the Greek stage—Prometheus, Oedipus, and so forth—are only masks of the original hero Dionysius."[20] Nevertheless, side by side with this masked appearance of Dionysius in Apollonian "form"—that is to say, as an individual distinct from the audience and standing over against it—there remains the chorus, a constant reminder of the forces of "primordial unity." In this balance and interplay lies, according to Nietzsche, the genius of the Attic tragedies.

Their decline began with Euripides, whose intention it was to "eliminate" *(ausscheiden)* the Dionysian element from tragedy, in order to rebuild it upon un-Dionysian foundations.[21] The result of Euripides's transformation, however, was paradoxical. Whereas the authentic tragedy balances and reconciles the forces of the Apollonian and the Dionysian, in Euripides the suppression of the Dionysian leads to an unmediated opposition between the "rationalistic method"[22] of his plays, on the one hand—Nietzsche cites the typical Euripidean prologue, which offers a detailed explanation of the action before the play itself even begins—and the passion with which many of his scenes are filled, thus producing uncontrolled outbursts of emotion on the part of the audience, on the other. Moreover, as Euripides's "rationalism" can no longer accommodate the divine, mystical, and ecstatic, his plays come to center on characters of a "bourgeois mediocrity."[23]

The strange dialectic[24] between the rationalistic and emotional tendencies in Euripides's plays is indicative of a greater tragedy that was to be triggered by the demise of the Dionysian-Apollonian drama. For Nietzsche, Euripides was "in a certain sense only a mask"[25]—a mask of a new god called Socrates! Nietzsche believes that the tendencies verified in Euripides's plays correspond exactly to what he derogatorily terms Socrates's "optismism": that is to say, the conviction that "virtue is knowledge; sinning is due to ignorance; the virtuous person is the happy one."[26] In this philosophy, there is no room for the dark and irrational forces of the Dionysian; the clarity of a despotic logic triumphs everywhere. Analyzed from this perspective, the Socratic-Platonic aversion to the classical tragedy, and against art in general, is not surprising. Art is acceptable to Socrates/Plato only to the extent that it obeys the dictates of reason. However, what is wrong with that? Where is the tragedy we alluded to at the beginning of this paragraph? Nietzsche maintains that when the Platonic worldview became dominant in classical Greece, it drove music out of tragedy, annihilating the chorus and, with the chorus, it drove out the only way for the Dionysian to articulate itself in a setup capable of channeling its horrible unifying force.[27] Yet the Dionysian did not just disappear. Since Socratic times, it has led a subterranean existence. And when it emerges from its secret hiding place, it shows itself all the more violently and dangerously—just like the passions and emotions in Euripides's plays . . . :

> Dionysius, as before, when he fled from Lycurgus, the king of the Edonians, took refuge in the depths of the sea, that is to say, in the mystical floods of a secret cult slowly encompassing the whole world.[28]

In his own day, Nietzsche believes, the limits of Socratic optimism are for the first time in history beginning to dawn upon humanity.[29] This is the merit of Kant's and Schopenhauer's philosophical achievement. From them, we have learned that the innermost core of things is forever inaccessible; that all our knowledge concerns nothing but "appearances." This insight has inaugurated our contemporary culture, which Nietzsche calls a "tragic" one—a culture where the boundless optimism of science is once again being replaced by wisdom that acknowledges the inevitability of suffering.[30] About a century after Nietzsche's death, this statement rings truer than ever. After the guilt heaped upon humanity by slavery, two world wars, the Holocaust, and other abominations, have we not come to realize that progress of knowledge alone will not guard us against fearful eruptions of pent-up violence and cruelty?

But let us break off here. We shall leave the judgment about the historical accuracy of Nietzsche's theses about Greek tragedy to the classicists. For our own purposes, it is more important to understand the philosophical core of his theory. Nietzsche's thought in *The Birth of Tragedy* is thoroughly dialectical. There are two opposing forces at work in human history, whose ideal relationship is a state of reconciliation in which both are at once preserved and overcome (*aufgehoben,* Hegel would say; "sublated"). Nietzsche's dialectics of history is of course not Hegelian in the strict sense. For Hegel, history was the teleological process of substance becoming subject, a continuous enrichment and unfolding that culminated in absolute knowledge. By contrast, Nietzsche interprets the history of the West as a decline from an original perfection, a decline stopped only recently through the genius of such thinkers as Kant and Schopenhauer. Nietzsche's "Hegelianism" is therefore resolutely anti-teleological. Moreover, the Kantian and Schopenhauerian ideas that Nietzsche incorporates into his own thought are equally important as the Hegelian elements—though he was later to regret the presence of "Schopenhauerian and Kantian formulations" in his treatise.[31] With Kant, *The Birth of Tragedy* holds that reality is characterized by a fundamental duality between what *appears* and what is *behind that appearance*. Nietzsche's fleshing-out of this duality, however, is much more Schopenhauerian than Kantian in nature. Kant believed any positive statement about this "behind," the *Ding an sich,* to be impossible, whereas Schopenhauer identified it with the Will. For the Nietzsche of *The Birth of Tragedy,* the Will is the Dionysian. We can also trace other elements, such as the dialectical interplay between a centripetal movement toward unity (the Dionysian), and a centrifugal movement toward differentiation (the Apollonian), to Schopenhauer's *World as Will and Representation.* These brief remarks obviously merit considerable elaboration; here, they are only meant to cast some light on the intellectual background of *The Birth of Tragedy,* a treatise that can in many ways be read as the source, not only of Foucault's historical methodology, but of the Continental philosophical movement in the twentieth century.

Foucault and the History of Limits

We are now in a position to understand the background of Foucault's Nietzschean project "to confront the dialectics of history with the immobile structures of the tragic." Following Nietzsche, Foucault is convinced that the history of Western civilization as a whole can be analyzed in terms of a dialectical and perpetual tension between the two poles of tragedy—the Apollonian and the Dionysian. He also shares Nietzsche's belief that the repression of the Dionysian element has "bound the tragic" to this dialectics, that is to say, it has given the history of the West an indelible tragic coloring. This, according to Foucault, can be verified in numerous other experiences that "gravitate" around the original Fall. Before turning to Foucault's analysis of these experiences (or at least of one of them), let us briefly examine his generalized reformulation of Nietzsche's theory of the tragic dialectics of history:

> One could write a history of *limits*—of those obscure acts, necessarily forgotten as soon as they have been accomplished, by which a culture rejects something which will be for it the Outside *(l'Extérieur); and throughout the course of its history, this hollowed-out void, this white space by which it isolates itself, designates it as much as its values. For, its values it receives and

maintains in the continuity of history; but in that sphere of which we want to speak, it exercises its essential choices, it makes the division which gives it the face of its positivity; here is found the original density [literally, "thickness"] where it forms itself. To question a culture about its limit-experiences, is to question it at the confines of history, about a tearing-apart which is like the very birth of its history. In a tension which is always in the process of resolving itself, there occurs the confrontation between the temporal continuity of a dialectical analysis and the unveiling of a tragic structure at the threshold of time.[32]

This rich and beautiful passage depicts the dialectics of history as involving three principal phases (see fig. 1.1):

(1) The constitution of a culture involves, first, an element of historical continuity. No culture creates itself ex nihilo, as it were, but rather depends for much of what it is upon "values" that it "receives and maintains." This seems fairly obvious: postmodernity did not start without any historical heritage, but is a movement defining itself through modernity, and to a considerable extent in continuity with it; the Middle Ages cannot be understood without their roots in antiquity; Christianity is a movement that arose out of Judaism; in many respects, the ancient Greek civilization can be traced back to Egyptian, and perhaps even Indian sources; and so forth. However, there was a moment in history when postmodernity had not yet distinguished itself from modernity; when the Middle Ages did not yet exist (though we can now, in retrospect, say that they were germinally contained in antiquity); when Christ had not yet reshaped his Judaic heritage into a new religion. This is what Foucault terms the "zero degree" (degré zéro)[33] of history—a state where the "old" and the "new" are not yet distinct.

(2) Yet, as much as by the positive values it inherits from history, each culture, civilization, tradition, etc. is also characterized by its Outside (l'Extérieur)—by what it rejects and decides not to be. Indeed, it is the very act of rejecting what will henceforth be its "other" that gives a culture its distinctness, or "the face of its positivity."

(3) Now what about the relationship between the outside and the inside of a culture once the division between the two, with the rejection of the Exterior, has occurred? Foucault's answer to this question is that the rejection of the element now destined to be the culture's "other" does not create a relationship of mere exteriority. In a sense, the excluded element will, paradoxically, stay within the culture that has eliminated it—namely, as a "hollowed-out void," a "white space." These metaphors are meant to

Figure 1.1   The Dialectics of History according to Foucault

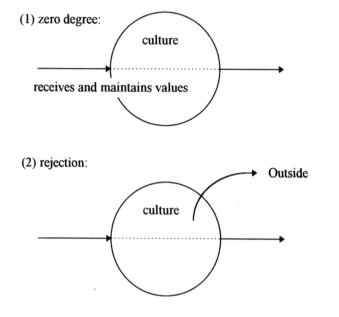

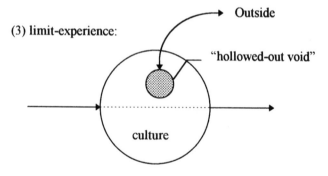

convey the fact that the division giving birth to the history of a new culture will remain this culture's central "limit-experience" throughout its
whole history. In other words, the new culture will continue to experience
the tension between the inside and the outside; indeed, in a sense, it will
be nothing but this tension. Therefore, throughout the course of its history,
every culture will be determined by the conflict between its inside and its

outside, and by the various ways in which this conflict will play itself out at different stages, in its ceaseless attempts to resolve itself. Consequently, a culture will never manage to divorce itself totally from its "other"; it will never fill the "hollowed-out void" that lies at its very center. Rather, as a commentator on Foucault's thought has incisively formulated it: "*the absolutely other is inextricably within.*"[34]

As I have already pointed out, when *Madness and Civilization (Folie et déraison)* first appeared in 1961, Foucault was convinced that "at the center of these limit-experiences of the Western world, that of the tragic itself obviously stands out."[35] He therefore conceived of his own project as a complement to the original Nietzschean insight into the dialectics of the Apollonian and the Dionysian; what he hoped to accomplish, for his part, was to spell out some of the ways in which this tragic structure manifested itself again and again, under different forms, throughout the history of the West. To this end, Foucault envisaged undertaking studies of the relationship between the West and the Orient, between the "luminous unity of appearance" and the dream, between the realms of legitimate and illegitimate desire, and, of course, between reason and madness. Not all of these projects were to be realized; others, not mentioned in the preface we are analyzing, took their place.[36]

Madness and Civilization is thoroughly Nietzschean in many other respects. It shares Nietzsche's anti-teleological reading of history, viewing the development of the West in terms of decline rather than progress.[37] It is also imbued with a spirit of nostalgia, that is to say, the desire to "return" to a state of affairs before the Fall, to the "zero degree" that obtained before the tragic divisions characterizing the history of the West took place, to the "charred root of meaning."[38]

Nevertheless, for all its Nietzschean overtones and even explicit references, the 1961 preface cannot be adequately understood as a mere offshoot of *The Birth of Tragedy.* Foucault is already much more skeptical than Nietzsche as to the possibility of entering, once again, into a more authentic relationship with the Dionysian. "This is perhaps an impossible task," he writes, as it would require the undoing of the cultural foundations upon which we stand, and upon the basis of which we speak.[39] Foucault also throws the dialectical nature of the Nietzschean vision of Western history much more clearly into relief than did Nietzsche himself, often employing those paradoxical phrases so typical of the dialectical tradition. "History is possible only against the background of an absence of history"[40]—for, the formless and conceptless Dionysian force leaves no trace in our rational accounts of time. Thus, "the great work *(œuvre)* of the history of the world is ineffaceably accompanied by an absence of any work."[41] "This structure" of the inside and the outside "is constitutive of what counts as meaning and non-meaning, or rather of that reciprocity by which they are linked to one another."[42]

Another difference by comparison to Nietzsche: even in the preface to *Folie et déraison,* at the beginning of his career, we see foreshadowed what Foucault would later describe in great detail as his "archaeological" method.[43] As we shall discover in the next section, it is an important feature of this method to analyze the genesis of an historical structure in such a way as not to privilege intellectual, "abstract" history over against the history of social, political, institutional, and other material conditions. In other terms, "mind" and "matter" belong together. Whereas Nietzsche, in *The Birth of Tragedy,* focuses upon developments in art and philosophy, Foucault conceives of the history of madness in the following terms:

> To write the history of madness therefore means: to undertake a structural study of the historical factors—notions, institutions, juridical measures and measures of the police, scientific concepts—which keep captive a madness the savage state of which can never be reconstructed in itself.[44]

Before completing our description of the Foucauldian method through a consideration of some of the principal points in the *Archaeology of Knowledge,* let us first consider Foucault's analysis of the relationship between reason and madness, which will serve to illustrate many of the points made so far.

The Transformation of Madness into Discourse

One can summarize Foucault's central thesis in *Madness and Civilization* as follows: whereas the Western world had, up to the early seventeenth century, been "strangely hospitable"[45] to madness, it subsequently began to confine mad people to those institutions that had been created during the Middle Ages to house lepers; then, in an apparent act of humanity, toward the end of the eighteenth century, it began to establish asylums where madness was to be treated and healed. Foucault interprets this movement from "hospitality" through confinement to healing as the gradual annexation of madness to the realm of reason. Hence the suggestive title of the first French edition of this work: *Folie et déraison* ("Madness and Unreason"). Strangely, Foucault never explains this title, which was jettisoned in later editions. However, what it insinuates is exactly the transformation of madness, as a state coexisting with reason in relative autonomy, into un-reason—a condition defining itself as the negative of reason, that is to say, strictly through and over against it.[46]

According to Foucault, "from the fifteenth century on, the face of madness has haunted the imagination of Western man."[47] At this stage, however, madness had not yet become the totally "other" of rationality; rather, it still signified the "familiar foreignness of the world" *(l'étrangeté familière du monde)*,[48] the presence of monstrous animality at the heart of sinful man, disfigured by forbidden knowledge. Madness was not yet absence of reason but a "difficult, hermetic, esoteric learning"[49] presaging the end of the world. In the artistic vision of Hieronymus Bosch, the Forbidden Tree in the Garden of Eden is transplanted onto the ship of fools, to serve as its mast. At the end of the Middle Ages, the ship of fools *(stultifera navis)* was a common sight on the rivers of Europe, transporting mad people from their hometowns to unknown exile. Despite this exclusion, what manifested itself in the madman was considered a necessary, if disturbing, part of the human condition.

Foucault notes that, as early as the sixteenth century, the relationship between madness and rationality began to be reevaluated. Madness was no longer regarded as a form of knowledge and existence that was independent of reason, though also constituting a threat to it (in the same way in which, since the Fall, sin poses an ineluctable threat to human nature), but came to be conceived as the dialectical "other" of rationality. The Letter to the Corinthians played a crucial role in this development: "Where is the wise man? Where is the scribe? Where is the debater of this age? Has not God made foolish (ἐμώρανεν) the wisdom of the world?" (1 Cor. 1.20) In this and similar quotations, thinkers such as Calvin, Tauler, and Nicholas of Cusa found folly linked to rationality as its highest form. Human wisdom is mere folly by comparison with the divine, and conversely, God's wisdom cannot but appear like foolishness to the eyes of the world. "It [madness; *la folie*] is taken up into the indefinite circle which attaches it to reason; they affirm and negate each other."[50]

In 1656, the Hôpital Général was founded in Paris. Foucault views this date as a landmark. For the Hôpital Général, like so many similar institutions soon to be created throughout Europe, served to confine mad people. Rather than being allowed to roam from place to place on the purifying waters of rivers, they were now rigorously segregated from society. But why? The answer Foucault gives is not of a philosophical or theological order. He links the confinement of mad people to economic considerations:

Throughout Europe, confinement had the same meaning, at least if we consider its origin. It constituted one of the answers the seventeenth century
gave to an economic crisis that affected the entire Western world: reduction
of wages, unemployment, scarcity of coin—the coincidence of these phenomena probably being due to a crisis in the Spanish economy.[51]

In fact, mad people were not confined insofar as they were mad, but insofar as they were seen as idling. From this point of view, they fell into the
same category as beggars and destitute or unemployed people, who at the
time started populating the streets of European cities in increasing numbers. Confinement, then, did not serve any medical or even religious purpose—as Foucault points out, the Church had no hand in the
establishment of the *hôpitaux généraux,* which were "structure[s] proper to
the monarchical and bourgeois order."[52] Confinement was meant to take
care of unemployment. As a result, madness, caught accidentally in its net,
changed its meaning entirely; no longer a reminder of the fallenness of humankind and the dangers of arcane knowledge, it now became one of the
forms of the inability to function in the economy.

In the same way in which the fifteenth century had embarked mad
people onto ships in order to expose them to the purifying powers of
water, the seventeenth century sought redemption for its "idlers" through
forced labor. The people confined in the prisons were made to work
there, so as to contribute to the prosperity of society. "The prisoner who
could and who would work would be released, not so much because he
was again useful to society, but because he had again subscribed to the
great ethical pact of human existence."[53] Here we can see that there is
something more to the origins of confinement than just economics. In
the "monarchical and bourgeois order" of the seventeenth century, labor
had come to acquire quasi religious connotations, so that idleness was
viewed as going hand in hand with all manner of moral transgression and
depravity. Interestingly enough, the reinscription of the incarcerated idlers
into the mainstream economy, albeit superficially successful, tended to
produce a paradoxical result. As soon as the unemployed and otherwise
"useless" people of a certain region were imprisoned and subjected to
forced labor, their very productiveness would drive manufacturers of similar goods out of business, creating more unemployment. In Nietzschean
terms, one could say that the "Dionysian," the "other" always continues to
reaffirm itself.

Toward the end of the chapter of *Madness and Civilization* that deals
with the "great confinement," Foucault writes that "'confinement' conceals

both a metaphysics of the state and a politics of religion,"[54] all enforced by the police. This quotation enables us to seize one of the hallmarks of the Foucauldian method of archaeological research. Rather than privilege one cause over all the others in a reductionist manner, Foucault analyzes the new seventeenth-century experience of madness as the result of a complex web of "indissociable"[55] factors. To be sure, confinement constitutes the response of the monarchical-bourgeois state to certain economic developments, a response enforced by the police. However, this reaction has to be viewed in the context of the ethico-religious connotations acquired by the idea of labor. Economics, politics, power, religion, ethics, and metaphysics all contribute to the constellation of factors in which madness is reduced, by reason, to idleness.

However, confinement is not the final step in the annexation of madness to reason. The famous liberation of the insane at Bicêtre, a house of confinement in Paris where they had been held in cells and chains, is usually hailed as a victory of humanitarian values. Foucault disagrees. What happened at Bicêtre in 1794 is, for him, only a sign that reason's suppression of madness had turned to subtler and, indeed, more efficient means. For, the more "humane" treatment of madness, advocated by reformers such as Philippe Pinel, finally silenced madness—both figuratively and literally. In his *Traité médico-philosophique sur l'aliénation mentale,*[56] Pinel develops a "cure" for madness that responds to its perceived moral challenge by moral means, rather than by physical violence, as had previously been the case. Like his seventeenth-century predecessors, Pinel associates madness with a transgression of social norms, although purged of its former religious connotations (this is, after all, the time of the French Revolution). Now in order to restore the madman's conformity with these norms, Pinel invents a number of techniques for "moral syntheses,"[57] as Foucault calls them—syntheses meant to reintegrate the mad immorality of the insane into the rational morality of the bourgeois order. More concretely, Pinel suggests the punishment of particularly recalcitrant patients—he cites the example of a former ecclesiastic who stubbornly believed he was Christ—by depriving them of communication. Foucault comments:

Compared to the incessant dialogue of reason and madness during the Renaissance, classical internment had been a silencing. But it was not total: language was engaged in things rather than really suppressed. Confinement, prisons, dungeons, even tortures, engaged in a mute dialogue between reason and unreason—the dialogue of struggle. This dialogue itself is now disengaged; silence is absolute; there is no longer any common language

between madness and reason . . . a common language will become possible
again, insofar as it will be one of acknowledged guilt.[58]

A common language will become possible again only on the terms of
reason, once the patient, worn down by total linguistic isolation, gives in
and admits: Yes, I am guilty; you are right, I am insane, I am not Christ.
That the madman has now, through judgment and guilt, internalized the
rational standards of his environment, signifies, for Foucault, the ultimate
absorption of the difference of madness, with its threatening opacity, in the
transparent medium of reason.

The creation of the asylum for the humane treatment of insanity is accompanied by another development, namely, the conceptualization of
madness as a medical condition. This, according to Foucault, marks the beginning of our own "modern experience of madness."[59] As the asylum
transforms into a medical space, the person of the doctor becomes central
to the cure. However, it is not from his specialist knowledge of medical
therapeutics that he derives his powers of healing. Pinel himself already realized, so Foucault claims, that the psychiatrist administers morality rather
than medicine; he is the "Father and Judge, Family and Law"[60] to which
madness, appropriately scolded, must succumb. Contemporary psychiatry
and psychoanalysis—that is Foucault's final thesis concerning the history
of madness since the end of the Middle Ages—are still deeply steeped in
Pinel's heritage. "What we call psychiatric practice," Foucault provocatively
writes, "is a certain moral tactic contemporary with the end of the eighteenth century, preserved in the rites of asylum life, and overlaid by the
myths of positivism."[61] The Freudian talking cure, with its emphasis upon
the patient-analyst relationship, is nothing but the dissolution of madness
in the medium of bourgeois order, through the moral authority of the analyst. Moreover, since the fundamentally moral structures of contemporary
psychiatry and psychoanalysis have come to be "overlaid" by the myths of
positivistic science, in whose categories the process of healing cannot adequately be accounted for, the psychiatrist is credited with a "daemonic secret of knowledge."[62] Foucault's final criticism of psychoanalysis could not
be more damning: "Psychoanalysis has not been able, will not be able, to
hear the voices of unreason."[63] For historically, psychoanalysis is a mere
outgrowth of the long "conspiracy"[64] that has aimed to transform madness
into discourse, in the same way in which it has transformed another
Dionysian force into discourse; namely, sex.[65]

However, Foucault follows Nietzsche in his conviction that the
Dionysian force cannot remain repressed for good. It will always return,

eventually; remember Nietzsche's oracular quotation about the "mystical floods of a secret cult" that will "slowly encompass the whole world." It is fascinating to discover that for Foucault, Nietzsche is not only the oracle of Dionysius, but in a sense he is Dionysius himself. In fact, several times in the course of *Madness and Civilization,* Foucault states that the repressed forces of madness have reasserted themselves in the madness of the philosopher, Nietzsche himself.[66] Of "Nietzsche's last cry, proclaiming himself both Christ and Dionysos,"[67] Foucault writes in a tone of awe and admiration. If we are to believe his recent biographers, Foucault himself was, toward the end of his life, pulled into the vortex of Dionysian forces.[68]

Our rapid summary of the argument of *Madness and Civilization* serves two purposes: first, to illustrate Foucault's archaeological method of historical research through a concrete example; and secondly, to provide some historical material enabling us to fill Foucault's tripartite schema of the dialectics of history with "data." I should now like to return, for a moment, to Foucault's analysis of the three phases that constitute the "tragic structure from which the history of the Western world develops," in order to show how the history of madness can be mapped onto it (see fig. 1.2).

(1) In commenting upon a quotation from the preface to the first French edition of *Madness and Civilization,* we said that the constitution of a culture involves an element of historical continuity. There is a "zero degree" *(degré zéro)* in history where the "old" and the "new" are not yet distinct: where Christianity has not yet differentiated itself from Judaism, where there is no difference between antiquity and the Middle Ages because medieval culture has not yet constituted itself in its specificity, and so forth. In the history of reason and madness, is there anything that corresponds to this "zero degree"? Certainly. Foucault himself speaks of "that zero degree of the history of madness where it is an undifferentiated experience."[69] But undifferentiated from what? From reason? Yes, but not in the sense of there being no distinction whatsoever between reason and madness. Rather, we must think of a closeness and *proximity*[70] between the two, a kind of a coexistence in relative autonomy, enabling what Foucault calls an "exchange."[71]

(2) In the tripartite schema sketched out in the preface, the second step is the rejection, from the center of culture, of what will henceforth become its "Outside" *(l'Extérieur).* However, it would seem that in the account offered in the body of *Madness and Civilization,* there is a stage preceding this division. At this stage, madness, without yet being rejected, comes for the first time to be construed as the "other" of reason. The two are brought into a dialectical relationship, in which they define each other mutually: "Has not God made foolish the wisdom of the world?"

Figure 1.2   The History of Madness according to Foucault

(1) zero degree:

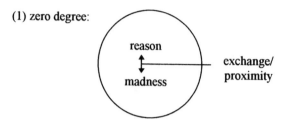

(2) construction as "other":

(3) rejection:

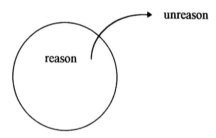

(4) return:

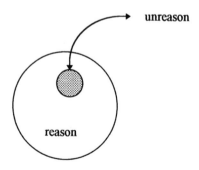

(3) It is only now, once madness has come to be constructed as non-reason, as un-reason, that reason begins to gain a purchase upon it. It starts distancing itself from its other, relegating it to its margins, and finally rejecting it altogether. This is the philosophical meaning of confinement. However, rejection is, as we have seen, more than the affirmation of otherness; paradoxically, it is also its denial, in the following sense. Confinement and, later, the treatment of the mad in asylums, and still later psychoanalysis, do not content themselves with distinguishing and separating reason from unreason while leaving unreason alone. All their efforts are directed at *dissolving* unreason in the (moral) medium of rationality, through external (confinement) or internal (asylum, psychiatry, psychoanalysis) pressure. Thus, the rejection of madness by reason is at the same time an attempt to absorb madness into reason; reason's very movement of distancing itself from unreason is, in its truth, a movement toward the elimination of distance.

(4) Yet the distancing/collapsing of distance between reason and unreason will never be wholly successful. When rationality deludes itself with the idea of having finally rid itself of its "other": that is precisely when madness will reaffirm itself at its very heart. This is, indeed, what has happened in the history of modern reason. The Enlightenment believed it had at last overcome the superstitions of the dark ages, asserting the reign of reason in all aspects of human existence. Enter Nietzsche, and the whole beautiful edifice of modernity crumbles.

We shall see in the next study that Foucault's schema of the dialectics of history can help us understand much more than just the relationship between reason and madness, as it evolved from the end of the Middle Ages up to the present day. It lends itself to a reformulation that will enable us to define the historical locus of the Scholastic tradition in the history of the West. I should like to conclude the present study with some remarks about the development of Foucault's methodology of historical research after *Madness and Civilization*. There is no final statement by Foucault on his methodology; indeed, Foucault would have found the idea of such a "final word" repugnant, a sign of intellectual arrest. Nevertheless, he has given us a detailed account of his method in *The Archaeology of Knowledge*, which is his only work exclusively devoted to methodological questions.

Archaeology, Episteme, Historical a priori

Madness, as we have seen, is not a thing-in-itself, a condition or state that is fixed, so that it could be defined once and for all. Arcane knowledge of disfigured sinners, idleness and immorality, sickness; these are, according to Foucault, the different meanings madness has taken on in the West since the fifteenth century—meanings that are held together by an historical evolution (whose steps can be retraced), though not because they all belong to an identical "substance" of what madness "really" is. For, any decision about such a "substance" of madness would necessarily have to be made from within one of the paradigms that are products of historical processes.

In *Madness and Civilization*, Foucault focuses upon the analysis of these processes. *Madness and Civilization* therefore constitutes what its author would later call an "history of the Other,"[72] that is to say, the history of the relationship between a given culture and its "outside." However, in order to complete the analysis of culture and its constitution, the "history of the Other" must be complemented by an "history of the Same,"[73] that is to say, an investigation into the way in which a given culture conceptualizes itself, rather than its relationship to its "other." This investigation is what, from *The Order of Things* (1966) onward, Foucault terms "archaeology." What archaeology unveils is the "episteme" of a culture, its "historical *a priori*."[74]

Both terms, "archaeology" and "historical a priori," have a Kantian background. Although this is less obvious in the former case than in the latter, it was Foucault himself who identified the Kantian parentage of "archaeology" in an article published in 1971,[75] claiming that Kant employed the term "philosophical archaeology" in the sense of "the history of that which renders necessary a certain form of thought."[76] The Boston philosopher James Bernauer has located the passage Foucault had in mind;[77] it is to be found in a page of posthumously published notes that Kant took for the 1798 treatise devoted to the progress of metaphysics in Germany since Wolff and Leibniz.[78] As this reference to an extremely obscure text shows, Foucault knew Kant's work well.[79] In fact, Foucault's project is deeply rooted in Kantian philosophy. In the early 1980s, Denis Huisman, the editor of the *Dictionnaire des philosophes,* approached François Ewald, Foucault's assistant at the Collège de France, with a request to revise the entry on Foucault. The result of this request was an article coauthored by Ewald and Foucault himself, who signed the piece pseudonymously as "Maurice Florence."[80] The article opens: "*To the extent that Foucault fits into the philosophical tradition, it is the critical tradition of Kant,* and his project could be called a *Critical History of Thought.*"[81]

The Kantian connotations of the term "historical a priori" are evident. Kant, in the *Critique of Pure Reason,* set out to define the "conditions of possibility" of all human knowledge. He argues that, while empirical data are knowledge's first element in the order of time, logically they come only second. For empirical knowledge is a composite of matter and form; and while the matter of sense perception and thought is furnished by the objects perceived, it is the subject's instruments of cognition by which they are formed. The subjective elements in human knowledge—space, time, and twelve "categories"—are, unlike the variable data of experience, constant and universal; in a word, they are a priori. From this brief description, one can already see that Foucault's idea of an historical a priori—one changing with time—would have been unacceptable to Kant, who, in his philosophy of "transcendental idealism," pursued the goal of safeguarding the objectivity and universality of human knowledge, precisely through the unchangeability and universality of the a priori. Foucault himself acknowledges in the *Archaeology of Knowledge* that "juxtaposed, these two words [i.e., *historical* and *a priori*] produce a rather startling effect."[82] Explaining this "rather barbarous term,"[83] he continues:

> ... this *a priori* does not elude historicity: it does not constitute, above events, and in an unmoving heaven, an atemporal structure; it is defined as the totality of rules that characterize a discursive practice: but these rules are not imposed from the outside on the elements that they relate together; they are caught up in the very things that they connect ... [84]

The historical a prioris account for the conditions of possibility of the emergence of certain kinds of discursive practices in history. Let me try to give an example, lest our discussion become too abstract. In his essay, "The Question Concerning Technology," Heidegger compares the way in which the river Rhine used to be experienced in preindustrial times to how it is experienced in our own days.[85] In former times, the Rhine would have been the mythical incarnation of the German spirit, a force of nature inspiring awe; today, it has become a mass of H_2O flowing at a certain speed, whose inherent power can be made to serve as a source of electrical energy. One could object that it is still possible for us to encounter the Rhine independently of the technological paradigm. Not according to Heidegger. Nowadays, when people come to visit the Rhine, they do so as "tourists," that is to say, as part of the "vacation industry." Technology again ... What Foucault means by "historical a prioris" is, roughly, the set of cultural (economic, social, political, philosophical) presuppositions that make us experience the Rhine in a certain fashion, rather than another. Due to these historical a prioris, the Rhine is part of a "discursive practice" in which it is thought about, spoken about, and *dealt with* in a certain way (rather than another). The historical a prioris do not determine our experience of the Rhine *absolutely;* we can still approach it from the industrialist's perspective, the environmentalist's point of view, the vantage point of the tourist . . . yet all these perspectives remain within the technological paradigm. The historical a prioris can be compared to the rules of a game: the rules dictate what game you play (basketball, football, baseball), but not each and every move within it.

Let us summarize what Foucault means by "episteme," "historical a priori," and "archaeology" through an admirably concise passage taken from the preface of *The Order of Things:*

> Quite obviously, such an analysis . . . is . . . an inquiry whose aim is to rediscover on what basis knowledge and theory became possible; within what space of order knowledge was constituted; on the basis of what historical *a priori,* and in the element of what positivity, ideas could appear, sciences be established, experience be reflected in philosophies, rationalities be formed, only, perhaps, to dissolve and vanish soon afterwards . . . what I am attempting to bring to light is the epistemological field, the *episteme* in which knowledge . . . grounds its positivity and thereby manifests a history which is not that of its growing perfection, but rather that of its conditions of possibility . . . Such an enterprise is not so much a history, in the traditional meaning of the word, as an "archaeology."[86]

Archaeology, thus, is the non-teleological reconstruction of the conditions of possibility of knowledge (and, more generally, discursive practices) prevailing at a given period; a reconstruction not of that knowledge itself, but rather of the bases upon which knowledge is possible, that is to say, of the element of positivity or the epistemological field in which it can appear. In short, archaeology is the reconstruction of the episteme[87] and the historical a prioris of a given culture.

The fact, pointed out above, that the historical a priori "does not elude historicity," produces an important consequence for the conception of the subject in archaeology. If the structures of subjectivity that the archaeologist attempts to unveil in the cultures he or she studies are all subject to history, then the Kantian quest for sovereign "powers of a constituent consciousness"[88] becomes impossible. Put differently, in archaeology there is no longer a subject whose ways of constituting objects are guaranteed by any kind of transcendence. As a consequence, the archaeological subject becomes truly that: a sub-ject, "sub-jected" to the historical a priori as much as the objects it constitutes. This is exactly what Foucault means in the famous last sentence of *The Order of Things,* according to which "one can certainly wager that man [will] be erased, like a face drawn in sand at the edge of the sea."[89] What Foucault is predicting here is not the final demise of the human race, but rather the disappearance of the modern subject conceived of as sovereign and transcendental.

Foucault profoundly detested all labels attached to his thought, and especially all labels connecting him with structuralism.[90] Nevertheless, it is exactly this movement from the Kantian transcendental subject to the subject that allows us to place Foucault in the postmodern, or post-structuralist, current of thought.[91] Structuralism applied a certain method of formal analysis to domains such as language (Ferdinand de Saussure, Nikolai Trubetskoi), ethnology (Franz Boas), or literature (Roland Barthes). This method implied a rigorous distinction between the synchronic and the diachronic points of view. De Saussure, for instance, insisted that in order to explain the meaning of a word in a given language, it was not sufficient to trace its history (etymology), but that this diachronic approach needed to be complemented by focusing upon the place of the word in question in the overall semantic structure of the language under consideration. Why is "I" a word signifying the speaker of the sentence? Two answers are possible: (1) because it ultimately derives from the Indo-European root *ego;* (2) because it is part of a meaning structure (I, you, he/she/it, etc.) in which it occupies a specific position. This position, and nothing but this position, gives it its "identity." In other words, the synchronic analysis of the structuralists attempts to understand a structure through its own internal organization and laws, without any reference to extrinsic factors—including the subject itself. Example: a structuralist interpretation of a poem does not ask what the author "wanted to say," "meant," or "felt" when he or she was writing the poem, but rather endeavors to account for the poem's status as literature through an analysis of its formal features.[92] Now post-structuralism/ archaeology takes the "successes" of structuralism "to turn the analysis back *(faire refluer l'analyse)* on to the forms of discourse that made them possible, and to question the very locus in which we are speaking today."[93] In this quotation, Foucault presents archaeology as a kind of "structuralism of structuralism,"[94] that is to say, as a type of structural analysis that does not leave unquestioned the subject conducting structural analyses.[95] However, if the "archaeologizing" subject can be sub-jected to such an analysis, then it is itself an effect of structure.

Let us follow Foucault one step further. Given that archaeology recognizes the historical contingency of its own "locus," it no longer aspires to be a "science" in the traditional sense. It is just "the name given to a part of our contemporary theoretical conjuncture,"[96] an enterprise inextricably bound to the intellectual and political situation of the moment. Once this situation changes—and archaeology is about "change in the order of discourse"[97]—the archaeological approach "may disappear with the figure that has borne it so far."[98]

Archaeology is not for those who find objectionable or troubling the idea of an historical methodology that does not promise to reveal the eternal truths of history. It is, like other forms of post-structuralist thought, a philosophy of the radical finitude of the human subject. Archaeology does not aspire to free us from that finitude, but to make us understand it in greater depth and detail. Archaeology is, ultimately, an option in favor of difference, against the belief that it is possible to reduce the different forms of human subjectivity and culture—the different historical a prioris—to one identical structure, from which it then becomes possible to analyze and evaluate all the others.

This option is not without political implications and perhaps even motives. Whether this fact makes archaeology an "ideology-driven" project is for my reader to decide. Yet is it not true that metaphysics, psychology, ethics, and politics have always formed—since the very beginnings of our Western tradition, since Plato's *Republic*—a constellation of interdependent factors?

> What is that fear which makes you seek, beyond all boundaries, ruptures, shifts, and divisions, the great historico-transcendental destiny of the Occident?
> It seems to me that the only reply to this question is a political one. But let us leave that to one side for today.[99]

Categories of Archaeological Analysis[100]

Apart from theoretical reflections upon the methodology of historical research, *The Archaeology of Knowledge* contains information of a more "practical" nature. Indeed, with this book, Foucault has created a kind of manual of archaeological research, providing a comprehensive list of all the factors that need to be taken into consideration in the analysis of an episteme. To these factors we now briefly turn, as they provide signposts for our own work in this book.

"Discursive formations," that is to say, cultures or parts of a culture which are based upon the same episteme, are governed by historical a prioris that can be called "rules of formation." These rules of formation, which correspond to Kant's "categories," define the conditions of possibility for the discursive formations, whose constitution can be analyzed according to four principal axes.

(1) How are the *objects* formed that are part of the discursive formation in question? According to what rules do these objects appear in the discursive formation, are transformed in it, differentiated, etc.? (a) To begin with, objects require *surfaces of emergence.* Let us take mental illness as an example. Where does mental illness manifest itself? In the family, in the workplace, in sexual behavior, in criminal activities? What counts as mental illness in a given discursive formation, the way it is broken down into subtypes, etc. depends on the surfaces in which, a priori, it is expected to emerge. (b) Secondly, objects are constituted by *authorities of delimitation.* Who has the right to identify mental illness as such? Is it doctors, priests, art critics—or perhaps all of these? The object "mental illness" and its "dispersion" do not remain unaffected by these possibilities. (c) Finally, objects of discursive formations are subjected to certain *grids of specification.* For instance, what is the grid underlying the distinction of different kinds of mental illness? Is the grid constituted by the parts of the soul? If so, the object "madness" resulting from such a differentiation looks very different from the "madness" categorized according to the life history of the individuals affected by mental illness.

(2) What are the *enunciative modalities* of the discursive formation being analyzed? In other words, what criteria do the subjects have to satisfy who, in a given culture at a given time, are authorized to make statements recognized as belonging to a certain discourse—even if the statements contradict each other? (a) *Who* is accorded the right to speak? To use an example of our own, what qualifications does a subject need to possess in order to pronounce him- or herself authoritatively on the birth of tragedy in ancient Greece? In German academia at the time of Wilamowitz-Möllendorff, an "undistinguished doctor of philology" was not qualified! (b) What are the institutional *sites* of discourse? To become part of today's medievalist discourse, for instance, where do you have to publish your ideas? In a peer-reviewed journal: yes; in a book published by a vanity press: no. It is more difficult to make oneself heard in this discourse from the site of a small college than from an Ivy League university. (c) From what *coign of vantage* can the subject legitimately approach the object of discourse? To return to Foucault's own example of mental illness, is the subject diagnosing and treating madness a questioning and listening subject (as in psychoanalysis), or rather an observing subject employing scientific instruments (as in neurology)? Both vantage points are acceptable in contemporary discourse about mental illness, but others no longer are (the exorcising subject, for instance).

(3) A discursive formation possesses a certain set of rules for the formation of concepts. One should emphasize that the concepts making up

a discursive formation do not have to be homogeneous. A discursive formation does not owe its unity to the fact that it is possessed of an absolute conceptual coherence, but rather to the similarity with which the different subsystems belonging to it produce their concepts—concepts that, as such, may be quite incompatible. (Take "theism" and "atheism"; these are incompatible concepts. Nonetheless, in many debates about the existence of God, the same rules of concept formation are applied, with radically differing results.) (a) The similarity just mentioned will, first, be one involving particular *rules of succession,* which govern the way in which concepts are interrelated. Example: in the Middle Ages, from the twelfth century onward, the "body politic" came to be conceptualized as an organism. As a consequence, the concepts describing the parts of the state, with their respective functions and relationships, were organized into a discourse articulated according to the semantic field of "living body." By contrast, to understand the state as a political "structure" involves a different conceptual architecture. (b) Furthermore, rules of concept formation place concepts in a *field of coexistence.* For instance, the neurological discourse on mental illness employs concepts that are quite different from those of the psychoanalyst; yet the psychoanalytic discourse coexists with the neurological one, such that the latter measures itself with the former, attempts to refute it, etc. To this "field of presence," as Foucault calls it, is added a "field of concomitance," which comprises concepts that, although belonging to a different domain, serve to confirm the conceptual structure of the discursive system in question. For example, neurology is different from chemistry, but a neurological approach to mental illness finds confirmation and support in the concepts of chemistry. Lastly, concepts are formed against the foil of a "field of memory," made up of concepts that are considered to be "out of date," yet situate a discourse in its own past. Alchemy is the field of memory for chemistry, for instance. (c) The formation of concepts obeys rules regulating *procedures of intervention.* For instance, what techniques of rewriting are legitimate in incorporating old ones into new conceptual structures? Can one transcribe Aquinas's "five ways" according to the rules of formal logic? Can one recycle Aristotle's insights by reading him as a linguistic analyst? Or are we translating the concepts of medieval thought according to the procedures of intervention characteristic of post-structuralism?

(4) Fourthly and finally, discursive formations are subject to rules which give rise to different *strategies.* What is a strategy? It is a theory or idea emerging from a discursive formation in competition with a different one, yet according to the same rules. In order to describe the emer-

gence of strategies, again three aspects need to be taken into consideration. (a) What are the possible *points of diffraction* where strategies come to
be differentiated from each other? Within a discursive formation, what are
the crossroads where certain a priori possibilities allow for paths to part?
Within the discourse of postmodernism for instance, what are the options
generated by similar rules of formation for thinkers as different as Foucault, Lacan, Deleuze, Marion? (b) Not all of the potential paths opened
up by the points of diffraction of a discursive structure will actually be followed up in reality, this being due to the *economy of the discursive constellation* to which the structure in question belongs. Thus, post-structuralism
might hold in store discursive possibilities that, due to its position in the
intellectual situation of the day, remain unseen, others being favored in
their place. Therefore, any "insertion in a new discursive constellation"[101]
always opens up new avenues for the interpretation of a discursive structure. An important hint for our own enterprise to reread medieval
thought from a postmodern point of vantage . . . (c) The constellation just
mentioned is not limited to "discursive" factors. Rather, the rules of formation of a discourse include a *field of non-discursive practices*. Into this category enter, among others, "Marxian" considerations: what is the social
and political function exercised by a particular discourse? And, in spite of
his archaeological deconstruction of psychoanalysis, Foucault does not
exclude that psychological factors may determine strategies. "[D]is-
course," he writes, "may in fact be the place for a phantasmatic representation, an element of symbolization, a form of the forbidden, an
instrument of derived satisfaction."[102]

Conclusion

The preceding outline of Foucault's archaeological method, its "field of
memory" and application, should give us a fairly precise idea as to what is
implied in the use of a post-structuralist methodology for the study of medieval thought—not just any post-structuralist methodology, of course, but
that developed by Foucault in such works as *Madness and Civilization* and
The Archaeology of Knowledge. In the following studies, I shall attempt to
apply some of the principal categories of Foucault's historical method to
Scholastic thought. Let me quickly say how, without repeating the
overview already provided at the end of the preface.

First, I shall try to reconstruct the Scholastic tradition from the point of
view of an "history of the Other" (study 2), showing that there is a dialectical interplay of two forces at work in medieval thought, an interplay of

an "inside" and an "outside." I shall then endeavor to write an "history of the Same" for Scholastic thought, by investigating the constitution of its episteme (studies 3 through 6). This step falls into four parts that are difficult to map exactly onto the Foucauldian schema, but are inspired by Foucault nonetheless. Study 3 will deal with the "intellectual practices" developed by the Schoolmen; for instance, we shall try to understand the importance of the literary form of the *quaestio* in Scholastic culture (a crucial "form of succession" of concepts), we shall investigate the "institutional sites" of Scholastic thought (most characteristically, the university), etc. Studies 4 and 5 will be devoted to the "content" of Scholastic thought, which I shall attempt to capture in one central problematic, namely, the clash of the Greek "circular" mode of thought with Christian "linearity." These studies will take their point of departure in Foucault's description of the medieval episteme in *The Order of Things,* upon which they will, however, elaborate considerably. The clash between the "circle" and the "line" opens up a discursive field some of the most important "points of diffraction" of which I shall examine in study 6. This study discusses a heterodox, and hence condemned, strategy that emerged from the Scholastic episteme in the thirteenth century, together with the transformation of the Scholastic episteme on the road to modernity. Let me repeat that any attempt to map the study of Scholastic thought—a field with its own history and structure—exactly onto Foucault's methodology would be artificial. However, I shall avail myself of Foucauldian approaches throughout the following analyses.

STUDY 2

DEFINING THE SCHOLASTIC TRADITION

"Yeut-il une philosophie scolastique au moyen âge?" ("Was there a Scholastic Philosophy in the Middle Ages?") is the surprising title of an article published by Maurice De Wulf, founder of the Louvain school of the study of medieval philosophy, in 1927.[1] When was there a Scholastic philosophy, if not in the Middle Ages? Who would want to dispute the existence of Scholastic philosophy in the Middle Ages? However, the paradoxical title of De Wulf's article reveals a genuine problem in the study of medieval thought, a problem that has already occupied several generations of medievalists. We can formulate this problem in the following way: What (if anything) characterizes and distinguishes medieval intellectual culture, beyond the mere historical fact that it took place during a period we call the "Middle Ages"? And can the term "Scholastic" be used to convey such distinguishing characteristics?

The Doctrinal Approach

De Wulf's article was directed against three critics of his work, *Histoire de la philosophie médiévale,*[2] two of whom—Marie-Dominique Chenu and Étienne Gilson—were themselves at the beginning of outstanding careers as medievalists. De Wulf's *Histoire de la philosophie médiévale* is a powerful, scholarly, and highly influential, yet also idiosyncratic book. Throughout almost half a century of continuous amplification and rewriting, from the first edition in 1900 (500 pages) to the sixth edition completed in 1947 (1,000 pages in three volumes)[3], De Wulf held fast to his conviction that there is a "doctrinal body"[4] to be discerned in medieval philosophy which is common to all the great thinkers of the Middle Ages. This conviction is reflected in the very organization of his *Histoire,* which is especially striking in the first two editions. On the one hand, De Wulf deliberately marginalizes thinkers—notably the "pantheist" John Scottus Eriugena—whose ideas do not fit into his conception of Scholastic philosophy. As these thinkers undeniably lived and worked in the period treated in the *Histoire,* so that it would hardly have been justifiable to exclude them altogether, they come to be classified as "anti-Scholastics." For De Wulf, "Scholastic philosophy" is therefore not synonymous with "medieval philosophy," but only with its "best part," as he declares.[5] On the other hand, De Wulf makes the "Scholastic synthesis" largely coincide with the thought of Thomas Aquinas. As a consequence, in the section devoted to his thought, text printed in roman letters signifies doctrines common to all the Scholastics, whereas italics are reserved for positions specific to Aquinas, and not shared by the Scholastic tradition as such.

One understands why De Wulf's *Histoire* should have given rise to prolonged and heated controversy. Even Fernand Van Steenberghen, his loyal pupil and successor at Louvain, had to admit that De Wulf's stance became more and more difficult to defend as "rapid progress in medieval studies" during the first decades of this century "increasingly revealed the richness and diversity of the philosophical systems" in the Middle Ages.[6] This "richness and diversity" ultimately dooms any attempt to define the unity of thought in the Middle Ages materially, through a "doctrinal core."

Nonetheless, is there not something that all the Scholastic thinkers had in common, namely, their Christian faith? As a consequence, is it not true that doctrines such as the existence of God or the immortality of the soul were shared by them all? Although this is correct, it does not constitute anything specific to medieval Christian thinkers. As De Wulf quite rightly points out in "Y eut-il une philosophie scolastique au moyen âge?," if it is Christianity that unifies Scholastic thought, why then do we not consider Descartes, Jacob Böhme, Pascal, or Schelling as Scholastics?[7]

The difficulties of the doctrinal approach to the unity of the Scholastic tradition seem unsurmountable. To speak of a core of philosophical doctrine or a "Scholastic synthesis" in the Middle Ages does violence to the historical facts. To define the specificity of the Scholastic movement through its Christian character is insufficient, as evidently there continued to exist Christian thinkers after the Middle Ages.

The Formal Approach

In contradistinction to the doctrinal approach, the formal approach does not claim a fundamental homogeneity on the plane of the ideas elaborated by medieval thinkers. Rather, this approach focuses upon the structure of medieval thought, that is to say, upon the methods developed and utilized by the medievals in their intellectual work. Study of the Scholastic method has made considerable progress in the last few years,[8] yet it remains indissociably connected with the name of the great Bavarian medievalist Martin Grabmann.[9] His chef-d'oeuvre, entitled *The History of Scholastic Method*, appeared in two volumes in 1909–1911.[10] *Die Geschichte der scholastischen Methode*, as the title runs in German, is a meticulous investigation of the origins of the Scholastic method in patristic times, and its development up to the beginning of the thirteenth century. *The History of Scholastic Method* has remained incomplete however, as its third volume, although announced in the preface of volume two for the immediate future, never appeared.

One can summarize Grabmann's thesis in this magisterial work in very few words.[11] Medieval thought centered around one paramount issue— the reconciliation of authority *(auctoritas)* and reason *(ratio)*. The tension between these two poles was felt from the very beginnings of Christianity, a religion founded upon the authority of a text—namely, Scripture— as interpreted by the church. However, this text raised innumerable questions concerning its internal coherence, as well as its external concordance with human thought and science. Thus, it is from patristic times onward that thinkers started developing "a certain external technique, an external form,"[12] devised to cope with this tension and, ultimately, resolve it. The seeds of the Scholastic method sown in patristic times came to fruition in the thought of St. Anselm of Canterbury, whom Grabmann dubs "the father of Scholasticism." The Scholastic method continued to mature until the thirteenth century.

Note that in Grabmann's definition of the Scholastic method, it is not the Christian faith as such that lends the intellectual endeavors of the medievals their unity; rather, it is the *relationship* between this faith and the exigencies of reason that, according to Grabmann, is paramount for an understanding of Scholasticism. Furthermore, the Scholastic method needs to be studied through the manner in which it has "as it were sensualized and incarnated itself"[13] in a certain technique.

The conviction that it is only through an investigation of the Scholastic *method* in its historical development and reality that we can discern the specificity of the Scholastic project is widely shared by contemporary medievalists. In the recently published first volume of his *Scholastic Humanism and the Unification of Europe,* Sir Richard W. Southern, doyen of medieval studies in Britain, writes: "[I]t must be remembered that scholastic thought was not a system of ideas, but a method, or rather a combination of methods."[14] However, as such, or as a structure, the tension between *auctoritas* and *ratio,* which Grabmann identified as the central issue of Scholasticism, is not peculiar to medieval culture. It is literally an ancient problem—a problem that first manifested itself at the very origins of Western civilization in ancient Greece. Let us try to describe it, and thereby situate the Scholastic tradition in the intellectual history of the West.

A Foucauldian Approach[15]

(1) Μῦθος and λόγος in Ancient Greece

The Christian Scriptures offer what one could call a "narrative" account of reality, that is to say, one based upon "stories" rather than upon argued demonstration. There are no proofs for the existence of God to be found in the Bible, no "five ways" or "ontological arguments" as would be developed in later centuries; instead, God is a reality, an agent present in the stories told through the Bible. The verity of these stories is guaranteed by a living tradition of faith.

At the beginning of Western civilization, there existed nothing except such narrative accounts of reality. The Greeks called them μῦθος, or "myth." For us, "myth" means something false, fictitious, and irrational. According to Jean-Pierre Vernant, a colleague of Foucault's at the Collège de France and an outstanding authority on comparative religion, this negative attitude toward myth is a fundamental characteristic of Western civilization:

> The concept of myth . . . belongs, by reason of its origins and history, to a tradition of thought peculiar to Western civilization in which myth is defined in terms of what is not myth, being opposed first to reality (myth is fiction) and, secondly, to what is rational (myth is absurd).[16]

As we just said, the negative definition of myth is not the way in which μῦθος was originally understood. In the period before the eighth century B.C., Vernant tells us, the Greeks saw no opposition between μῦθος and λόγος (speech, reason). Consequently, they also found no contradiction in using words that combined the two concepts, such as μυθολεγεῖν (to tell myths) or μυθολογία (the telling of myths). The story of the gradual differentiation between μῦθος and λόγος is the story of the birth of Western civilization.[17] It is also the story of the dialectical interplay between two poles that, even after being differentiated, continue to act upon each other.[18] Finally, as we shall see, the story of μῦθος and λόγος is a more sober retelling of another story, namely, the one of the conflict between Dionysius and Apollo. The whole history of Western civilization, including that of the Scholastic tradition, can be reconstructed along its lines.

According to Jean-Pierre Vernant, the invention of writing played a crucial role in the gradual movement from narrative to argued demonstration in ancient Greece. In the same way in which, according to Nietzsche, Dionysius objectivized himself when he first assumed an Apollonian form on the stage of Attic tragedy, so myth, with its presentation in the mode of an incantation, its charming and magic qualities, fundamentally changes character when committed to writing. "To put a text in writing is to set down one's message *es meson,* at the center of the community—that is, to place it openly at the disposal of the group as a whole."[19] The text as "object" of public scrutiny, no longer spellbinding the audience, comes to be susceptible of critical discussion. Of course, the differentiation between μῦθος and λόγος emerged slowly; there was no radical move directly from, say, the *Iliad*'s "being accepted by the public as if it had really happened"[20] to Plato's or Aristotle's radical critique of myth. Vernant distinguishes several factors and steps. Hesiod, in his *Theogony,* already does much more than just recount ancient tales. Sifting and recasting the mythical material transmitted to him, he creates "an original integrated construction."[21] Similar techniques of intervention are used by early poets. Pindar, for instance, frames traditional stories with an introduction and conclusion of his own, also feeling justified in interrupting the mythical account when it attributes unworthy deeds to the gods. In a similar way, Aischylos and Sophocles modify Homer's story of Oedipus. By making him "a man blinded by his own hand, an exile rejected by the world of men,"[22] they transform the legendary hero into an example of the mystery and tragedy of the human condition. As Vernant concludes: "When tragedy takes over the mythical traditions, it uses them to pose problems to which there are no solutions."[23] Still, there is no disavowal of myth yet to be found at this stage of the development of Greek culture. Even the first philosophers, the Presocratics, whose rejection of the supernatural as a valid explanation of natural phenomena marks another important aspect in the transition from μῦθος to λόγος, not only employed narrative structures (think of Parmenides's *Poem*), but were sometimes direct descendants of priest-kings. Thales, Anaximander, and Heraclitus are examples.[24] Thus, in ancient Greek civilization, the movement from μῦθος to λόγος went hand in hand with the transformation of the role of the magus into that of the philosopher. Moreover, the aforementioned objectivization of the text in the public sphere was made possible by the creation of the social institutions of the city. Vernant therefore, without reducing intellectual developments to social, political, and economic ones, points to a certain parallelism in the development of these different spheres. He believes that even an economic factor, such as the objectivization of value through the creation of coins in the seventh century B.C., has to be taken into consideration if we want to understand the emergence of λόγος-centered culture in ancient Greece.[25]

The gradual differentiation of μῦθος and λόγος culminates in Plato's and Aristotle's utter rejection of the narrative account of reality: "There is now such a gap between *muthos* and *logos,*" states Vernant, "that communication between the two breaks down; dialogue becomes impossible since the break is complete."[26] Compare this stage to Nietzsche's description of the triumph of the Apollonian in Socratic philosophy, and to Foucault's interpretation of the forces at work in the 1794 events at Bicêtre. Of course, there exists a difference between Plato and Aristotle, in that Plato, despite all his criticisms of myth, nevertheless employs narrative structures to a much greater extent than the Stagirite. When it comes to the realm of Ideas, especially the Idea of the Good, λόγος fails, so that one must make do with storytelling. The simile of the sun, the allegory of the cave, and the myth of Er in the *Republic* are examples of this approach of "mythos at the service of logos."[27]

Appearances notwithstanding, there is no contradiction involved in Plato's twofold attitude toward myth. We can analyse it along the lines of the paradoxical relationship between reason and madness described by Foucault. Reason employs different techniques in order to negate the challenge of madness; exclusion is one, but hand in hand with it goes the attempt to "cure" the mad, that is to say, to reintegrate them into the economic and moral order of bourgeois society—albeit on the conditions of that society. Now, according to Vernant, something very similar occurs in Plato's (and, less obviously, in Aristotle's) treatment of myth. On the one hand, myth is rigorously excluded from the realm of reason. On the other, it is "granted the rights of citizenship"[28] in the world of philosophical reason as a vehicle for the allegorical expression of truths that, albeit difficult to formulate in the language of λόγος, are not fundamentally opaque to its logic. In this way, μῦθος is reduced or enslaved to λόγος. This reductionist tendency has persisted right into modern scholarship about myth.[29]

(2) Christian Folly (μωρία) and Greek Wisdom (σοφία) in the Scholastic Tradition

The developments sketched out in the preceding section dealt the mythical culture of the Greeks a deadly blow. A return to myth became im-

possible once its spell had been broken. To be sure, some forms of the ancient mythical religion of the Greeks survived well into the first Christian
centuries, but only in syncretistic combinations with oriental cults and
mystery religions. In general, "philosophy had taken the place of [mythi-
cal] religion."[30]

This situation changed radically with the advent of Christianity:

> For the word of the cross is folly (μωρία) to those who are perishing, but to
> us who are being saved it is the power of God. For it is written, "I will de-
> stroy the wisdom (σοφίαν) of the wise, and the cleverness of the clever I
> will thwart." Where is the wise man? Where is the scribe? Where is the de-
> bater of this age? Has not God made foolish the wisdom of the world? For
> since, in the wisdom of God, the world did not know God through wisdom,
> it pleased God through the folly of what we preach to save those who be-
> lieve. For Jews demand signs and Greeks seek wisdom, but we preach Christ
> crucified, a stumbling block to Jews and folly to Gentiles, but to those who
> are called, both Jews and Greeks, Christ the power of God and the wisdom
> of God. For the foolishness of God is wiser than men, and the weakness of
> God is stronger than men. (1 Cor. 1.18–25 Revised Standard Version)[31]

For us post-Scholastics, the full import of this passage from the First
Letter of St. Paul to the Corinthians is difficult to appreciate. If, perchance,
we have been educated in institutions dominated by traditional "Aristotelico-Thomistic" philosophy and theology, its meaning must be altogether obscure. For, we have come to take it for granted that there exists
some kind of continuity between the culture of classical antiquity and
Christianity. Thus, we speak of the "being" and "essence" of God, discuss
the three "Persons" of the Trinity and the fact that Christ possesses two
"natures," human and divine, we learn about "transubstantiation" . . . all
notions borrowed from ancient philosophy. St. Paul and the first Christians, however, found the "wisdom of the Greeks" quite incompatible with
the Christian faith. In order to understand the Scholastic tradition, we
must not soften the Pauline stance vis-à-vis Greek wisdom; St. Paul was
simply against it. That we, if we are Christians, no longer have to be
"against" Greek wisdom, that we are even able to accept it as a legitimate
tool for the formulation of our faith—that is the result of the Scholastic
tradition. The Scholastic tradition is the bridge between St. Paul's attitude
toward Greek wisdom and ours. How this bridge came to be built is what
we shall endeavor to find out in the next few studies.

Before that, however, a more detailed explanation of the relationship
between Christian "folly" (μωρία) and Greek "wisdom" (σοφία) is called

for. First, some historical remarks. That St. Paul and the first Christians regarded Greek learning and philosophy as being incompatible with the
message of the Gospel, and in fact antagonistic to it, is easily understood
when we consider the fundamental differences between the two world-
views. Let me cite but one example: deeply entrenched in the Greek
philosophical tradition, from Plato and Aristotle right to the Neoplatonism of the first centuries A.D., is the belief in a radical inferiority of matter
to mind. This is very clear in Plato—only think of the hierarchy of the
parts of the soul—and even more so in the Neoplatonists of later centuries.
Plotinus's pupil Porphyry relates that the great thinker was "ashamed of
being in the body"![32] Even Aristotle, whose thought is said to be more
"empirical" in orientation, does not fundamentally diverge from this attitude. Hence Aristotle's intellectualist conception of the divine. Aristotle's
God, the "Unmoved Mover," is not only totally immaterial and un-
changeable, but is pure thought. Indeed, the thought of Aristotle's God is
so pure that it cannot possibly be conceived as extending to anything
below the level of the God himself. Therefore, the Unmoved Mover is
"thinking of thinking," pure self-reflexivity.[33] Now consider the stark contrast of this type of divinity with the God of the Old and, even more so,
the New Testament. This God reveals himself through prophets, he is prov-
idential, cares about his chosen people, punishes and rewards them, inter-
venes in history—he even sends his own Son to live among humanity and
"take away the sin of the world." This happens through the horrible and
humiliating death of Christ on the Cross. To believe any of this must indeed have seemed totally absurd from the point of view of traditional
Greek wisdom. It is this apparent incompatibility of pagan philosophy with
the message of the Cross that explains St. Paul's option for "folly."

On a more systematic plane, we can interpret the tension between
μωρία and σοφία in early Christian culture as a continuation of the dialectics between μῦθος and λόγος in ancient Greece. The Christian rejection of σοφία in favor of μωρία marks the return of the previously
excluded and marginalized element of myth into the center of culture.
One could object that faith in the foolishness of the Cross is not a myth.
This is true. The Christian religion—every religion, for that matter—is
fundamentally different from myth in that it replaces the centripetal, fu-
sional, "Dionysian" logic of myth with a heightened awareness of the otherness of God and the dignity of the individual.[34] Nonetheless, insofar as
it is a narrative account of reality, religion remains connected with the
structures of myth. It can never be fully translated into, or reduced to, pure
λόγος. Like those of myth, the "stories" of religion do not demonstrate

anything, but aim to gain the adherence of their audience. Religion is not susceptible of total "objectivization"; or rather, it is thus susceptible—like myth—but only at the price of losing its character as religion. Totally "demythologized"[35] and historically dissected, it is deprived of its binding *(religere)* force.[36]

Given the preceding considerations, we are authorized to interpret Christianity as a force that reinscribed μῦθος/μωρία into the center of Mediterranean culture, thereby displacing λόγος/σοφία and relegating it to the margins. And was Christianity not highly successful in its struggle against Greek philosophy and wisdom? In 529, the Emperor Justinian closed the Platonic Academy in Athens. In the very same year, Benedict of Nursia is said to have founded the Abbey of Montecassino. These two events are often considered to mark the beginning of the Middle Ages. However, 529 is a plausible date for the beginning of the medieval period only if one wants to associate the Middle Ages with the death of ancient civilization, and the beginning of a long period of intellectual darkness that was dominated by the "foolishness of the Cross," and overcome only by the revival of the Classics in the Renaissance. This was certainly the perspective adopted by Wilhelm Nestle, among many others, when he published *Vom Mythos zum Logos* in 1940.[37] However, this is a distorted and historically indefensible view. In reality, ancient σοφία survived to some extent within the Christian faith that had originally rejected it.

It is true that right into early patristic times, that is to say, the period when Christian thinkers started reflecting upon their faith in a systematic manner and transforming it into theology, the original Pauline distrust of Greek wisdom persisted. Tertullian's (ca. 160–after 220) famous outburst against "Athens" in his *Prescription against Heretics* is perhaps the best known example of this attitude:

> What has Athens to do with Jerusalem? What the Academy with the Church? What heretics with Christians? . . . Away with those who have professed a Stoic and Platonic and dialectical Christianity! We need no curiosity after Christ Jesus, no inquiry after the Gospel.[38]

Tertullian's bilious attacks against those seeking to interpret Christianity through categories of ancient Greek thought notwithstanding, he is himself considered one of the first theologians to have started a reconciliation of Greek λόγος with the Christian faith. For instance, he reflects upon the nature of the Trinity (it is in Tertullian that the word *trinitas* occurs for the first time) by means of the philosophical terms *persona* and *substantia.* Indeed, this reconciliation is at the very heart of the patristic movement, which is why Grabmann was more than justified in locating the origins of the Scholastic method in the patristic period. We can go so far as to say that the Scholastic tradition, interpreted, following Grabmann, as the reconciliation of the authority of faith with the exigencies of reason, started in the first Christian centuries.

This, then, is our definition of the Scholastic tradition: the Scholastic tradition is a movement characterized by the tension between μωρία and σοφία, a tension that constitutes the continuation, in Christian times, of the ancient Greek dialectics between μῦθος and λόγος. The Scholastic tradition attempted to reconcile these two poles, that is to say, to return Greek wisdom to the center of Christian culture—from which it had been excluded by the first Christians[39]—without sacrificing the integrity of the faith (see fig. 2.1).

Although in a sense the Scholastic tradition can be traced to patristic origins, it did not reach its fullest development until the thirteenth century. Such a statement might appear to be diametrically opposed to our "postmodern" approach and Foucauldian method, precluding as these do a teleological reading of history. However, to view the thirteenth century as the proverbial "golden age" of Scholasticism is not an arbitrary decision. This reading is imposed on us by the historical fact that, before the thirteenth century, the Scholastic tradition did not have at its disposal the sources necessary to reconcile "Athens" and "Jerusalem." Quite simply, it did not know Athens well enough.

The Greek Intellectual Heritage until the Thirteenth Century: The Aristotelian Tradition

Let us start with a general remark. The history of the Western intellectual tradition is, like all human history, replete with all manner of accidents and vicissitudes. It is not simply the history of continuous growth, but also one of loss and decline. An insight acquired, a work written, a step made is as likely to be lost as to be built upon in subsequent generations. Take the Aristotelian tradition as an example.[40] Aristotle died in 322 B.C. Does this mean that from this date onward, the corpus of Aristotelian writings as we know it enjoyed a continuous presence in the Western world, being accessible to whoever cared to read it? Not at all. Aristotle produced two types of writings: those published during his own lifetime, and manuscripts of his lectures delivered at the Academy (Plato's school), and at the so-called

Figure 2.1   Scholastic Thought in the Dialectics of the Western Tradition

(1) zero degree (before 800 B.C):

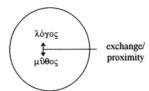

(2) construction as "other":

(3) rejection of narrative account
(Plato, Aristotle):

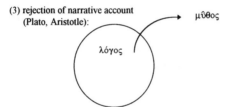

(4) return of narrative account
(early Christianity):

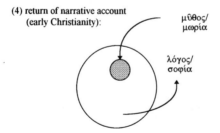

(5) return of Greek wisdom (Scholastic method):

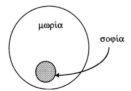

Lykeion. We know nothing about the fate of the works that Aristotle cir-
culated himself, the so-called exoteric writings. They were lost sometime
toward the beginning of the Christian era. Paradoxically, all that has been
handed down to us is the part of Aristotelian oeuvre which Aristotle never
bothered to publish; hence the sometimes highly fragmentary character of
these treatises—we have already had an occasion to discuss this problem
earlier, in the introduction. However, even Aristotle's lectures disappeared
from his school in 288 B.C., when his last living disciple, Neleus of Skepsis, decided to take them to his hometown (Skepsis near the old Troy).
Neleus's descendants buried them there. Remaining unread and unknown
for about 200 years, they were rediscovered only at the beginning of the
first century B.C., by a bibliophile called Apellikon of Teos. Andronikos of
Rhodes then edited Aristotle's works for the first time sometime in the
first century B.C., not including the exoteric writings. The order of the
Aristotelian corpus as we know it today is due to Andronikos; he, too, is
responsible for the structure of such works as the *Physics* and *Metaphysics,*
which he assembled from independent lectures. Andronikos called the
Metaphysics thus because he placed the treatises brought together under this
name "after the *Physics*" (τὰ μετὰ τὰ φυσικά).[41]

It would be a mistake to assume that, once Aristotle's writings had been
made accessible by Andronikos of Rhodes, all the following generations
were fully conversant with his teachings. From the time of the Emperor
Diocletian (reigned 284–305 A.D.) onward, the Roman empire started
drifting apart, the Eastern part separating itself gradually from "West
Rome," which it would survive—as the Byzantine empire—for a whole
millennium. The division was as much a cultural as a political, military, and
economic one.[42] Thus, by the time of the downfall of the Western part of
the empire (conventionally, the date 476 is assigned to this event), Greek
was no longer widely understood by educated Romans. This is why
Boethius (ca. 475/480–524) undertook the ambitious project of translating the entirety of Plato's and Aristotle's works into Latin, and elucidating
them by means of commentaries.[43] Boethius, however, fell out with the
Ostrogothic king Theodoric, in whose service he worked; accused of trea-
son, he was executed. As for his project to "render into Latin" *(Romanum
stilum vertere)* all the works of Plato and Aristotle, he only ever completed
translations of some of Aristotle's logical writings. Consequence: due to
this tragic accident of history, the bulk of the Platonic and Aristotelian heritage was to remain inaccessible to the Latin-speaking world for many centuries to come. For the Christian reconciliation of μωρία and σοφία, this
meant that for hundreds of years it would simply lack the sources enabling

it to appreciate Greek wisdom, except for a few morsels—in Aristotle's
case, some works dealing with logic. The full force of the challenge that
ancient thought represented for Christianity was not to be felt until the
middle of the twelfth century onward—we shall consider these developments in a moment.[44]

The Greek philosophical tradition continued to flourish in Byzantium
long after the fall of the Roman empire in the West. The rich philosophical culture of the Byzantine empire is still one of the most underresearched
areas of the history of philosophy.[45] At the margins of the philosophical
and theological mainstream of Byzantine culture, Christian monks in Syria
also continued the tradition of Aristotelian learning.[46] After the Muslim
conquest of Syria, the culture of these Syriac-speaking Christians, with
their background in Greek learning, found itself marginalized again in its
new Arabic environment. Yet this history of continued marginalization—
which ultimately led to the virtual disappearance of Syriac Christianity—
secured the Syriac Christians a crucial role as cultural mediators. Already
under the first caliphs, the Umayyads (661–749), the original Arabic culture started to undergo profound transformations. The Arabs had little experience in the practical matters of running their ever-expanding empire,
and learned eagerly from their subjects, whom they often employed in
their service. Moreover, under the rule of the 'Abbāsids, who succeeded
the Umayyads, a systematic effort to improve the intellectual level of Arabic culture was initiated. In order to obtain important scientific and philosophical literature, the 'Abbāsid caliph "al-Ma'mūn sent emissaries to
Byzantium to seek out and purchase for him books of 'ancient learning,'
which were then ordered to be translated by a panel of scholars."[47] One of
the most eminent and prolific of these scholars, Ḥunain b. Isḥāq (809–873),
was a Syriac Christian, as were many other members of the original team
of translators and commentators. Ḥunain is one of the greatest figures in
the history of translation, as well as translation theory (on which he reflected in a famous epistle written in 856). Unfortunately, we often tend
to forget the crucial role played by translations and translators in the
processes of cultural transmission. What texts are translated, how and how
well, when . . . all these are questions that often prove central in the building and development of a tradition.

The efforts made by the Islamic culture to assimilate the Greek heritage
bore copious fruit. Between the ninth and the thirteenth centuries, a rich
and diverse intellectual culture developed in the Islamic world, drawing
upon many sources—including Aristotelian and Neoplatonic philosophy,
Greek astronomy, medicine, and other sciences—that were unavailable in

the West. From the tenth century, Spain became one of the centers of Islamic thought—indeed, of the Mediterranean intellectual culture in general. Ibn Rushd or, according to the Latinized form of his name, Averroës (1126–1198) lived and worked there, as did his contemporary Moses Maimonides, who, despite his Jewish faith, composed his works in Arabic.[48] When Toledo was reconquered in 1085, it soon developed into a hub of Christian intellectual activity. From the middle of the twelfth century onward, it became a center of translation, not unlike Baghdad 300 years earlier.[49] Thus, in the words of the great American medievalist Charles Homer Haskins, "[t]he great adventure of the European scholar lay in the Peninsula."[50] Works by Islamic and Jewish philosophers, as well as Arabic versions of Greek works hitherto unknown to the West, were rendered into Latin by translators such as Dominicus Gundissalinus and Gerard of Cremona (twelfth century), Alfred of Sarashel, Michael Scotus, and Herman the German (thirteenth century). Michael Scotus left Spain sometime before 1220, having been hired to work at the court of Emperor Frederick II in Sicily, another important center of translating activity.[51] The translation of Averroës's meticulous Aristotelian commentaries, which is due in part to Michael, was to constitute one of the dominant influences upon the intellectual development of the Latin West in the thirteenth century. Averroës's so-called "Long Commentaries" were accompanied by full quotations of Aristotle's text, so that the translation of Averroës also rendered the Philosopher's own thought accessible.[52] Ibn Sīnā (Avicenna, ca. 980–1037), too, was translated and proved influential, though he defended an Aristotelianism much more colored by Neoplatonic strands of thought than that of Averroës.[53]

The Latins rapidly discovered the difficulties involved in reading Aristotle through Arabico-Latin translations. When new contacts with Byzantium (in 1204, Constantinople was invaded by the Crusaders) made it possible to gain access to Greek manuscripts, the Arabico-Latin translations gradually came to be superseded.[54] William of Moerbeke, a Dominican confrère of St. Thomas Aquinas and one of the most important medieval translators, was responsible for numerous excellent Graeco-Latin versions of Aristotle.[55]

This massive influx of new material, all of pagan or non-Christian origin, brought a renewed challenge to the "foolishness of the Cross." To respond to this challenge, philosophical and theological doctrines had to be reformulated in decisive ways. That this work of assimilation and restructuring succeeded is the result of a combination of many factors, to the study of which we now turn.

STUDY 3

SCHOLASTIC INTELLECTUAL PRACTICES

" "Intellectual practices" *(pratiques intellectuelles)* is a term coined by the Dutch medievalist Olga Weijers, who uses it in the subtitle of her study, *Le maniement du savoir.*[1] Weijers does not offer an explicit definition of the term, although in the preface of her book she speaks of certain "approaches and methods," as well as "notions and mechanisms," which she says were the "basis" of what was taught at the early Scholastic universities.[2] These "intellectual practices" correspond to what Foucault calls the "rules of formation" of a discourse, that is to say, the constellation of intellectual procedures, institutional conditions, subject positions, etc. that opens up the epistemological field in which a given kind of discourse becomes possible. Traditional medievalist research into the intellectual conditions prevailing in Scholastic times differs from the Foucauldian approach, in that it distinguishes rigorously between the "form" and "content" of Scholastic thought, studying the intellectual practices for their own sake, as it were, rather than envisaging them as conditions of possibility for a certain kind of thought. This distinction, or even separation, which is quite artificial from a Foucauldian point of view, translates itself right onto the institutional plane. Mostly, medievalist philosophers or theologians have neither interest nor competence in the domain of intellectual practices, while the historians investigating such practices keep, for their part, a certain distance from philosophical and theological questions. One of the aims of this book is, of course, to overcome this artificial separation.

Weijers's *Le maniement du savoir* is a masterly summa that reflects the state of the art in our knowledge of many Scholastic intellectual practices. In the course of this study, we shall speak of most of the issues Weijers addresses in her book, though we shall also deal with others strikingly absent from it. Thus, we start with an intellectual practice, or an historical a priori, of

which neither Weijers nor Foucault seems to have appreciated the fundamental importance: handwriting.

Gothic Handwriting as an Historical a priori

The claim that a particular style of handwriting can constitute an historical a priori in the Foucauldian sense might seem rather farfetched. Handwriting is nothing that shapes our thoughts; we shape our handwriting!
But perhaps this alternative is misleading. On the one hand, it is clear that
it is human subjects who write, thereby creating styles of script. However,
even at this most basic level of intellectual tools, the "tool" might turn out
to possess a life of its own, being much more than merely a passive instrument. This, at least, is the claim that the French paleographer Robert
Marichal advanced in an article published in 1963 under the title "L'écriture latine et la civilisation occidentale du Ier au XVIe siècle."[3] In this excellent piece, Marichal argues not only that the cultural and intellectual
developments which took place in the Latin world from patristic times to
the beginning of the Renaissance are faithfully mirrored in the respective
handwriting styles of these periods; he goes further and contends that these
developments were *foreshadowed* by stylistic changes:

> In other words, it appears that, in the history of the Occident, every change
> of mentality is accompanied, and most often even foreshadowed, by a
> change in the morphology and style of writing.[4]

Marichal's thesis seems to be, then, that styles of writing exercise a formative influence in the development of cultures.[5]

Gothic script was the result of a transformation of the so-called Caroline minuscule, that is to say, the style of handwriting that prevailed in the
Latin West from the time of the Carolingian renaissance, in the eighth
century, until the middle of the twelfth. After centuries of cultural "darkness," the Emperor Charlemagne—himself illiterate—initiated a series of
educational and liturgical reforms that encouraged learning and scholarship in the Church, the education of whose representatives had declined
to a pitiful level. Under the propitious conditions created by these reforms, the Caroline minuscule spread rapidly in the monasteries and
schools of the Carolingian empire, where its was appreciated, above all, for
its improved legibility.[6] Generally speaking, the Caroline minuscule is
more sober, harmonious, and well-balanced, and therefore clearer, than its
Roman predecessors. It gave a more characteristic shape to certain indi-

vidual letters—Marichal mentions the *g* as an example—thereby making them easier to distinguish and, thus, to read (see plate 1 for a manuscript in Caroline minuscule).

The exact origin of Gothic script is one of the most difficult and hotly debated issues in Latin paleography. According to a thesis recently put forward by Christopher de Hamel, the first tendencies toward Gothic style can be discerned in manuscripts containing Peter Lombard's Gloss of the Bible.[7] The Gloss offers explanations of individual words and phrases in Scripture, to which it adds illuminating extracts from the commentaries of the church fathers. The first standardized Gloss on the whole Bible was prepared at the school of Laon, starting to circulate around 1130.[8] It was later revised by the great theologian Peter Lombard (ca. 1100–1160), who expanded further upon the Psalter and the Pauline Epistles. Now the page layout of the manuscripts containing Peter Lombard's *Magna Glosatura,* or "Great Gloss," differs radically from the layout of the earlier Glosses. In the first glossed books of the Bible, the text of Scripture invariably occupied the center of the page, which was created first; then, as a second step of the writing process, the glosses were added in the margins (see plate 1). However, in copies of Peter Lombard's *Magna Glosatura* made from the 1160s onward, "a complete change occurred."[9] The text and the gloss came to be conceived as forming a unity on the page. This can be seen by the process in which the layout was now created. The text of Scripture was no longer copied first, with the glosses being added later as a kind of appendix. Rather, the scriptural text and the gloss were placed on the same ruled lines, the only difference between them being that Scripture was written in larger letters on alternate lines (previously, the marginal text had been written on lines ruled separately from those for the main text). Moreover, after Peter Lombard's revision, the glosses themselves had come to represent a continuous text, rather than isolated notes. The Bible still occupied the center of the page, but was made "to fit neatly around the blocks of gloss on either side of it"[10] (see plate 2 for an example of the new layout). Again: the Bible was made to fit neatly around its commentary! Let us not, in the present context, dwell on the implications of the remarkable shift of emphasis in the relationship between the text of Scripture and its glosses—a shift of emphasis that indicates, in Foucauldian terms, a change in "procedures of intervention." Here, it is only interesting to note that, according to de Hamel, the new display script devised by the scribes for the alternate-line biblical text was a precursor of the Gothic style.[11] According to this thesis, then, Gothic script emerged as part of a process in which medieval theology began to take a more systematic shape; no longer presented in the form of isolated notes, Peter Lombard's Gloss becomes a text in its own right, with its own coherence, claiming to be written on the same lines as the Bible.

The most important difference between the Gothic style of handwriting and the Caroline minuscule is the "fracturing" or "breaking" that occurs in the Gothic letters.[12] This is especially clear in *i, n, u,* and *m,* the "minims." These letters, like the Gothic script as a whole, acquire an increasingly angular quality as they come to be composed of vertical shafts that are written in several movements: a perfectly vertical center part, a stroke at the top added at an angle inclined to the left, and a stroke at the bottom added at an angle inclined to the right. Similarly, the *o,* which was round in Caroline minuscule, is broken up into a series of six straight strokes. (According to Marichal, the breaking of the Gothic letter first occurred at the bottom of the line, when scribes devised angular "feet," which are comparable to the serifs of our modern printed letters.) The already complex shafts were then, in the case of letters such as *n, u,* or *m,* which have many "legs," written side by side and connected by means of hair-strokes.

The procedure of building letters from clearly discernible, homologous elements in an almost geometrical fashion repeats itself analogously at the level of the words. Word divisions, as well as the beginning and end of individual words, are much more clearly marked in Gothic handwriting than they were in Caroline minuscule. Some letters, such as the *s,* acquire different forms as they occur at the beginning or end of the word (the *s* of our modern Latin alphabet was originally designed to be used at the end of words; the "long" *s* reserved for the beginning or middle of a word still survives, in the form of a ligature with *z,* in the German character *ß*). Within the boundaries of the word, the individual letters are joined together more densely, this compression being brought about, on the one hand, by touching feet and, on the other, by so-called "biting" connections between adjacent letters; these are ligatures of letters such as *o* and *c,* which come to be written so closely together that their strokes partially overlap.

Finally, moving from the level of the word to that of the text, we see the same Gothic preoccupation with clarity repeat itself in the typical page layouts of the time. The Gothic layout endeavors to throw the structure of the written text into as clear a relief as possible. This is accomplished through the use of large, often illuminated initials and the chapter sign "¶" to mark the different hierarchical levels of a text in a systematic fashion. (It is interesting to know that the symbol "¶," omnipresent as it is on our computer screens, is a medieval invention.)

However, let us return to the main thesis of this section, according to which handwriting is not merely a neutral tool, but exercises a formative influence upon the thought to which it gives expression. Marichal claims that Gothic script is animated by "a certain dialectics."[13] What the eminent paleographer has in mind here is, first, the "breaking up" of Gothic letters into a series of small units of similar structure and, subsequently, the systematic composition of these homologous units into more and more complex wholes, all (letters, words, and texts) following the same basic law of clear articulation. It would certainly seem as if this method rendered the form of the text eminently suitable to be grasped by the discursive structure of human reason. For reason, too, "builds up" its idea of reality by means of analysis and synthesis. The characteristics of Gothic script, then, seem to reflect and reinforce a certain confidence in the powers of human reason, a confidence that can be perceived as well in the daring new layout of the Gloss—and as we shall see, in other intellectual practices that will be analyzed in the present study. Yet, Gothic handwriting is perhaps characterized by a dialectics even more profound than the structure to which Marichal drew attention.

Abbreviations: Traces of Negative Theology?

Marichal does not make much of the proliferation of abbreviations in Gothic manuscripts, although he is of course fully aware of this phenomenon, so vexing for the untrained modern reader.[14] Abbreviations had been employed in Latin handwriting since Roman times. In the Middle Ages, their use underwent a first standardization during the Carolingian reform. Then, as a result of the massive influx of new sources we sketched out in the previous study, the greatly increased scholarly activity to which it contributed, and the foundation of the universities, many new abbreviations were created in the later Middle Ages to speed up the writing process and economize on parchment. In combination with the other transformations of Gothic script—especially the greater internal density of its words—the increased use of abbreviations transformed many words into veritable ideograms, which were no longer deciphered letter by letter, but rather recognized as a whole by their general shape, their gestalt.[15] This tendency, while not necessarily impinging upon the legibility of the texts, rather obviously runs counter to the desire for a display of clarity and "rational" structure (see plate 3 for a typical page from a Gothic Bible). The tension is explained, to a certain extent, if one considers the historical development of the medieval abbreviation system.

Adriano Cappelli, in his *Dizionario di abbreviature latine ed italiane,* distinguishes six methods of abbreviation utilized in medieval manuscripts: truncation (such as "AUG." for "Augustus"), contraction (such as "d̄s" for "Deus"), abbreviation by means of signs with a fixed meaning (such as "⁹cedo" for "concedo"; the "9"-shaped sign stands for "con" or "com"), abbreviation by means of signs that are context-dependent (such as "omnib;" for "omnibus," and "quilib;" for "quilibet"), abbreviation by means of superscripted letters (such as "aᵃ" for "anima") and, finally, abbreviation by means of conventional signs (such as "÷" for "est").[16] There are many subtypes and combinations of these six basic methods. It is contraction, however, that has a particularly interesting history. According to Ludwig Traube, one of the pioneers of paleographical studies in this century, the technique of contraction originated in a special treatment accorded to the "holy names" of God.[17] When the Bible was first translated into Latin, *nomina sacra* such as "Dominus" or "Christus" were not spelled out in full letters, but rather contracted, thus: "D̄M̄S̄," "X̄P̄S̄"—the latter contraction representing a combination of the Greek letters X and P (from "ΧΡΙΣΤΟΣ") with the Latin S. Already from the fifth century onward, however, the practice of contracting the holy names of God came to be extended to other terms, first to words related to the religious sphere ("Ē̄P̄S̄" for "episcopus" is an example), then to any profane word whatsoever.[18] It is not clear to what extent later medievals were aware of the religious origins of the technique to create abbreviations by means of contraction. Traube discovered a remarkable, yet apparently isolated, passage in a commentary on Matthew authored by the ninth-century exegete Christian of Stablo.[19] This author still offers a religious explanation for the abbreviation of holy names:

> In fact, in our culture *(apud nos)* "Jesus" is written iota, and eta, and sigma, with a stroke on top. Now in the books of the Greeks, one finds it written only by means of iota, and sigma, and a stroke on top, in the same way in which the other names of God, too, must be written in a contracted form *(comprehensive),* as the name of God cannot be spelled out in letters.[20]

Earlier in his commentary, Christian had already remarked, in a very similar context, that "the Trinity cannot be understood nor explained by means of letters, but is ineffable."[21] We therefore witness, in this author, a very clear understanding that there is a religious background to the practice of abbreviating the names of God. Christian attributes this practice to the inability of language, and hence of writing, to give adequate expression to the nature of the divine. God is too great to be spelled out; all we can do is stammer, as it were, his holy names.[22]

Furthermore, Christian of Stablo points in the right direction when he associates the Latin and Greek traditions of contracting the *nomina sacra*. Indeed, Traube has provided evidence showing the Greek roots of the contracted Latin forms. The Latin contractions "$\overline{\text{DMS}}$," "$\overline{\text{XPS}}$," and "$\overline{\text{SPS}}$" ("SPIRITUS") are directly modeled upon Greek equivalents, in this case "$\overline{\text{KC}}$" ("KYPIOC"), "$\overline{\text{XPC}}$" ("XPICTOC"), and "$\overline{\text{ΠNA}}$" ("ΠNEYMA").[23]

According to Traube, the Greek contractions of the divine names were originally devised by Hellenistic Jews who translated the Old Testament from Hebrew into Greek.[24] At the beginning, only one or two contracted forms existed, namely, "$\overline{\text{KC}}$" and "$\overline{\text{ΘC}}$" ("ΘEOC"). Their purpose was to render the Jewish name of God, the tetragram יהוה. The tetragram was considered so holy, magic, and ineffable that the rabbis did not disclose its pronunciation to the ordinary faithful, arbitrarily reading "adonai" wherever יהוה occurred in the text of the Old Testament. Indeed, for the uninitiated it was not clear how to pronounce the unvocalized יהוה, even when they were face to face with the letters—for in Hebrew, as in other Semitic languages, the basic script does not include any vowels. Therefore, on the one hand, we see in the Jewish tradition a desire to keep the holy name of God concealed. At the same time, in the manuscripts containing the Old Testament, the tetragram was often lavishly illuminated in gold, so as to highlight it especially. This proves to be "a strange dialectics" *(ein eigentümlicher Widerstreit),* as Traube remarks.[25] For the name of God was at once concealed and thrown into high relief. The Hellenistic translators were faced with the difficult problem of having to reproduce this dialectics in the Greek version of the Old Testament. Illuminating posed no difficulty; but how could they render the tetragram adequately in Greek, that is to say, in a language in which both the vowels and the consonants are represented by letters, so that there can be no unvocalized words? According to Traube, the contracted forms "$\overline{\text{KC}}$" and "$\overline{\text{ΘC}}$" were the best solution the translators could offer to this problem.

If this interpretation is correct—and contemporary scholars deem it at least "possible"[26] that the Greek contraction has to be traced to Jewish attitudes toward the tetragram—this means that the abbreviation through contraction, which was to become so pervasive in Latin script, is, historically speaking, an element of negative theology; in other words, it originated in the insight that God infinitely transcends the capacities of the human mind and of human language. In this logic, even to utter God's name, as if one could possess him through words, is ultimately an act of blasphemy. From the historical perspective, then, the contractions occurring in Scholastic texts contain traces of a negative theology, reminding the reader of the limitations of reason, and its inability to grasp the divine. At the same time, on all their levels—letters, words, paragraphs, chapters—Gothic texts are constructed in such a way as to reflect the discursive structure of reason, thus underscoring the powers of the human mind to order and elucidate. As a consequence, Gothic handwriting contains an amazing tension; a tension, which we shall encounter again and again in analyzing the Scholastic episteme, between confidence in human reason and awareness of its radical finitude.

Manifestatio **and** *concordantia* **in Gothic Architecture**

Medievalists from the art historian Charles Rufus Morey to the paleographer Robert Marichal have adverted to the similarities between Gothic manuscripts and Gothic architecture. Whereas Marichal offers a comparison between the style of Gothic handwriting and that of Gothic building,[27] Morey suggests that the medieval book illuminators "reveal in many . . . ways . . . their dependence on cathedral art."[28] I propose to consider manuscript-making and building as fields of concomitance in the Scholastic episteme, that is to say, as analogical structures confirming and reinforcing each other.[29] It would be very strange if the intellectual practices of the Scholastics had not been shaped and influenced by the architectural surroundings in which they lived and worshipped day by day. Indeed, there is a growing body of philosophical literature—inspired both by Heidegger's reflections on architecture and by the architectural roots of postmodernism—that reflects on the relations between the forms of our architecture and the forms of our thinking.[30]

The best account of the intellectual significance of High Gothic architecture is still the book *Gothic Architecture and Scholasticism,* by the illustrious art historian Erwin Panofsky.[31] While some of Panofsky's theses in *Abbot Suger on the Abbey Church of St.-Denis*[32] have recently come under attack[33]—especially his claim according to which Abbot Suger's ideas for the remodeling of his church were directly inspired by a Neoplatonic metaphysics of light—*Gothic Architecture and Scholasticism* remains authoritative.[34] According to Panofsky, there are two "controlling principles" at work in Scholasticism and, hence, High Gothic architecture,[35] namely, *manifestatio* and *concordantia*.[36] By *manifestatio*, Panofsky understands the elucidation and clarification of reality through reason, accomplished by a quest for totality, an arrangement of this totality in a structured system of homologous parts, and distinctness and cogency in the relation between these parts.[37] The Romanesque churches had been like castles for the defense of the faith, their structure conveying, as Panofky writes, "the impression of a space determinate and impenetrable."[38] In contrast to the display of solidity in the Romanesque edifice, the Gothic cathedral is infinitely "fractionized"[39]:

> . . . this principle of progressive divisibility (or, to look at it the other way, multiplicability) increasingly affected the entire edifice down to the smallest detail. At the height of the development, supports were divided and subdivided into main piers, major shafts, minor shafts, and still minor shafts; the tracery of windows, triforia, and blind arcades into primary, secondary, and tertiary mullions and profiles; ribs and arches into a series of moldings.[40]

This fractionization, combined with features such as larger windows and thinner walls, allows the Gothic cathedral to radiate a high degree of transparency. Its construction gives the impression of lying open to the eye. Moreover, the whole of the edifice seems to be contained in each of its smallest parts, thus rendering the whole accessible through the parts. In this regard, Panofsky draws attention to the ingenious construction of the compound piers, whose complex combination of core, shafts, and colonnettes enabled them to "express" the entire superstructure resting on them, and, so to speak, flowing together in them.[41] Finally, the famous flying buttresses project the inside structure to the outside, making it possible to "read" the cathedral even from without.[42] This last feature again contrasts sharply with the fort-like character of the Romanesque edifice, emphasizing the "openness" of the Gothic cathedral.

Before moving on to the second "controlling principle" of Gothic architecture, let us stop for a moment to consider a point made by Charles Morey that complements Panofsky's analysis. One aspect of the Gothic cathedral that is strangely absent from Panofsky's account is the Gothic "quest for greater and greater height."[43] As Morey observes, the soaring space of the Gothic cathedral is "no longer rational, commensurable, and geometric"; it is "space in movement" linking the observer with infinity.[44] Anybody who has ever stood in a Gothic cathedral—such as the *Dom* in Cologne—and looked upward, knows the truth of this description. As "rational" as the Gothic structure may be, it manages to combine its logical transparency with an intimation of the infinite; it expresses both the greatness and the limits of rationality, both self-confidence and humility. In this regard, the Gothic cathedral mirrors the dialectics of Gothic script, with its characteristic combination of rational clarity and opaque abbreviations.

The second principle that, according to Panofsky, animates the religious architecture of the twelfth and thirteenth centuries is *concordantia*. *Concordantia* is defined as the "acceptance and ultimate reconciliation of contradictory possibilities."[45] The Gothic architect was sometimes faced with architectural possibilities that appeared equally valid, though, on the face of it, irreconcilable. Panofsky shows that, in these cases, an effort was made to reject neither of the conflicting solutions. One striking example of this pursuit of *concordantia* is the rose window, which typically appears in the west façade of the Gothic cathedral. This round window posed a number a difficulties of both a technical and stylistic nature. To mention but one difficulty, in an otherwise "angular" Gothic environment, an isolated circular element gives a strange impression! Some architects, mostly in Normandy and England, thus refused to incorporate the rose window into their edifices, but, as Panofsky suggests, the example of the abbey church of St.-Denis seems to have proven authoritative.[46] In different building projects, various experiments were undertaken over the years, until the architect of the now destroyed abbey church of St.-Nicaise in Reims finally found the solution: the rose was simply inscribed within the pointed arch of a "typical" Gothic window, thus reconciling the circular and angular forms (see plate 4).

Similar "synthetic" solutions were found in other cases of architectural conflict. We need not investigate these in detail here. The main point to remember from our discussion of the principle of *concordantia* in Gothic architecture is that the reconciliation of opposite forms constitutes an important element in the design of High Gothic architecture.[47] It will become clear later in this study that the theme of *concordantia* is mirrored in the Scholastic culture of the time.

Digression: Textual Transmission and Textual Criticism

In a previous section, I briefly treated the nature of Gothic handwriting considered as an intellectual practice. In connection with this subject, it will be useful if we familiarize ourselves with the basic principles of the transmission of texts in the Middle Ages. Evidently, in the Middle Ages there were no printing presses to ensure the dissemination of texts. It is important to render explicit some of the consequences that ensue from this rather obvious fact.

From the time of the Carolingian renaissance until about the middle of the twelfth century, the centers of scribal activity in the Latin West were the monasteries. The larger monasteries in particular were equipped with *scriptoria,* writing rooms, in which specially trained monks were engaged in the production of books—everything from the pricking and ruling of the page to writing, illuminating, and binding. As we shall see a little later in this study, the monastic culture of the Middle Ages was extremely text-centered; together with the chapel, the refectory, and the library, the *scriptorium* constituted one of the most important focal points of community life. Unfortunately, not much is known about precisely how the monasteries acquired books for their libraries. No doubt they sometimes borrowed books from each other to have them copied in their *scriptoria;* more often, however, they sent one of their own monks to a library possessing the desired book, to transcribe it there. This procedure obviated the need to borrow from a monastery that might only have possessed one copy of a certain volume, thus being reluctant to see it depart into the vicissitudes of a long and perhaps dangerous journey to some faraway place. Moreover, some of the smaller monasteries were not equipped with all the facilities needful for bookmaking. Finally, it was not unheard-of for monasteries to hire professional *scriptores* to seek out and copy certain texts.[48]

As Christopher de Hamel has shown, the advent of the glossed books of the Bible and their increasing popularity around 1160–1170 created the conditions for an urbanization, professionalization, and commercialization of scribal activities. When, in the new intellectual conditions of the twelfth century, the rhythm of book production picked up, the traditional monastic techniques for the dissemination of texts no longer proved adequate. Monks could travel, but being tied by their Rule to one specific house, they were not supposed to spend their time chasing after the latest, most up-to-date books. Thus, the function of book production shifted, first to secular priests and thence to lay professionals. Studying the large library that St. Thomas Becket acquired during his exile in France between 1164 and 1170, de Hamel found evidence of clerics from Becket's household who were charged with the task of systematically obtaining books for their employer. According to de Hamel, "the cleric doubling as a scribe in the household of a wealthy patron provides the link . . . between the declining monastic scriptoria (struggling without exemplars and equipment) and the earliest resident professional scribes."[49]

In the thirteenth century, the universities created the institution of the *stationarius,* or university stationer, where authorized copies of the most important textbooks were kept for the students to borrow. Having obtained such an official exemplar—longer works were made available in several separate gatherings or *peciae*[50]—the student could either transcribe the text himself, or hire a professional to do so. This practice, together with the intense literary activities of the masters (we would say, "professors"), gave rise to a flourishing booktrade.[51] In Paris, one of the centers of Scholasticism, the businesses of the scribes, illuminators, and binders soon came to occupy several streets. The *peciae* are of particular interest for the enterprise of textual scholarship; for, unlike ordinary copies, they were proofread—either by the authors of the writings thus disseminated or, as in the case of Scripture or the works of Aristotle, by competent masters familiar with the texts.[52] The *peciae* are therefore often precious textual witnesses for the modern editor struggling to eliminate scribal mistakes.

The inevitability of errors is one of the characteristics of textual transmission by means of handwriting.[53] While the invention of the printing press made it possible to circulate large numbers of identical copies of the same book, it is well nigh impossible for two handwritten copies of even a short text to be without divergences. Transcription requires an enormous amount of practice, unbroken attention, and discipline. Of course, the typographical method does not in itself guarantee error-free texts; yet typographical errors do not spread unpredictably from copy to copy, as is the case with handwriting. The well-known textual scholar David C. Greetham has produced a useful list of different types of scribal errors that the student of medieval (and other) manuscripts has to reckon with:[54]

(1) Misreadings. There are a number of misreadings that are especially prone to occur in Gothic manuscripts. Thus, minims broken up into identical parts and written side by side closely together are difficult to distinguish. As a consequence, in a Gothic manuscript, there might be no discernible difference between words such as *nummis* and *minimus;* the quick reader, or copyist, might easily misread one for the other. The small *c* and *t* also look alike, as do the long *s* and the *f.* It is well to remember that the Gothic style was originally used as a display script for biblical text, intended not for quick reading but careful meditation.[55] The transposition of letters also belongs to the category of "misreadings" (for instance, *latera* for *altera*), as does the confusion of words with similar meaning or spelling (for example, *Dominus* for *Deus*).

(2) Omissions. Omissions are often due to either "haplography" or "homoeoteleuton." In the case of haplography, the eyes of the scribe move forward too fast in the text, so that letters or syllables resembling each other get skipped. Example: *quidquid id est* becomes *quidquid est*. The term "homoeoteleuton" designates an error caused by the fact that the scribe accidentally moves from a word on one line to an occurrence of the same word a line or more further down, thereby omitting the entire text between the two occurrences.

(3) Additions. Dittography is the opposite of haplography, meaning that the scribe's eyes, in returning to the text after focusing on the page of the copy, go back too far, so that words come to be copied twice.

(4) Apart from the three aforementioned kinds of variants caused inadvertently, there is also what Greetham calls "determined variation." In this case, the scribe deliberately "improves" upon the text he reads—for instance, suspecting a mistake where he does not understand a word—thus introducing errors.

That a manuscript does not necessarily reflect a text as it was originally written or dictated by its author, indeed that every manuscript is likely to diverge from this original in many conspicuous and (worse) inconspicuous ways, usually in proportion as it is further removed from the author's copy: these are not facts it took modern philology to discover. Textual criticism—the critical interrogation of a text with regard to its fidelity to the original and the preparation of an edition attempting to eliminate divergences from it—is not a modern invention. During the Carolingian renaissance, for instance, systematic efforts were made to eliminate errors that had become widespread in the texts central to the religious life of the time—above all Scripture, liturgical texts, and St. Benedict's *Rule for Monks*. To this end, Charlemagne ordered scribes to obtain less contaminated, "purer" texts from sources such as the papal curia. Also during Carolingian times, Lupus of Ferrières (ca. 805–862) prepared editions of such classical authors as Cicero, Livy, and Macrobius, collating manuscripts from different sources.[56] From the thirteenth century, Robert Grosseteste's meticulous edition of the writings of Pseudo-Dionysius the Areopagite still survives in a famous Oxford manuscript.[57] Many other examples could be added to these. However, what distinguishes the textual criticism practiced by modern philologists from medieval editorial techniques is its ability to determine the value of a given manuscript with much greater certainty. If we are confronted with a number of different, and differing, manuscript witnesses of the same text, what criteria allow us to decide which of these witnesses is to be followed in establishing an edition? Note that not all variants necessarily fall into the category of obvious mistakes, such as misspellings or grammatical errors; thus, sometimes one reading will seem as good as any other. Can we just count the occurrences of a particular reading, adopting the one that is better represented quantitatively? That seems an unsatisfactory approach, given that there is no reason why an isolated manuscript cannot be closer to the original than all the others. Neither is the age of a manuscript always decisive for ascertaining its value. For a very old manuscript written by a negligent scribe can be more corrupt than a less ancient copy that was made more meticulously.

Failing a reliable solution to the kinds of problems just sketched out, editions of classical and medieval texts remained unsatisfactory until as recently as the last century. It was then that a genealogical method for the classification of textual witnesses was discovered, which has come to be associated with the name of one of its greatest pioneers, the German philologist Karl K. F. W. Lachmann (1793–1851). This method, rigorously applied by Lachmann in his edition of Lucretius's *De rerum natura*,[58] rests upon the insight that the history of the transmission of a text can be reconstructed through the errors made in the different manuscripts. The discussion on Lachmann's method has become extremely complex over the years; however, the basic principles of this approach are clearly laid out in an almost Euclidean fashion by Paul Maas in his classical study, *Textual Criticism*.[59] Before trying to summarize these principles, let us note that the Lachmannian method was originally designed for classical texts, and has only later come to be applied to medieval texts. Until quite recently, there has been almost no theoretical reflection on this method by medievalists.[60]

If of a given text we have only one manuscript witness *(codex unicus),* either because only one survives or because others have not yet been discovered (European libraries are still full of unsifted medieval material), the philologist's task in this case is at once easy and difficult. It is easy insofar as there are no variants; thus, the unique manuscript in question obviously does not need to be compared with others. It is difficult insofar as there is no way, except by conjecture, to amend the text where it appears faulty or lacunar. One possible way of dealing with this dilemma is the so-called "diplomatic" edition, which attempts to reproduce the manuscript as faithfully as possible in modern typography.[61] The diplomatic edition ensures that a given text is available in print for scholars to study, without their having to consult a microfilm and laboriously decipher medieval script; moreover, it renders the text accessible in a format that gives the modern reader a taste of its actual state in the manuscript in which it is found. The diplomatic edition thus respects the historical reality of the text to a greater degree than does the "critical" edition, which is, in many ways, an artifact.

Faced with a multiplicity of manuscript witnesses of the same text, the editor must start by attempting to reduce the number of manuscripts he or she needs to take into consideration for the edition *(eliminatio codicum descriptorum).*[62] A manuscript is worthless for the constitution of the text if it depends entirely upon a surviving exemplar (another manuscript from which it was copied). How can this be ascertained? By the fact that it contains all the errors (misspellings, grammatical mistakes, lacunae, etc.) of the exemplar, plus at least one peculiar error of its own—the assumption being that the scribe, importing all the errors from the exemplar, also introduced an error or errors of his own. Such a manuscript can be disregarded. Now, the principles of this method can be extended, making it possible to reconstruct even a lost exemplar. For, if two (or more) manuscripts have a large number of errors in common, each exhibiting only a small number of peculiar ones, the lost exemplar can be assumed to correspond to the text that the manuscripts have in common; the peculiar errors, by contrast, can be eliminated *(eliminatio lectionum singularium).*

It is clear that the *eliminatio codicum descriptorum* and the *eliminatio lectionum singularium* yield much more than a merely quantitative reduction of, respectively, manuscript witnesses and errors. By identifying exemplars, and even reconstructing lost ones, they make it possible to ascend to an antecedent stage in the process of textual transmission—a stage closer to the original because it contains fewer errors. The same procedure (called *recensio*) is now applied to the surviving or reconstructed exemplar. Let us call it exemplar δ. It will now be treated like an ordinary manuscript and compared with other witnesses that do not "fall under it," as it were. These witnesses will either show an agreement with exemplar δ with regard to a significant number of errors—then it will be possible to ascend to another exemplar on a yet higher level, explaining the provenance of these common errors—or they will exhibit an independent tradition of errors, that is to say, errors too different from exemplar δ to be traceable to a common source. Let us assume the independent tradition of errors is in itself coherent, depending on another exemplar γ. In this case, we are dealing with a "split" in the tradition. This split creates variants that one cannot reduce by means of the procedure outlined so far. Exemplars δ and γ now represent "hyparchetypes." These contain readings that, from the technical point of view hitherto adopted, have an equal chance of representing the archetype from which they were copied.[63]

At this stage, the variants need to be "examined" *(examinatio).* This step is crucial, leading as it does to the discrimination of scribal errors from the authentic text of the archetype. Sometimes the selection *(selectio)* of the correct reading is easy, because one of the two variants is a plain mistake: in a poem, the word or phrase in question might not fit the meter; in a philosophical text, it might just not make sense. Of course, in the latter case, there is already room for discussion, as editors might disagree on what makes sense and what doesn't. If both variants are clearly erroneous, the editor must proceed by *divinatio,* that is to say, conjecture as to what

the archetype will most likely have said through an "inspired self-identi-
fication with one's author."[64] *Divinatio* is something like the dialectical
counterpart of the technical procedures used by the Lachmannian
method; it requires an intimate acquaintance with the edited text, its terminology, style, idiosyncracies . . . in short, it is the unscientific "other" of
Lachmannian positivism (see fig. 3.1 for an example of a simple stemma).

The principles of the Lachmannian method, then, are clear. It is a genealogical method designed "to demonstrate incontestably [*sic*] the inter-
relationship of all surviving witnesses, as well as the number and position
of all intermediate splits in the tradition"[65] of a text, thereby enabling the
editor to "backtrack" step by step from the manuscripts to their archetype.
The most important tool for the stemmatization of witnesses (that is to say,
for their arrangement in a graph showing their interrelationships) is the
identification of textual variants, or errors. Ultimately, however, the goal of
the Lachmannian method is the elimination of these variants, through
technical and philological considerations—including, as a last resort, *divinatio.*

Lachmann's method has never been uncontested. In a celebrated and
witty lecture entitled, "The Application of Thought to Textual Criticism,"
the English classical scholar and poet Alfred Edward Housman derided
what he believed to be the pseudo-scientificity of the "palaeographical
method," provocatively declaring: "If the sense requires it, I am prepared to
write *Constantinopolitanus* where the MSS have the monosyllabic interjec-
tion *o.*" He concludes: "Knowledge is good, method is good, but one thing
beyond all others is necessary; and that is to have a head, not a pumpkin,
on your shoulders, and brains, not pudding, in your head."[66]

Housman and other champions of what Greetham terms the "belletris-
tic" approach to editing[67] criticize the Lachmannian method for its emphasis upon historical detail. Interestingly enough, more recent
discussions[68] seem to have gone in the opposite direction. Indeed, contemporary textual scholars tend to regard the Lachmannian method as
being ill-equipped to do full justice to history. First of all, its theoretical
schemes do not accord with the historical reality of textual transmission,
where the phenomenon of so-called contamination is extremely frequent.
As we have seen earlier on, textual criticism has been practiced in some
form since the Middle Ages (if not since ancient times). Hence, the manuscript witnesses with which the contemporary editor has to deal very
often cannot be arranged neatly according to branches of transmission, because frequently each of these witnesses already depends upon two or
more different strands of the tradition. However, as Maas himself admits,

Figure 3.1   A simple stemma illustrating the steps followed in textual criticism

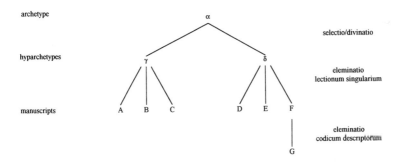

"if individual scribes have 'contaminated' several exemplars, the process of *eliminatio* within the area of these 'contaminations' is greatly hindered, if not made impossible."[69] More recently, efforts have been made to adapt the Lachmannian method to the complicated problems caused by contamination[70]; yet other, more fundamental, questions remain. In the introduction, we have already quoted Horst Fuhrmann's critique, according to which the traditional editorial method wrongly privileges "a state of the text which, from an historical point of view, might have been without influence or of substantially less influence than that of the derived and, in the eyes of Lachmann, corrupted versions."[71] This "tendency to idealize the original"[72] is thrown into high relief in Martin West's striking phrase in his book, *Textual Criticism and Editorial Technique,* where he writes: "The textual critic is a pathologist."[73] Now if the textual critic is a pathologist, then the tradition of a text is nothing but a pathology, a progressive degradation of a pure and authentic original. However, does this characterization do justice to the historical processes to which we owe our knowledge of a text? Are these processes not to be viewed, more positively, as the condition of possibility for the dissemination and continued existence of a work? And if, historically speaking, the "corrupt" version of a text has come to be more influential than the "authentic" one, is it wise to treat it like a mere pathology? It is for the reasons indicated by these questions that contemporary editorial techniques place a great deal of emphasis upon the appreciation of the history of the transmission of a text,[74] its *Überlieferungsgeschichte*—a term that Housman, for his part, considered to be merely "a longer and nobler name than fudge."[75] This shift of emphasis manifests itself in the critical apparatus of many recent editions, which no longer record exclusively those variants that have a chance of reflecting the original text, but even readings that are "just" historically interesting and influential. Father Édouard Jeauneau's edition of the *Periphyseon,* briefly described in the introduction, is an outstanding example of this tendency.

Scholastic Curricula

Let us continue our consideration of some important Scholastic intellectual practices, or historical a prioris. In the study of the history of thought in the Middle Ages—indeed, in the study of the history of thought *tout court*—we are accustomed to a certain manner of presentation by which intellectual history is depicted as a succession of "great authors": after Augustine comes Boethius; after Boethius, Eriugena; after Eriugena, Anselm; and so forth. This tendency is quite evident in older textbooks, but also in the manner in which we teach philosophy even today. Nevertheless, the outstanding medievalists of this century—scholars such as Grabmann, Chenu, Van Steenberghen[76]—realized that in the study of the history of thought, we cannot jump from mountaintop to mountaintop without crossing the valleys. We cannot, because the mountains rise up from the valleys, as it were. In order to appreciate the achievement of, for example, the towering intellectual figures of the thirteenth century, we need to understand the context in which they worked; the structures that have given shape to their thought; in a word, the "epistemological field" in which their ideas appeared. Now, one of the most decisive factors in the constitution of an epistemological field consists in the organization of studies in a given culture, that is to say, in its curricula. Van Steenberghen perspicaciously remarks that

> if the organization of studies is an effect, a result, the expression of a culture,
> it exercises in turn a decisive influence, for it is an essential factor in the sub-
> sequent development of that culture.[77]

Since Roman times, theoretical knowledge had in the Latin West come to be conceived as being divided into seven branches, the seven "liberal arts" *(artes liberales).* Within this scheme, a first group, called *trivium,* embraced the more literary branches of knowledge represented by grammar, rhetoric, and dialectic (we would say, logic); the second group, the *quadrivium,* included the sciences of arithmetic, geometry, music, and astronomy. Roman Christians, such as Boethius, accepted this division, although with an important modification; all human knowledge was now seen as being ordered toward the most worthy object of the intellectual and spiritual life of the Christian, namely, the contemplation of the Holy Writ. The explicit recentering of the classical heritage of profane learning around the Bible was accomplished by St. Augustine, whose treatise *De doctrina christiana* (On Christian Teaching) was to remain decisive for the medieval curriculum until the twelfth century.[78]

If we remember the terms in which Tertullian attacked what he regarded as the dangerous conflation of Christianity with elements of pagan learning ("What has Athens to do with Jerusalem?"), the tone of the *De doctrina christiana*, completed about two centuries after Tertullian's death, has changed entirely:

> Any statements by those who are called philosophers, especially the Platonists, which happen to be true and consistent with our faith should not cause alarm, but be claimed for our own use, as it were from owners who have no right to them. Like the treasures of the ancient Egyptians, who possessed not only idols and heavy burdens which the people of Israel hated and shunned but also vessels and ornaments of silver and gold, and clothes, which on leaving Egypt the people of Israel, in order to make better use of them, surreptitiously claimed for themselves (they did this not on their own authority but at God's command, and the Egyptians in their ignorance actually gave them the things of which they had made poor use)—similarly all the branches of pagan learning *(doctrinae omnes gentilium)* contain not only false and superstitious fantasies and burdensome studies that involve unnecessary effort, which each one of us must loathe and avoid as under Christ's guidance we abandon the company of pagans, but also studies for liberated minds which are more appropriate to the service of the truth, and some very useful moral instruction, as well as the various truths about monotheism to be found in their writers. These treasures—like the silver and gold, which they did not create but dug, as it were, from the mines of providence, which is everywhere—which were used wickedly and harmfully in the service of demons must be removed by Christians, as they separate themselves in spirit from the wretched company of pagans, and applied to their true function, that of preaching the gospel . . . This is exactly what many good and faithful Christians have done. We can see, can we not, the amount of gold, silver, and clothing with which Cyprian, that most attractive writer and most blessed martyr, was laden when he left Egypt; is not the same true of Lactantius, and Victorinus, of Optatus, and Hilary, to say nothing of people still alive, and countless Greek scholars? This is what had been done earlier by Moses himself, that most faithful servant of God, of whom it is written that he was trained in "all the wisdom of the Egyptians." . . . As students of the

divine scriptures, equipped in this way, begin to approach the task of studying them in detail, they must ponder incessantly this phrase of the apostle
Paul: "knowledge puffs up, but love builds up."[79]

The strategy employed by Augustine in order to justify the application
of pagan knowledge to the study of Scripture is complex and fascinating.
Dispossessing pagan Greece and Rome of their learning, so to speak, he
argues that the Christians have a greater claim to this learning than the
pagan authors themselves. For, if knowledge is based on the investigation
of creation, in which God exercises his providence, then all human knowledge is owed to God—whom the Christians recognize, while the pagans
do not. By this fact, they forfeit as it were their right to their own knowledge. For this strategy, Augustine invokes a biblical precedent—the Israelites' use of Egyptian goods on one side, and Moses's training in "all the
wisdom of the Egyptians" on the other—as well as the authority of such
predecessors as Victorinus, Hilary of Poitiers, and Ambrose (no doubt one
of the "people still alive"). All in all, an ingenious move, which suggests that
the appropriation of pagan learning is done "at God's command," just as
the actions of the Israelites in Egypt stood under God's immediate guid-
ance. At the end of the passage just quoted, Augustine explicitly recenters
all profane learning on Scripture, cautioning his reader that all knowledge
must be pursued in the spirit of Christian love.

The branches of knowledge that Augustine deems particularly useful
for the understanding and contemplation of Scripture are dealt with in detail in the whole of book II of *De doctrina christiana*. They include languages, especially Latin, Hebrew, and Greek (2.30–58), paleography (2.37,
41),[80] biology and petrology (2.59–61), arithmetics (2.62–65), music
(2.66–67), history (2.105–109), astronomy (2.112–114), medicine, agricul-
ture, navigation, as well as dancing, running, and wrestling (!) (2.115), logic
(2.117–131), rhetoric (2.132–133) and, as we have seen, philosophy
(2.144–147).

The Augustinian conception of the structure of Christian teaching,
together with the heritage of the seven liberal arts and, of course, the un-
availability of many sources of classical learning, determined the nature of
Christian thought until the middle of the twelfth century. Early medieval
thought, thus, was centered upon Scripture, which it approached through
the branches of knowledge recommended by Augustine—to the extent to
which these branches of knowledge could be studied in the seven liberal
arts and by means of classical texts. As we have already discovered in the
preceding study, the transmission of the classical tradition to the early Mid-

dle Ages was anything but trouble-free. The premature death of Boethius, in particular, caused a large part of the Greek heritage to be lost to the Latin-speaking world for hundreds of years. Boethius translated only some of the logical treatises from Aristotle's oeuvre before his ambitious project was interrupted; this fact, combined with the lack of physics, metaphysics, and ethics within the scheme of the *artes liberales,* accounts for the complete absence of the core elements of philosophy from the pre-twelfth-century medieval curriculum. In this light, the "relative poverty of the High Middle Ages with regard to philosophical productions properly speaking" can be no surprise.[81]

It was the inflow of fresh, hitherto unknown literature beginning in the twelfth century—a phenomenon outlined at the end of the last study—that was ultimately to lead to a revision of the medieval curriculum, especially when, from 1200 onward, studies came to be organized in the newly founded universities. The most detailed and elucidating document that we possess on the structure of the revised curriculum was discovered by Martin Grabmann in 1927. It is the famous "study-guide" contained in a manuscript of the *Arxiu de la Corona d'Aragó* in Barcelona, namely, codex Ripoll 109.[82] Debates regarding the study-guide have received a fresh impetus in recent years, due to the scholarly activities of Claude Lafleur of the Université Laval in Québec, who has both prepared an edition of the text,[83] and organized a colloquium held at his university in 1993.[84]

The study-guide was composed around 1240 by an unknown master teaching at the faculty of arts of the University of Paris.[85] Its purpose is, as suggested by the title contemporary scholars have given to it, to guide this master's students through their studies, and especially to prepare them for their examinations. The study-guide thus presents the material and questions that a student at the Parisian faculty of arts around 1240 would have had to know in order to pass his exams. In no respect is it a "great book," expounding "original" ideas and developing grand new syntheses. However, the very fact that the study-guide is an anonymous text, reflecting the day-to-day teaching of an average master, allows us to catch a glimpse of the historical a priori presupposed by the intellectual productions of the time. The study-guide informs us about the sources available around 1240, enables us to infer how well they were known and how profoundly (or superficially) they were studied, and it lays out the structure of knowledge as taught at the faculty of arts. It is a crucial document for the reconstruction of the Scholastic episteme.

It will be useful for our discussion to have an overview of the contents of the study-guide to which we can refer:[86]

I.   Introduction
II. Definition of philosophy
III. Division of philosophy (2 questions)
    1.   Natural philosophy
        a)   Metaphysics (books: *Vetus methaphisica, Methaphisica noua, De causis;* 1 question about the subject matter of metaphysics)
        b)   Mathematics (3 questions about the subject matter of mathematics; the division of mathematics into astronomy, geometry, arithmetic, and music; literature used: Ptolemy, *Almagest,* Martianus, Euclid, Boethius—24 questions about these authors)
        c)   Physics (the subject matter of physics; further subdivision; books used: Aristotle, *Physics, On Heaven and Earth, On Generation and Corruption, On Meteors, On Plants, On Animals, On the Soul,* etc.; 3 questions about these works)
    2.   Moral philosophy
        a)   Subject matter and subdivision: revealed theology, economics, politics, ethics; literature: Cicero, Aristotle: *Nicomachean Ethics*
        b)   The *Nicomachean Ethics* (*Noua ethica* and *Vetus ethica;* the division of the *Ethics;* 35 questions)
        c)   Plato's *Timaeus* (5 questions) and Boethius's *Consolation of Philosophy* (2 questions)
    3.   Rational philosophy
        a)   Rhetoric (the subject matter of rhetoric; literature: Cicero, *On Invention;* 6 questions)
        b)   Grammar (subject matter and detailed subdivision; literature: Priscian and Donatus; 189 questions)
        c)   Logic (introduction: the subject matter and division of logic; detailed analysis of Aristotle's *Categories, On Interpretation, Prior* and *Posterior Analytics, Topics,* and *Sophistical Refutations;* further literature: Porphyry (*Isagoge*), *Liber sex principiorum;* 404 questions in all)

Let us note that the teaching at the Parisian faculty of arts as witnessed to by this study-guide no longer follows the traditional structure of the seven liberal arts. Rather, what we see is an Aristotelian tripartite division of philosophy into natural (theoretical) philosophy, practical philosophy, and logic. Indeed philosophy, which in the scheme of the *artes liberales* possessed no proper place as a unified branch of knowledge, has as it were turned the tables, absorbing both the *quadrivium* (see III.1.b) and the *trivium* (see III.3.a–c). Even revealed theology becomes a subdivision of philosophy! Such self-confidence on the part of the philosophers would, some thirty years after the publication of the study-guide, lead to a deep crisis in the arts faculty and the Condemnation of 1277. Aside from the general structure of the curriculum, it is interesting to analyze the sources upon which it draws. Some of Aristotle's logical writings had been known in the West since Boethius's times; that they should figure prominently in the study-guide is not surprising. Of the more recently discovered Aristotelian works, the study-guide mentions, most importantly, the *Posterior Analytics, Metaphysics, On the Soul,* and the *Nicomachean Ethics.* The *vetus methaphisica* to which our anonymous master refers, that is to say, the "old metaphysics," is a translation of books I through IV that dates back as far as 1125–1150 and was made, directly from the Greek, by James of Venice. The *methaphisica noua,* on the other hand, is the "new" translation, based upon the Arabic and due to Michael Scotus, who finished it in the years 1225–1230. It contained more books than the *vetus methaphisica,* namely ten, but was still incomplete.[87] As a complement to the *Metaphysics,* the study-guide names the *Liber de causis.* It was not before Aquinas composed his commentary upon this treatise that the medievals came to realize that the Neoplatonism espoused in the "Book of Causes" is not consonant with Aristotle's doctrines, so that the treatise itself cannot have the Stagirite as its author.[88] It is obvious that this misunderstanding had serious consequences for the proper appreciation of Aristotle's thought. With regard to the *Nicomachean Ethics,* the study-guide again distinguishes a "new" and an "old" version, a *Noua ethica* and a *Vetus ethica.* The "old" *Ethics* had been available since the end of the twelfth century, but contained only books II and III. The "new" *Ethics,* translated around 1220, then added book I. The complete translation of all ten books, prepared by Robert Grosseteste in 1246–1247, is yet unknown to the author of the study-guide. To conclude, it is worth pointing out that the only Platonic work figuring in the text of manuscript Ripoll 109 is the *Timaeus.* The two other dialogues to which the medievals had access, the *Phaedo* and the *Meno,* are not mentioned. Neither are any Arabic or Jewish writings— which does not mean they were not known to the masters teaching at Paris around 1240. Yet the texts of such "heretic" authors as Avicenna or Averroës were not taught; they provided the backcloth for the assimilation of the Aristotelian tradition, without themselves appearing on the stage of the curriculum.

Thus, by 1240 Aristotle's *Metaphysics* and *Nicomachean Ethics,* among other writings, seem to have become an integral part of the university colloqium, being taught and discussed on a regular basis. The reinscription of Greek wisdom into the center of Christian culture was therefore complete. Or was it? Let us not rush to conclusions. For, it is curious that the master who compiled the study-guide asks his students so few questions about anything but logic. Indeed, apparently he expected his students to prepare nothing but one single question on the whole of the *Metaphysics!* The three questions on all the books being studied as part of physics are not very impressive either. Even the thirty-five questions bearing upon the *Nicomachean Ethics* pale beside the 599 devoted to rhetoric, grammar, and logic. These numbers indicate that what we witness in the study-guide is not the finished result of the old liberal-arts-centered curriculum transforming itself into a university curriculum, but that, rather, we are in the middle of a process of transformation. Why does the master ask only one question about the *Metaphysics?* Answer: most likely, he had not understood much more about it than its basic outline. Remember that in 1240, only ten years had elapsed since the completion of Michael Scotus's new, more comprehensive version. Ten years are not a lot of time to assimilate and digest a completely unfamiliar worldview. Moreover, in 1240 the teaching of some of Aristotle's writings (especially the *Metaphysics*) was still officially prohibited at the University of Paris.

The Universities: Methods of Teaching and Literary Forms

We now turn to the "institutional site" of Scholastic discourse, the university. In this context, we shall determine who participates in that discourse and what kinds of discourse are considered legitimate in Scholastic thought, in other words, by what rules concepts are ordered ("rules of succession") and statements systematized ("procedures of intervention").

The University of Paris—probably the first university—can be considered to have been officially founded in 1200, when the then king of France, Phillip Augustus, removed the masters and students from the jurisdiction of the ordinary courts, placing them instead under the authority of the bishop of Paris and his delegate, the chancellor.[89] By this move, the king recognised the body of masters and students as an entity in its own right, creating a space for study, research, teaching, and learning under the judicature of the church that was exempt from the rules of ordinary life in the city. The emergence of the university in 1200 marks the result of a process in which several schools that had operated independently under the direction of their respective masters in the twelfth century gradually came to cooperate and coalesce—without, however, losing their independence altogether. The medieval model of the university as composed of a number of colleges collaborating on issues like the recognition of masters, the conferral of degrees, and the standardization of curricula survives to this day, in universities such as Cambridge and Oxford in England, or Toronto in Canada. At any rate, the schools of Paris gradually standardized their curricula and agreed upon a certain order of degrees certifying the competence of their students and masters. Moreover, the different disciplines were demarcated by the creation of faculties. Significantly, despite the position of the university as an outsider within the juridical order of the city, the organization of the university closely followed the model of the guilds. Thus, the faculties of the university corresponded to the various crafts of the guilds; furthermore, within each of these, there existed a distinction between masters, craftsmen (bachelors), and apprentices (students). Originally, the University of Paris was composed of only four faculties, namely, arts, theology, law, and medicine. In this setup, the arts faculty played a preparatory role, roughly comparable to the function of our contemporary liberal arts colleges, where students are acquainted with the foundations of culture before going on to learn a "job." In the medieval university, too, you "did not grow old in the arts": *non est consenescendum in artibus,* as the Schoolmen used to say. As a matter of fact, most of the great so-called "philosophers" of the thirteenth century—such as Bonaventure, Albert the Great, Thomas Aquinas—were masters in the theology faculty. Bonaventure, Albert the Great, and Thomas Aquinas were also friars—members of the new religious orders founded by St. Francis and St. Dominic, who envisaged the lives of their followers not in the solitude of some isolated abbey, but rather as preachers of the gospel amidst the townsfolk. This constitutes an important aspect of the shift from "monastic" to "Scholastic" culture, which we shall analyze in greater detail in the next section.

But back to the structure of the University of Paris. A student would usually enter the university at the age of fourteen or fifteen.[90] As was already pointed out, all students had to start their careers at the faculty of arts. There, undergraduate studies usually took four years. The boys would attend lectures mostly on grammar and logic, and participate in formal discussions, the so-called "disputations"—we shall consider these forms of teaching in more detail later in this section. After their first two years, the students were expected to take a more active role in the disputations—a role not just of listening but of intelligent participation as "respondents" to certain arguments. The examination for the bachelor's degree consisted of two parts:[91] first, the student and his master had to satisfy a board of examiners that all the curricular requirements of attending lectures and disputations had been fulfilled (whether the candidate had to answer questions is not clear); secondly, the student had to "determine" during a series of disputations, that is to say, offer the final synthesis of the discussion by expounding a philosophically sound solution to the problem at hand. After graduation, the bachelor continued to attend lectures and disputations, but now on the full range of subjects taught at the faculty of arts under the name of "philosophy," including metaphysics, mathematics, physics, and moral philosophy. He also continued to "respond" and "determine" in disputations, and even started to give his first own lectures. These further studies would normally take three years, after which the bachelor took the examination for the license. This comprised thorough questioning by two examination boards and, again, a series of disputations. Here we already see the central role played by formal discussions in the life of the university. Subsequently, the new licentiate had to commit himself to two years of teaching at the arts faculty, during which he would, as "master," lecture and preside over disputations. Thereupon, he would move on to another faculty and start all over again as an ordinary student.

Of particular interest for us is, of course, the theology faculty, where most of the outstanding thinkers of the time taught as masters. Members of the mendicant orders did not enter theology through the faculty of arts, but received their preliminary training (structured very similarly) at study-houses, *studia,* established by their orders. Undergraduate studies in theology took longer than in the arts—six to seven years, during which time the student followed lectures on the books of Scripture, as well as on Peter Lombard's *Book of Sentences.*

This *Liber sententiarum* is one of the most influential books in the Christian tradition, although it holds little attraction for the contemporary reader—which is why it is virtually unread nowadays, even by specialists.[92] Compiled by Peter Lombard, whose name we already encountered in discussing the glosses of the Bible, the *Sentences* were a first attempt to construct theology as an ordered body of doctrines. In the *Liber sententiarum,* Peter Lombard presents a collection of biblical quotations and patristic authorities on theological questions, arranged systematically. The *Book of Sentences* served as the standard textbook for the teaching of theology, from the beginning of the thirteenth century until the Council of Trent in the middle of the sixteenth, thereby exercising an enduring influence upon the structure of the "epistemological field" of theology in the West. All the great theologians lectured and wrote commentaries on it, up to and including Martin Luther.

After meeting the requirements for the baccalaureate by attending lectures on the Bible and the *Liber sententiarum,* as well as disputations, the student of theology became a *baccalaureus biblicus.* While continuing to deepen his own knowledge of theology, he was now also required to give introductory lectures on biblical books and to "respond" in disputations. This second stage lasted another two years, after which he became *baccalaureus sententiarum,* which entailed, as the name suggests, the duty of lecturing upon the *Book of Sentences.* Another two years later—and always under the condition that his progress continued to satisfy the masters supervising him—our young theologian reached the stage of *baccalaureus formatus,* with the requirement to participate in disputations for a period of four more years. Only then, and after a detailed examination and another series of special disputations, could his "inception" as master take place— if he was lucky, and a chair happened to be vacant. The new master of theology would have spent an average of twenty-four years of studying, lecturing, and actively participating in disputations, before receiving the authority to give the main lectures on Scripture and preside over disputations concerning theological matters. A long time for what might seem to us a limited task; for the curricula of the arts faculty and the theology faculty taken together can hardly rival the amount of knowledge that a contemporary student is expected to digest in any course of study within a few years. However, there remains a difference between depth and breadth.

Having acquainted ourselves with the basic organization of the institutional site of Scholastic thought, we shall now examine more closely the methods of teaching that so far have only been characterized, rather vaguely, as "lectures" and "disputations." It is only against the background of these forms of teaching that we shall be able to understand the forms of writing, or literary genres, employed by the Scholastics, as these closely mirror the teaching methods. Why is this important? Because the literary genre in which ideas are expressed is not an external garment, an element extrinsic to thought, but an important and intrinsic part of its formation. Our ideas are formed in their expression, and thus the mode and genre of this expression are essential to our understanding of thought. The literary genre is yet another form of historical a priori, although philosophers have been slow to recognize this fact.[93] Whether an idea is framed in a Platonic dialogue, in a Scholastic *quaestio,* in a chapter of Kant's *Critique of Pure Reason,* or in a seminar of Jacques Lacan, is far from inconsequential. In fact, an idea could not remain the same by being framed in these different ways. Our discussion of the Scholastic literary genres will render this point evident.

At the beginning was the *lectio,* or lecture; the disputations *(disputationes)* were originally part of it, at least in the pre-thirteenth-century schools.[94] The *lectio* at the medieval university was always text-based (as the name suggests, for *lectio* is more correctly translated as "reading"). The modern "lecture," in which a professor explains a topic according to his or her own ideas, or even engages in spontaneous discussion with the students, did not exist in the same way in the Middle Ages. Rather, a lecture always consisted in the commentary of an authoritative text—and we have seen, in studying codex Ripoll 109, what range of texts was included in that category, at least in the faculty of arts. These texts were expounded upon three levels: *littera, sensus,* and *sententia,* each level "digging deeper" than the preceding one, as it were. Thus, an explanation of the "letter" *(littera)* of the text was followed by a first paraphrase of its meaning *(sensus),* before the master would embark upon a more detailed examination of doctrinal issues *(sententia).* Note that the explanation of the letter was crucial, given the often extremely literal translations *(verbum de verbo)* that were used, necessitating the elucidation of individual words and phrases, as well as of grammatical constructions. In the statutes of the University of Paris, we find a distinction between *lectio ordinaria,* "ordinary lecture," and *lectio cursoria,* "cursory lecture," which can be mapped upon the three levels of textual commentary. For it appears that—at least after the transformation of the schools into the university—the different types of commentary had come to be assigned to different types of lecture. Thus, the "cursory" lectures would have concentrated upon the literal meaning, perhaps also offering quick paraphrases, while the "ordinary" lectures were devoted to scrutinizing the *sententia.* The *lectio ordinaria* always had to be given by a master; on the other hand, the less exacting *lectio cursoria* could be delegated to a bachelor. Moreover, the *lectiones ordinariae* were held early in the morning, when the students and masters were fresh and alert, whereas the *lectiones cursoriae* were relegated to the afternoon. Now to the question as to whether medievalists have been able to identify which literary genres correspond to these different kinds of *lectio.*

According to Olga Weijers, whose impressive account of these matters we are summarizing here, the practice of the *lectio* is reflected in three kinds of textual commentary. In the first half of the thirteenth century, the masters tried to incorporate all the aspects of the *lectio* into one literary form, which combined the tasks of basic explanation and more probing enquiry, the latter often through questions raised in connection with the text. However, this hybrid literary genre was replaced, in the second half of the thirteenth century, by commentaries in the form of questions, on the one hand, and commentaries following the text more closely, on the other. Thus, the *quaestiones* commentary provided the master with the opportunity to develop certain doctrinal issues suggested by a text in greater length and more independently, while the *sententia* commentary remained more literal.[95] If we remember what was said earlier about the development of the glossed versions of the Bible, we can see a clear evolution in which medieval thought gradually detaches itself from its immediate textual bases, emancipating itself as it were and assuming an increasingly independent character, and finally culminating in the "elaboration of systematic disciplines."[96]

This evolution becomes even more evident if we consider the second form of teaching employed at the medieval universities—namely, the *disputatio*—along with the literary genre corresponding to it, the *quaestio*. The *disputationes* in the faculty of arts dealt with the whole gamut of questions raised in the various branches of "philosophy": physics, biology, psychology, logic, etc.; in theology, in turn, metaphysical questions were often considered.[97] The disputations were organized in two ways, as *disputationes in scolis*—disputations held in the individual masters' schools for the benefit of their own students—and as *disputationes sollempnes,* "solemn" disputations in the presence of the masters and students of the whole faculty. For the latter, which were arranged once a week and often functioned as examinations, all other courses were suspended. For their part, the *disputationes in scolis* were scheduled in the mornings, immediately after the *lectiones ordinariae.* This underscores the importance accorded to the culture of disputation. As for the structure of the disputation, a master would start with a basic statement of the question under consideration, followed by a few arguments in favor of different possible solutions. The students assigned the role of "respondents" *(respondentes),* who were usually divided into a "yes" and a "no" group, then attempted to formulate more arguments supporting these solutions. Other students, "opponents," countered these arguments. Finally, the master would offer a detailed "determination" of the problem—his suggestion for a solution, based upon a careful weighing-up of the different arguments advanced in the course of the session. In the arts faculty, the *determinatio* apparently took place right at the end of the session; in the theology faculty, the session was adjourned after the exchange between the *respondentes* and the *opponentes,* to be resumed only on the next day.[98] That obviously gave the master more time to prepare his "determination." The practice and structure of the disputations are crucial for our understanding of the historical setting of Scholastic thought, its institutional and intellectual a prioris. Olga Weijers remarks that the disputations—in particular as practiced in the arts faculty—were much more than mere exercises in logic:

> One is struck by the open-mindedness which characterizes the [*disputatio* at the arts faculty]: this search for a "scientific" truth is typical of an epoch and of a milieu. Even in this milieu, it was to be lost later. But it favored a mentality which appears modern to us: to make ideas concerning a certain subject matter evolve by means of argumentation, and to do so by respecting and appreciating [even] those arguments which would finally be rejected. It certainly encouraged people to adopt a critical attitude with respect to texts and statements, but also to respect other opinions and to be demanding in the search for the truth.[99]

The *quaestio disputata* is the literary equivalent of the oral disputations, although not every collection of questions that has come down to us necessarily reflects an actual disputation. Indeed, the literary form of the *quaestio,* modeled as it is upon the structure of the *disputatio,* soon became the most characteristic form of Scholastic writing. In Thomas Aquinas's *Summa theologiae,* for instance, the *quaestio* form is used to create a systematic manual of theology, in which complex *quaestiones* are broken up into articles and bundled into "parts." Historically speaking, the question (mirroring in this the disputation) "separated itself from the basic text in stages."[100] First, questions were always raised with regard to particular problems encountered in commentating upon authoritative texts; then, the more elementary elucidation of the text was separated from the discussion of more difficult issues (*sententia* commentary vs. *quaestio* commentary); finally, questions came to be discussed as problems in their own right—still with references to authoritative texts, but no longer bound to the scope and order dictated by any one text in particular.

So what exactly is the structure of a Scholastic *quaestio?* Let us take an example pulled from St. Thomas Aquinas's commentary on Peter Lombard's *Book of Sentences.* Large parts of this commentary—composed in the second half of the 1250s, that is to say, toward the beginning of Aquinas's career as a master—exhibit the *quaestio* structure, although it also contains short summaries of Peter Lombard's text: "more and more neglected vestiges," as Père Chenu writes, "of the old litteral commentary."[101] However, the questions are always raised apropos of the text, and follow its order. There is therefore less room for a new theological "system" in the *Sentences* commentary than there will be later in the *Summa theologiae.* The work is divided into books, "distinctions," questions, and articles. An article is a kind of sub-question. Now, not only does each article follow the structure of the *quaestio*—enunciation of the problem, arguments pro, arguments con, solution, response to the arguments—but even parts of the articles are sometimes organized like smaller *quaestiones*. That is precisely the case with the text we are going to examine now, taken from book II of the *Sentences* commentary, a text that combines a very typical structure with certain explicit statements about the Scholastic method.

One of the articles making up distinction 9 (qu. 1, art. 2) discusses the rather subtle theological point as to whether the angels are capable of "purging" *(purgare)* each other from such shortcomings as may afflict them, so as to render their souls more similar to God. As "purging" goes hand in hand with illuminating, it becomes necessary to look into the related question as to whether the angels are able to illuminate each other: *de illuminatione quaeritur*. This is the topic addressed in the response to the third argument:

> About this, certain people *(quidam)* have expressed contrary opinions *(contrarie opinati sunt)*. For certain people *(quidam)* have said that the lower angels can never see the essence of God, but that they can gain a notion of God by an illumination from the higher [angels], who see Him immediately. Against this stands what is said in Matt. 18.10: "their angels always behold the face of my Father," where he speaks of the angels of the lower order, who have been deputed to guard human beings. Others *(alii)*, however, say on the contrary that all the angels receive an illumination immediately from God, denying that the lower ones are illuminated by the higher ones, and denying everything that Dionysius hands down *(tradit)*, which is proven by the authority *(auctoritatem)* of the Sacred Scriptures and is consonant with the teaching of the philosophers. Hence, choosing a middle course *(mediam viam)* we say that, on the one hand *(quidem)* all the angels see the essence of God immediately, which is why they are blessed; yet *(sed)* it is not necessary that someone who sees a cause, see all its effects, nor [is it necessary] that he comprehend that cause according to its full potency, like God who, in comprehending Himself, knows everything. However, each of the other beings who do not comprehend Him by seeing Him, knows more things in Him in proportion as he grasps Him more fully through the enjoyment of grace—just as *(sicut)* someone who is of a better intellect can also draw more conclusions from speculative principles. Hence *(unde)*, the higher angels illuminate and instruct the lower ones with regard to those divine effects that pertain to the state of nature or of grace, which are dispensed by the office of the angels, as is expressly said in book VII of the *Celestial Hierarchy* and at the beginning of book IV of the *Divine Names.*[102]

Let us closely analyze the structure of this text, which is pregnant with information on the functioning of the *quaestio* method.

The discussion is opened with the phrase, "about this, certain people have expressed contrary opinions." Why the vague "certain people," *quidam?* Why does Aquinas not "name names"? Along with other similar expressions, such as *alii* ("others"), which occurs a few lines later in our text, *quidam* is the conventional Scholastic way of referring to the participants of a debate, especially if these participants are contemporaries. In fact, ancient and patristic thinkers are rarely referred to as *quidam*. The *quidam* has two functions: first, it anonymizes the debate, lifting it from the level of individual people's opinions to a purely doctrinal plane. What is at stake in the debate is not whether master X is right or wrong, but whether a certain position is helpful for our understanding of philosophical or theological matters. The anonymization thus plays the useful role of minimizing factors such as personal prestige or pride. A master is not humbled if his views turn out to be rejected. Secondly, the *quidam* makes it possible to create fictitious views that were never actually held by anyone. Through this device, one could represent the extremes of a spectrum of possible opinion. Again, we see that the Scholastic *quaestio* is concerned less with the historical reality of ideas (and the people holding them), than with the very structure of these ideas.

"Certain people have said": Aquinas now summarizes the first pole in the spectrum of possible opinion concerning the question under consideration. Some authorities have opined that the lower angels, who can never themselves attain to the vision of God's essence, are illuminated by the higher angels who, for their part, do enjoy this vision—the result of this illumination being that the lower angels participate in the higher angels' knowledge of God. This view, however, is unacceptable, for it contradicts scriptural authority, as represented by what the Gospel according to St. Matthew states about the guardian angels' vision of the Father face-to-face (the guardian angels of course belong to the lower angelic orders).

Thomas therefore turns to the opinion of the opposite camp: "others, however, say on the contrary . . ." In fact, these "others" *(alii)* defend a view that is diametrically opposed to the first position. For, according to the *alii,* all the angels receive a direct illumination from God. The need for any kind of reciprocal illumination is thus obviated. Aquinas, however, finds that this idea too falls wide of the mark; for in putting forward their erroneous conception, the *alii* deny authority *(auctoritas)* and tradition (that is to say, what Dionysius "hands down," *tradit*).

If we look more closely at the kind of authority Thomas cites, we find that it falls into three categories: the authority of Sacred Scripture, the authority of an important sub-apostolic writer (namely, Pseudo-Dionysius the Areopagite, who by the medievals was considered to be the disciple of St. Paul mentioned in Acts 17.34[103]), and the authority of the philosophers. The fact that in the case of both of these opposed views a simple reference to authority suffices to refute them might confirm a longstanding prejudice about Scholastic thought, namely, the idea that the Schoolmen built their systems upon the foundation of uncritically accepted views considered as authoritative. It is true that the use of authority was of central importance in the Scholastic project. However, the role played by authority is a rather complex one. Aquinas uses authority and tradition both to refute views, and, later on in the text, to confirm his own solution. Oftentimes in the *Summa theologiae,* the opposing views set out at the beginning of the article are each supported by weighty authorities. In other words, the mere reference to authority is not used to solve the problem. Rather, for the Scholastics the reconciliation and weighing up of authoritative positions helps in the investigation of reality—indeed, for them, the investigation of reality can only be achieved through the reconciliation of authoritative texts. At the end of this section, we shall see why.

Neither mediate nor immediate illumination is reconcilable with the testimony of the different *auctoritates;* given that the angels must nevertheless have some knowledge of God, we have reached an impasse. For Aquinas, the only way out of it is to choose a "middle course," a *via media.* This "middle course" avoids the extremes of both the refuted positions, while not rejecting such valuable insights as they might contain.[104] But to find out where exactly the middle path lies, what the common ground is between the seemingly irreconcilable positions, it is necessary to make a distinction. Linguistically, this distinction is thrown into relief in our text by combination of the adverb *quidem* and the conjunction *sed:* "on the one hand . . . yet . . ." Aquinas attempts to determine the respective points of view, or perspectives, from which each of the opposing viewpoints were formulated, and from which each of them is therefore justified—but justified only if seen literally "in perspective," rather than absolutized. Aquinas concedes that the *alii* are right in claiming that all the angels enjoy the vision of God face-to-face; yet the *quidam* also caught a glimpse of the truth, as this does not necessarily entail they know all God's effects. This distinction makes room for the possibility that the lower angelic orders are illuminated by the higher ones, specifically with regard to those effects of the supreme Cause that the lower angels are not able to see in the Cause Himself.

An example, introduced by the word *sicut* ("just as") illustrates this point. Just as the angels are able to grasp more of God's effects depending on how close they are to Him and how much grace they enjoy, so human beings are able to draw more conclusions from the basic principles of human knowledge (such as "the whole is greater than each of its parts") in direct proportion to their intelligence. The possibility of illustrating a point made about angels by means of an example taken from the human realm depends upon an important conviction shared by all the Scholastics, namely, that all levels of being are held together by a basic similarity, by an all-embracing structural analogy. According to this view, no being can be totally exterior to any other being, as everything bears some traces of the cosmos, the all-pervading order. We shall have to discuss this view in greater detail in the next study.

After this example, Aquinas offers his final solution to the original problem discussed in our excerpt: are the angels able to illuminate each other? His answer, introduced by the conjunction *unde,* is a qualified "yes"; yes, but only with regard to certain divine effects. This solution is then shown to be in accordance with authority. In a fully developed *quaestio,* another more detailed discussion of the opposing positions presented at the outset would now follow, with the goal to show exactly where they were right and where they went astray, and why.

The method of the *quaestio* is clearly dialectical in nature; proceeding from a thesis and an antithesis, it works toward a synthesis. Or, to use a more authentically Scholastic terminology, it works toward a *collectio,* a "collection" of opposing viewpoints. As Aquinas writes in his commentary on Aristotle's *Metaphysics:*

> [I]n spite of the fact that what one human being is able to contribute to the understanding of the truth, by means of his own study and talent, is something small by comparison to the whole consideration *(totam considerationem)* of the truth, nevertheless what comes together from all the collected partial views *(quod aggregatur ex omnibus "coarticulatis," idest exquisitis et collectis)* becomes something big. This can be seen in the individual branches of knowledge: through the study and talent of various individuals, the latter have reached an admirable growth *(incrementum).*[105]

As fallen human beings do not enjoy divine omniscience, nor even the beatific vision granted to the angels, the truth, as opposed to partial truth*s,* is accessible to them only as the goal of a *collectio*—a painstaking gathering together of such scraps of truth as individual researchers have discovered throughout the course of history. The hope which animates this *collectio* is that the sum of these pieces of knowledge will "collectively" bring us closer to the whole of the truth. Put differently, the truth can only be attained through an unflagging effort aiming at the unification of partial perspectives, each of which captures *something of* the truth while none of them can capture the truth *as such:* "while each of the predecessors has discovered something of the truth *(aliquid de veritate),* the product of all these discoveries brought together into *one (simul in unum collectum)* leads posterity to a great knowledge of the truth."[106] The method of the *quaestio,* as employed by Thomas Aquinas, is animated by a dialectic not unlike the one we discovered in the Gothic cathedral (and, indeed, Gothic script); both combine great confidence in the powers of human reason with a humble recognition of human finitude. For Aquinas, the truth is not a possession but a task; indeed, it is an open-ended task, because ultimately it *is* the transcendent God,[107] of whom "we cannot know what He is, but only what He is not."[108] That "growth" *(incrementum)* of our knowledge is possible and necessary—that the last word can never be spoken—is a natural consequence of this conception.[109]

The World as Text

The *quaestio* is, by its very nature, a method for the reconciliation of authoritative texts. In the *quaestio,* reality is revealed to us insofar, and only insofar, as it is treated in texts. If, therefore, the *quaestio* is the most characteristic literary genre in which the Schoolmen couched their ideas—the typical Scholastic "form of succession" of concepts—one wonders where this method leaves the natural sciences, in which progress is difficult to make without direct observation. For Sir Richard Southern, it is precisely this text-centeredness of the Scholastic method that explains its eventual downfall. It was, he believes, structurally unable to accommodate the natural sciences:

> The established texts all required—and only required—the meticulous study of their words and the systematization of their doctrines to make them fully intelligible, and lecture rooms were the ideal place for studying them. But, in the physical sciences, a commentary and elucidation of the texts had to be sought by observing afresh such phenomena as the movements of the stars. None of this work could be done inside the classroom.[110]

But why were the Scholastic masters so obsessed with their texts? Did they not realize that there was a reality outside their lecture rooms, a reality for which the existing texts accounted perhaps but insufficiently? Lest we fall prey to the facile prejudice according to which the Scholastics, in their bookishness, ignored the "real world," let us stop for a moment to investigate the relationship obtaining between text and reality in Scholasticism.

The author to turn to in this context is the Franciscan St. Bonaventure (1217/1221–1274), a contemporary of St. Thomas Aquinas and, for a few years in the 1250s, his colleague at the University of Paris. St. Bonaventure states most clearly the conviction that underlies the text-centeredness of Scholastic culture: "the creation of the world," he writes in his *Breviloquium,* a handbook of theology, "is like a kind of book."[111] The world is a text.[112] This is so because the world can be read; like a text it refers to something that it signifies. Now the ultimate "signified" of the world—to use Saussurean terminology—is God:

> The creation of the world is like a kind of book *(quasi quidam liber),* in which the creative Trinity is reflected, represented, and can be read, according to three levels of expression, namely, in the mode of a trace, an image, and a similitude.[113]

We can "read" the triune God in the text of creation, but not all parts of this text are equally expressive; a stone, for instance, tells us less about the work of the ultimate Author than an intelligent human being. Unfortunately, human beings have lost the ability to read the text of creation properly. This is a result of the Fall. Instead of tracing the signifiers of creation back to what they signify—God—we have acquired the habit of taking them at face value, for what they are in themselves.[114] Consequently, the book of the world has "died" for us, its text being tragically "effaced" *(deletus).* That is why God has written another book for our benefit, Scripture, so as to give humanity a second chance to interpret correctly the "similitudes, properties, and metaphors of those things which are written in the book of the world."[115] Thus, the book of the world and the book of Scripture contain the same basic text, the only difference between them being that the *liber Scripturae* is easier to read for humanity after the Fall. This point is of the highest importance; not only is reality itself a text, but there can never be any contradiction between it and the text of Scripture. In other words, it is by attempting to understand

Scripture (and, of course, the authorities commenting upon it in order to elicit its full meaning) that we have the best chances to decipher the meaning of reality correctly.[116] The German theologian Winthir Rauch writes that, for Bonaventure, Scripture is the "dictionary and key for the language of the book of creation."[117] The reasons for the "bookishness" of Scholastic thought should now already be much clearer; there is, in the Scholastic episteme, no contradiction between reality and text, because the real is itself of a textual nature. Moreover, both the reality-text and the Scripture-text have the same Author, Who has composed the latter in order to help us read the former. For a Scholastic, the idea that the explanation of Scripture somehow fails to take the "real world" into consideration would hardly have been intelligible.

However, we have not yet followed Bonaventure's book metaphysics to its highest point, namely, to what the "Seraphic Doctor" calls the "book of life" *(liber vitae),*[118] or the "book written within" *(liber scriptus intus).*[119] The "book of life" is written within God Himself, for it is His Wisdom. What Bonaventure wants to say here is that God Himself, or at least an aspect of God Himself, is textual. As we all know, this idea is suggested by Scripture itself:

> In the beginning was the Word (ὁ λόγος), and the Word was with God, and the Word was God. He was in the beginning with God; all things were made through him, and without him was not anything made that was made (John 1.1–3).

For those who see God face-to-face in the hereafter, the text of the book of life bears a testimony to the Trinity that is "through itself and in itself explicit and express"; indeed, it is "irrefragable."[120] This absolute certainty is not granted to us in this life. Nevertheless, even here we are allowed to catch a glimpse of the book of life through the natural light of reason and, if we enjoy the gift of faith, through the light of grace, too. The fact that St. Bonaventure describes the beatific vision in terms of reading the book of God's Wisdom has a very important corollary; for us humans God *always* remains a book to be read, which means, to be interpreted. For us, there will never be a complete coincidence of the text that signifies God and its signification, even if the signification will ultimately become "through itself and in itself explicit and express." Put differently, there will always remain a distance between God as we see Him through the text of His Wisdom, and God as He is in Himself.[121] In other words again, there will be no end to interpretation, ever.

Reading Techniques and the New Subjectivity of Thirteenth-Century Scholasticism

Although the understanding of reality as a complex web of words ultimately signifying the Word is brilliantly epitomized in the book metaphysics of St. Bonaventure, a thirteenth-century author who in many ways
belonged to the mainstream university culture of his day, the attitude of
High Scholasticism toward textuality has its roots in monasticism.
Nonetheless, it can be argued—and the present section will be devoted to
this problem—that in thirteenth-century Scholasticism we find the first
germs of a dissociation of text from reality—not a breaking of the bond,
to be sure, just a loosening of the grip of the text over reality, and indeed
over the subject. In order to understand this subtle shift, we shall have to
study the difference between monastic and High Scholastic reading techniques. This will then enable us to define the kinds of "subject positions"
generated by these different reading techniques. Tell me how you read, and
I shall tell you who you are.[122]

In the medieval monastery, following the recommendations of St.
Benedict's Rule, reading was one of the principal activities. First of all, the
day of the monks was of course structured by the rhythm of the liturgy, in
which the recitation of the Psalms was central. Yet even outside the
chapel—and, as Dom Leclercq notes, in some monasteries there was little
life outside the chapel, for the liturgy occupied almost the whole day[123]—
the monks read or listened to readings in the refectory, as well as during
hours of study and meditation. This *lectio divina*, "divine" reading or reading as part of a greater quest for God, not only pervaded most aspects of
the lives of the monks; it was also of a different quality than the kind of
reading to which we have come to be accustomed. For, the monks would
usually read aloud. Silent reading was not totally unheard-of in antiquity
and the Middle Ages, but it remained an exception—precisely up to the
times of High Scholasticism, as we shall see. One problem with silent reading was that its practice required a script featuring well-developed word
divisions, which emerged only gradually from the eighth century onward;
before then, and throughout the whole of antiquity, texts formed undivided strings of letters that could not be read silently with ease.[124]

However, such paleographical considerations aside, oral reading has extremely powerful anthropological and psychological, even cultural implications. Reading a text (above all, Scripture) aloud, and doing so over and over,
leads to what Dom Leclercq has aptly termed, "total memorization."[125] This
means that oral reading is not just an intellectual exercise—as silent reading

tends to be—but rather engages the whole person. The memory of a text learned by heart through oral reading is intellectual and visual, but also auditory and even muscular; that is to say, thoroughly physical. In this way, the *lectio divina* "inscribes . . . the sacred text in the body and in the soul."[126] The whole existence of the monk comes to be assimilated, as it were, to the holy text, including of course his mind. It has been pointed out that monks made little use of written concordances when composing their works, the reason for this being that their entire minds were themselves complex fabrics of scriptural and patristic cross-references and associations. Thus, each word read (=heard) represented, as Leclercq says, a kind of "hook"[127] linking it to other words associated with it. These associations were often half haphazard—at least this is how they appear to our more "logical" minds. In monastic literary compositions, ideas are arranged in associative chains, the key to which lies in the structure of the monk's imagination:

> As it had for the Fathers, reminiscence on the part of the monastic authors of the Middle Ages had a profound effect on their literary composition. The mere fact of hearing certain words, which happen to be similar in sound to certain other words, sets up a kind of chain reaction of associations which will bring together words that have no more than a chance connection, purely external, with one another.[128]

In monastic culture, the author is therefore less a controlling, mastering "subject" than a being "subjected" to the text that *lectio divina* has inscribed in his mind and body. Following the associations suggested by this text(ure), he refrains from imposing a more "logical" structure upon it. For this text is the Word of God, and the texture of reality; it cannot be manipulated at will. The monk attempts to copy the book of Scripture, first in his own body and soul, and then in the books that he himself eventually produces. Hence, in the monastic culture of the Middle Ages, writing is an extension of reading. As the Hispanicist John Dagenais observes in his fascinating work on *The Ethics of Reading in Manuscript Culture*, "in the Middle Ages the primary 'literary' activity was not writing, and certainly not 'authoring' or 'creating,' but reading."[129] Moreover, this writing, which is always a rereading, is an ethical, even religious activity. In pagan Rome, writing had been a servile task, delegated to slaves, even gladiators; in the Christian Middle Ages, it is a religious duty.[130]

This situation changed with the advent of the Scholastic universities; it changed, though not completely, as Scholastic culture remained text-centered. Yet the attitudes toward textuality underwent an important transformation.[131] For, the influx of a large body of new sources containing ideas both complex and challenging, and the creation of more efficiently organized institutions to "digest" this material, rendered the monastic approach to textuality obsolete. The monks' technique of slowly reading, ruminating, and reciting over and over again a relatively small body of texts—Scripture, as well as a selection of patristic and classical authors—proved unable to rise to the challenge posed by the new material. Oral reading was slow, a fact evidenced by the monastic libraries' practice to lend each monk one book per year, which would be given out at Lent.[132] One book sufficed to nourish a monk's meditations for a whole year! The masters of the thirteenth century could not content themselves with such a contemplative approach. Not only did they have to give lectures and hold their own in disputations on a wide variety of subjects; in doing so, they also had to confront the task of comparing the new Greek, Islamic, and Jewish sources in a systematic way with the Christian heritage, weighing up their merits and demerits, and finally harmonizing the diverse material in some way. This is, of course, what the *quaestio* structure was meant to facilitate. The bottom line is that, as a result of the university culture, reading had to become quicker (that is to say, silent) and more efficient, more systematic.

The more systematic character of university reading was achieved by the creation of a number of research tools, such as concordances, indexes, and library catalogs. The goal of these reference works was to make it possible to *statim invenire,* as Mary and Richard Rouse have put it in the title of one of their articles: to "find at once."[133] Texts now came to be "used," rather than "read" and pondered in the old fashion of *lectio divina:* used to prepare a disputation and compile a *quaestio;* used to provide further arguments on a specific issue in Scripture, the Fathers, or, indeed, Aristotle; used to write a study-guide. One of the most ingenious indexes of scriptural, patristic, and secular authorities was prepared by the Oxford theologian Robert Grosseteste and his circle. It has been handed down to us in only one copy, contained in a manuscript at Lyons, Bibliothèque municipale, MS 414.[134] Grosseteste's index, completed around 1230, is remarkable in a number of respects. The *Tabula,* or "table," as the text is called in the surviving manuscript, does not use the method of alphabetic indexing that was current in other research tools made around the same time, especially biblical dictionaries. Apparently the author, a rather conservative theologian, was unhappy with the idea of imposing the arbitrary order of the alphabet upon his material. Therefore, he chose an order better reflecting the "texture" of things divine and profane. In fact, his index is divided into nine *distinctiones,* or subject categories, which group topics together systematically: *de Deo* deals with the existence and nature of God, His unity and trinity, and so forth; *de Verbo* is divided into topics relating to the Word; *de creaturis* then contains subjects regarding creation; and so on. Grosseteste had planned to treat 440 different subjects in his *Tabula,* but the entries are completed only up to number 217. Each entry contains references to scriptural authorities, followed by references to patristic and medieval Christian authors. Added in the margins are ancient and Islamic writers such as Aristotle or Avicenna. The references are identified by book and chapter numbers, not, as was common practice in the case of indexes attached to particular books, by folio numbers. In this way, Grosseteste's *Tabula* could be used with profit by anyone possessing copies of the books it mentions. Finally, we must draw attention to the unique system of logographic signs employed in the *Tabula.* Each entry is accompanied by a symbol—for example, a dot standing for *de unitate Dei* or a triangle for *de trinitate Dei.* (A large number of the signs are conventional, though, that is to say, they are not images of what they represent.) The idea of these symbols, which form a complex system comprising 440 different signs, was to facilitate the compilation of the index. In perusing a given work, Grosseteste would systematically mark all the passages appearing to be of interest to him with the appropriate symbols. His assistants could then use the volume later to incorporate the newly discovered references into the *Tabula.* Moreover, when going the other way, from the index back to the books, Grosseteste and his circle could avail themselves of the logographs in order to identify indexed passages at one glance on the pages (see plates 5 and 6).

The cultural revolution brought about by the Scholastic indexes was such that Ivan Illich considers it "reasonable to speak of the pre- and post-index Middle Ages."[135] Generally in the universities, the masters and their students no longer contemplate texts, in the sense of subjecting themselves to their rhythm and allowing their bodies and souls to be impregnated by them. Rather, they manipulate these texts by means of dictionaries and indexes in order to "master" and then "use" them for doctrinal syntheses. Reading, in this period, starts becoming an "intellectual" activity, which it has remained to this day. Further, the silent reading outside the monastic community renders study and research more individualistic.[136] It also eliminates the element of peer correction and control for readers driven by curiosity to consult heretical works—or indeed to compose them.[137] The libraries, for their part, are transformed from places where mumbling was an accepted practice to those silent spaces we have come to associate with

serious study.[138] As memory starts playing a less important role in education, the libraries also establish reference sections, with chained-up books
to be consulted by everyone. Last but not least, the idea of authorship itself changes. As A. J. Minnis has argued, in the thirteenth century we witness an increased interest in the meaning of human authorship. Even in the
context of the books of the Bible, it becomes acceptable to be interested
in the "instrumental cause" responsible for the text of the Holy Writ, that
is to say, in the inspired human authors with their particular styles and ways
of expressing themselves.[139] This, of course, in no wise involves denying
the ultimate divine authorship of Scripture. Yet there is a subtle shift of emphasis here, a new significance attached to the human self and its role in
writing. Perhaps writing is gradually developing into something more, or
at any rate something different from, rereading; it becomes the conscious
"creating" of "original" ideas.

Conclusion

Let us conclude this lengthy study, which has examined the textual bases
of Scholastic thought, as well as the intellectual practices associated with
them. Scholastic thought is eminently "embodied." If we try to study it
in anything but the most superficial manner, we cannot abstract from the
strangeness of its material support: the manuscripts with their unusual
layouts, penned in Gothic characters. In order to be able to establish editions, we must learn how to read these manuscripts. However, by thus
engaging in textual scholarship, we already discover that the "body" and
the "soul" of Scholastic thought cannot be separated from one another.
We have formulated the thesis that Gothic script itself is animated by a
dialectics of confidence in human reason, on the one hand, and deep respect for the mystery of the divine, on the other. This tension is also discovered in other fields of the Scholastic episteme: in the Gothic
cathedrals, for instance.

In the thirteenth century, Christian knowledge undergoes its most profound restructuring since Augustinian times, as an inflow of new sources
challenges the limits of the age-old curriculum. We have learned that the
analysis of such a seemingly dull document as a study-guide can sometimes
tell us more about the internal organization of a field of knowledge than
the sophisticated arguments of a much more "original" author.

The influx of Greek, Islamic, and Jewish material might have over-
thrown the Augustinian curriculum, but it does not change the text-
centeredness of medieval culture. In medieval times, thinking is text-based,

and solving problems means to commentate upon and then reconcile textual authorities contradicting each other. The culture of commentary *(lectio)* and disputation *(disputatio)*, which is such a characteristic feature of the medieval university, is designed to effect this reconciliation. In the *quaestio,* that is to say, the literary equivalent of the *disputatio,* we see a dialectical structure at work. Deliberately juxtaposing the most extreme authoritative opinions on a subject, the Scholastic author attempts to find a middle course *(media via,* as Aquinas says) incorporating the insights of the contradictory (and hence, partial) views. This work of "collecting" *(colligere)* limited human perspectives into a greater whole comes to a provisional end in the conclusion of the *quaestio;* yet the transcendence of the ultimate object of enquiry—God, the Truth—makes this conclusion itself subject to further questioning.

The "bookishness" of the Scholastics, together with their seeming indifference with regard to the world "out there," outside the lecture room, led us to consider the relationship between reality and text in the Middle Ages. For St. Bonaventure, the greatest representative of a "book metaphysics" in the thirteenth century, God is quite literally the "Author" of reality. Reality is a text copied from the book of life—God's Wisdom itself—which can be read, even though after the Fall its correct interpretation requires the succor of a third book, Scripture. The interpretation of these books is susceptible of various degrees of accuracy; indeed, the meaning of the book of life, which only the blessed in heaven are allowed to read directly, is absolutely certain. Still, even its reading necessitates interpretation, as it retains the bipolar textual structure of signifier and signified. Thus, in the Scholastic episteme, the confidence in the powers of human reason to discover the texture of the real is counterbalanced by the insight that God, ultimately, transcends the text—every text.

The history of medieval reading techniques reflects the conviction that texts, and especially the Text, are more than faint images of reality—which has been the typically modern view of the matter. To assimilate oneself to the Text is, in the medieval monastery, part of the ascetic quest for deification—the assimilation of the human creature to the Creator. The masters of High Scholasticism (who had to deal with many more pagan texts than their monastic counterparts) read their sources less intimately, less holistically. In their new reading techniques, with their increased sense of privacy and "mastery" over the text, we can discern the seeds of many of the dualisms of modernity: the text versus the real, the individual versus the community, the body versus the soul. The seeds are sown, but their full development is as yet far away.

Plate 1: The Gospel of St. Mathew with glosses (ca. 1130–40). Private collection, by permission of the owner.

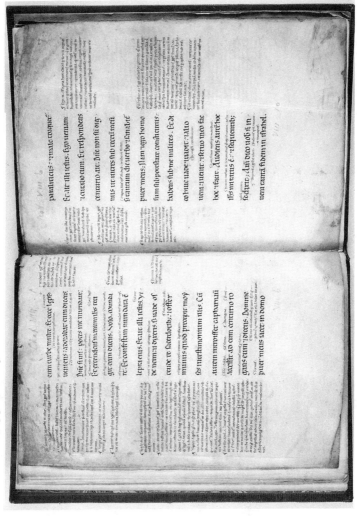

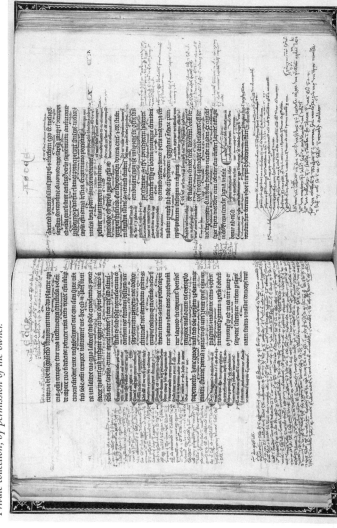

Plate 2: Ecclesiastes with glosses (thirteenth-century manuscript). Note the new layout, in which the biblical text is written around the glosses.

Private collection, by permission of the owner.

Plate 3: A Gothic Bible (thirteenth-century manuscript). The opening shows the beginning of the First Letter of St. Paul to the Corinthians. Note especially the shape of the Gothic letters and the abundance of abbreviations.
Special Collections, Bridwell Library, Perkins School of Theology, Southern Methodist University.

Plate 4:   *Rose window in the west façade of the abbey church of St.-Nicaise, Reims. The church was destroyed in the French Revolution.*
Drawing by Sarina Fuhrmann, of the University of Dallas.

10/20

Plate 5: Robert Grosseteste's Tabula *(mid-thirteenth century manuscript). The page shows part of the list of Grosseteste's indexing symbols at the beginning of the* Tabula. *Lyons, Bibliothèque municipale, MS 414, fol. 18r.*

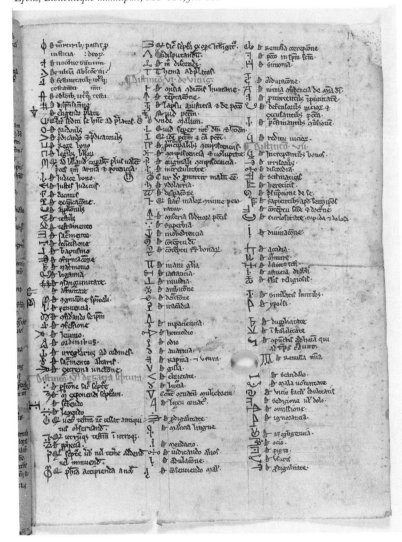

Plate 6: Robert Grosseteste's Tabula: *a typical page with index entries. Lyons, Bibliothèque municipale, MS 414, fol. 20v.*

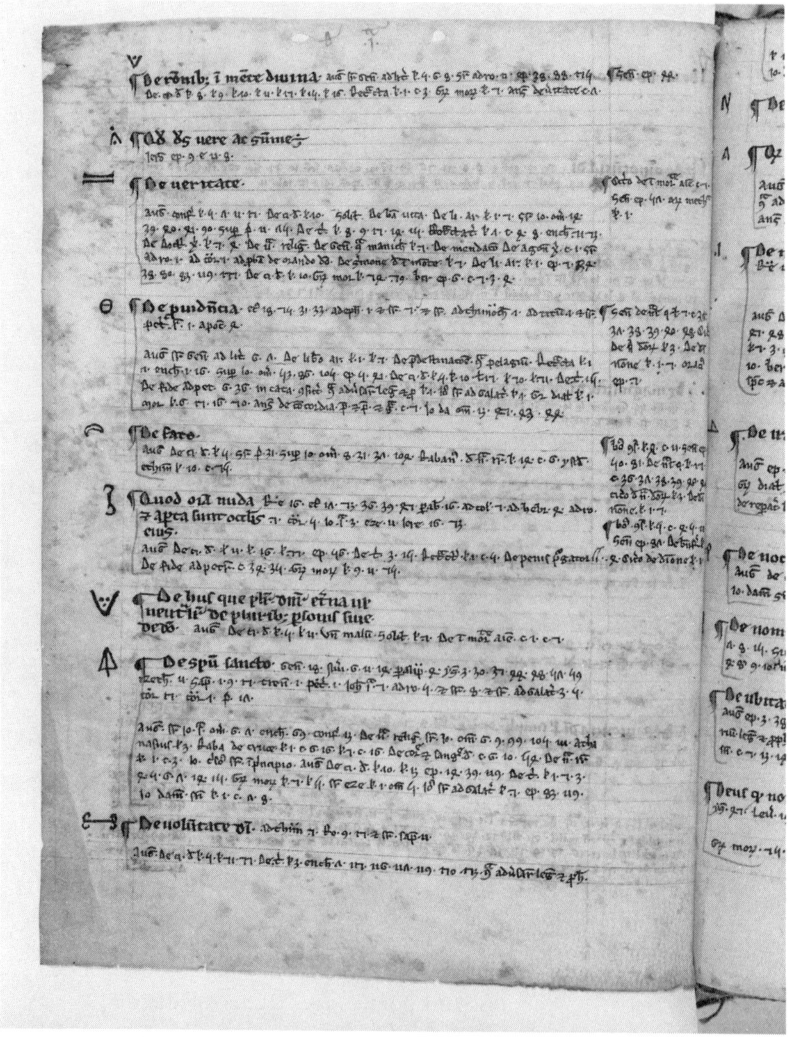

STUDY 4

THE PROSE OF THE WORLD—
THE GREEK CIRCLE AND THE CHRISTIAN LINE

A lthough Foucault never wrote a work devoted explicitly to the medieval period, the Middle Ages function as a kind of backcloth against
which he conducts his analyses of the modern age. Regrettably, the one
book of his which comes closest to a study of medieval Christian culture—volume 4 of the *History of Sexuality*—was not released before its author's death. As Foucault's will prohibits the publication of texts not
printed during his lifetime, it will probably remain inaccessible, except in
manuscript form.[1] *Les aveux de la chair* (The Confessions of the Flesh) contains the history of sexuality during the first Christian centuries. A short
essay that, according to Foucault's biographer David Macey, "is presumably
part of the unpublished fourth volume,"[2] was printed in 1982.[3] An earlier
work of Foucault's, *The Order of Things* (1966), includes a chapter that, dealing with pre-seventeenth-century culture, also somewhat obliquely treats
of the Middle Ages. About this book, I shall say more in a moment.

Concerning the function of the Middle Ages as a kind of foil for Foucault's studies of the modern period, the medievalist Anne Clark Bartlett
has criticized what she considers "Foucault's view of the Middle Ages as
sort of a utopian realm." "In Foucault's work," she continues, "all of Western history before the seventeenth century functions nostalgically—
though ambivalently—as a lost and golden age."[4] One of the examples
Bartlett cites is Foucault's idealization of pre-modern sexuality in his essay,
"A Preface to Transgression," written in 1963 as a contribution to a
Festschrift for Georges Bataille:

> [N]ever did sexuality have a more immediately natural meaning, and never
> did it know a greater "felicity of expression," than in the Christian world of

fallen bodies and of sin. The proof is a whole [tradition of] mysticism and spirituality which were quite unable to divide the continuous forms of desire, of rapture, of penetration, of ecstasy, of that outpouring which fails (épanchement qui défaille); they felt that all these movements led, without interruption or limit, right to the heart of a divine love of which they were the last flaring (évasement) and the returning source (source en retour). What characterizes modern sexuality, from Sade to Freud, is not the fact that it has found the language of its logic or of its nature, but rather the fact that it has, through the violence of their discourses, been "denatured"—cast into an empty space where it finds nothing but the meager form of the limit, and where it has no beyond (au-delà), no prolongation, except in the frenzy that disrupts it. We have not liberated sexuality . . .[5]

The thesis expressed in this passage is not totally unknown to us; for it was touched upon in study 1. Foucault claims that, in the same way in which modernity has marginalized madness and dissolved it into rational discourse, modern culture has reduced sexuality to a marginal existence at the limits of reason. Hence the provocative statement holding that de Sade and Freud, rather than liberating sexuality, have done violence to it.

The passage just quoted does indeed, as Bartlett notes in her critique, place modern attitudes toward sexuality against the background of an idealized "natural immediacy" and "felicity of expression" that it supposedly enjoyed in the pre-modern Christian tradition. There is no doubt a measure of nostalgia to be detected here, reminiscent of the preface to Madness and Civilization, which, written just two years before "A Preface to Transgression," expresses a similar longing for the "zero degree" in the relationship between madness and reason, for the hypothetical time when the two were still engaged in dialogue. However, the very same preface also formulates doubts about the possibility of such a return. By the time of the publication of The Archaeology of Knowledge, in 1969, the nostalgic element has entirely disappeared from Foucault's thought. He is now more interested in historical a prioris as conditions for the possibility of certain kinds of discourse, rather than as limitations. Nonetheless, every condition of possibility can also be read as a limitation; hence the statement made in a 1983 interview: "My point is not that everything is bad, but that everything is dangerous, which is not exactly the same is bad. If everything is dangerous, then we always have something to do."[6]

The nostalgia to which Bartlett adverts in Foucault's treatment of the Middle Ages, at least in his earlier works, does not invalidate his ideas about medieval culture. Indeed, the very passage that we have just read concerning pre-modern sexuality contains an observation about medieval civilization upon which Foucault was to expand a few years later in *The Order of Things,* and which is consonant with our own findings concerning the nature of the medieval episteme. Modern sexuality, Foucault writes, has been relegated to an "empty space" where it no longer has any "beyond" *(au-delà)* or "prolongation" *(prolongation);* in a word, it has come to be severed from the experience of the divine. Unlike the medieval cosmos, the modern world, including the modern experience of sexuality, no longer signifies anything, because the signified of the text, God, is "dead."[7] As a consequence, language, like sexuality, is destined "to grow with no point of departure, no end, and no promise."[8] This quotation leads us to *The Order of Things* and its second chapter, entitled, "The Prose of the World."

The Prose of the World

Foucault states his thesis right at the beginning:

> Up to the end of the sixteenth century, resemblance *(ressemblance)* played a constructive role in the knowledge of Western culture. It was resemblance that largely guided exegesis and the interpretation of texts; it was resemblance that organized the play of symbols, made possible knowledge of things visible and invisible, and controlled the art of representing them. The universe was folded in upon itself *(s'enroulait sur lui-même):* the earth echoing the sky, faces seeing themselves reflected in the stars, and plants holding within their stems the secrets that were of use to man.[9]

Although "The Prose of the World" presents an analysis of "the sixteenth-century *episteme,*"[10] as Foucault himself states a few pages later, the opening sentence of the chapter claims that this analysis equally applies, more generally, to Western culture "up to the end of the sixteenth century." However, there is not a single reference to a medieval text in the chapter's footnotes. In fact, in the course of his discussion, Foucault occasionally draws attention to differences between the sixteenth-century episteme and its predecessors.[11] Nonetheless, as we shall see, much of what is said in "The Prose of the World" can indeed be taken as commentary, extremely insightful commentary even, on medieval culture.[12]

"Resemblance," Foucault says, "made possible knowledge of things visible and invisible." In order to understand this claim, it will be necessary to look more closely into the nature and functioning of resemblance. Foucault distinguishes four principal kinds of similitudes, namely, *convenientia, aemulatio, analogia,* and *sympathia.* The latter cannot adequately be described without its dialectical counterpart, *antipathia.*

(1) *Convenientia* designates less an explicit "resemblance" between things, than the fact that they are made to coexist harmoniously in "the vast syntax of the world."[13] God fashioned the human soul so that it could exist in a body; mosses grow "on the outsides of shells, plants in the antlers of stags, a sort of grass on the faces of men,"[14] attesting to a kind of universal symbiosis. Why does the multifarious multiplicity of created beings form a web of coexistence and mutual adjustment? The answer that the Western episteme up to the sixteenth century gave to this question was *convenientia.*

(2) The second form of resemblance, *aemulatio,* differs from the first in that it does not require any proximity between the factors it involves; it is also more dynamic than *convenientia.* Emulation is at work, for instance, in the relationship between divine wisdom and the human intellect, for the latter is but a faint reflection of the former, which it endeavors to imitate. Likewise, the whole earth mirrors and emulates the sky. If *convenientia* constitutes a chain between the beings it relates, *aemulatio* can be likened to "a series of concentric circles."[15]

(3) *Analogia,* the third form of resemblance, obtains between relations, or groups of beings, rather than between individual objects. Thus, there exists, for example, an analogy between the stars and the heavens they occupy, on the one hand, and plants and the soil in which they grow, on the other. Foucault does not mention the analogy that, in medieval Christian culture, served as the paradigm of all the others—namely, the analogy between the three Persons of the Trinity and the innumerable triads reflecting it in creation. Most important in this context is the "trinity" of mind, knowledge, and love first described by Augustine in his treatise, *De trinitate.*[16] In the Western episteme up to the sixteenth century, the complex network of analogies is viewed as centering upon the human being, in whom analogies are found both for the world above him and for the world below him. The human being, Foucault writes, "is the great fulcrum of proportions—the center upon which relations are based and from which they are once again reflected."[17]

(4) Together with its antipode, *antipathia,* the fourth form of resemblance, *sympathia,* is not just one kind of similitude amongst the others; rather, they are "resumed and explained by it."[18] *Sympathia* functions in a way that is comparable to *aemulatio,* drawing things together. However, where *aemulatio* contents itself with imitation, sympathy is a power capable of changing the fundamental nature of things, transforming them into

one another. As Foucault remarks: "Sympathy is an instance of the *Same* so strong and so insistent that it will not rest content to be merely one of the forms of likeness; it has the dangerous power of *assimilating,* of rendering things identical to one another, of mingling them, of causing their individuality to disappear."[19] For instance, fire, warm and light, moves upwards into the air, but in doing so, it becomes air itself. "Sympathy transforms."[20] Sympathy is what is at work behind the other three forms of resemblance; it is the root from which they derive their power. It is so strong that, were it not counterbalanced by a force opposed to it, "the world would be reduced to a point, to a homogeneous mass, to the gloomy form of the Same."[21] Antipathy *(antipathia)* therefore plays the role of the necessary counterpoise of sympathy. For things are not only attracted to each other, they also repugn each other. Foucault, who likes gory examples, cites a text (which he does not identify) describing the antipathy that obtains between rats and crocodiles: taking advantage of an opportune moment when the crocodile is asleep, the rat is known to enter its mouth, whence it will proceed to eat its way through the tormented beast's bowels. In the episteme of Western culture before the sixteenth century, it is the interplay of dialectically opposed forces that defuses the danger of resemblance turning into identity. As we shall discover at the end of this study, Foucault's analysis of resemblance is incisive in many ways; for it is true that similitude was an essential feature of medieval thought, and it is also correct to claim that resemblance was understood as an interplay between the forces of identity and difference.

So far, it has not yet become evident why the chapter we are interpreting is entitled, "The Prose of the World." Resemblances, hovering as they do between identity and difference, sympathy and antipathy, are not obvious. Or rather, a resemblance is "both the most obvious and the most hidden of things"[22]: it is obvious once discovered, yet hidden as long as it remains undetected. But how do we recognize the element of identity in the relationship between two things, isolating it from the element of difference? After all, there are no two objects in this world that are exactly the same! What are the criteria that enable us to bracket this difference and say that, for instance, the kernel of a walnut is "like" a little brain? The distinction of the similar from the dissimilar is impossible without *signs* that bring hidden similarities to the surface of the world. Hence, "the world of similarity can only be a world of signs."[23] Things form chains, concentric circles, and analogies only inasmuch as they refer to each other. Without signs—which act like hooks linking things together—everything would remain isolated. At this point, Foucault's discussion of the pre-classical[24] episteme joins the theme of the world as text, which is already familiar to us:

> [T]he face of the world is covered with blazons, with characters, with ciphers and obscure words—with "hieroglyphics," as Turner called them. And the space inhabited by immediate resemblances becomes like a vast open book; it bristles with written signs; every page is seen to be filled with strange figures that intertwine and in some places repeat themselves.[25]

Now what is the nature of these signs that enable us to read the world as a text, that is to say, as an ordered and coherent set of similar things? Answer: signs are themselves resemblances. Let us consider an example provided by Foucault. In sixteenth-century medicine, the walnut was seen to possess a twofold sympathy with regard to the human head: for while its thick green rind was believed to be able to cure wounds of the pericranium, internal head ailments could, according to the science of the day, be positively affected by the kernel. This twofold resemblance between the walnut and the human head would remain hidden, however, if there were not a sign indicating it. This sign is the analogy obtaining between the walnut, its kernel and its shell, on the one hand, and the human head, the brain and the skull, on the other. But what about this analogy itself? Is it obvious? No, of course not, as the elements of similarity between the human head and the walnut are counterbalanced by many other elements of difference, which always threaten to overshadow them. Thus, we need a further sign identifying the analogy. And so forth. A resemblance is indicated by a sign, which is another resemblance (of a different type), which is indicated by a sign, which . . . "And so the circle is closed," remarks Foucault.[26]

The world is an enormous text, the deciphering of which requires endless interpretation. In this task, other texts can help us. For, the "profound kinship of language with the world"[27]—the fact that the world itself "speaks"—means that all the different types of "texts" complement and comment upon each other:

> There is no difference between the visible marks that God has stamped upon the surface of the earth, so that we may know its inner secrets, and the legible words that Scripture or the sages of antiquity, who have been illuminated by a divine light, have set down in the books preserved for us by tradition. The relation to these texts is of the same nature as the relation to things: in both cases there are signs that must be discovered . . . The truth of all these marks—whether they run through nature or exist in lines on

parchments and in libraries—is everywhere the same: coeval with the institution of God.[28]

Many of these ideas do, of course, seem familiar to us from our own
analysis of the Scholastic episteme in the previous study.[29] As God is the
Author of both the book of nature and the book of Scripture, any fundamental incompatibility between the two is excluded. Moreover, pagan authors can be integrated with the texts of nature and Scripture, as all
genuine knowledge ultimately originates from God. This is, in fact, precisely the point made by Augustine in the passage of *De doctrina christiana*
where he justifies the Christian appropriation of ancient thought. Pagan
wisdom, inasmuch as it is true wisdom, can never be in contradiction with
either revelation or nature. As a consequence of the fundamental harmony
that obtains between the texts of nature, of Scripture, and of human wisdom, knowledge in the pre-classical episteme "consists in relating language
to language; in restoring the great uniform plain of words and things; in
making everything speak."[30]

This relating of language to language privileges, as Foucault acutely observes, the literary form of the commentary. At the universities, as we remember, the *lectio* constituted one of the fundamental forms of teaching.
The task of the commentary is to restore the "original Text" *(Texte primi-
tif)*,[31] the Text in which the languages of the various texts (Scripture, nature, human wisdom) are finally reconciled with each other. To put it in
Thomistic terms with which we are already acquainted, the philosopher or
theologian is called to "collect together" *(colligere)* such partial truths as are
contained in the different texts written by human authors—truths that, in
turn, serve for the interpretation of Scripture. However, the Text, written
in a language that is "an absolutely certain and transparent sign for
things,"[32] proves to be elusive. We know why from our reading of
Bonaventure: the Fall has impeded our ability to read. Consequently, the
Text has been transformed into a future promise; it is the book of life that
will be open to those granted the beatific vision. In this life, however, there
is no end to the quest for the Text. Foucault frames this insight in the following way:

> Perhaps for the first time in Western culture, we find revealed the absolutely
> open dimension of a language no longer able to halt itself, because, never
> being enclosed in a definitive statement, it will express its truth only in some
> future discourse and is wholly devoted to what it will have said; but this dis-
> course itself does not have the power to halt the progression, and encloses

what it says like a promise, bequeathed to yet another discourse . . . The task of commentary can never, by definition, be completed . . . The language of the sixteenth century—understood not as an episode in the history of language, but as a global cultural experience—found itself caught, no doubt, in this game, in this interstice occurring between the primal Text and the infinity of Interpretation.[33]

A few pages earlier in "The Prose of the World," Foucault had already formulated a characterization of the Western episteme up to the end of the sixteenth century in similar, albeit much more critical terms, speaking of "the plethoric yet absolutely poverty-stricken character of this knowledge": "sixteenth-century knowledge condemned itself to never knowing anything but the same thing, and to knowing it only at the unattainable end of an endless journey."[34] This characterization is correct, but its critical overtones are irritating. Has Foucault failed to appreciate that the "one thing" which pre-classical culture pursued in its endless quest for knowledge was so precious that it regarded all its travails as being more than warranted? Did he not realize that the Text which scholars were trying to decipher was God's Wisdom itself? Of course, "The Prose of the World" focuses upon the sixteenth century, making claims about the Western episteme "up to the end of the sixteenth century" only in passing. We should, therefore, be careful in simply projecting medieval categories into Foucault's analysis, or in castigating Foucault for not using them. One thing is certain, however: even if Foucault does not recognize it, in medieval times the episteme he describes is indissociable from a theistic metaphysics of creation.

The universal resemblance of things, with all that it entails (the dialectics of sympathy/identity and antipathy/difference, the conception of the world as a text, the idea of the kinship between world and language, so that all texts become tools in the quest for resemblances, etc.), cannot adequately be understood if the origin of the resemblances remains obscure. For the Scholastics, the whole cosmos is held together by an all-pervasive similarity that never allows the dissimilarity of individual beings to destroy the cosmic order. This order is captured by a theistic metaphysics of creation governed by the principle of causal similarity. In other words, for the Scholastics, all causes bring about effects that resemble them—*omne agens agit sibi simile,* as Thomas Aquinas puts it[35]—God being the First Cause, the Creator, the Author of the world. Therefore, creation, the text, mirrors its Creator/Author.

However, why does "every cause bring about an effect similar to itself"? Why this idea that a cause, rather than dispersing itself in its effect, returns to itself in and through its effect? What are the motives and origins of this reflexive metaphysics of causation, of this metaphysics privileging identity over difference? I have investigated this problem in some detail elsewhere[36]; for our present purposes, it will suffice to summarize the principal results of this previous inquiry.

Parmenides: Being as a "Well-Rounded Sphere"

The reflexive metaphysics of causation that is epitomized in the Thomistic principle *omne agens agit sibi simile,* and the philosophy of circularity, repetition, and identity of which it is part, have a long history in the Western intellectual tradition. Even before the birth of philosophy, Greek literature had a peculiar tendency to associate the perishable realm of human activity with straight movement, while reserving circular imagery for permanent cosmic processes, that is to say, for the more perfect types of existence. As the philosopher Lynne Ballew has demonstrated in her pioneering book, *Straight and Circular: A Study of Imagery in Greek Philosophy,* this trend can already be verified in Homer.[37] In the writings of the Presocratics, which contain the earliest evidence of speculative thought in the West, the tension between the straight and the circular continues to figure prominently. In Parmenides, the theme of circularity is given an explicitly metaphysical significance.[38]

In fragment 8 of his *Poem,* we find Parmenides describing the attributes of being (ἐόν). Being is said to be ungenerated (ἀγένητον) and imperishable (ἀνωλεθρόν) (l. 3)[39]; a whole (οὖλον) and complete (τελεστόν) (l. 4); one (ἕν) and continuous (συνεχές) (l. 6); indivisible (οὐδὲ διαιρετόν) (l. 22) and changeless (ἀκινητόν) (l. 26); it remains the same and in the same (ταὐτόν τ᾽ ἐν ταὐτῶι τε μένον) (l. 29), not lacking in anything (οὐκ ἐπιδευές) (l. 33). Then, just before the goddess ends this "trustworthy speech" (l. 50) concerning the nature of being, the description culminates in the following comparison:

> [It is] from every direction like the bulk of a well-rounded sphere
> (εὐκύκλου σφαίρης),
> Everywhere from the center equally matched (ll. 43f.).

But why liken being to a sphere? As I briefly indicated, since Homeric times Greek literature associated circularity and permanence, especially the permanence of cosmic processes, such as "the cycles of time and the seasons," "the paths of the stars,"[40] and so forth. These phenomena must have imposed themselves upon the Greek mind as paradigms of eternity and perfection, qualities that, by abstraction, then came to be attributed to circularity itself. It is perhaps in this way that Parmenides could come to employ the imagery of sphericity in his attempts to describe the perfection of being.

If for Parmenides being is spherical, so too is human knowledge of it— a conviction that line 29 of fragment 1 summarizes in the famous expression, "well-rounded truth" (ἀληθείης εὐκυκλέος):

> And it is right that you should learn all things,
> Both the steadfast heart of well-rounded truth
> And the beliefs of mortals . . . (ll. 28–30).[41]

Given the fragmentary state of the *Poem,* it is not easy to determine in exactly what sense Parmenides's conception of knowledge implies circularity, but the fact that a "spherical" ontology should be reflected in a "spherical" epistemology does not seem surprising in the context of the ancient principle that "like is known by like."[42] Perhaps this parallelism between the realms of thought and reality, that is to say, their likeness and commensurability due to a common circular nature, is also what the notoriously difficult fragment 3 expresses in its pointed affirmation of the "identity" between thinking and being: "τὸ γὰρ αὐτὸ νοεῖν ἐστίν τε καὶ εἶναι."[43]

Plato: "The Similar is Infinitely Fairer than the Dissimilar"

Plato's cosmology can in some important respects be regarded as an expansion and explanation of Parmenides's remarks concerning the sphericity of being. One passage, in particular, has attracted the commentators' attention for the closeness of its doctrine—indeed, the closeness even of its wording—to the *Poem.* This passage, 33B of the *Timaeus,* has variously been called a reflection,[44] a possible "conscious echo,"[45] or simply the "best explanation"[46] of Parmenides's hints about the "well-rounded sphere" of being. The text reads as follows:

> Now for that Living Creature which is designed to embrace within itself all living creatures the fitting shape will be that which comprises within itself all the shapes there are; wherefore He wrought it into a round (κυκλοτερές), in the shape of a sphere (σφαιροειδές), equidistant in all di-

rections from the center to the extremities, which of all the shapes is the most perfect and the most self-similar (ὁμοιότατον αὐτὸ ἑαυτῷ), since He deemed that the similar is infinitely fairer than the dissimilar.[47]

Like Parmenides's all-embracing being, Plato's cosmos forms a sphere. However, unlike Parmenides, Plato tells us why: the sphere is the "most perfect" of all the shapes, being as it is "the most self-similar," or similar to itself (ὁμοιότατον αὐτὸν ἑαυτῷ). What does self-similarity mean? Perhaps we can paraphrase it as "self-reflexivity," as the circle is, of course, the perfect example of a self-reflexive figure. We can view its circumference as the constant return upon itself of the same line. Or, to put it another way, when a circle is made to rotate around its center, the circumference never ceases to be coincident with itself throughout the process. The same holds good for the surface of a sphere. At any rate, its perfection, for Plato, stems from its self-similar, self-reflexive nature.

However, why should self-similarity or self-reflexivity be considered a perfection? Plato's reply, that "the similar is infinitely fairer than the dissimilar," is not self-evident. Yet it does lead us to one of Plato's most fundamental convictions, namely, the idea that the meaning of the cosmos consists in the pursuit of identity. The *Timaeus* conceives of the cosmos as a copy (εἰκών) of an eternal model or "paradigm" (παράδειγμα), after which Plato believes it has been fashioned by the demiurge.[48] Now this eternal model, the Form of the cosmos, is completely self-identical; it exists, as Plato says, "κατὰ ταὐτὰ καὶ ὡσαύτως,"[49] "according to the same and in a selfsame way." The self-identical paradigm, the "κατὰ ταὐτὰ ὄν/ἔχον,"[50] does not have a sensible nature, but rather belongs to a realm that can be apprehended only by means of thought and reason.[51] It would seem evident that only what is rational (and, hence, immaterial) can be completely self-identical, or one with itself; for everything sensible is necessarily extended in space, and thus somehow disperses its essence in the three dimensions. Now, the perfect self-similarity of the sphere is the closest the sensible cosmos can come to the self-identity of its eternal exemplar. Note Plato's equation of perfection, identity, and rationality! This triad would prove extremely influential throughout the Western intellectual tradition. Inversely, Platonic philosophy regards linear forces moving toward differentiation and dispersal as signs of irrationality and imperfection: "The motion characteristic of the vicious, ignorant soul," Lynne Ballew points out, "is invariably described as disorderly, and this disorder is normally described as the result of straight or rectilinear forces. The imagery of the *Gorgias* shows that the life of Callicles is devoted to and comprised of straight motions, and that Socrates is unable to convert him to a circular, philosophical way of life."[52]

In the *Symposium,* a fourth factor is added to the triad of perfection, identity, and rationality—namely, life. Indeed, together with the revolutions of the heavens, the cycle of life is perhaps the most natural sign of permanence in the changeable world. It is therefore not surprising that, in the *Symposium,* Plato portrays the circle of life as a privileged mirror and imitation of the eternal within the sensible realm. The well-known, justly celebrated and beautiful passage 207C–208B of the *Symposium* provides an excellent starting point for our discussion:

> [T]he mortal nature ever seeks, as best it can, to be immortal. In one way only can it succeed, and that is by generation; since so it can always leave behind it a new creature in place of the old . . . Every mortal thing is preserved in this way; not by keeping it exactly the same (τὸ αὐτό) for ever, like the divine, but by replacing what goes off or is antiquated with something fresh, in the semblance of the original (οἷον αὐτὸ ἦν). Through this device, Socrates, a mortal thing partakes of immortality, both in its body and in all other respects; by no other means can it be done.[53]

As has rightly been observed, these sentences constitute the historical origin of the idea according to which every cause brings about effects that are similar to itself[54]—the same idea that, as we know, would eventually be formulated in the Thomistic principle, *omne agens agit sibi simile.* The *Symposium* interprets the cycle of life in the following way[55]: transient beings, aspiring to immortality, strive for the permanence of sameness ("παντάπασι τὸ αὐτὸ ἀεὶ εἶναι," 208A/B) that characterizes the divine. But their materiality prevents them from attaining this goal. As a consequence, the closest they can come to the ideal of absolute self-identity is generic sameness, brought about by the continuous self-reproduction of a genus or species through its individual representatives. Now the permanence of the genus requires that the process of reproduction proceed from the same to the same; in other words, it requires that the individual be, through propagation, replaced by something like itself: "οἷον αὐτὸ ἦν," as our text puts it. In this way, the self-reflexivity of the genus is able to capture something of the divine self-identity. Therefore, Plato concludes: "it is a divine affair, this engendering and bringing to birth, an immortal element in the creature that is mortal."[56]

All living beings strive after the divine through procreation. However, it is the prerogative of the human being to be able to immortalize himself in two ways: "κατὰ τὸ σῶμα καὶ κατὰ τὴν ψυχήν"[57]—according to the body or according to the soul; physically or intellectually. Indeed, the human being is called to ascend from the merely physical manifestations of eros (ἔρως) to an intellectual level, where it is the contemplation of the beautiful that "brings forth in all their splendor many fair fruits of discourse and meditation in a plenteous crop of philosophy."[58] Plato believes that, although the physical and spiritual articulations of eros share a characteristic fecundity, the self-reflexivity of contemplation by far surpasses the generic self-reflexivity that belongs to procreation. For, in procreation, the individual disperses its essence to persist in a generically identical offspring, whereas in philosophical meditation the individual soul copies the self-presence and unity of the eternal by a movement in exactly the opposite sense: it withdraws and returns into itself in a kind of self-collection. The *Phaedo* describes the autarky and inner unity of the philosopher's soul in the following way:

> The lovers of knowledge, then, I say, perceive that philosophy, taking possession of the soul when it is in this state, encourages it gently and tries to set it free . . . exhorting it to collect and concentrate itself within itself (αὐτὴν δὲ εἰς αὐτὴν ξυλλέγεσθαι καὶ ἀθροίζεσθαι), and to trust nothing except itself and its own abstract thought and abstract existence.[59]

We have come full circle, as it were. The triad of perfection, identity, and rationality seemed to be transformed into a quadruplet by the addition of life; however, the best life is a life of inwardness, of reason. These, then, are the results of our brief examination of Plato's thought: In Plato, the principle of causal similarity arises within the framework of a metaphysics of identity that Plato adopted, and adapted, from his Presocratic predecessors. Plato defines similarity and self-reflexivity as a derivative of identity, which is the characteristic of true perfection. Such true perfection is possible only in the immaterial realm of reason.

The fact that Plato thus connects rationality with eternal self-sameness, moreover defining human rational activity as a quest for eternity, has made him the archenemy of all philosophers of difference. In a Platonic perspective, rationality cannot be internally differentiated: it is the pursuit of the Same. It could be argued that in the *Republic,* we see the consequences of this philosophy of identity in the authoritarian, indeed totalitarian structures of the Platonic state.[60]

Aristotle: "Human Begets Human"

Aristotle was both Plato's pupil and his critic; his thought is as much in continuity with Plato's as it revises a number of fundamental aspects of the

Platonic system. As Lynne Ballew has pointed out, this twofold attitude toward Plato is very clear in Aristotle's treatment of the problem of circularity. On the one hand, the Stagirite's cosmology is as thoroughly circular as that of his teacher—even more systematically so. But on the other, in his theory of syllogistic reasoning, Aristotle introduces a conception of linear rationality—of making deductions from known premises to unknown new conclusions—which contradicts Plato's claim that all true rationality has to proceed in a circular fashion.[61] In the following pages, I shall focus on the Platonic side of Aristotle's thought, as it is only in this light that the Aristotelian theory of causal similarity becomes fully intelligible.

As we discovered in the previous section, in the *Symposium* Plato sees a divine force at work in procreation, which he interprets as the mortal nature's way to participate in divine identity through causally transmitted similarity. This Platonic conception, couched in poetic language, has its counterpart in chapter 4 of the second book of Aristotle's treatise *On the Soul,* which has been called a "scientifically sober, unadorned echo"[62] of the *Symposium's* reflections on eros and eternity. While all things strive for participation in the eternal and divine, procreation is the specific form this universal tendency takes on in living nature. I quote the crucial passage:

> [F]or any living thing that has reached its normal development and which is unmutilated, and whose mode of generation is not spontaneous, the most natural act is the production of another like itself (τὸ ποιῆσαι ἕτερον οἷον αὐτό), an animal producing an animal, a plant a plant, in order that, as far as its nature allows, it may partake in the eternal and divine. That is the goal toward which all things strive, that for the sake of which they do whatsoever their nature renders possible . . . Since then no living thing is able to partake in what is eternal and divine by uninterrupted continuance (for nothing perishable can for ever remain one and the same [ταὐτὸ καὶ ἓν ἀριθμῷ]), it tries to achieve that end in the only way possible for it, and success is possible in varying degrees; so it remains not indeed as the self-same individual but continues its existence in something like itself—not numerically but specifically one (οὐκ αὐτὸ 'ἀλλ' οἷον αὐτό, ἀριθμῷ μὲν οὐχ ἕν, εἴδει δ' ἕν).[63]

This text contains a number of important claims:

(1) The whole universe exhibits one and the same finality; for *everything* desires to participate in the eternal and divine. The "eternal and divine" therefore is a universal final cause.

(2) While the eternal and divine is the object of a universal aspiration to participate in its perfect identity, participation in "the same and one in

number" is possible in varying degrees. The degree achieved by a given individual is a function of its individual nature, for it participates in perfection "as far as its nature allows."

(3) Therefore, living things, for which the most natural act consists in
producing another individual of the same species, participate in sameness
and oneness precisely through their most natural operation, and that is procreation. The propagation of their respective species does not, of course,
render living things eternally one and the same, like the divine. Rather, the
particular sameness and oneness that procreation secures them is generic,
their form or species persisting as one and the same, but not the individual. This was exactly Plato's claim in the *Symposium*.

The law of causal similarity—every cause brings about effects similar to
itself—is not formulated explicitly in the passage from *On the Soul* that we
have just read, any more than it was spelled out in the *Symposium*. Nevertheless, the clear implication of what Aristotle is saying is that a living being
always produces offspring generically similar to itself, as it is only through
this causal self-reflexivity of the form that the species can safeguard its
unity and sameness in the process of procreation. Indeed, if Aristotle does
not mention the law of similarity in generalized form, he gives two examples to illustrate it: "an animal [produces] an animal, a plant a plant."
However, this causal self-reflexivity of form appears to be limited to the
animate world, to ensouled beings.

In another treatise, *On Generation and Corruption,* Aristotle corrects this
impression. At the end of book two, chapter 11, he reflects upon the various forms that circularity, or "return upon oneself," can take in nature.
Here, self-reflexivity is depicted as a universal phenomenon of which the
return upon itself of species in the reproduction of living beings is only
one particular manifestation:

> Then why do some things manifestly come-to-be in this fashion (as, e.g.,
> showers and air come-to-be cyclically, so that it must rain if there is to be a
> cloud and, conversely, there must be a cloud if it is to rain), while men and
> animals do not return upon themselves (οὐκ ἀνακάμπτουσιν εἰς αὑτούς)
> so that the same individual comes-to-be a second time (for though your
> coming-to-be presupposes your father's, his coming-to-be does not presup-
> pose yours)? Why, on the contrary, does this coming-to-be seem to consti-
> tute a rectilinear sequence (εἰς εὐθύ)? In discussing this, we must begin by
> inquiring whether all things return upon themselves (ἀνακάμπτει) in a uni-
> form manner; or whether, on the contrary, though in some sequences what
> recurs is *numerically* the same, in other sequences it is the same *only in species*.
> Now it is evident that those things whose substance—that which is under-

going the process—is imperishable, will be numerically the same; for the character of the process is determined by the character of that which undergoes it. Those things, on the other hand, whose substance is perishable must return upon themselves (ἀνακάμπτειν) specifically, not numerically. That is why, when Water comes-to-be from Air and Air from Water, the Air is the same specifically, not numerically.[64]

From this passage, we learn, first of all and most importantly, that all coming-to-be is self-reflexive; for to ask "whether everything returns upon itself uniformly or not" implies that indeed everything does return upon itself. Thus, all antecedent-consequence relationships involve "ἀνα-κάμπτειν," which is Aristotle's term for return upon oneself or self-reflexivity.[65] Yet ἀνακάμπτειν is not the same in all cases. Imperishable substances, we are informed, return upon themselves numerically. What the Stagirite has in mind here are the heavenly bodies: considering that the celestial bodies remain unchanged in substance as they revolve, their circular motion can be described as a return upon itself of the numerically identical. Perishable substances, on the other hand, recur only specifically in the circle of generation. In the present passage from *On Generation and Corruption*, it is not animals and plants that serve as instances of perishable natures (as in *On the Soul*), but air and water. How the coming-to-be of water from air (and vice versa) involves a "specific" return upon themselves of these substances is explained in some detail in the treatise on meteorology.[66] Water and air describe a circle when one is transformed into the other and then transformed back again into its original state. But this cyclical transformation involves substantial change: exhaling water becomes vapor, vaporous air condenses into cloud, and cloud turns into rain. That is why air and water recur only specifically in the process, without returning upon themselves as the heavenly bodies do, that is to say, as numerically the same substances.

In the passage from *On Generation and Corruption* we are discussing, Aristotle does not elaborate upon the mode of self-reflexivity that is characteristic of the animate world. Indeed, from what he says in this text, one might be tempted to conclude that he does not regard natural procreation as an instance of ἀνακάμπτειν at all, confronting as he does the cyclical coming-to-be of water and air with the reproduction of humans and animals, which "seems to constitute a rectilinear sequence (εἰς εὐθὺ)." However, the lines immediately following already attenuate the contrast, as they specify that there can be no question of an individual recurrence of the same in the air-water cycle, any more than "men and animals return upon themselves so that the same individual comes-to-be a second time." Nevertheless, Aristotle leaves the question of the self-reflexivity of procreation unresolved in our text. We must complement it from what we have already learned about natural reproduction in *On the Soul,* where the same distinction between numerical and specific self-return is employed, the specific mode of self-return being attributed to procreation.

Everything desires to participate in the eternal and divine, Aristotle tells us in *On the Soul,* but success is possible in varying degrees, in accordance with each thing's nature. We have already examined some of the different levels of imitation of the perfect self-identity and unity that belong to the divine, namely, the circular motion of the heavenly bodies, the cyclical transformation of the elements, and the circle of life. To these we must now add the circle of history. Human history, for Aristotle, is an eternal cycle of civilizations being born, developing, flourishing, only to decline and disappear. As these civilizations are not fundamentally different from each other, they go through the same phases and experiences, even giving rise to the same thoughts and ideologies. As Aristotle writes in the *Meteorology:*

> the same opinions appear in cycles among men not once nor twice nor occasionally, but infinitely often.[67]

Yet it is possible, to some extent, to learn from the experiences of previous civilizations. Ancient proverbs and adages usually manage to transmit to us some of the wisdom accumulated in the cycles of history that occurred before our own time.[68]

However, the most important manifestation of "return upon oneself" in the Aristotelian system has not yet been touched upon. This is the self-thinking thought (νόησις νοήσεως) that Aristotle ascribes to God, the "Unmoved Mover."[69] Two chapters in book 12 of the *Metaphysics,* namely chapters 7 and 9, are devoted to a discussion of God's "thinking of thinking." Briefly, Aristotle argues that the Unmoved Mover, whose existence he has just proven, must be continually engaged in the best possible activity. Anything else (such as pursuing unworthy activities, or moving from one type of activity to another, or being asleep) is incompatible with his dignity. If we accept, upon the basis of our own experience, that intellectual activity is the best of all, the question still remains as to what the Unmoved Mover is thinking. Yet can he be thinking anything but himself? He would be lowering himself, as it were, if he were contemplating anything inferior to himself. Hence, Aristotle's conclusion: the Unmoved Mover is self-thinking thought, νόησις νοήσεως.[70] This νόησις νοήσεως functions as the "goal toward which all things strive, that for the sake of which they do whatsoever their nature renders possible" (*On the Soul,* see above). It is copied on all the lower levels of being, through their different kinds of self-reflexivity. Thus, self-reflexivity is for Aristotle a cosmic force. In the words of the German philosopher Klaus Oehler, "the Aristotelian cosmos reveals itself . . . as an ordered system of graded forms of self-reference."[71]

The characterization of the divinity in terms of self-reflexive intellectual activity is very significant for a proper understanding of the status of self-reflexivity in Aristotle. For if God's nature is itself intrinsically self-reflexive, then self-reflexivity is not per se an imperfect copy of unity and self-identity, as Plato had suggested. Rather, if God is essential νόησις νοήσεως (human beings can reflect upon themselves only "by the way," ἐν παρέργῳ,[72] as the self-reference of human thought always remains bound to the apprehension of other objects that are not the self[73]), then the unity and self-identity of the divine are synonymous with absolute reflexiveness. In other words, for Aristotle perfection and rationality at their highest point do not exclude circularity, as they did for Plato.

After the preceding survey of the different forms of self-reflexivity in Aristotle's cosmology, and of their dependence upon the circular thought of the Unmoved Mover, we are now in a position to examine the law of causal similarity more closely. The self-reflexivity of form in procreation, the fact that "an animal begets an animal, a plant a plant," is the specific way in which living beings manifest a self-reflexivity that is all-pervasive in the Aristotelian universe. However, is there any indication that the principle according to which a living being produces offspring generically similar to itself might lend itself to generalization? That is to say, does Aristotle envisage the possibility that all cause-effect relationships might be characterized by some kind of similarity between cause and effect? The standing example the Philosopher uses more often than any other to illustrate the law of similarity seems to indicate a negative answer, for the example is taken from the sphere of procreation: "ἄνθρωπος ἄνθρωπον γεννᾷ— human begets human."[74]

What is more, Aristotle himself points out that "man is born from man but not bed from bed"[75]—in other words, that causal similarity does not seem to obtain in the realm of artifacts.[76] However, from a certain perspective, it would be in keeping with the tenets of Aristotle's philosophy to say that even beds "beget" beds or, put less paradoxically, that the causal self-reflexivity of form is not limited solely to the reproduction of living beings. In book 7, chapter 7 of the *Metaphysics,* Aristotle analyses the nature of the causal processes leading to the production of artifacts. He comes to the conclusion that, as "human begets human" ("ἄνθρωπος ἄνθρωπον γεννᾷ"),[77] so "in a sense health comes from health and house from house."[78] Despite the fact that the efficient cause of health or of a house (respectively a physician and an architect) does not itself share the form of its product, there could not be health or a house without the idea (or, in Aristotelian parlance, the form) of health or of the house preexisting in the mind of the agent bringing either one about: "Health," as Aristotle says, "is the formula and the knowledge in the soul."[79] It is thus only in proceeding from the notion and knowledge of health that the physician can determine what steps to take in order to cause actual health to be present in a particular case; *mutatis mutandis,* the same holds true for the making of all artifacts. In *Metaphysics* 12.3 Aristotle gives this insight the explicit form of a general law:

> [W]e must observe that each substance comes into being out of something synonymous (ἑκάστη ἐκ συνωνύμου γίγνεται οὐσία). (Natural objects and other things are substances.) For things come into being either by art or by nature or by chance or by spontaneity. Now art is a principle of movement in something other than the thing moved[80], nature is a principle in the thing itself (for man begets man), and the other causes are privations of these two.[81]

"Each substance comes into being out of something synonymous" is the first explicit formulation of the law of causal similarity in the history of philosophy. Aristotelian scholars have often termed it the "law of synonymy,"[82] because Aristotle does not just maintain that the cause of a substance somehow vaguely "resembles" it, but that cause and effect are strictly "synonymous," in the Aristotelian sense of the word. In Aristotle, "synonymous" things have a common name and definition: "When things have the name in common and the definition of being which corresponds to the name is the same, they are called *synonymous.*"[83]

In the form, "each substance comes into being out of something synonymous" the law of synonymy is still limited to substances, albeit both natural and artificial ones. This limitation is not easily compatible with the fact that in *Metaphysics* 7.7, Aristotle uses health as his preferred example of causal self-reflexivity: health, in fact, is a quality. However, we find other passages where the law is expressed without any restriction, the scope of its applicability extending to everything that comes to be:

> And it is clear also from what has been said that in a sense everything is produced from something homonymous (τρόπον τινὰ πάντα γίγνεται ἐξ ὁμωνύμου).[84]

In this passage, the word "homonymous" (ὁμώνυμος) does not have the technical sense assigned to it in the *Categories:* "When things have only a name in common and the definition of being which corresponds to the name is different, they are called *homonymous.*"[85] Aristotle sometimes employs "homonymous" (ὁμώνυμος) as a synonym of "synonymous" (συνώνυμος), as indeed the two words bore the same meaning in ordinary Greek usage.[86]

We undertook our brief consideration of the origins of the metaphysics of reflexivity in Greek thought in order to elucidate the principle of causal similarity, which is crucial for understanding the Scholastic episteme. What is the basis for the assumption that God, the Creator, communicates his likeness to creation, such that all levels of creation can be read as one complex text signifying its Author? Of course, there is a biblical basis, especially the famous passage in Genesis 1.26: "Then God said, 'Let us make man in our image, after our likeness.'" This Old Testament idea is in profound harmony with some of the most primitive intuitions of the Greek philosophical tradition. As we have seen, since Presocratic times, the Greeks thought perfection in terms of identity, self-similarity, and self-reflexivity. The idea of being dispersing itself in a straight movement appears to have been not only irrational but repugnant to them. The reflexive metaphysics of causation that follows from this philosophy is already hinted at by Plato; it is only in Aristotle, however, that it finds its first full development. It was to exercise a crucial influence upon Christian thought through the form given to it by Neoplatonism, the form of "Greek wisdom" that proved most influential during the first Christian centuries, leaving its mark upon the writings of such authoritative thinkers as St. Augustine and Pseudo-Dionysius the Areopagite.

Plotinus: Outward Movements Backward

Despite its name, the Neoplatonic movement saw itself at the confluence of Platonism and Aristotelianism. In fact, one of its standard theses—which was to prove very popular in Islamic philosophy—was the profound harmony obtaining between the thought of its two great predecessors.[87] The highly speculative metaphysical system of Plotinus (204/205–270)[88] is an excellent example of these attempts to reconcile Platonic and Aristotelian elements; it combines Plato's insistence on the complete self-identity of the eternal model of the cosmos with Aristotle's more dynamic understanding of the Unmoved Mover's identity in terms of self-reflexivity.

At the summit of Plotinus's cosmos stands the One (τὸ ἕν) as the principle of all unity and identity in the cosmos. It is because all things have "one" origin that the world, too, is in a sense "one." For is it not amazing that the world, fragmented as it is into innumerable elements of untold multifariousness, does not break up and disintegrate into chaos? Plotinus's theory of the One is an attempt to explain this fact.

As one reads Plotinus, one quickly discovers that the oneness of the One is far from unproblematic. Its unity must certainly not be confused with some kind of stale emptiness, for surprisingly Plotinus declares, in the first sentence of *Ennead* V.2, that "τὸ ἕν πάντα—the One is all things." So is the One not one after all? It is, for Plotinus immediately adds: " . . . and not a single one of them (καὶ οὐδὲ ἕν)." The notion that the One is at once all things and none of them is difficult to grasp; it seems self-contradictory. However, Plotinus believes that all things coexist in the One in such a way that they are all present in it, yet concentrated in one point—like rays of light bundled together in the closest possible way by a magnifying glass. Thus, Plotinus writes:

> What then are "all things"? All things of which that One is the principle. But how is that One the principle of all things? Is it because as principle it keeps them in being, making each one of them exist? Yes, and because it brought them into existence. But how did it do so? By possessing them beforehand (τῷ πρότερον ἔχειν αὐτά). But it has been said that in this way it will be a multiplicity. But it had them in such a way as not to be distinct (ὡς μὴ διακεκριμένα).[89]

As is evident from this extract, Plotinus's theory of the One is thoroughly dialectical. It does not play off identity and unity against difference and multiplicity, but sees them reconciled at the highest point of the universe. Nevertheless, this dialectical theory is not without tensions. Oftentimes, Plotinus's thought seems to oscillate, as if undecided, between a more rigidly unified conception of the One and a more dynamic theory. This oscillation is particularly clear in connection with the problem of self-reflexivity. Is the One possessed of any kind of self-reflexivity? Or does it rather form a more static and simple unity, like a mathematical point without internal life? Plotinus's answer is ambivalent. In *Ennead* V.1, he criticizes Aristotle for ascribing self-thinking thought (νόησις νοήσεως) to the Unmoved Mover, whom he takes as corresponding to the One.[90] This is a contradiction in terms, he maintains, because thinking involves a structure composed of two elements, subject and object.[91] Such "otherness," however, is incompatible with the absolute self-identity that befits the first principle: "The Good itself, then, must not think anything: for the Good is not other than itself."[92]

Nonetheless, the unambiguous clarity of this statement does not prevent Plotinus from also defending the diametrically opposed view:

> [A]ll things belong to it and are in it and with it. It is completely able to discern itself (πάντη διακριτικὸν ἑαυτοῦ); it has life in itself and all things in itself, and its thinking of itself is itself (ἡ κατανόησις αὐτοῦ αὐτό), and exists by a kind of immediate self-consciousness, in everlasting rest and in a manner of thinking different from the thinking of Intellect.[93]

A. H. Armstrong has remarked that the passage just quoted "stands alone in the *Enneads* in the clarity with which it attributes a kind of thinking to the One."[94] That may well be true; yet there are other texts which indicate that Plotinus must at least have been seriously considering the possibility of ascribing self-reflexivity to the One. *Ennead* VI.8 is a powerful example:

> He himself therefore is by himself what he is, related and directed to himself, that he may not in this way either be related to the outside or to something else, but altogether self-related (πρὸς αὐτὸν πᾶς).[95]

The passage is not in need of much commentary, so plainly does Plotinus spell out what he takes the One to be: πρὸς αὐτὸν πᾶς, entirely turned toward itself, that is to say, completely self-reflexive.[96]

We can, however, reverse perspectives once again, turning to texts that contradict this position. Thus, in *Ennead* V.5, we find Plotinus wondering if "perhaps this name 'One' contains [only] a denial of multiplicity,"[97] that is to say, if perhaps it is entirely negative in its signification, so that we cannot make any positive claims about it at all. Quite simply, "it is what it is."[98] And even the predicative form of this sentence might still be too strong, suggesting as it does some kind of structure. As a matter of fact, Plotinus believes that if the One were to speak about itself, it would just say: "εἰμὶ εἰμί" or "ἐγὼ ἐγώ"—"am am," "I I"![99]

That there are tensions in Plotinus's frequent changing of perspectives upon the One is undeniable. Nevertheless, perhaps some scholars have been precipitate in castigating Plotinus for what they consider to be "the self-contradictory nature of the One."[100] Plotinus himself knew full well that his language concerning the One was replete with "perplexities" (ἀπορίαι).[101] However, it might well be the case that the dialectical nature of the One is situated in a sphere too far beyond the realm of human reason to be expressed in ordinary language, without tensions and even contradictions. In this case, Plotinus's "aporetic" statements would not bespeak his failure to present a coherent theory of the One. Rather, they would constitute an audacious experiment at the limits of language.

Once we have understood the two sides of Plotinus's theory of the One, we can take up the difficult problem of how the One—that is to say, absolute unity—can be conceived of as the origin of multiplicity and alterity. As one might have come to expect at this point, Plotinus offers two rival theories of how the One gives rise to the world of the many, a process that begins with the generation of Intellect (νοῦς). As two recent Plotinus scholars have noted, "ambiguity is at the very center of Plotinus's account of the generation of Intellect from the One."[102]

Let us first consider the conception of the generation of Intellect from the One that is in concordance with the more dynamic theory. If total self-identity and self-hood are regarded as not excluding some kind of internal structure (that is to say, the circular structure of self-reflexivity), then this structure can become the starting point of a process of further self-differentiation and multiplication. In other words, if the germs of multiplicity are already present within the One in any identifiable sense, then the generation, by the One, of a multiplicity external to it can be made intelligible. There is at least one text in the *Enneads* that would suggest an interpretation along the lines just indicated. In a much-debated passage from *Ennead* V.1, Plotinus writes:

> But we say that Intellect is an image of that Good; for we must speak more plainly; first of all we must say that what has come into being must be in a way that Good, and retain much of it and be a likeness of it, as light is of the sun. But Intellect is not that Good. How then does it generate Intellect? Because by its return to itself[103] it sees: and this seeing is Intellect. (. . . ἀλλ οὐ νοῦς ἐκεῖνο. πῶς οὖν νοῦν γεννᾷ; ἢ ὅτι τῇ ἐπιστροφῇ πρὸς αὐτὸ ἑώρα: ἡ δὲ ὅρασις αὕτη νοῦς.)[104]

If this rendering of the passage is correct,[105] Intellect, the first element of the world of the many, is born from the One's return upon itself in a reflexive act of self-vision. Indeed, on this interpretation Intellect is nothing but the One seeing itself. Thus, (1) the total unity of the One is not incompatible with self-reflexivity, and (2) the "circle" that the One describes in returning upon itself is already other than itself, a kind of self-alienation that Plotinus calls "Intellect." Intellect is the mirror in which the One sees itself—and what do we see in a mirror if not ourselves? Yet, the mirror image is at the same time already something "other" than ourselves.

Admittedly, this is not Plotinus's standard account of the generation of Intellect. From all the other texts dealing with the subject, the reader of the *Enneads* would gather that Intellect proceeds from the One in the following three steps, which are logically, though not temporally, distinct: (1) the One "overflows," producing something different from itself; (2) the "stream" of otherness comes to a halt and "turns back" toward its source, which gives it some consistence or being of its own; (3) this being contemplates the One and thus turns into Intellect. *Ennead* V.2 represents perhaps the clearest statement of the emanational theory of the generation of Intellect:

> This, we may say, is the first act of generation: the One, perfect because it seeks nothing, has nothing, and needs nothing, overflows, as it were, and its superabundance makes something other than itself. This, when it has come into being, turns back upon the One (εἰς αὐτὸ ἐπεστράφη) and is filled, and becomes Intellect by looking toward it. Its halt and turning toward the One constitutes being (τὸ ὄν), its gaze (θέα) upon the One, Intellect. Since it halts and turns toward the One that it may see, it becomes at once Intellect and being.[106]

In commenting upon this passage, it is fair to start by observing that Plotinus in no way explains why the One causes otherness to exist outside of itself: it "overflows, as it were" (οἷον ἡπερερρύη); but why? And how can that which is total self-identity overflow and "make something other than itself"? It must be acknowledged that if the One's self-identity is conceived of as debarring all internal relationship, then these questions remain unanswerable.[107]

The immediate product of the One's emanation is as yet wholly indefinite; indeed, Plotinus sometimes calls it the "indefinite dyad" (ἀόριστος δυάς),[108] a kind of inchoate duality that gains determination and, hence, being only once the formless flow from the One comes to a standstill. The movement outward changes direction, as it were, and by reversing toward the One is prevented from dispersing itself. Intellect is engendered as the product of emanation, being drawn to the One in an aspiration to recapture the simplicity of its origin, contemplates the One. The emanative process that leads to the genesis of Intellect is thus, as the German philosopher Karl-Heinz Volkmann-Schluck has very graphically termed it, a "hinausgehendes Zurück,"[109] an outward movement backward.

The two accounts of the origin of Intellect we have been considering are perhaps not entirely reducible to one another, reflecting as they do the two sides of Plotinus's dialectical theory of the One. Yet the two accounts, or rather, the two perspectives, are not altogether unrelated, having an important element in common, namely, the idea that *self-reflexivity is at the origin of being*. The world of multiplicity, which begins at the level of Intellect, emerges from the self-identity of the One in a movement turned back toward the One. Plotinus's theory of the relationship between identity and self-reflexivity is more complex than either Plato's or Aristotle's. He does not follow Aristotle in the idea that the circularity of the cosmos is merely the result of the attractive force of identity (the Unmoved Mover); rather, it is both as an efficient cause (overflowing) and as a final cause (object of contemplation) that absolute identity brings about multiplicity. However, like Plato and Aristotle, Plotinus assigns self-reflexivity the role of a cosmic principle. If we were to follow up the way in which Plotinus conceives of all the different levels of existence below the One (Intellect, Soul, and Nature), we should find that each level is characterized by a self-reflexivity analogous to that of the One, and that in each case, this self-reflexivity "opens itself up," as it were, to generate the respective lower level—just as the One itself does. In the last analysis, Plotinus can be interpreted as holding the view that all the strata of being are nothing but the increasingly differentiated self-vision of the One. Consequently, their difference with regard to the One, and with regard to each other, is not due to any fundamental caesura; rather, it stems from a gradual loss of the powerful centripetal force that, in the One, keeps difference unified:

> [T]hat which is produced must always be of the same kind as its producer, but weaker through losing its virtue as it comes down.[110]

As the universe comes to be through a succession of "outward movements backward," all ultimately originating in the One, the cosmos unfolds like a text recounting the story of the One. Yet the story differs according to the level on which it is told—Intellect, Soul, or Nature. How does the story differ? It differs not in terms of its content, but rather with regard to the mode of its telling. It is at this point that Plotinus introduces a most fascinating idea, which must have occurred to him as a result of his experience in Egypt.[111] At the level of Intellect, where we are dealing with a representation of the One that is still highly unified, the text of the world (which is that of the One) is written in hieroglyphs. For, a hieroglyphic inscription conveys its meaning not piecemeal and step-by-step, but in units made up of whole ideas. On the other hand, on the next level, that of Soul, the degree of unification has further declined, owing to an increasing dominance of the centrifugal forces of otherness. Therefore, the Soul's mode of apprehending the One is rather like the process of reading in a language that uses an alphabetical system of writing; units of meaning or ideas emerge discursively as the mind assembles letters into words, and words into propositions.

> The wise men of Egypt, I think, also understood this, either by scientific or innate knowledge, and when they wished to signify something wisely, [they] did not use the forms of letters (τύποις γραμμάτων) which follow the order of words and propositions and imitate sounds and the enunciations of philosophical statements, and by drawing images (ἀγάλματα δὲ γράψαντες) and inscribing in their temples one particular image of each particular thing, they manifested the non-discursiveness of the intelligible world, that is, that every image is a kind of knowledge and wisdom and is a subject of statements, all together in one, and not discourse or deliberation. But [only] afterward [others] discovered, starting from it in its concentrated unity, a representation in something else, already unfolded and speaking it discursively and giving the reasons why things are like this . . . [112]

Textuality is not the central metaphor Plotinus employs in order to elucidate the relationship between the One and its hypostases (Intellect, Soul, and Nature); that role is played by the concepts of archetype (ἀρχέτυπον) and image (εἰκών). Nevertheless, the passage just cited demonstrates how closely the ideas of self-reflexivity and of the textual nature of the world belong together, not only systematically but also historically. Plotinus's thought, in which self-reflexivity and self-reflexive causality function as the organizing principles of cosmology, provides the kind of soil in which a conception of the world as text can grow. The connection between the self-reflexive metaphysics of the Greeks and the understanding of the world as text would be further strengthened in Christian culture—but only in the course of a complex development to which we now turn.

Christ and Time

In the preceding sections, the ancient metaphysics of reflexivity was presented with the goal of elucidating the philosophical presuppositions that are implied in the Scholastic view of the world as text. We may remember that in *The Order of Things,* Foucault leaves off his analysis of the Scholastic episteme without penetrating to its philosophical foundations. The foregoing sections on Parmenides, Plato, Aristotle, and Plotinus might have created the impression that, with regard to the issue of the textuality of the world, there existed a seamless continuity between Greek philosophy and the Christian thought of the Scholastics. Such an impression would be misleading. The happy harmony obtaining between a metaphysics of the Aristotelian or the Plotinian type, on the one hand, and the text-centeredness of Christianity, on the other, was the result of a synthesis that Scholastic thought only reached in the thirteenth century. In truth, primitive Christian thought was profoundly inimical to the Greek cyclical view of the world, favoring, as we shall see, the straight line—the Greek symbol of imperfection, dispersal, and difference. This tension is so central to understanding the relationship between "Athens and Jerusalem" that the reinscription of Greek wisdom into the center of Christian culture which, in study 2, we defined as the core of the Scholastic project, can be described as the gradual reconciliation of the Christian line with the Greek circle.

In 1946, the Swiss theologian Oscar Cullmann published a groundbreaking study entitled *Christ and Time. The Primitive Christian Conception of Time and History*.[113] The principal thesis of this book was that the Christian faith of the New Testament authors is centered upon a tension between the present and the future, and *not* a tension between time and eternity, or this world and the Beyond.[114] The present is the crucial period in redemptive history after the decisive battle against sin has been won through Christ, yet before the final fulfillment is reached in the Second Coming of Christ and the Resurrection of the body. According to Cullmann, the first Christians expected this fulfillment to occur at the end of time, and within it; they had not pinned their hopes on an abstract Beyond. That, Cullmann pointedly remarks, is a conception which crept into Christianity as a result of a "heresy," namely "the dissolving into metaphysics of the Primitive Christian conception that redemptive history is bound to the progressing time line."[115] Cullmann's thesis, so clearly antimetaphysical in its quest for a primitive Christianity not yet affected by Hellenistic "heresies," triggered an animated debate amongst theologians, both Protestant and Catholic. Without wanting to take sides in a theological debate I am not competent to judge, let me say that Cullmann's ideas have remained highly controversial.[116] What has won wide acceptance, though, is another thesis that Cullmann developed in *Christ and Time,* and which concerns the fundamental difference between the Greek and the Christian conceptions of time. Cullmann writes:

> [W]e can clearly define the conception of the course of time which the New Testament presupposes by stating it in opposition to the typically Greek idea, and we must start from this fundamental perception, that the

symbol of time for Primitive Christianity as well as for Biblical Judaism and
the Iranian religion is the *line,* while in Hellenism it is the *circle.*[117]

We have already seen that for Aristotle, human history is a cyclical
process, with the result that "the same opinions appear in cycles among
men not once or twice nor occasionally, but infinitely often." This Aristotelian conception epitomizes the Greek view of time, which has a number of important corollaries. An history characterized by an eternal return
of the same is not directed toward any goal that could "fulfill" it, in the
sense of bestowing upon it any ultimate meaning. If such an ultimate
meaning is sought, it cannot be found in the course of history, but only
outside it. According to Cullmann, this explains the belief of the Greeks
that blessedness is possible only in a Beyond, that is to say, an "eternal"
realm entirely removed from the course of time.[118] In a word, what Cullmann argues is that the typically Greek "two-worlds theory," which was to
become one of the cornerstones of Western civilization—the division between this life and the hereafter, time and eternity—has its roots in a cyclical conception of time.

The Christian view of time that can be gathered from the New Testament is not circular or cyclical, but linear. Possessed of a definite beginning
and an end, Christian time "progresses" in a sense in which Greek time
cannot. It moves from creation through the Fall and the history of Israel
to the Redemption of humanity through Christ and the Coming of the
Kingdom. Only such a linear history can be teleological, that is to say, oriented toward a goal. What is more, the idea of historical uniqueness obviously makes sense only if history does not repeat itself. Therefore, what
seemed like "foolishness" to the Greeks—namely, the Christian belief in
the salvation of humankind once and for all through an historical individual, Jesus Christ—becomes intelligible if placed in the context of the
Christian linear understanding of time and history. In Christianity, every
moment in history matters, because it constitutes an unrepeatable step toward the end. Furthermore, some steps are more important than others,
depending on their relation to the two extremes, the beginning and the
end. Thus, the Incarnation matters more than the Battle of the Boyne or
the landing on the moon because it ushers in the end; indeed because, in
a sense, it *is* the end.

When the Scholastics came to be confronted with the full force of the
Greek philosophy of being and history, especially as represented in the
works of Aristotle, the opposition between the Greek circle and the Christian line crystallized in the famous debate over the eternity of the world.[119]

This debate reached its climax in the thirteenth century, when all the major thinkers elaborated solutions to the problem. Aquinas devoted a special treatise, *De aeternitate mundi,* to the controversy, finding himself unable to refute Aristotle's doctrine on the eternity of the world.[120] St. Bonaventure's stance toward the Hellenistic philosophy of history has been studied by the present Cardinal Ratzinger in his well-known book, *The Theology of History in St. Bonaventure.*[121] Despite his much less sympathetic attitude toward Aristotle, even Bonaventure endeavors to reconcile the circle with the line. Ratzinger draws attention to a beautiful passage from the *Hexaëmeron* in which Bonaventure summarizes his position in the following words:

> Now when the center is lost in a circle, it can be found only by two lines which intersect at right angles.[122]

In another version of the same work, he elaborates:

> How the center of a circle can be found by means of a cross becomes clear through a geometrical example. According to the teaching of Euclid, in the first book of the *Geometry,* let us fix one foot of a pair of compasses and describe a circle. Now the position of the center shall be designated by C, then the center C shall be deleted. Then, to find the center again, mark two separate points in whatever part of the circumference you like, and draw a straight line from one to the other, according to the proposition: "A line happens to lead from one point to another." Let this line be AB. In the center of this line, D shall be marked, and through D a line shall be drawn to the opposite circumferential points E[123] [and] F, and it will appear how the intersection of the lines in D at right angles forms a cross.[124]

What Bonaventure is trying to illustrate through this geometrical example (shown in fig. 4.1) is how the Cross of Christ enables the world to recover its center. In order to do this, it is not necessary to discard the circle; it suffices to give it a new meaning, by inscribing the Cross within it. Ratzinger comments:

> The lost middle of the circle is found again by means of two lines that intersect at right angles, that is, by a cross. This means that by His cross, Christ has definitively solved the geometry-problem of world history. With His cross He has uncovered the lost center of the circle of the world so as to give the true direction and meaning to the movement of the individual life and to the history of mankind as such.[125]

Figure 4.1   "How the center of a circle can be found by means of a cross."

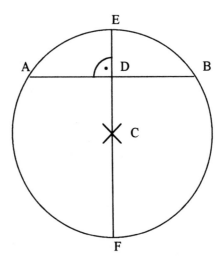

Of course, the problem of time, eternity, and history is only one facet of a larger issue, namely that of the compatibility of the reflexive metaphysics of antiquity with the Christian message. This issue can be discussed satisfactorily only at the most fundamental and most general level, which is that of the philosophy of being. In the next study, we shall investigate how one of the outstanding thinkers of the thirteenth century, Thomas Aquinas, attempted to rethink Greek self-reflexivity in the context of the Christian line.

STUDY 5

AQUINAS: THE OPEN CIRCLE

"We must forget Thomas Aquinas," Alain de Libera declared in his book on Albert the Great published in 1990—we remember the quotation from the introduction. Of course, one must not overlook the context of this claim. In a book on Albert—and not an history of medieval thought—de Libera wrote it out of frustration with an approach that, considering the great Swabian only as the teacher and precursor of Aquinas, was unable to do justice to Albert's originality.[1] Whatever de Libera's own intentions, the phrase, "we must forget Thomas Aquinas" characterizes a more general attitude among contemporary medievalists that was widespread until quite recently—especially among medievalists regarding their research as decidedly contemporary and state of the art. In these circles, interest in the thought of St. Thomas had been waning for a number of reasons, but in particular because of a certain over-ideologization of the field. In the one hundred years following the promulgation of *Aeterni Patris,* "Thomism" oftentimes became a label for a cluster of philosophical and theological "positions," rather than designating an original and challenging way of thought. The fact that these positions came to be regarded as the epitome of Catholic orthodoxy did not always help matters. In this climate, denying the validity of Aquinas's "five ways" of proving God's existence could come to be seen as bordering on heresy.[2] The effect of these developments was to prove stifling for Thomistic studies, which were reduced to an often monotonous discussion of the same themes, from the same angles, upon the basis of the same texts.[3] This ossification was further reinforced by a lack of historical consciousness. To cite but one example, the famous essence/existence distinction was discovered as a key to Aquinas's writings at a time when existentialism was on the rise, which indicates that this interpretation, without being "wrong," constitutes only one of a number of possible perspectives upon Aquinas's work; however, mainstream Thomism lacked this insight for a long time, and in many cases still lacks it today. Yet already in the 1970s, the French Thomist Michel Corbin formulated this insight most lucidly:

> No reading is perfectly true (in the sense in which truth is the perfect adequation of the reading and the work, or, to use modern terms, the perfect objectivity of the reading), but no reading is perfectly wrong; it is a human reading, partial and finite.[4]

As I indicated in the introduction, we have experienced the rise of a "new" Thomism in recent years. If nothing else, this new Thomism has the advantage of understanding and interpreting Aquinas's thought from new viewpoints, which bring out hitherto neglected aspects of the Thomistic oeuvre. Moreover, it corrects some overly rigid interpretations that, quite simply, do not stand up to close textual scrutiny. Thomistic ethics, for instance, tended to be used in a way that played down its complex and nuanced approach to the natural law, thus transforming thought into doctrine. Recent publications, from Martin Blais's *L'autre Thomas d'Aquin*[5] to Bishop Léonard's *Le fondement de la morale*[6] and Pamela Hall's *Narrative and the Natural Law*[7] have, despite all their differences in tone and substance, managed to correct some of these previous misconceptions.

In other words, there is no need to "forget" St. Thomas in the context of the new medievalism. Rather to the contrary. Apart from his undeniable intellectual achievements, Aquinas has played such a crucial role in the philosophico-theological tradition of the West that any effort to reevaluate the meaning of this heritage in the postmodern context cannot circumvent the task of reappraising his thought. In the course of such a reappraisal, we may discover that the Aquinas whom we imagined we knew turns out to be quite different.

Every Being is an "Other"

Let us begin our interpretation by a close rereading of a well-known passage.[8] In keeping with the nature of the present book, this rereading is inspired by the postmodern, and post-Hegelian, interest in "otherness."

In his *Disputed Questions on Truth,* question 1, article 1, Thomas presents a list of attributes of being that the tradition has come to call "transcendentals." A transcendental is a "mode which generally accompanies every being" *(modus generaliter consequens omne ens)*[9]; put differently, everything that *is,* insofar as it is, is characterized by these different "modes" of being.

The list we are examining mentions five of them; for our purposes, it will suffice to consider the first three. First of all, every being *(ens),* insofar as it *is,* is something—or some "thing," for Aquinas terms the first mode "thing" *(res).* Nothing that is, is ever just some vague and general existence; it has an essence that makes it some specific kind of being: a house, a horse, a book, a can of dogfood, and so on. *Res* is a positive characteristic of every being considered in itself. In a second step, Aquinas lists a negative mode, that is to say, something every being is *not* insofar as it is. Every being, insofar as it is, is not divided *(indivisum).* A book, for instance, may be composed of many different parts—hundreds of pages, flyleaves, the binding, and so forth—yet insofar as it *is,* we consider it as one. We say, "This is a book"—one book, treating the many different parts as one *(unum).* Similarly, the being "tree" has a trunk, a bark, branches, leaves, roots, and so on; yet it is *one* tree. There is no being that "is" two or three. Thus, the second transcendental (not counting being, *ens,* itself) is "one" *(unum).*

Aquinas's next step is to consider being, not in itself but with regard to the ways in which it relates to others:

> If the mode of being is taken in the second way, namely, according to the order [of beings] one toward the other *(secundum ordinem unius ad alterum),* there are two possibilities. The first concerns the division [of beings] from one another, and this is what the noun *aliquid* expresses: for *aliquid* is said like "an 'other' what" *(aliud quid).* This is why, just as being is called "one" *(unum)* insofar as it is not divided *(indivisum)* in itself, so it is called *aliquid* insofar as it is divided from others.
>
>   The second [mode] concerns the agreement [of beings] with one another . . . [10]

Every being, insofar as it is, is *aliquid.* If one looks up *aliquid* in a Latin dictionary, one finds such meanings as "something" or "anything" given as its English equivalents. This nontechnical meaning has frequently misled commentators. Indeed, the overwhelming majority of Thomists have failed to understand the profound metaphysical insight St. Thomas tries to convey through the transcendental *aliquid.*[11] If *aliquid* just meant "something," it would not be different from *res.* Yet *aliquid* does not mean "something"; St. Thomas explicitly tells us that he understands *aliquid* etymologically, that is to say, as *aliud quid,* "an 'other' what." Every being, just as it is *one* with regard to itself (because it is undivided), relates to other beings as "an 'other' what" (because it is divided from them). Thus, for a being to *be,* it is not enough that it be some "thing" *(res)* and "one" *(unum);* it must also be a "what" that is "other" than others, that is to say, different from them. In short, in the same way in which being requires identity *(res)* and unity *(unum)*, so it requires difference *(aliud quid)*. A being is not itself, and then happens, in a second movement and as a kind of afterthought, to relate to others—rather, a being is itself only insofar as it relates to others and, in relating to them, distinguishes itself from them. Aquinas is a dialectical thinker for whom identity and difference are thoroughly co-constitutional; one does not exist without the other.

Let us take this interpretation one step further before responding to possible objections. For a being to be other than another, it has to relate to this "other" being; it is not by accident that St. Thomas speaks of an ordering of beings one *toward* the other *(ordo unius ad alterum)*. Otherness, or difference, is not the absence of any kind of relationship, but rather, a being must enter into a relationship with the "other" (something that is different from it) before it can affirm itself as *aliud quid,* as something that is "other than another." To give an anthropological example: how can I say that I am other than you if I do not know you at all? But this means that a being can affirm itself only in an "outward movement backward" (we remember the expression): in a movement *toward* the other *back* to itself. This is a circular movement. For a being to be some "thing" *(res)* and "one" thing *(unum)*, it must leave itself behind and affirm itself as "other" than another *(aliud quid),* thereby returning to itself.

Now to the objections. Have we not wildly overinterpreted the excerpt from the beginning of the *Quaestiones disputatae de veritate?* Is it not true that there is no other text in the Thomistic oeuvre which even mentions the transcendental *aliquid?*[12] How can we justify making such an extremely marginal text the starting point of an overall interpretation of Aquinas's thought?

First of all, the insight expressed in the text on *aliquid* is true phenomenologically. It corresponds to our experience of the world. For, there is no object in this world that has any meaning whatsoever if it is given in isolation. All objects, in order to be what they are, require a context in which they are placed, yet from which they are also distinct.[13] What is a window? A hole in the wall, basically. Is it the wall? No. But what would it be without the wall? Who are you? James or Joan Smith. Okay, but that information does not help anyone who does not already know you. It does not even help yourself, for your name, as such, does not tell you "who you are"—what kind of person, with what goals, etc. You need a context to define yourself, such as, "James (or Joan) Smith, a student at the University of Dallas." Now you have an identity—but only through something that is not yourself (namely, your college). That this phenomenological description corresponds to our interpretation of *aliquid* is a fact which certainly militates in its favor.

Furthermore, the text on *aliquid* from the *Quaestiones disputatae de veritate* is not so isolated and marginal as it might seem. Admittedly, there is no other passage in St. Thomas that treats of the transcendental *aliquid*. Yet there are many other passages that render the insight of the *Quaestiones disputatae de veritate* more explicit, spelling out its consequences and applying it. To some of these texts we now turn.

Substantiality as Self-Reflexivity

In the tradition of Aristotelian metaphysics, the kind of being that *is* in the fullest sense of the word is substance, whereas accidents like quantity or quality possess being only insofar as they attach to a substance. This position makes sense, for there is no such thing as, for instance, just "black." The quality "black" always belongs to something that acts as its support, such as skin, hair, a tire, and the like. From this description, we can already see why the Aristotelico-Thomistic standard definition of substantiality is self-subsistence: a substance is a kind of being that exists in itself, rather than in another.[14]

Self-subsistence may be the standard definition Aquinas offers of substance, but it is not the only one. In a few passages whose import, again, many Thomists have failed to see, he identifies substantiality with self-reflexivity. Here is an example:

> For a thing to return to its own essence *(redire ad essentiam suam)* means nothing other than for it to subsist in itself.[15]

Read against the background both of the Greek metaphysics of self-reflexivity and Aquinas's own reflections upon the transcendental *aliquid,* the text makes perfect sense. It means that substantial being is inherently self-reflexive or circular. It "goes back" *(redire)* to its own essence because this essence cannot be itself without the "outward movement backward" in which it defines itself through, and over against, an "other."

The accuracy of this interpretation finds further confirmation in the fact that St. Thomas himself adverts to the Neoplatonic origins of his definition of substantiality in terms of self-reflexivity. In the *Quaestiones disputatae de veritate* he writes:

Note, however, that in the *Liber de causis* the return to its own essence *(red-itio ad essentiam suam)* is called the very subsistence of a thing in itself.[16]

The *Liber de causis,* or "Book on Causes," was mentioned in study 3. As Aquinas correctly points out in the proem to his commentary, the *Liber de causis* is a compilation, of Arabic provenance, of the *Elements of Theology* by the Neoplatonic author Proclus (ca. 412–485). This links Aquinas's conception of substantiality as self-reflexivity directly to Neoplatonic metaphysics.

"Operation" as a Condition of Being

Let us follow the "unfolding" of the transcendental *aliquid* and its implica-tions one step further. So far, the question has remained unanswered as to what exactly the return upon itself of substance consists in. Does it consti-tute nothing more than an abstract metaphysical principle that it is impos-sible to verify; or is there some phenomenological evidence that such a *reditio ad essentiam suam* does actually take place in an observable fashion?

According to St. Thomas, there is no such thing as static, inert being. "Every thing is said to be in virtue of *(propter)* its operation," he maintains; or, even more succinctly: "Every thing *is* in virtue of *(propter)* its opera-tion."[17] In these sentences, the preposition *propter* expresses a final causal-ity that it is difficult to render in English. By *propter,* Aquinas wants to convey the idea that it is the *purpose* or *goal* of being to "operate," that is to say, to be active. However, his understanding of such "purposive" or final causality differs substantially from our modern conception, in which final causality tends to be regarded as insignificant, if not as an unscien-tific figment of the imagination; all that matters is the "efficient" cause, which alone is viewed as actually "doing" anything.[18] For Aquinas, on the other hand, the goal is everything; indeed, he calls it the "cause of causes" *(causa causarum),*[19] without which nothing would ever come about. In a passage from his commentary on the *Book of Sentences,* we read the pithy phrase, *subtracto enim fine, relinquitur vanitas* ("if the end is taken away, all that remains is emptiness").[20] Being without its end, "operation," would be nothing.

It is clear why this is so. A being that does not move outside itself, re-maining statically self-enclosed, cannot constitute itself as *aliquid,* as other than another. This is possible only in a return *(reditio)* to its own essence, that is to say, an outward movement backward in which it becomes some "thing" *(res)* through the mediation of an "other."

The nature of "operation" *(operatio)* is in keeping with the dialectics of identity and difference that we have discovered on the level of the transcendentals, as well as being concordant with the outward/backward movement characteristic of *reditio.* Insofar as operation, as an expression of the transcendental *aliquid,* pulls being toward the "other," it manifests itself as what one could call a centrifugal force[21]; but insofar as it expresses the transcendentals *res* and *unum,* which emphasize each being's identity and unity, it shows itself as a centripetal force. Put differently, operation is possessed of a dialectical nature that "oscillates"—or even "circulates"—between self-communication and self-dispersal.

Operation as Self-Communication

Each being, in operating, that is to say, in moving through an "other" to itself, exerts an attraction upon the other that pulls it toward its own center of identity. In more traditionally Thomistic terms:

> It is to be pointed out that the nature of any act is to communicate itself *(seipsum communicet)* inasmuch as that is possible *(quantum possibile est).* Thus, every agent acts *(agit)* in accordance with what it is in act. But acting is nothing but communicating *(communicare)* that by which the agent is in act, inasmuch as that is possible.[22]

That which makes an agent what it is in act, is its form. It is the form of tree, for instance (which is a kind of primitive soul, according to ancient and medieval thought), which bestows upon the tree its actual being, making it a living, growing, and breathing creature. Likewise, it is the form of house through which brick, concrete, windows, wood, and tiles are structured in such a way as to make these materials "behave" like a house (affording shelter from bad weather, having its foundations cracked by drought, etc.). Now Aquinas's claim in the text just quoted is that in operating, or "acting" *(agere),* each being communicates its form to other beings "inasmuch as that is possible." This statement is another way of formulating the principle that *omne agens agit sibi simile* ("every agent brings about something similar to itself"), a principle we previously identified as being at the very core of the Scholastic episteme:

> As every agent, insofar as it is an agent, brings about something similar to itself *(omne agens agat sibi simile),* each thing acting in accordance with its form, it is necessary that there be a similitude *(similitudo)* of the form of the agent in the effect.[23]

Let us recapitulate. Each being (*ens*), insofar as it is, is some "thing" (*res*) and one (*unum*), as well as "other than another" (*aliquid/aliud quid*). This transcendental dialectics crystallizes in an operation (*operatio*) in which each being constitutes itself, or indeed its self, by returning to itself through another (*reditio ad essentiam suam*). However, this movement to the self through an "other" does not leave the other being unaffected, but draws it into the sphere of the being that acts. The being acted upon therefore becomes "like" (*simile*) the acting being. The degree of assimilation varies (*quantum possibile est*), resulting in different types of causal similarity that range from univocity to the faint "resemblance" an effect bears to a tool that helps to cause it.[24] Following Aristotle, Aquinas often uses the "human begets human" example in order to illustrate univocal causality, in which cause and effect fall under the same definition.[25]

Earlier on, we asked if there is any evidence that the circularity of being, the *reditio ad essentiam suam,* is not a mere figment of an overheated metaphysical imagination, but actually takes place in an observable fashion. The answer to this question can now be given: wherever we see causal similarity, that is to say, a cause returning to itself in and through an effect bearing its similarity, we are in the presence of *reditio.*[26]

Operation as Self-Dispersal

Each being, as we have seen, is intrinsically operative, for in order to *be,* it must establish itself as "an 'other' what." In this process of defining itself over against the other, it draws it into its own circle by communicating its own form to it, at least "inasmuch as that is possible." Yet, through this same operation, being also loses itself. By returning to itself through the mediation of the other, it does not only leave its own stamp upon the other, but also takes the other into itself, as it were, so that its own identity comes to be affected by the otherness of the other. An example is in order here.

We have already noted that each being, in order to *be,* requires a context in which to situate itself, and indeed from which to distinguish itself. We mentioned the example of the University of Dallas students James and Joan Smith, who define their identity, at least partially, through the institution at which they study—as well as through their family and friends, interests, beliefs and convictions, avocations, and so on. To use a common metaphor, it is through the different roles that we play upon the stage of life that we come to be who we "are." However, these roles can never completely exhaust our identity, so that they will always leave us, to some extent, dissatisfied. There is always "more": opportunities we have had to

decline, possibilities we have allowed to pass, hopes we have had to aban-
don. The distance existing between all we could be, were all the potential-
ities lying within our identity realized, and the roles we have come to play
on the stage of life, is expressed in the very word that designates human
existence in most European languages: *person.* Etymologically, *person,*
which derives from the Latin *persona,* which again is a translation of the
Greek πρόσωπον, means "mask." Originally, *persona* designated the mask
worn by an actor on the stage.[27] Later on, the word came to signify the
actor himself, then any human being considered from the point of view of
the role he or she played in society. Finally, *persona* took on the meaning of
any human being whatsoever.[28] From this etymology, it is clear that, in
calling human beings "persons," or *personae,* the Western tradition implicitly recognizes the distance between ourselves and our "roles." For, the
context which we need to define ourselves over against (the "other") constantly threatens to alienate us from our "true" selves. This alienation occurs when we freeze in the roles society expects us to play, not realizing
that they are just "masks."

In medieval thought, etymological considerations occupy an important
place; Aquinas himself often introduces them at key points of his arguments—
as, for instance, in the list of transcendentals in the *Quaestiones disputatae de veritate.*[29] In the case of *persona,* St. Thomas does not draw any far-reaching
conclusions based upon the etymology; nonetheless, he is vividly aware of the
word's origins:

> According to Boethius, the word *persona* is derived from *personare,* due to the
> fact that in tragedies and comedies those reciting used to put on some kind of
> mask *(sibi ponebant quamdam larvam)* to represent the personage whose deeds
> they would relate in their chants. And it is hence that [*persona*] has come to be
> the object of a usage such that any individual human being of whom such a
> relation is possible, is called *persona.* For the same reason, in Greek *prosopon* is
> derived from *pro,* which means "before," and *sopos,* which means "face,"[30] be-
> cause they used to wear these kinds of masks before their faces.[31]

Back to our original point about operation as self-dispersal. In operating—which, for human beings, means acting on the "stage" of life—beings
ineluctably distance themselves from their own identity, which paradoxically happens precisely in their quest for it. This dialectical paradox is due
to the necessary mediation of their identity through otherness. How does
St. Thomas frame the loss of identity that is involved in operation? Let us
turn to the following text from the *Quaestiones disputatae de veritate:*

When, therefore, we ask if things exist more truly in themselves than in the Word, we must make the distinction that *more truly (verius)* can designate the truth of the thing *(veritas rei)* or the truth of predication *(veritas praedicationis)*. If it designates the truth of the thing, then undoubtedly the truth of things as they exist in the Word is greater than [that which they possess] in themselves. However, if it designates the truth of predication, then the opposite is the case. For *human being* is more truly predicated of a thing which is in its own nature than of a thing which is in the Word.[32]

What Aquinas is saying here is that when we refer to "human being" or "horse" in ordinary language, we do not understand these words to designate the being of these creatures as they preexist in the mind of their Creator. In formulating a predication such as, "A horse is a type of large strong animal with mane, tail, and hooves which people ride on and use for pulling and carrying heavy things," we have in mind the concrete, material being (the *esse hoc,* as St. Thomas sometimes calls it[33]); we are not thinking of the horse as a divine idea. Nevertheless, when we turn from the order of predication to the order of being (the *veritas rei*), each thing does indeed exist more truly in the Word than in itself. For, in the order of predication, its identity is always broken, being the object of a never completed quest in which identity is indissociable from otherness. By contrast, in the mind of God, its Creator, each thing exists in pristine purity, for it does not have to be "other than another" in order to be itself.[34]

The Open Circle

After the preceding considerations, it is already possible to provide a provisional description of how Aquinas has resolved the problem of the Greek circle and the Christian line.

Thomistic metaphysics regards being as self-reflexive in its very core: substance, we have seen, is indissociable from *reditio.* However, it is not only each individual being that possesses a circular structure; the cosmos, as the totality of beings, also performs a circular movement. This is not difficult to understand, as the world is the effect of its divine Creator, so that the reflexivity which is to be found in innerworldly cause-effect relationships also exists, in an analogous way, between God and the universe:

In the issuing forth of the creatures from their first principle, a certain circling *(circulatio)* or wheeling around *(regiratio)* is to be considered, due to the fact that all things turn back, as to their end, to that from which they have come forth as from their principle.[35]

This passage shows the extent to which Aquinas has allowed Greek circularity to penetrate to the very heart of his thought. But what has happened to the Christian line? It is present in the circle—in the following way. If we return for a moment to self-reflexivity on the "microcosmic" level of individual substance, it was said that the return upon itself of substance in its operation is frustrated by the mediating role of the "other." In this fashion, the ultimate truth of each thing *(veritas rei)* is withdrawn from the order of predication, coming to be situated on the level of the Word. The self-reflexivity of substance is thus prevented from coming full circle in the finite order (see fig. 5.1). In somewhat naive terms, one could say that substance, in exteriorizing itself in an operation, leaves its identity behind in order to constitute itself as *aliquid* through an "other," but finds its original identity has disappeared after its contact with the other. Of course, substance has always already "left its identity behind," for there is no being that is not "an 'other' what" *(aliquid),* that is not self-reflexive, that does not operate. Therefore, the dialectics of identity and difference that characterizes operation has always already cut open the circle of creaturely being. Like a straight line, this circle has a beginning and an end which do not join—although, in a sense, the end is the beginning (namely, the *veritas rei*

Figure 5.1   Aquinas's "Open Circle"

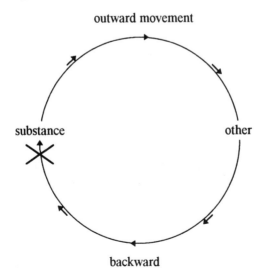

outward movement

substance

other

backward

in the divine Word). There is therefore no eternal repetition of the same *circulatio,* but a teleological movement from the beginning to the end.

God, in Thomistic metaphysics, is the Other at the heart of each being's self-reflexive operation.[36] The constitution of each substance involves the quest for an identity which is lost in that very quest—albeit not lost absolutely. For, the *veritas rei* of every substance, rather than being annihilated, comes to be situated in an "other" world: the Word. This means that a being's truth, the identity it seeks in operating, is both its own essence and God, or rather, its own essence *in* God. In light of these considerations, it is not surprising that Aquinas depicts the operation which is constitutive of each thing's being as a quest for likeness with the divine:

> The created thing strives after divine similitude *(divinam similitudinem)* by means of its operation *(per suam operationem).* Now through its operation one thing becomes the cause of another. Therefore, things strive after divine similitude also in that they are the causes of others.[37]

A remarkable affirmation, if one thinks about it: causality, even in its most humble manifestations, is always a divine affair.

The Meaning of Creation and of the Beatific Vision

In order to throw into even higher relief how St. Thomas's metaphysical circle remains open, thus accommodating the linear worldview of the Christian faith, it will prove useful to examine briefly his theories of creation and of the beatific vision. Creation and the beatific vision are, in fact, the two extremes of the Christian line, in the former case absolutely speaking—everything begins with creation—in the latter with regard to each individual's life (assuming, of course, that the individual proves worthy to receive the grace of the beatific vision). By the same token, creation and the beatific vision constitute the beginning and end, respectively, of the "circling" movement that Aquinas describes in the passage from the *Sentences* commentary cited above: "In the issuing forth of the creatures from their first principle, a certain circling or wheeling around is to be considered, due to the fact that all things turn back, as to their end, to that from which they have come forth as from their principle." Creation and the beatific vision are, as it were, the points of transition between God and creation: the former, as the point where creation emerges from the Creator; the latter, as the point where the human being returns to his or her Maker. The nature of these two thresholds is extremely important in determining the kind of circle we are dealing with in the case of Thomistic metaphysics. The question is, can we recover the pristine identity of our being in the Word either retrospectively (by "deriving" the finite order from the sphere of the *veritas rei* in which being is unaffected by finitude) or prospectively (by looking forward to a time when our identities broken by otherness will, once again, be perfectly reconciled with their truth in the Word)? Can we close the circle, as it were? St. Thomas's answer to this question is a clear "no." Let us examine the case of creation first. In the *Summa contra gentiles,* Aquinas declares:

> In fact, creation is no change *(mutatio),* but the very dependence *(ipsa dependentia)* of created being upon the principle by which it is posited, and thus creation pertains to the genus of relationship *(est de genere relationis) . . .* Yet it seems that creation is some kind of change [, but that is so] only according to a way of understanding *(secundum modum intelligendi),* that is to say, insofar as our intellect takes one and the same thing as non-existent first, and then as existent.[38]

Creation is not a transition from the nonexistence of the world to its existence. If we choose to envision matters in this way, we must be aware that this conception is a mere *modus intelligendi*—a convenient, perhaps facile, way of understanding that has no basis whatsoever in reality. In truth, creation signifies nothing but the relationship between created beings and their "Other"—that is to say, creation is the quest of finite being for divine similitude, which is at the same time a quest for its own fullest truth and identity. Let us quote another text to confirm this interpretation:

> Now, as has been said, creation cannot be taken as a "being moved" *(moveri)* existing before the result of the movement *(ante terminum motus),* but it must be taken as something that belongs to being as already made *(ut in facto esse).* That is why creation does not involve any passage into being *(accessus ad esse),* nor any transformation *(transmutatio)* by the Creator, but only the beginning of being *(inceptio essendi),* and the relation *(relatio)* to the Creator from which it has its being. Thus, in reality creation is nothing but some kind of relationship with God, together with the novelty of being *(relatio quaedam ad Deum cum novitate essendi).*[39]

Creation cannot be envisaged as a movement from nonbeing to being because such a transition is unintelligible. How can *something* be "moved" by God into existence if it is *nothing?* Therefore, Aquinas again defends a conception of creation as a relation between the created and the Creator.

While we can understand the structure of this relation, its origins are not susceptible of further investigation; they must be taken as a "given" *(ut in facto esse)*. This position is not tantamount to a denial of the "beginning" and "novelty" of being; however, we should regard this beginning and novelty as a result of the structure in which each being, in the very process of constituting its own identity through the mediation of an "other," is referred to the Other that is God. It is this circle of self-reflexivity that *is* creation itself; the circle has no further origins. Its open structure is a fact that has to be accepted as the mystery of creation.

If the circle of self-reflexivity cannot be closed at its origins, neither can it at its end. As we remember, the *circulatio* or *regiratio* leads each being to its Creator, striving as it does after divine similitude. In the case of the human being, the quest for God finds its final fulfillment in the beatific vision, where the human being is reunited with the fullest truth of its own essence. Nonetheless, the beatific vision is not the simple absorption of creation into its Other, God; there must remain a distance, or difference, between the two, or else the being of creation would disappear altogether. St. Thomas attempts to express this necessary distance by means of a distinction:

> No created intellect, however abstract it may be either by death or by [natural] separation from the body [as in the case of the angels], is in any way capable of comprehending *(comprehendere)* the divine essence in seeing it. Hence it is generally said that, although the divine essence is seen as a whole *(tota)* by the blessed, as it is most simple and without parts, still it is not seen totally *(totaliter)*, because this would mean to comprehend it . . . Now somebody is properly said to "comprehend" something by knowing it *(cognoscendo)*, who knows that thing to the degree to which it is in itself knowable *(in se cognoscibilis)*; otherwise, although he may know it, he does not comprehend it . . . Now any thing is knowable to the degree to which it participates in being and truth; the knower himself, however, only knows to the degree that he participates in knowing power *(quantum habet de virtute cognoscitiva)*. But every created intellectual substance is finite; thus it knows in a finite way *(finite cognoscit)*. Therefore, as God is of infinite power and being, and consequently infinitely knowable *(infinite cognoscibilis)*, He[40] cannot be known by any created intellect to the degree to which He is knowable, and thus He remains incomprehensible *(incomprehensibilis)* to every created intellect.[41]

God is "known" in the beatific vision, but not "comprehended." In order to understand this distinction, we must attend to the literal meaning of the Latin verb *comprehendere*, which Aquinas himself explains in another text. "It must be pointed out," he notes in the *Quaestiones disputatae de veritate*, "that something is properly said to be 'comprehended' by someone if it is included by him *(ab eo includitur)*; for someone is said to 'comprehend' something when he can apprehend it at once with regard to all its parts, which is to have it included from all sides *(undique inclusum habere)*."[42] "Comprehension" thus implies total mental mastery, the ability fully to "take in" and as it were contain the object comprehended. However, it is obvious that no finite mind can contain divine infinity. Hence Aquinas's insistence that the beatific vision, even if it consists in a contemplation of God's "total" essence (for God's essence is simple, so that there are no parts that could remain unseen), nevertheless does not reveal God "totally." In other words, the beatific vision does not put an absolute end to the human quest for completion; even in the very presence of God, there always remains more to be discovered and enjoyed.[43] That God ultimately remains "incomprehensible" means that, just as the metaphysical circle cannot be closed at its starting point, so it cannot be closed at its end.

The Incomprehensibility of the Knowable God: Negative and Positive Theology

The tension obtaining in the beatific vision between the knowledge of God that the blessed enjoy, and His utter incomprehensibility to any created intellect, epitomizes a dialectics that is not foreign to this life. On the one hand, God is the ultimate final cause of every operation, so that there is not in this world the tiniest motion, physical or spiritual, that could come to pass without Him. Indeed, the fact that the *veritas rei* of each created thing—its own innermost truth—is located in its Maker makes it necessary to assume that God is not only each operation's final cause, but also its ultimate origin; a thesis that in fact Aquinas defends in several places of his oeuvre.[44] Moreover, given the principle of causal similarity, the whole of creation bears the stamp of its Maker, being, as St. Thomas formulates it, "the mirror of God" *(speculum Dei)*.[45]

Epistemologically, the presence of God in creation through these various modes translates into a position according to which knowledge of God is indeed possible in this world. Indirectly, the existence and nature of God can be inferred upon the basis of His effects; this is what Aquinas himself does, for example, in the famous "five ways."[46] In addition, just as God is intimately present in each being's operation, so His presence in the order of knowledge, too, is more intimate than that of a mere logical conclusion:

indeed, God speaks in us through the very principles which make knowledge possible. Thus, in the *Quaestiones disputatae de veritate,* we read:

> The certainty of knowledge is wholly the result of the certainty of its principles: in fact, one knows conclusions with certainty when they are traced back to their principles. Hence, that something is known with certainty comes from the light of reason which is inwardly given [to us] by God, and through which God speaks in us *(ex lumine rationis divinitus interius indito quo in nobis loquitur Deus).*[47]

In nobis loquitur Deus ("God speaks in us")! For, He is intimately present to our minds through the first principles of knowledge, which Aquinas maintains are the result of divine infusion.

His belief in the intimate presence of God in our minds notwithstanding, St. Thomas also maintains, in a dialectical fashion, that God is ultimately absent in human knowledge. Thus, the incomprehensibility of God in the beatific vision is reflected in the fact, reaffirmed by Aquinas time and again, that we cannot know anything positive about God in this life: "We cannot know about God what He is, but only what He is not."[48] How could we know anything positive about Him? He is infinite, we are finite. Besides, if God were not hidden from us, together with our own innermost truth *(veritas rei),* what reason would there be to act? For, remember: *subtracto enim fine, relinquitur vanitas.* Hence:

> [W]hatever our intellect conceives of God, falls short of a representation of Him; that is why what pertains to God Himself *(quid est ipsius Dei)* remains forever hidden *(occultus)* from us. And this is the highest knowledge *(cognitio)* that we can have of Him in this life: to know that God is beyond everything that we think of Him.[49]

There is no contradiction involved in Aquinas's simultaneous affirmation and denial of our ability to know God. The tension is just another manifestation of the fundamental dialectics at work in creation; of the constant "circulation" of being between identity and difference. God is the Other; but as each individual being's own truth and fulfillment, He is also the Same. (Operation is the constitution of each being's identity; but also its loss.) The tradition of Christian thought expresses this insight by maintaining a necessary complementarity of "positive" and "negative" theology. In the quest to learn whatever we can about God (positive theology), we must always be prepared humbly to admit that "whatever our intellect conceives of God, falls short of a representation of Him" (negative theology).[50]

"A Doctrine of Negative Theology for Morals"

Toward the beginning of this study, we noted that recent discussions have already gone some way toward dispelling the impression that Thomistic ethics is necessarily "legalistic and aridly theoretical," as Pamela Hall put it in her recent study of the topic.[51] In the contemporary reappraisal of Aquinas's ethical thought, one important step, however, remains to be taken. So far, no attempts have been made to apply the dialectics of positive and negative theology to the interpretation of St. Thomas's ethics. It is in line with this important desideratum that Mark Jordan, a medievalist from the University of Notre Dame, rightly calls for "a doctrine of negative theology for morals," in which he sees hope for "a genuinely Thomist project of moral theology."[52] But what exactly is the challenge that negative theology poses for ethics? In the Thomistic natural-law context, we can answer this question quite easily. If God's nature is ultimately incomprehensible, so that "whatever our intellect conceives of God, falls short of a representation of Him"; if, moreover, the innermost truth *(veritas rei)* of creation is located in the Word, that is to say, in God; then any ethics deriving its principles from the "law of nature"—that is to say, from what beings intrinsically are—will have its ground cut from under its feet. Ernst Cassirer well observed the connection between negative theology and our knowledge of human nature in the *Essay on Man:*

> Religion, therefore, never clarifies the mystery of man. It confirms and deepens this mystery. The God of whom it speaks is a *Deus absconditus,* a hidden God. Hence even his image, man, cannot be other than mysterious. Man also remains a *homo absconditus.*[53]

However, negative theology must not be divorced from its positive counterpart; the two theologies are complementary. We shall now attempt to see how this dialectical complementarity manifests itself in St. Thomas's ethics.

Thomistic ethics is thoroughly metaphysical, being based as it is upon a transposition of the principles of ontology onto ethical terrain. Each being operates—which means, *is*—with a view to attaining divine similitude. Yet God is not, or not only, the absolutely Other of creation, but also contains, in His Word, the truest nature of each individual being. Therefore, "what holds the world together in its innermost core," to use Goethe's phrase, is each individual being's quest for itself. Thomistic ethics does nothing but draw the consequences of this fundamental metaphysical insight. As the former Louvain philosopher and now bishop André Léonard formulates it, "the essential precept of the natural law could therefore be expressed in the terms: 'Become what you are,' that is to say, 'Become practically, intelligibly, and freely what you are ontologically.'"[54] Nothing could be more mistaken than to interpret the natural law as a set of "commandments" extrinsically imposed upon human nature. On the contrary, the natural law expresses the inherent teleology of creation, and in particular of the human being. The problems of ethics are due to the necessary transition from the ontological to the practical level; for, in order to "become what I am," I must not only *realize* who I am, but I must also *freely embrace* my true self. This is the point where negative theology and its corollary, negative anthropology, render "the matter of morality varied and deformed, so that it does not possess total certainty."[55]

However, before turning to these problems, let us analyze the ontological roots of ethics in the finality of creation—that is to say, in its quest for its self, which is a quest for God. In the *Summa theologiae,* St. Thomas explains:

> Every agent acts for *(propter)* an end, which has the meaning of a good *(rationem boni).* That is why the first principle in [the realm of] practical reason is that which is founded upon the definition of good *(ratio boni),* which is: *The good is what everything desires.* This is, therefore, the first precept of the law, that the good is worthy to be done and to be pursued, and evil deserves to be avoided *(bonum est faciendum et prosequendum, et malum vitandum).* Upon this all the other precepts of the natural law are founded.[56]

This text shows impressively how naturally Aquinas accomplishes the transition from the ontological principle that everything desires what is good for it, to the ethical "precept" that the good is worthy to be done and pursued. As this precept arises from within each creature's being, it is something that we all "possess" in an ineradicable fashion; St. Thomas speaks of a *habitus,* a "having" of the universal principles of the natural law.[57] Indeed, as we cannot *not* pursue the good in this most general sense, we all desire beatitude, insofar as it constitutes our perfect good. Admittedly, many people fail to see what exactly beatitude entails, namely the vision of God.[58] This gap between our natural desire for the good and the deliberate pursuit of it is exactly where the crux of ethics lies. To this we now turn.

Like every other creature, the human being cannot help but desire perfection and fulfillment. Short of the beatific vision, about which we can only speculate in this life, what do these consist in? In answering this question, it is important to remember that "the created thing strives after divine similitude by means of its operation," that is to say, through the exercise of causality in all its manifestations. To put it bluntly, the pursuit of divine similitude is not something in which human beings are engaged only in prayer or at Sunday Mass, but in every moment of their lives. From this, it follows that the finality of those operations which come most naturally to the human being can be taken as indicative of the path leading to beatitude. Aquinas terms these most natural operations *inclinationes naturales* (natural inclinations), distinguishing three kinds:

> First, there is in the human being an inclination toward the good in accordance with the nature which he shares with all substances, namely, insofar as any substance desires the conservation of its being according to its nature. And according to this inclination, that by which the life of the human being is preserved and what is opposed [to it] prevented, pertains to the natural law. Secondly, there is in the human being an inclination toward some more specific [goods], according to the nature which he shares with the other animals. And according to this, that "which nature teaches all animals"[59] belongs to the natural law, such as the union of male and female, the education of children, and the like. In a third manner, there is in the human being an inclination toward the good according to the nature of reason *(secundum naturam rationis),* which is proper to him; for instance, the human being has a natural inclination to know the truth about God and to live in society. And according to this, that which concerns this kind of inclination pertains to the natural law—for instance, that the human being avoid ignorance, that he not offend the others with whom he must keep company, etc.[60]

These three natural inclinations form a hierarchy which culminates in the inclination that is most proper to the human being, namely, to pursue the good rationally. It is thus that Aquinas can declare, in another text, that "good and evil in moral matters are spoken about in accordance with what agrees or disagrees with reason."[61] To act morally, thus, is to act rationally. However, the relationship between reason and the other natural inclinations is not unproblematic. St. Thomas refers to reason as "ordering" and "directing" the nonrational inclinations:

> It is necessary that all the natural inclinations which pertain to the other powers be ordered according to reason *(ordinentur secundum rationem).* Hence, this is generally right according to everyone, that all the natural inclinations of human beings be directed according to reason *(secundum rationem dirigantur).*[62]

"Ordering" and "directing" can mean a variety of things. First, reason draws conclusions from the most general and obvious precepts of the natural law in order to apply them to concrete situations. For instance, the natural law to preserve the family and rear children cannot prevent me from committing adultery unless I recognize that this particular adulterous action in which I am on the point of engaging right now contravenes the good highlighted by the law. It is this recognition of the validity and implications of the natural law in a particular case that depends upon the mediation of practical reason; however, as we know from experience, reason often fails in performing its task, due to *error rationis*.[63] Second, in certain cases reason is authorized to annul precepts of the natural law, if they stand in the way of higher goods. For instance, the preservation of human life is a precept that may be overruled for the good of the community. Thus, "if a human being poses a danger to the community and corrupts it due to some sin, he is laudably and salutarily killed, so that the common good may be preserved."[64]

But which precepts may be overruled, and which may not? As one sees, the position of reason within the field of the natural inclinations causes serious tensions. Indeed, reason is part of human nature, and even its most precious one; but it is also an ambiguous part that seems to call nature itself into question. Bishop Léonard summarizes this paradox in a provocative formulation when he writes: "man is, according to his proper nature, transgression of nature, he is an animal whose nature it is to be cultural, his specific nature is not to remain a merely natural being."[65] Of course, the word "transgression" is not to be as understood as "violation" here, but in a more literal sense of "stepping beyond." Nonetheless, Léonard's statement shows well that some of the difficulty involved in ethical decisions stems from the tension obtaining between reason and the other natural inclinations. That there is such a tension does not mean that anything goes in moral matters—far from it. Aquinas himself develops an elaborate ethical system. What the tension does underscore is the distance existing between, on the one hand, the spontaneous adherence to "the Good" in general that is characteristic of human actions and, on the other hand, the extreme difficulties that often arise in the attempt to determine what exactly the good amounts to in a given situation. Matters are further complicated by the fact that even the nonrational natural inclinations are subject to cultural and historical variation:

> As human actions are necessarily varied according to the diverse conditions of persons and times and other circumstances *(actus humanos variari oportet secundum diversas conditiones personarum et temporum, et aliarum circumstantiarum)*, the aforesaid conclusions from the first precepts of the law of nature do not

follow in such a way that they are always effective, but [only] for the most part *(in majori parte)* . . . With regard to itself *(quantum est de se)*, the natural law *(jus naturale)* always and everywhere has the same power; yet accidentally and through some impediment *(impedimentum)* it can vary sometimes and in some places . . . for, according to nature, the right hand is always and everywhere better than the left. However, through some accident it comes about that someone is ambidextrous, because our nature is variable, and so is the natural right *(natura nostra variabilis est; et similiter etiam est de naturali justo)*.[66]

Thus, it is not only in the transition from the natural inclinations and corresponding precepts to their practical consequences that the difficulty of ethical judgments lies; the fact that human nature itself is subject to historical, cultural, and even personal variation makes natural-law judgments liable to exceptions, applying as they do only *in majori parte,* and not always. In the same way in which we can be said paradoxically to have some knowledge of the incomprehensible God, so we possess some knowledge of the Good, which nevertheless remains highly elusive.

Remedy for the Weaknesses of the Natural Law: Divine Law and the Rule of Conscience

The difference between theory and practice is that, in the face of theoretical uncertainty, I can always suspend judgment in the hope that further evidence, reasoning, and discussion will clarify the matter under consideration; but with regard to ethical problems (except when they are themselves discussed theoretically, as we are in the process of doing right now), I have to come to decisions that will translate into actions of sometimes momentous consequence. For instance, if I believe that the natural law to preserve human life suffers exceptions, as Aquinas does, I may decide to give my vote at the next election to an advocate of the rigorous implementation of the death penalty. If the candidate wins, this will result in more people being executed. However, if ethical judgments are so difficult to make as the previous section suggested, how could one ever come to such a decision? Aquinas's answer to this problem is twofold: first, he maintains that divine, or revealed, law is indispensable in helping us come to ethical decisions. Second, he argues that someone faithfully following the voice of his or her conscience does not sin, even if the decision to which this person comes proves to be objectively wrong.

Let us first examine the divine law as a remedy for the shortcomings of the natural law. In the *Summa theologiae,* St. Thomas adduces four reasons why a divinely revealed law is indispensable to ensure the moral well-being of humans. We immediately turn to the second reason:

> Secondly, [it was necessary to have a divine law for the direction of human life] because, owing to the uncertainty of human judgment *(propter incertitudinem humani iudicii)*, especially concerning contingent and particular matters, it so happens that there are diverse judgments on different human acts, and from these, diverse and contrary laws also follow. Therefore, in order that the human being might know without any doubt what, for him, is worthy to be done and what deserves to be avoided, it was necessary that he be directed in his proper acts by a divinely given law, of which it is certain that it does not err.[67]

In other words, human reason cannot be trusted to come to sufficiently certain judgments on vital moral matters without the aid of laws directly revealed by God. What Aquinas has in mind here are the moral guidelines contained, explicitly or implicitly, in the Bible. Of course, Scripture can serve as a moral guide only for those who recognize its divine origin; moreover, it is itself subject to interpretation. The divine law, therefore, cannot represent the ultimate solution to the ethical dilemmas of human life. This solution is contained, at least to some extent, in Aquinas's teaching on conscience.

In his commentary on the *Sentences,* Aquinas defines conscience as follows: "conscience designates the application *(applicationem)* of a natural law to something that is to be done, by way of some kind of conclusion."[68] Another pithy definition is to be found in the *Quastiones disputatae de veritate:* conscience is "a judgment of reason deduced *(deductum)* from the natural law."[69] In its most general form, *bonum est faciendum et prosequendum* ("the good is worthy to be done and pursued"), the natural law is the direct expression, on the ethical plane, of the human being's ontological adherence to the Good. This adherence constitutes, even if sometimes unbeknownst to the human agent, an inalienable link with the Creator. There is no other way for us to remain faithful to God/the Good (which of course also means to ourselves) than by applying the natural law to each of our own particular lives. No one can adhere to the Good "for" us, any more than bring the precept *bonum est faciendum* to bear upon our lives "for" us. Consequently, each person has to rely upon his or her own conscience in order to find out what it means, for himself or herself, in this or that particular situation, to do the Good and be obedient to God. After all that has been said in the preceding section about the uncertainty of human judgments in moral matters, it is clear that there will be errors in the way we apply the natural law, making deductions from it. Yet, if we are not aware of these errors, does our adherence to the Good not remain faithful nonetheless? Of course it does, Aquinas replies, holding that conscience is always morally binding, even if it is erroneous:

> An erroneous conscience *(conscientia erronea)* does not suffice to absolve [someone] if he sins in the error itself, as when he errs about matters that he is obliged to know. If, on the other hand, the error occurs with regard to matters which a person is not obliged to know, then he is absolved in virtue of his conscience.[70]

In this text, Aquinas underscores the moral obligation to educate one's conscience, so that errors of judgment can be avoided as often and as reliably as possible. For instance, as a voter exercising my right to choose between a candidate who is in favor of the death penalty and one who opposes it, it is not enough for me to follow my "instincts" with regard to this matter; rather, I have the moral obligation to consider the issue seriously before casting my vote. If I am a Christian, the teachings of the Bible and of the church will also have to play a role in my decision-making process. But then, once I have, after careful and responsible weighing-up of the evidence, come to a conclusion, I have the right, nay the obligation, to follow my conscience. Moreover, in doing so, I do not have to fear that I am being unfaithful to the Good, God, or myself.

That this position leads to a moral paradox is undeniable, and St. Thomas is well aware of the fact. For, situations are likely to occur in which "the subject acts with a righteous and virtuous will whereas, objectively, his act is contrary to right reason. Thus, it can happen that I have merit on the moral plane for engaging in acts that are nevertheless in themselves reprehensible."[71] Aquinas himself provides a startling example of such a situation: if someone believes, in all conscience, that fornication is a good, then that person has to follow his or her conscience and fornicate. Anything else would be sinful![72] The point that St. Thomas is trying to convey by means of this drastic example is clear. However, it is also clear that it needs to be interpreted in its full context. To fornicate without committing a sin, one would have to be totally ignorant that this might constitute a morally reprehensible act, as well as not being obliged to know about the problematic moral status of fornication. Alternatively, one would, after carefully and responsibly considering the matter, have had to come to the conclusion that fornication is good, and this beyond any possible doubt. For, any lingering doubt requires the agent to abstain from the act in question.[73]

One could cite other, more lifelike examples of the possible conflict between the moral Good and one's individual perception of it. However, there is no need to discuss the problem further in this context. The point of our brief examination of Thomistic ethics was only to illustrate the fundamental structure of St. Thomas's thought. Thomas is convinced that "all things turn back, as to their end, to that from which they have come forth as from their principle." Cosmologically, as well as on the level of each individual substance, being is circular. But the circle does not, and cannot, close. This is why human beings, much as they long for perfection and fulfillment, constantly hover between their inalienable adherence to the Good and the threat of moral error. Hence, too, why the distance that exists between the objective exigencies of the natural law and individual conscience can be reduced, but not eliminated.

Conclusion

Apart from providing an introduction to the structure of St. Thomas's thought from a postmodern point of view, the intention of this study was to throw light upon the epistemological field in which this thought develops, and upon the historical a prioris in which is it rooted. In the conclusion of study 3, on the "intellectual practices" of the Scholastics, we remarked that the "body" and "soul" of Scholastic thought cannot be divorced from one another. I think our findings on Aquinas prove this point. One of the most salient features of Thomism is the way it is governed by confidence in the powers of human reason, on the one hand, and profound respect for the mystery of the divine, on the other. In this respect, the structure of Thomism does nothing but reflect a dialectics that we have already found to be at work in Gothic script, or in Gothic architecture. Aquinas believes that, on one side, we can arrive at knowledge concerning God, who is our most intimate truth and perfection, creation being nothing but His mirror; on the other side, however, we can never attain this truth and perfection in this life, with the consequence that, epistemologically too, God remains shrouded in darkness. This tension is reproduced on all the different levels of Aquinas's system; operation is both self-communication and self-dispersal, and in the ethical realm, ineradicable attachment to God/the Good is coupled with the vicissitudes of our finite rational struggles to discern what goodness practically means.

In the circular or self-reflexive structure of Aquinas's thought, we have discovered the condition for the possibility of the Scholastic understanding of the world as text—although Aquinas, unlike his contemporary Bonaventure, does not develop a book metaphysics. Yet the idea that causes return to themselves in and through their effects, thus weaving the world into a texture of similarity, is central to the Thomistic system. As we have seen in the preceding study, the Scholastics inherited the self-reflexive conception of being from Greek philosophy; given the incompatibility of this circular worldview with biblical Christianity, some synthesis had to be worked out. After our discussion of the intellectual practices of *quaestio* and *disputatio*, it was not surprising to see Aquinas cite his Greek predecessors with great respect: for example, he explicitly embraces the Proclean principle according to which substantiality implies self-reflexivity. Of course, Thomistic thought develops as much in dialogue with the Greeks as it is grounded in Scripture and the Christian tradition. This is why St. Thomas cannot accept the Greek philosophy of self-reflexivity and identity without rethinking it at its deepest, ontological level. Thomas's emphasis upon the impossibility of "closing the circle" anywhere in this life—ontologically, epistemologically, ethically—underscores the finitude of the human being, and of creation in general. The course of the world and history are not, as in Plato and Aristotle, an infinite and vain attempt to imitate the divine, but a finite and ultimately successful endeavor. That the beatific vision does not constitute a kind of absorption of the blessed into a seamless identity with God might, on the face of it, appear like a limitation. However, this ineffaceable distance between God and creation is a necessary consequence of the Christian belief that life, individually and cosmologically, is finite and unrepeatable. This finitude and unrepeatablity, in turn, bestow a dignity upon the particular that is absent from Greek thought.

Non est consenescendum in artibus ("there is no point in growing old in the arts"). We quoted this Scholastic adage in study 3. In the curriculum, philosophy gained a heightened importance in the universities, but it continued to be conceived, like the liberal arts preceding it, as being preparatory. With a few exceptions, which we shall examine in the next study, all the great Scholastic thinkers were thus professional theologians. The theological finality of philosophy has become very clear in our discussion of Aquinas's thought. If we tried to avoid mentioning God in interpreting a Scholastic thinker such as Aquinas, everything would become incomplete, if not unintelligible. Ontologically speaking, "creation is nothing but some kind of relationship with God"; epistemologically speaking, without the first principles of knowledge, which are God's voice itself, nothing could be known; finally, on the ethical plane, reason would be lost in determining the practical goods to be pursued without the aid of the divine law. Moreover, the confidence we are entitled to have in the judgment of our individual consciences stems from our adherence to God and the Good, without which we would not be what we are—indeed, without which we would not be.

THE SCHOLASTIC EPISTEME AND ITS OTHERS

> One could write a history of *limits*—of those obscure acts, necessarily for-
> gotten as soon as they have been accomplished, by which a culture rejects
> something which will be for it the Outside (*l'Extérieur*); and throughout the
> course of its history, this hollowed-out void, this white space by which it
> isolates itself, designates it as much as its values.

The time has come to consider once again this quotation that figured so
prominently in study 1, on Michel Foucault's philosophy of history. This
book has tried to reconstruct the Scholastic episteme in its fundamental
features, through an analysis of the place it occupies in the Western tradition (study 2), the Schoolmen's intellectual practices (study 3), the philosophical presuppositions underlying these practices and the major
challenge faced by Scholastic thought in the thirteenth century (study 4),
and the manner in which one of the great Scholastics, St. Thomas Aquinas,
attempted to address this challenge (study 5). However, as every culture defines itself not only through the positivity of some identity, but also—and
in an equally crucial way—through the rejection of something foreign,
something "outside" of itself, it is also necessary to raise the question as to
what constituted the "other" of Scholastic culture. The answer is not difficult to provide.

The Condemnation of 1277

On March 7, 1277 the bishop of Paris, Étienne Tempier, condemned 219
philosophical and theological propositions. In the document containing
the Condemnation, the bishop claims that these "manifest and execrable
errors, or rather vanities and false insanities" *(manifestos et exsecrabiles errores,*

immo potius vanitates et insanias falsas) have been defended by professors in the faculty of arts. He threatens these teachers and their students with excommunication, unless they make themselves known within seven days, either to the bishop himself or to the chancellor of the university.[1]

What are these "manifest and execrable errors"? The condemned propositions range over a wide variety of topics, and scholars have often drawn attention to the apparent disorder in which they are presented.[2] They cover everything from the nature of philosophy, the eternity of the world and the famous dispute over the Averroistic doctrine on the unicity of the intellect, to astrology, sexual ethics, and religious and theological matters. Of course, we cannot examine all 219 condemned propositions here. For our purpose, we need to discuss only the beginning of the document, and then single out a few significant examples.

In his prologue, Bishop Tempier accuses certain masters at the faculty of arts in Paris of defending a theory of "double truth," following which certain ideas are said to be "true according to philosophy, but not according to the Catholic faith, as if there were two contrary truths *(quasi sint due contrarie veritates),* and as if against the truth of Sacred Scripture there were truth in the enunciations of the damned pagans."[3] The list of condemned views begins with an anti-Christian thesis maintaining that God is not triune. After going on to condemn two other heresies concerning the nature of God (theses 2 and 3), the document mentions three theses defending the eternity of the world (4–6), moves on to the problem of the body-soul relationship (7 and 8), censures a version of Aristotle's view that the generation of the human being is circular ("human begets human"; 9 and 10), and cites the Averroistic doctrine according to which humans only participate in thought, without being its ultimate subjects (11–14). Thesis 16 contains one of the "most radical"[4] propositions of this document, claiming that one should not worry about heresy: *de fide non est curandum* ("one should not care about the faith"). Theses 17 and 18 deny the Resurrection of the body. The nineteenth condemned thesis disputes the reality of purgatory as a physical fire, and thesis 20 makes the vegetarian claim that the natural law forbids the killing of animals almost as much as that of humans. All this is, of course, condemned.

Let us now turn to some of the most interesting remaining propositions. "One of the most aggressive theses of our document,"[5] according to the German medievalist Kurt Flasch, is stated under number 40: "That there is no more excellent state [in life] than to devote oneself to philosophy" *(Quod non est excellentior status, quam vacare philosophie).* Somewhat later in the list, we find a cluster of propositions devoted to sexual ethics:

166 maintains that the "sin against nature" (that is to say, homosexual acts, bestiality, and generally all nonreproductive sex), while indeed being incompatible with the nature of the species, is not contrary to the nature of the individual; 168 states that continence is not essentially virtuous; 169 makes the claim that complete abstinence in sexual matters destroys both virtue and the human race; 172 holds that the pleasure resulting from sexual activity does not necessarily impinge upon the ability to think; 181 disputes that the chastity required of ordained and religious people is morally superior to lay abstinence; 183 advances the view that "simple fornication" between unmarried people does not constitute a sin. Interspersed with these attacks against Christian sexual ethics are other, more radical challenges against the truth of the faith. Thesis 174, for instance, denounces Christianity for containing "fables and untrue things" *(fabule et falsa),* while 175 accuses it of standing in the way of learning. In a similar vein, propositions 179 and 180 discourage confession and even prayer.

It is no wonder that Kurt Flasch should have entitled his recent study on the 219 condemned propositions *Enlightenment in the Middle Ages?* The theses contain a critical onslaught against the Christian faith from every possible point of view. Research into Bishop Tempier's Condemnation has passed through a number of stages, which have gradually led to a better appreciation of this remarkable historical document.

Initially, there prevailed a certain naivety with regard to the historical import of Tempier's Condemnation. The assumption was made that the theses Tempier censured must necessarily have been defended by one or more of the masters in the arts faculty, because Tempier, in his prologue, explicitly speaks of *nonnulli Parisius studentes in artibus.*[6] It is true that in the ten or fifteen years preceding the Condemnation, a number of masters at the Parisian faculty of arts had started professing what Van Steenberghen has termed an "heterodox Aristotelianism."[7] This interpretation of Aristotle's thought, which was often inspired by the commentaries of Averroës, distinguished itself from the approach taken by theologians such as Bonaventure and Aquinas by its disregard for the exigencies of synthesis. In other words, the "heterodox Aristotelians" read Aristotle's ideas without immediately being concerned about their compatibility with the Christian faith, rather choosing to expound Aristotle's writings according to their own internal logic. The fact that Aristotle's circular view of the world and its history stands in sharp contrast to the Christian conception of time did not dissuade these thinkers from exploring Aristotle's theory on the eternity of the world, any more than belief in the immortality of the soul prevented them from scrutinizing Averroës's thesis (developed in his

commentary on Aristotle's *On the Soul*) according to which all human beings think by participating in one and the same intellect. The best-known
representatives of heterodox Aristotelianism were Siger of Brabant († between 1281 and 1284)[8] and Boethius of Dacia.[9]

Now given the presence of these radical masters at the arts faculty of
the university of Paris, and given also that Bishop Tempier no doubt had
the group of heterodox Aristotelians in mind when writing his prologue,
historians concluded that the theses contained in the Condemnation were
actually held by representatives of this group. Hence, for example, Pierre
Mandonnet's claim in his study on Siger of Brabant, that the latter defended a theory of "double truth" like the one described by Tempier.[10]

The second stage of scholarship inaugurated a more critical attitude toward the Condemnation. Did Siger really maintain that two opposing theories could be true at the same time, one from a philosophical, the other
from a theological point of view? After careful examination of all of Siger's
surviving works, Fernand Van Steenberghen concluded: "Siger regularly affirms that, in case of a conflict between philosophical conclusions and the
teachings of the faith, the truth is to be found on the side of the faith."[11]
Van Steenberghen's line of inquiry was subsequently taken up by his pupil
Roland Hissette, who extended the scope of the examination to the entirety of the 219 condemned propositions.[12] For each of the propositions,
Hissette attempted to identify an historical source in the writings of a
Parisian master. The results of this inquiry were striking. For many of the
theses, especially the most radical of them, Hissette was unable to locate
any trace in the teachings of the Parisian masters. Thus, for example, theses 1 and 2 (concerning the nature of the Christian God) do not seem to
have been defended by any Latin thinker of the thirteenth century.[13] In
point of the scandalous proposition 16, according to which "one should
not care about the faith," Hissette states: "source unknown."[14] The Belgian
medievalist comes to the same result with regard to the ideas that Christianity contains fables and falsehoods (thesis 174), that it stands in the way
of learning (175),[15] and that confession is futile (thesis 179).[16] As far as the
propositions that touch upon sexual ethics (166, 168, 169, 172, 181, 183)
are concerned, Hissette believes that they might reflect ideas played with
in a work by the twelfth-century author Andreas Capellanus and entitled
De amore ("On love"),[17] but not any doctrine entertained by the masters
at the Parisian arts faculty.[18] All in all, out of the 219 propositions, 68 cannot be attributed to any contemporary author.[19]

What conclusion should one draw from this diagnosis? Van Steenberghen sought the answer to the problem in the personality of the

bishop who promulgated the Condemnation: "Étienne Tempier," he wrote in his 1977 work on Siger of Brabant, "originally from Orléans, had been master in theology and chancellor of the university from 1263 through 1268. Authoritarian and impulsive, he belonged to the conservative theological school."[20] In Van Steenberghen's opinion, the Condemnation of 1277 thus betokens Tempier's "tempestuous zeal."[21] In his own study, Hissette fully aligns himself with this position, speaking of the bishop's "lack of objectivity and discernment." The Condemnation, resulting from an "hasty and disorderly inquiry, betrays the partisan spirit of Tempier and certain theologians."[22]

Recent discussion,[23] however, has led to a surprising reevaluation of the role played by Bishop Tempier in the intellectual movement of the thirteenth century. In the eyes of such a postmodern medievalist as Alain de Libera, Tempier was not at all so *borné* as Van Steenberghen, Hissette, and others[24] have made him out to be. According to de Libera, Tempier might have been conservative, but he was also perspicacious and farsighted in his condemnation.[25] The reason why there is no thirteenth-century thinker to be found who defended the theory of "double truth" is that Tempier "invented" this "doctrine that never existed."[26] And what about the other 68 theses of which there is no evidence that any thirteenth-century master ever espoused them? Here too, de Libera maintains that Tempier made them up, and indeed not in an arbitrary fashion, but rather in accordance with the "latent logic"[27] inherent in the kind of philosophy that was developing at the Parisian arts faculty at the time. De Libera also questions the hypothesis that, due to the haste with which the Condemnation was drawn up, the 219 propositions are listed in a totally chaotic manner, so that, in order to become intelligible, they need to be rearranged (which is what Roland Hissette did in his own study, following the example of Pierre Mandonnet). In marked contrast with this common assumption, he speaks of the "system" formed by the condemned theses.[28] According to de Libera, the nature of the system we are dealing with in the 219 propositions is a "declericalized Arabism,"[29] that is to say, a renaissance of the ancient ideal of a philosophical life, as it was transmitted to the Latins through Arabic philosophers, especially through Averroës.

If the Condemnation is interpreted along these lines, thesis 40 becomes the central element of the philosophical project "invented" by Bishop Tempier: "That there is no more excellent state [in life] than to devote oneself to philosophy." That had indeed been the opinion of the ancient philosophers, for whom philosophy was not just the acquisition of useful knowledge and of insights into the structure of the world, but rather a path–and indeed the only path—to happiness.[30] "'Η γὰρ νοῦ ἐνέργεια ζωή," Aristotle declares in the *Metaphysics*, "the activity of the intellect is life."[31] He makes this statement in a discussion of the self-thinking thought of the Unmoved Mover, who is the paradigm of life. All other kinds of life—nonintellectual kinds—fall short of this ideal. As we have already seen, the message of the Gospels challenged the intellectualism of the Greeks and eventually overthrew it: "Has not God made foolish the wisdom of the world?" The Christian faith requires a "linear" movement in which the soul opens itself to grace; reflection[32] can, at the most, play an ancillary role in this movement, but it cannot constitute its essence. Viewed in this light, the strategy adopted by the heterodox Aristotelians of the Parisian arts faculty, namely to expound Aristotle's writings according to their own internal logic, abstracting from the problem of their compatibility with the Christian faith, could not but pose a serious threat to Christianity. For, this strategy involved a reconstruction of the Greek ideal of philosophy as a way of life. It is significant to note that thinkers such as Siger of Brabant and Boethius of Dacia (who remained personally committed to their faith) opted to remain masters in the arts faculty, contrary to the Scholastic proverb that "there is no point in growing old in the arts" *(non est consenescendum in artibus)*. Thus, these "artists" *(artistae)* do indeed seem to have made philosophy their way of life.

It is in this light of a renaissance of the Greek ideal of philosophy as a way of life that, according to de Libera, we have to consider the propositions which deal with sexual ethics. Analyzed more closely, these theses do not, in fact, advocate lawlessness and excess. On the contrary; de Libera speaks of a "renaissance of philosophical asceticism."[33] When, for instance, thesis 181 claims that chastity (understood as a comportment required of ordained and religious people) is not morally superior to lay abstinence, it is obviously not advocating immoral behavior; on the other hand, this thesis does defend a secular ethics of Greek (and Arabic) inspiration. Similarly, propositions 168 (continence is not essentially virtuous), 169 (complete abstinence in sexual matters destroys both virtue and the human race), and 172 (the pleasure resulting from sexual activity does not necessarily impinge upon the ability to think) are in keeping with an Aristotelian ethics of moderation, according to which virtuous comportment in sexual and other matters consists in avoiding extremes, both of excess *and* of abstinence. Thesis 166, on the "sin against nature," and 183, on "simple fornication," mark a similar return to an Aristotelian, pre-Christian ethics. As far as the most explicitly anti-Christian propositions are concerned (for example, 174, 175, 179, and 180), they represent nothing but the logical consequence of this return to paganism; if philosophy is the way leading to happiness, and if the lifestyle advocated by Aristotle is superior to the Christian way of life embodied, above all, in the monastic communities, then indeed there is little room left for the Christian faith.

However, let us repeat again that no one in the Parisian arts faculty seems to have drawn these radical consequences of what, on the face of it, was merely the desire for an exact and faithful, nonsyncretic exegesis of Aristotle. Thus, Bishop Tempier, in explicitating the implications of Siger's and Boethius's Aristotelianism, paradoxically "contributed to bringing into existence something that did not yet exist"[34]; in other words, it was, in a sense, he himself who created "errors yet to come" and, in this fashion, "accelerated the trouble."[35] The Condemnation of 1277 was not aimed at an already existing non-Christian intellectualism of Greco-Arabic inspiration; it helped formulate its system. Already in the next century, the next steps in the development of this system were to be taken by Dante and Meister Eckhart.

We now know the "other" of Scholastic culture, over against which it explicitly defined itself through Bishop Tempier's Condemnation. The "other" of Scholastic culture is Greek intellectualism–the belief in philosophy as a way of life, in the primacy of reason and reflection, and in a lay ethics of moderation. The element of intellectualism especially played an important role in the transformation of the Scholastic episteme that led to modernity.

The Transformation of the Scholastic Episteme: Heinrich Kramer's *Malleus Maleficarum*

In 1487, some two hundred years after St. Thomas's death, there appeared in Strasbourg a work entitled *Malleus maleficarum,* or "Witch Hammer." Its author, Heinrich Kramer, was a member of the Dominican order, like Thomas himself.[36] Unlike Thomas's works, however, the *Witch Hammer* does not make for edifying reading—for the *Malleus* ushers in "the bloody age of witch-hunting."[37]

In popular imagination, the witch-hunt has always been associated with the "dark" and "superstitious" Middle Ages. That the "Middle Ages were practically free from witches"[38]; that, in reality, the witch-hunt did not start before around 1430, in the twilight years of the medieval period;[39] and that it culminated in the sixteenth and seventeenth centuries, that is to say, in the ages of the Renaissance, humanism, and the Reformation: these are perplexing truths. So is there no connection at all between the Middle

Ages and the witch-hunt? And why is the modern age—the age of reason—inaugurated by blind intolerance and madness? In this section, I shall
argue that indeed there exists a connection between Scholasticism and the
witch-hunt, but also between the witch-hunt and modernity. I shall argue
it is a transformation of the Scholastic episteme which made the witch-
hunt possible, and that modernity is to be understood as the reaction to
this transformation.

Günter Jerouschek, the recent editor and commentator of the *Malleus
maleficarum,* has called the work a "'summa diabolica,' the monstrous counterpart of St. Thomas's magnum opus."[40] The unlikely comparison of this
manual of witch-hunting with the *Summa theologiae* is not so preposterous
as it might seem. While Aquinas's intention in his *Summa* was to provide a
complete and systematic survey of Christian theology, the *Malleus maleficarum* represents a complete and systematic survey of witchcraft, which it
covers in three parts.[41] Part I lays the theological foundations of the belief
in witches and witchcraft, falling into eighteen questions. This starts with
the most basic one, "whether to assert that there are witches is so Catholic
that to pertinaciously defend the opposite is totally heretical."[42] Each of
the questions is discussed in the traditional Scholastic manner, that is to say,
according to the *quaestio* structure of arguments and counterarguments, author's solution, and final analysis of the original arguments. Among the authorities that Kramer adduces in favor of his positions, Scripture and St.
Thomas (often referred to as *Doctor*) figure prominently, but there are also
citations from Aristotle, Ptolemy, Augustine, the Pseudo-Dionysius, the
Gloss, Avicenna, and many others. Thus, with regard to its composition, this
first part of the *Malleus* is a typical product of Scholasticism. Part II turns
to more "practical" problems, namely, the kinds of witches and the effects
of witchcraft, as well as immunity from witchcraft and remedies for it. All
the different sorts of witches, according to Kramer, have the common
characteristic that they engage in sex with the devil or with demons representing him: *spurcicias carnales cum demonibus exercere.*[43] The worst witches
are capable of a wide range of evil deeds: they devour children, cause thun-
der and hail, bring about infertility in humans and animals, vow children
to the devil, and scare horses so that they throw off their riders. They can
fly, predict future events, remain silent even under torture, kill people by
means of the evil eye, cause impotence, and wreak havoc in numerous
other ways.[44] Other, less powerful kinds of witches are more limited in the
ways they express their malice. As for the question of immunity from
witchcraft and remedies for it, it is interesting to note that Kramer pro-
nounces the inquisitors themselves immune to witchcraft,[45] while the only

effective protection against the most pernicious deeds of the witches is *ut per suos iudices de medio tollantur* ("that they be removed from our midst by their judges") or at least punished.[46] Other forms of remedy, such as pilgrimages, confession, prayer, and exorcism are effective especially with regard to certain sexual effects of witchcraft (for example, the disappearance of the male organ), and with regard to sickness, hail, and excessive hatred or love. The 24 chapters of Part II are written in the form of a treatise, but each of the two main sections of Part II (on the effects of witchcraft and remedies for it, respectively) is introduced by a question that follows the traditional Scholastic format. Kramer knows the Scholastic method of reconciling opposing opinions by means of distinctions very well. After citing Augustine, Albert the Great, Aquinas, Bonaventure, Duns Scotus, and other authorities on the question of the legitimate means of removing spells, he declares at the beginning of his own solution:

> As it is expedient that such outstanding doctors be concordant *(concordare)* in their teachings as far as that is possible, and as this can be accomplished by means of a single distinction, hence it is to be noted that . . .[47]

Part III of the *Malleus maleficarum* deals with the procedural details that, according to Kramer, should govern the trials against people accused of witchcraft. It includes several questions on torture, also detailing the principles of sentencing. This part begins with a fundamental question discussed in the Scholastic mode, which is followed by 35 questions answered in treatise form. We shall examine some of its content more closely later. However, we must return to the issue of the "Scholastic" nature of the *Witch Hammer.*

The fact that parts of the *Malleus* are argued in the Scholastic *quaestio* form, that the purpose of the work is to present a summa of witches and their eradication, and that Heinrich Kramer was, like St. Thomas, a member of the Dominican order, connect the work with the Scholastic tradition in a rather tenuous fashion. Is there any more conclusive evidence to back up Günter Jerouschek's claim that the *Malleus maleficarum* represents the "monstrous counterpart" of the *Summa theologiae?* Or, more precisely, that the witch-hunt is the "other" of Scholastic thought—this time not in the sense of what it rejected, but in the sense of an internal perversion that turned the Scholastic project into its opposite? According to the Louvain medievalist Jos Decorte, the connection between Scholasticism and the witch-hunt is indeed more than accidental. In his work, *De waanzin van het intellect* ("The Madness of the Intellect"), Decorte argues that the witch-hunt brings out the madness into which Scholastic rationality turned when it absolutized itself, thus becoming totalitarian. Following Decorte, every kind of rationality becomes its "other," madness, not through a complete transformation of its structure, but rather through a rigidification of that structure, a "closure." In *De waanzin van het intellect,* Decorte explains:

> Rationality turns mad *(waanzinnig)* . . . when in one way or another it undermines itself and thus, in the long run, becomes self-destructive, and when it becomes a system revolving upon itself that is immune to all counterevidence. The refusal of counter-evidence, through which rationality becomes a self-enclosed totalitarian system, is a first step in the process of absolutization which will, in the long run, inescapably lead to self-undermining. Paradoxically enough, a [system of] rationality seems to destroy itself by desiring to protect itself (absolutization).[48]

Decorte's point with regard to the Scholastic thought is, again, that the episteme based upon the concept of similitude,[49] which proved so fruitful during the golden age of Scholasticism, transformed itself into monstrous madness when it closed itself to all elements of criticism and limitation.

That the demonology underlying the witch-hunt obeys the laws of similitude is not difficult to show. In fact, the world of evil, of the devil, demons, and witches is an antinature, or order of things "other" than the one instituted by God, which remains perfectly parallel to nature itself;[50] hence, for example, the idea that witches swear allegiance to the devil in a kind of antibaptism.[51] As the witch is the sign of the presence of evil in this world, she enters into the dynamism of *convenientia, aemulatio, analogia,* and *sympathia:* the witch emulates the devil, attempting, in analogy to him, to replace the order of the world with the anti-order of evil. We remember that, according to Foucault's analysis, *sympathia* is at the root of all similitude, being defined as "an instance of the Same" which assimilates things, mingles them together, and destroys their identity. Decorte applies the concept of sympathy as the root-power of all similarity to the relationship between the witch and the devil, using it to elucidate why the idea of a sexual union between the witch and the devil (or his demons) appears to be so central to the ideology of the witch-hunt. We already know that for Kramer, *spurcicias carnales cum demonibus exercere* ("to engage in acts of carnal filthiness with the demons") is the common characteristic of all witches. According to Decorte, the coital union most palpably symbolizes the oneness of the witch and the devil, that is to say, their *sym-*

pathia, which is at the root of the witch's furthering of the anti-order of evil.[52]

If the conceptualization of witches and witchcraft is in accordance with the basic laws of the Scholastic episteme, wherein lies the difference between Scholastic rationality and the madness of the witch-hunt? It lies in the perfectly circular, self-enclosed logic of the witch-hunt, its exclusion of any "otherness" that could enfeeble its system. Let us examine an example taken from the *Malleus maleficarum.*

According to the rules of the Inquisition, no witch could be sentenced to death without a confession.[53] Other people's accusations and independent evidence did not suffice. At this point, we should note that there were people during the period of the witch-hunt who did practice witchcraft; in the words of Brian P. Levack: "when writers and judicial authorities tried to wipe out witchcraft, they were not dealing with an entirely fabricated threat."[54] However, given the nature of the acts that often gave rise to accusations, many "witches" were obviously innocent and thus refused to confess. Kramer relates, for example, the following case, which he says occurred in the German town of Speyer (the *Malleus* is peppered with many "real-life" stories of the deeds, arrest, trial, and torture of witches).[55] An "honest man" is accosted by a prostitute who suggests to sell him "a certain thing." He refuses, whereupon the prostitute shouts after him: "Shortly you will wish to have agreed!" Angrily, the honest man turns around to look at the woman, but as he does, he suffers a "horrible deformation" of his face. For Kramer, it is obvious that this contortion, which takes a while to disappear, is the result of witchery. He does not discuss the case any further, but no doubt the prostitute was arrested and accused of witchcraft. According to the rules of the trial, she had to confess her alliance with the devil in order to be convicted. As that would mean death, the accused people were obviously reluctant to confess their real or imagined misdeeds. Therefore, torture constituted an integral part of the trial. The *Malleus maleficarum* contains a circumstantial description of the brutal, humiliating, and deceitful methods employed by the inquisitors in torturing their victims.[56] Hardly anything was considered out of bounds in this combat with the devil. However, worse still is the fact that the circular, self-enclosed logic of the witch-hunt made it extremely difficult not to confess, even for the most steadfast victims determined not to be broken by the horrific methods of torture. Thus, according to Brian P. Levack, well over 50 percent of witch-trials ended in the victim's execution.[57] Why was it so difficult not to confess? Because according to the logic of the Inquisition, denying the crime did not indicate innocence, but rather betokened

the *maleficium taciturnitatis,* that is to say, silence as the result of special succor granted by the devil only to his most committed followers:

> [With regard to his less committed followers,] the devil relinquishes them in
> any case, even if he is not forced by an holy angel, which is why they con-
> fess their crimes more easily. On the other hand, those others who adhered
> to him as with their mouths, so even more with their hearts, are defended
> by him with might and main and hardened into the crime of taciturnity
> *(maleficium taciturnitatis).*[58]

The logic at work in this extract is that of a catch–22. If the victim con-
fesses, as a result of torture or out of fear of the expected sufferings, she is
guilty and will be sentenced to burn at the stake. If, however, she denies
her involvement with Satan, she represents a particularly dangerous species
of witches, whose confession must be obtained by even more gruesome
methods of torture.

In the passage from *De waanzin van het intellect* cited earlier, Decorte
identifies the refusal of counterevidence as the first step toward the absolutization and, eventually, self-destruction of a system of thought. The refusal to accept counterevidence seems, on the face of it, to strengthen the
system, rendering it virtually unassailable. The logic of the "same" becomes
so strong that any "otherness" contradicting it is excluded. In terms of the
witch-hunt, the concept of *maleficium taciturnitatis* is designed to ensure that
there is no escape for the "other" of evil and witchcraft once the trial has
started. Ironically, the purpose of the system—*ut per suos iudices de medio tollantur* ("that they [the witches] be removed from our midst by their
judges")—comes to be served so well that the system undermines itself, by
producing evil in the very process of fighting for the good. This dynamism
shows that the "same" will not work without the "other"; hence, the elimination of the "other" from the sphere of the "same" will inescapably lead
to a return of the "other" within the same, or in the guise of the same.

The existence of evil in the world has always constituted one of the
most serious challenges to Christian life and thought. As we have seen in
the previous study, for Aquinas to do evil, or to sin, means to act against
one's own conscience, that is to say, against the innermost core of one's
own being. This split *within* the human being, this division of the self
against itself, is at the same time a split *outside* the human being, that is to
say, a division between the sinner and God. But what is it that causes this
split? Why would anyone ever sin, if sinning is directed as much against the
self as against God? Since apostolic times, Christians have been forced to

acknowledge the obscure nature of sin, its opacity, its otherness. In the Letter to the Romans, St. Paul describes the inner "war" of the human being against itself in a well-known passage:

> I do not understand my own actions. For I do not do what I want, but I do the very thing I hate.
> Now if I do what I do not want, I agree that the law is good.
> So then it is no longer I that do it, but sin which dwells within me.
> For I know that nothing good dwells within me, that is, in my flesh. I can will what is right, but I cannot do it.
> For I do not do the good I want, but the evil I do not want is what I do.
> Now if I do what I do not want, it is no longer I that do it, but sin which dwells within me.
> So I find it to be a law that when I want to do right, evil lies close at hand.
> For I delight in the law of God, in my inmost self,
> but I see in my members another law at war with the law of my mind and making me captive to the law of sin which dwells in my members.
> Wretched man that I am! (Rom. 7:15–24)

"Evil lies close at hand," St. Paul recognizes; it dwells right within him, so that he no longer understands himself. In this passage, evil is conceived of both as the "other" that threatens human existence, and as the "proximate" that is inextricably connected with that existence.

In the witch-hunt, the construction of the otherness of evil undergoes marked changes by comparison with the Pauline conception. Whereas St. Paul recognizes the presence of the split between good and evil within his own person, the inquisitors pronounce themselves free from the threat of witchcraft: "There are three kinds of people," Heinrich Kramer writes in the *Malleus,* "who are so favored by God that this most horrible race [of witches] cannot harm them through its witchery; the first are those who exercise public jurisdiction against them or who work diligently *(insistunt)* against them in some public office."[59] Thus, Kramer draws a clear line between groups of good and groups of evil people, so that the distinction can become a matter of "us" against "them." The whole trial is dominated by the idea that the witches must confess, that is to say, bring their real or imagined evil deeds into the open, so that nothing remains hidden and opaque. The inquisitors aim at a precise identification of evil, with the intention to root it out utterly.

Against this background, it is not a coincidence what kind of people fell victim to the witch-hunt most frequently. The title of the *Malleus maleficarum* already indicates this group: women. For *maleficarum* is the genitive plural of the *feminine* word for "witch": *malefica*. Kramer explains:

> With regard to the first point, why in the weaker sex of women a larger number of witches is to be found than amongst men, it is not expedient to deduce arguments for the contrary, as apart from the testimony of words and trustworthy men experience itself renders this claim worthy of credit.[60]

It is no surprise, then, that 75 to 90 percent of the people prosecuted for witchcraft were women.[61] Of course, Christianity has always been characterized by tendencies to associate evil and sin with women; nevertheless, Günter Jerouschek notes that these misogynist tendencies are brought to a rare point of culmination and systematization in the *Malleus*.[62] In a society of males dominated by the ideal of sexual abstinence and the constant fear of sin, women could very easily come to symbolize the threat of temptation and, indeed, of evil itself.[63] That the witches were to be undressed and shaved before being tortured gives the trial a perverse twist.[64]

Another point will throw into even higher relief the Inquisition's desire to eliminate the "otherness" of evil by targeting cultural symbols of that otherness. For, it was not mainstream women who usually fell victim to the witch-hunt. Older women, sometimes ugly, often unmarried, eccentric or acerbic, or with a history of social and sexual deviance, were most likely to find themselves accused of witchcraft. Levack writes that, "[i]f we need one word to describe the witch of the early modern period, we might refer to her as a non-conformist."[65]

To sum up, the witch-hunt can be characterized as resulting from a perverse transformation of the Scholastic episteme. Based upon the Scholastic concept of similitude, sometimes even employing the typical Scholastic methods of argumentation and literary genres, the witch-hunt constructs a rationality whose principal danger lies in its closure to all elements of otherness. Thus, Heinrich Kramer in his *Malleus maleficarum* devises strategies to forestall the possibility of counterevidence. Furthermore, the whole witch-hunt is animated by a systematic attempt to remove the otherness of evil from human life. This metaphysical or theological otherness, elusive as it is, comes to be identified with the culturally marginal group of nonconformist women. Of course, we must not forget that witchcraft existed and was practiced in the early modern period. Yet the brutal, perverse, and fanatical excrescences of the witch-hunt demonstrate the fearful effects that occur when a rational system turns totalitarian. Rationality itself, alas, contains the germs of insanity.[66]

Reason Absolutized: Further Examples

The witch-hunt is not the only phenomenon in which we witness a process of "closure" or absolutization of rationality in the early modern period. Other examples of this process are to be found in the literary form that philosophico-theological discourse takes in the early modern age, in the doctrine of the univocity of being, and in the rise and abuse of indulgences. These three phenomena will briefly be discussed in the following pages.

The Demise of the Quaestio

The *quaestio* is, as we know, the Scholastic literary genre par excellence. Its dialectical structure of arguments and counterarguments, solution, and return to the original arguments reflects one of the central methods of teaching practiced at the medieval university, namely, the disputation. The goal of the *quaestio* is the reconciliation of opposing authorities, or points of view, through distinctions; and its spirit is one of the greatest possible intellectual openness. It is clear that the *quaestio* does not, as such, constitute an infallible safeguard against doctrinal aberrations. Indeed, we have seen Heinrich Kramer use the form of the *quaestio* in his theoretical justification of the witch-hunt. It is perhaps no coincidence, however, that the *Malleus maleficarum* abandons the *quaestio* form in its most perverse parts, which deal with the trial and torture of witches. For, the traditional *quaestio* always takes its starting point in the opinions of authorities, such as Scripture, the fathers of the church, philosophers, and so forth. But there was no precedent in this tradition for the aberrations of the witch-hunt.

Characteristically, in the transition from the Middle Ages to the modern age the literary form employed not only by professedly antitraditional thinkers such as Descartes, but even by representatives of the so-called "silver age" of Scholasticism changes radically. Francisco Suárez (1548–1617), in his *Metaphysical Disputations,* which proved extremely influential in shaping Thomism for many centuries to come, abandons the *quaestio* form.[67] He still quite frequently develops his argumentation upon the basis of authoritative opinions, whose merits and demerits he considers, yet paradoxically the so-called "*Metaphysical Disputations*" are no longer formally structured like Scholastic disputations, or *quaestiones.* Very often, Suárez abandons even his own reduced form of "disputation," presenting his ideas in the form of a modern textbook. Does this matter? Very much so, according to the German philosopher Christiane

Schildknecht. In an excellent article on literary form in Descartes (1596–1650), she argues that there exists an intrinsic connection between the monological form of such Cartesian works as the *Meditations* and the *Discours,* on the one hand, and the foundation of Descartes's philosophy in an autonomous subject, on the other.[68] In her incisive analysis, Schildknecht draws attention to the fact that in Descartes's one dialogical work, *Recherche de la vérité* (which has, significantly, remained a fragment), opinions are merely juxtaposed; there is no evidence of genuine discussion leading to a more complete discovery of the truth through a "collective" effort. Schildknecht concludes, then, that there is indeed a "systematic connection between form and content"[69] to be found in Descartes's oeuvre—and, we may add, generally in the development and transformation of forms of thought, or *epistemai.* The "appropriate" form for Scholastic thought, which is a collective, open-ended quest for an ultimately transcendent truth, is the *quaestio.* The abandonment of the *quaestio* in favor of the textbook, as in Suárez's case (or the meditation, as in the case of Descartes), symbolizes the birth of the modern subject, with its characteristics of autonomy and self-sufficiency.[70]

The Univocity of Being

A second phenomenon testifying to the transformation of the Scholastic episteme at the dawn of modernity is the development of the doctrine of the univocity of being. As we discovered in the previous study, St. Thomas Aquinas, in his thought, is anxious to maintain a careful balance between positive and negative theology. The dialectical relationship between the two theologies is verified on the ontological level as much as in epistemology and ethics. Ontologically speaking, God is the *veritas rei* of every created being: its self, its own innermost truth, which is nevertheless infinitely "other." Epistemologically, this dialectics translates into the paradox that God speaks in us, that we can know Him, and that nonetheless He remains incomprehensible even in the beatific vision. Finally, on the ethical terrain, our inalienable adherence to the Good that is God, is often distorted by our failure to see what the good amounts to in particular situations. In ethics, this tension is to a certain extent reconciled in Aquinas's teaching on conscience, for someone who follows his or her conscience (after efforts to educate it) does not sin, even if that person acts in a way that disaccords with the objective moral law.

On the ontological level, Aquinas attempts to reconcile positive and negative theology in his doctrine on analogy, which has not been discussed so far. Analogy essentially means that the relationship between God's being and created being is such that they are neither entirely the same nor entirely different. In his commentary on the *Book of Sentences*, St. Thomas explains:

> There are three kinds of agent cause. Namely, a [kind of] cause which acts equivocally *(causam aequivoce agentem)*, and this [kind of causality] obtains when the effect does not agree *(non convenit)* with its cause in either name or definition: the sun, for example, which is not hot [according to medieval astronomy], creates heat. Also, there is a [kind of] cause which acts univocally *(causam univoce agentem)*, when the effect agrees with its cause in name and definition, as, for instance, human begets human or heat creates heat. God acts in neither of these ways. Not univocally, because nothing agrees univocally with Him. Not equivocally, because the effect and the [divine] cause somehow agree in name and definition according to priority and posteriority *(secundum prius et posterius)*; as, for instance, God makes us wise through His wisdom, in such a way that our wisdom always falls short of the definition *(ratio)* of His wisdom, as the accident [falls short] of the definition *(ratio)* of being insofar as it is in the substance. Hence, there is a third mode of cause, which acts analogically *(tertius modus causae agentis analogice)*. Hence, it appears that the divine being *(esse)* produces the being of creation in imperfect likeness to itself *(in similitudine sui imperfecta)*: and thus the divine being is said to be the being of all things *(esse omnium rerum)*, from which all created being flows as from its efficient and exemplary cause *(effective et exemplariter manat)*.[71]

As being belongs to both the Creator and creation, there obtains some kind of similitude between them. However, as God is the creator of the finite world, He possesses being primordially, whereas creation *is* only in a derivative sense. Therefore, being is not quite the same in the case of God as it is in the case of creation. Thomas's doctrine on analogy is ultimately nothing more than a way of expressing the identity and difference that hold God and creation together, while at the same time separating them.

In Suárez's metaphysics, Thomas's analogy of being is given up in favor of univocity. It is Jean-Luc Marion who has identified the considerations that proved decisive for Suárez's revision of the original Thomistic theory.[72] Amongst created beings, we find a difference between necessary facts that could not possibly be different, and things and facts that are merely contingent. For instance, that God created the particular soul of such and such a person is a contingent event; however, that a human being is a "rational animal," or that $2 + 2 = 4$, or that the whole is always greater than its parts taken severally—all these facts are necessarily so. How, Suárez asks, is this important difference reflected in the way God creates contingent beings, on the one hand, and necessary ones, on the other? Answer: these necessities are necessary even in the divine mind, from which they do not derive. God creates in accordance with certain logical rules that are represented in His mind, without owing to it their necessity. God does not have to create this human being, or even human beings as such (contingency); but *if* He creates human beings, they have to be "rational animals," in virtue of the intrinsic properties of the essence of human represented in the divine mind (necessity).

It is this theory of the relationship between God and the logically necessary that, according to Marion, leads Suárez to his doctrine of the *conceptum objectivum entis ut sic* ("the objective concept of being as such"). According to Marion, this doctrine is characterized by an "internal contradiction that renders it unthinkable,"[73] because it attempts to reconcile too many contradictory elements. Meant to be part of a theory of the analogy of being, the *conceptum objectivum entis ut sic* undermines this theory from within, positing as it does a concept of being that can be predicated of God and creation univocally. Suárez himself admits as much in a famous text in the *Disputationes metaphysicae* 2.2.36.[74] In fact, the *conceptum objectivum entis ut sic* denies the fundamental difference between the being of creation and God's being, regarding both as being captured in the same *conceptum*. The connection between this idea and that of the representation of the logical necessities in the divine mind is clear: God is not the ultimate end[75] of all human understanding, but is himself subject to necessity, and subsumable under the general concept of being. Again we see a totalizing rationality triumph over the opacity of the "other."

From Grace to Economics—the Indulgences

In order to understand the nature of indulgences and their importance in the process of the absolutization of reason, whose history we are attempting to trace, it is necessary to examine briefly the development of the sacrament of penance.[76] In the primitive church, sin was viewed as excluding the sinner from the saving community of the church, that is to say, as ex-communication. For the excommunicated individual to be received back into the church, it was considered indispensable that he or she performed works of penance commensurate with the seriousness of the transgression against God. Reconciliation with the community could thus not take place before the sinner had, through penance, reconciled him- or herself with God. These two aspects (reconciliation with the community and with God) were very closely connected. The community was intimately involved in the process of penance itself, not only through the public character of the sinner's confession, but also because the community would, through prayer, assist the penitent in his or her efforts toward reconciliation with God. In this assistance, the prayers of the priests were regarded as playing a particularly important role, due to their special closeness to God. However, the priests' prayers always remained supplications; they never functioned, in the early church, as authoritative acts through which sins were ipso facto forgiven. Rather, the forgiveness of sins consisted in the reconciliation with the community, which, in turn, presupposed reconciliation with God through penance.[77]

In the early Middle Ages, from the ninth century onward, the sacrament of penance underwent a series of transformations, which resulted in the appearance of the absolution (absolutio). First, the confession of sins became a private act taking place between the sinner and a priest. As a consequence, there no longer occurred a public exclusion of the sinner from the community, which is why the public act of reconciliation also lost its function. It is in this context that the prayers of the priests gradually grew in importance. The role of the priest in penance now came to be viewed as directly effecting the forgiveness of sins—not through supplications addressed to God, nor through the reintegration of the sinner into the community, but rather through an authoritative act: the absolution. At the beginning, absolutions remained "deprecative" in form, that is to say, they retained something of the character of supplications entreating God to forgive the sinner. Indeed, the performative formula, *Ego te absolvo* (I absolve you), spoken by the priest, is not attested before 1439.[78] The transformation of confession into a private act, as well as the appearance of the absolution, are accompanied by a third element of change, namely, the combination of confession and reconciliation/absolution in one rite. We have seen that in the early church, the sinner's confession of his or her sins to the community was followed by acts of penance, after the performance of which the penitent could be received back into the community. Now, on the other hand, the priest would pronounce the absolution immediately after the confession. In this way, the actual acts of penance were not made superfluous, as the absolution remained conditional upon their performance. Nonetheless, the immediate granting of the absolution could not but diminish the importance of the atonement.

We must view the indulgences against the backdrop of the developments just sketched out. In essence, they did nothing but further emphasize the authority of the church and its representatives to forgive sins, while at the same time continuing previous tendencies to reduce the importance of penance as a necessary precondition for reconciliation with God. For, in the indulgence, the church assured the sinner not only, as in an ordinary absolution, that his or her sins were forgiven, but granted this forgiveness without acts of penance, while at the same time waiving all further temporal punishments in the hereafter. In other words, the indulgence forgave the sinner, freed him or her from the obligation to do penance, and—speaking for God, as it were—included a guarantee that the recipient would not be subject to any further punishments in purgatory.[79] (In earlier times, the possibility that the penance done here on earth might not entirely satisfy God, so that complete forgiveness might necessitate a certain time spent in purgatory, had never been excluded.) We must note that the characterization of the indulgence just proffered only applies to the fully developed practice.

Originally, indulgences were granted for exceptional acts of piety or commitment to God and the church. The German theologian Bernhard Poschmann traces the appearance of the first indulgences to the eleventh century.[80] In the course of the twelfth century, they became more frequent, though usually remained partial—that is to say, they did not altogether free their recipients from the obligation to do penance, but rather reduced the amount of penance necessary to achieve reconciliation. Thus, giving alms or visiting a certain church could lead to a reduction in the number of days of fasting that had been prescribed as penance for some transgression. The indulgences granted to the Crusaders for their outstanding valor and commitment were the first ones to be "complete" *(indulgentia plenaria)*. Nevertheless, even these indulgences (first issued by Pope Alexander II in 1063) did not yet extend their jurisdiction to possible punishments in the hereafter.[81] This last step was taken only in the thirteenth century, when Schoolmen such as Albert the Great and Thomas Aquinas developed elaborate theological justifications for the practice of granting indulgences.[82] In fact, Thomas was a particularly avid advocate of indulgences, taking "the new theory to radical consequences," as Herbert Vorgrimler remarks.[83]

I think the meaning of the indulgences in the context of our present discussion has become sufficiently clear. Like absolutions, they forgive sins authoritatively, rather than constituting mere prayers of supplication. Thus, the function to forgive the sinner is "taken away" from God, as it were, instead being vested in the church. Unlike absolutions, the indulgences make the forgiving of sins possible without the sinner's having acquitted himself or herself of the penance prescribed by the confessor; other works—such as giving alms, pilgrimage, participating in a Crusade—can substitute for it. Finally, the indulgences guarantee that there will be no further punishment in the hereafter. Their tendency, then, is to make God's will subject to human jurisdiction—in analogy to Suárez's *conceptum objectivum entis ut sic*, which subsumes God under a human concept.

Critical voices concerning the indulgences existed as early as the twelfth century. Peter Abelard rejected the practice of granting indulgences in his *Ethics*, composed between 1125 and 1138.[84] Later on, as we have already seen, the developing theology of the indulgences defended their status. However, the "serious abuse"[85] that accompanied the practice since its very beginnings, especially the unscrupulous selling of indulgences by corrupt ecclesiastics, continued to draw criticism.

The indulgence trade debased divine grace and forgiveness by making them available for purchase. Thus, the transcendent God was represented as being part of the economic order. The indulgence trade practiced by Archbishop Alrecht of Brandenburg gave rise to the first great controversy in which Martin Luther became involved. Indeed, the issues of penance and indulgences formed the major focus of the famous Ninety-five Theses the reformer nailed onto the door of the castle church of Wittenberg on October 31, 1517. As the German Luther scholar Bernhard Lohse notes, "Luther did not reject every use of indulgences, but rather limited their efficacy to the remission of temporal punishments imposed by the church."[86] In other words, the Reformation started as a movement to defend God's freedom and transcendence, which the theory and practice of the indulgences had more and more come to limit. In fact, Luther himself characterized his entire work as pursuing one principal goal: "to let God be God."[87] It is well known, too, that there is a negative theology at the heart of Luther's thought; Luther believed God to be *absconditus sub contrario*, "hidden under contradiction."[88]

Modernity: The "Other" of Scholasticism or Its Transformed Revival?

Luther's criticism of the indulgences and his negative theology lead us to a final consideration, with which we will conclude this study. The thinkers of modernity are frequently presented as having radically broken with the tradition of medieval thought and culture. Indeed, this conception is so deeply rooted and widespread that it is institutionalized in our curricula for higher education. Many philosophy departments, for instance, do not teach medieval thought at all, rather envisioning modernity as a continuation of the great philosophical debates of antiquity. According to this view, the Middle Ages, a period of intellectual and cultural darkness, have little or nothing to contribute to our understanding of the modern age. In truth, some declarations of thinkers who played key roles in the creation of the modern project seem to support this interpretation. Does Descartes not claim an absolute novelty for his thought when he uses phrases such as "no one before me" *(nemo ante me)*, or "by no one before me" *(a nemine ante me)*?[89] Is Luther not the author of an acerbic *Disputation against Scholastic Theology*?[90]

But then again, we must ask the critical question as to what precisely modern "reformers" such as Luther in theology and Descartes in philosophy were reacting to: against the basic assumptions of Scholastic thought, or rather against the transformed version of Scholasticism with which they came to be acquainted through its contemporary representatives? With regard to Descartes, Jean-Luc Marion has attempted to answer this question in his magisterial study, *Sur la théologie blanche de Descartes.*[91] Marion argues that Descartes's "new" philosophy developed from the desire to restore the sense of divine freedom and transcendence which had come to be menaced by Suárez's transformation of the Scholastic doctrine of analogy into a doctrine of univocity. Descartes's project, then, would bear some fundamental similarity with Luther's theological concerns. In his interpretation of Descartes's oeuvre, Marion takes as his starting point the doctrine of the "creation of the eternal truths" that Descartes first developed in 1630, in his correspondence with Father Marin Mersenne.[92] According to this doctrine, the same eternal truths that Suárez had declared to be of equal validity in God's mind as in ours are mere creations, and as such totally subject to God's will. That $1 + 2 = 3$, that the angles of a triangle add up to 180°, that all the radii of a circle are equal, or that a human being is a "rational animal"—all this God could have ordained differently.[93] The reason why Descartes introduces such a radical discontinuity between God and creation is clear: he wants to safeguard the divine transcendence.[94] Paradoxically, however—this is what Marion argues in *Sur la théologie blanche de Descartes*—it is precisely Descartes's desire to return to the insights of negative theology which had always played a central role in traditional Christian thought, that removes him from the Scholastic tradition. For, Descartes simply inverted Suárez's position concerning the eternal truths, without challenging the presupposition that these truths are exterior to God. Following Suárez, the eternal truths are in God's mind only as representations, possessing an intrinsic validity not derived from God; following Descartes, they are created by God arbitrarily, that is to say, they also remain exterior to God, albeit in a different way. This radical departure from the Scholastico-Thomistic position, according to which God *is* the innermost truth of creation, leads Descartes to the question that has never ceased to preoccupy and trouble modernity: How can human knowledge be founded, and its validity guaranteed? Where can the truth be "anchored," if it is not God Himself? As one knows, the Cartesian answer to this problem is the *ego cogito*. Once I have indubitably ascertained my own existence (I can doubt everything, but not that fact that I am doubting; hence I exist), I can deduce the existence of God and of the world from within my own mind. However, as Marion impressively shows in *Sur la théologie blanche de Descartes,* even in the writings of the philosophical father of the modern age, the foundationalist solution to the problem of truth remains internally unstable, undermining itself from within. For while Descartes considers the *ego* as the epistemological foundation of human knowledge (including knowledge of God), the *ego* in turn is ontologically defined as being made in the image and likeness of God.[95] Descartes's attempt to safeguard the divine transcendence without the Scholastic doctrine of analogy leads to an irremediable opposition between the epistemological and ontological aspects of his system.[96]

Is modernity really the radical "other" of the Scholastic episteme? Our brief discussion of Luther and Descartes has yielded a paradoxical answer: the otherness of modernity seems to have been born from a thwarted desire to return to the Middle Ages.

CONCLUSION

It is time for an attempt to pull the threads of the preceding studies together and see what picture of the Scholastic episteme emerges from our analyses.

Using the Nietzschean-Foucauldian model of the dialectical development of the Western tradition, we situated Scholastic thought in this tradition by defining it as the endeavor to reinscribe Greek wisdom (σοφία) back into the center of Christian culture. The first Christians, such as St. Paul, had rejected it from this center, considering Greek intellectualism to be incompatible with the "foolishness" (μωρία) of the Cross. Already during the first Christian centuries, patristic authors started questioning the exclusion of Greek learning. However, due to the loss of large parts of the Greek heritage—in particular, the works of Aristotle—the movement of reinscription that the church fathers initiated could not come to full fruition before the thirteenth century, when contacts with the Islamic and Byzantine cultures rendered Greek thought more fully accessible to the Latin West.

Scholastic thought, understood as the reconciliation of Greek σοφία with Christian μωρία, constitutes a moment in the dialectics of μῦθος and λόγος that, I submit, represents the fundamental structure of the Western tradition.

After situating Scholastic thought in this way in the intellectual history of the West, we went on to analyze the Scholastic episteme in its internal constitution. Taking seriously Foucault's claim that discourse is formed by historical a prioris that open up a certain epistemological field for it, we began our analyses by a consideration of what Olga Weijers has termed Scholastic "intellectual practices." These include such factors as the institutional setting of Scholastic thought (namely, the early university), the curricula structuring this institution, rules of succession for concepts and procedures of intervention used to systematize statements (the disputations and *quaestiones*), the positions assigned to the subject in this epistemological field (monastic subject vs. Scholastic subject), and so forth.

A number of important insights emerged in the course of considering these factors. First, Scholastic culture is thoroughly text-centered. From monasticism, Scholastic thought inherits the conviction that texts, especially Scripture and its commentaries, put us into direct contact with the divine, such that the continued contemplation and, indeed, assimilation of these texts lead to a union with God Himself. "In the beginning was the Word (ὁ λόγος), and the Word was with God, and the Word was God."The central importance of authorities and commentaries upon these authorities in Scholastic thought must be understood against this background. For the Schoolmen, authoritative texts are tools believed to help us decipher the ultimate Text, namely, the Book of Wisdom.

However, the fact that the Book of Wisdom is identified with God locates it in a realm that remains fundamentally inaccessible. Hence the "openness" of Scholastic thought; hence its conviction that the Text is so inexhaustibly rich that there can be no end to human efforts to grasp it more fully. This interminable quest requires that further commentaries must be added relentlessly to the great authoritative texts, especially Scripture, and that the different authorities must be "collected together" carefully, lest valuable facets of meaning be lost.

In the Scholastic episteme, confidence in the powers of human reason (as it manifests itself, for example, in the powerful structure of the disputations and *quaestiones*) and humility in the face of the divine do not contradict each other. Moreover, their dialectical connection is mirrored in other aspects of contemporary culture: in Gothic handwriting, for instance, but also in the design of the High Gothic cathedral.

Our findings concerning the text-centeredness of the Scholastic episteme found confirmation in Foucault's own work. In *The Order of Things,* Foucault depicts the Western episteme up to the end of the sixteenth century as being based upon the concept of similarity—a universal similarity of all things that weaves reality into a texture of signifiers. The whole world thus becomes "prose," as Foucault says, the ultimate interpretation of which eludes us. Foucault does not investigate the metaphysical bases of the pre-seventeenth-century episteme, that is to say, the question of what founds the belief in a cosmos of similarities. These bases lie in a metaphysics of self-reflexivity, according to which beings are held together by a universal resemblance due to the fact that they form a chain of causes and effects, and that the causes communicate themselves to their effects. *Omne agens agit sibi simile,* as St. Thomas Aquinas puts it: "every agent brings about something that resembles it." Moreover, the entire chain is anchored, as it were, in a First Cause. That "every agent brings about something that

resembles it" can be understood only in the context of a metaphysics according to which being is fundamentally self-reflexive, or circular. I have
shown that the circularity and self-reflexivity of being constitutes one of
the most primitive assumptions of the Western intellectual tradition.

However, as Oscar Cullmann has pointed out, the Greek metaphysics
of self-reflexivity stands in sharp contrast to the Christian conception of
time and history as witnessed in the texts of the Old and, especially, the
New Testament. Christian history is not an eternal repetition of the same,
but rather constitutes a teleological order of irrepeatable events leading,
through different steps, to a final solution. The conflict between Greek wisdom and the "foolishness of the Cross" can thus, from another coign of
vantage, be viewed as a conflict between Greek circularity and Christian
linearity. I submit that, when the heritage of Greek thought became fully
accessible to the Latin West in the thirteenth century, the tension between
the "circle" and the "line" was the basic structure underlying the Schoolmen's attempts to reconcile the newly discovered sources with the Christian tradition.

St. Thomas Aquinas in his thought manages to bring Greek self-
reflexivity and Christian linearity together in a convincing synthesis. We
interpreted Aquinas's system as being in close continuity with the dialectical structures of Neoplatonism. Thus, each being constitutes itself only
in a relationship with, and over against, an "other." Each being *(ens)* is an
aliud quid ("an 'other' what"). In this relationship, being both affects its
"other" and is affected by it, such that its pristine identity comes to be inaccessible to it. This is why, according to Aquinas, each being is more "itself" in the divine Word than in the world of causality and "operation."
God, then, is for each being the Other that is the Same, its innermost yet
inaccessible core.

The Thomistic conception thus reconciles self-reflexivity and linearity
in an ingenious way. Each being, in order to be itself, must open itself to
the Other who is God; in other words, it must leave itself behind in a linear movement. However, this linear movement toward the Other is at the
same time nothing but a quest for each being's most authentic self; thus, as
a quest for the self (Same), it is self-reflexive.

Foucault maintains that, in order to understand an episteme, we must
understand its "Outside," that is to say, that which it rejects in the process
of constituting itself. The Scholastic episteme rejected unlinearized (and
hence un-Christianized) Greek self-reflexivity. According to the interpretation advanced by Alain de Libera, the 219 propositions that Bishop Tempier condemned in 1277 epitomize a revival of the Aristotelico-Arabic

ideal of the philosophical life. This philosophical life, however, is a life of "reflection," taken literally as a "turning back" of the self upon itself. The Christian faith, on the other hand, requires the soul to avow its radical heteronomy, or dependence upon the "Other." Therefore, philosophical reflection in the Aristotelico-Arabic sense can play only a secondary role in an authentically Christian quest for wisdom and holiness.

Finally, we considered the Scholastic episteme in relationship with the "other" that it was to become, namely, modernity. Toward the end of the medieval period, the Scholastic episteme transformed itself. This transformation amounted to an elimination of the linear element of Scholastic thought, which thirteenth-century thinkers had been so careful to defend in their dialogue with the heritage of Aristotelian and Arabic philosophy. The witch-hunt constitutes the most brutal evidence of the effects resulting from the closure of the Scholastic mind—that is to say, from the closure of the circle. In an attempt to capture goodness, to possess it, the Inquisition set out to eliminate all evil from human society. In doing so, it devised a totally circular rational structure from which witches, real or imagined, had little chance to escape once they were caught in the inquisitors' net. The obsession with the eradication of evil, coupled with the logical "perfection" of the rules for the witch-trial, created a kind of rationality that, fanatically convinced of its own goodness, excluded all possible counterevidence from its circle, and thus absolutized itself. From the Nietzschean-Foucauldian perspective we have adopted in this book, it is no surprise that the excluded evil and irrationality tragically reinscribed themselves within the very circle of the witch-hunt itself. The perfected pursuit of a good untainted by any traces of evil perverted itself, and turned evil. We remember Nietzsche's warning:

> Dionysius, as before, when he fled from Lycurgus, the king of the Edonians, took refuge in the depths of the sea, that is to say, in the mystical floods of a secret cult slowly encompassing the whole world.

Modernity can be interpreted as a reaction against the closure of the Scholastic mind, which manifested itself not only in the witch-hunt but also, less palpably, in the decline of the *quaestio,* a new metaphysics of the univocity of being, and the theology and practice of the indulgences.

Much remains to be done in the task of rereading Scholastic thought in the postmodern context. In any future work, it would be interesting, for instance, to take broader historical and social factors into consideration in analyzing the Scholastic episteme, thus following more closely the example Foucault set in his own research. Similarly, the privilege that this book has accorded to Paris in the mid-thirteenth century, while not without historical justification, must not be allowed to conceal the great diversity of the philosophical and theological movement in the period I have called "Scholastic." The perspectives this book has attempted to open up in its six studies are simply meant as an encouragement for future research along the methodological lines suggested. To show the fruitfulness of this methodology, inspired by some work of Foucault, has been my principal aim.

APPENDIX

THE LIBRARY OF THE
MEDIEVALIST PHILOSOPHER

In 1974, Fernand Van Steenberghen published a book entitled *La biblio-thèque du philosophe médiéviste* (The Library of the Medievalist Philosopher).[1] It contains reviews, written by the author over the years, of many of the most significant publications that appeared in the field of medieval philosophy during a career spanning five decades. *La bibliothèque du philosophe médiéviste* paints a fascinating picture of trends of research that prevailed from the 1930s until the early 1970s. Of course, we have moved on since then. Here are, therefore, my own suggestions for "the library of the medievalist philosopher" of the late 1990s. My "library" contains literature I consider indispensable to anyone interested in embarking upon serious study of the intellectual life of the Scholastic period in a postmodern perspective. There are gaps and idiosyncrasies, of course, as I have constituted the "library" in light of the principal questions addressed in this book.

Manuals on the History of Scholastic Thought

While several of the older histories of medieval thought—such as the well-known works by Étienne Gilson[2] and Dom David Knowles[3]—retain some of their value, they no longer represent the state of our knowledge in the field. Admittedly, the recent introductions and histories cannot always rival the coherence and philosophical vision of their predecessors, but perhaps this is simply due to the fact that the "postmodern" renaissance of interest in medieval thought needs more time to come to full fruition. The following three contemporary introductions to medieval thought are especially recommendable:

Alain de Libera, *La philosophie médiévale,* Collection Premier Cycle (Paris: Presses universitaires de France, 1993). This book is unique in that it covers the four great traditions of medieval thought: Byzantine, Islamic, Jewish, and Latin, giving equal weight to each.

Medieval Philosophy, ed. John Marenbon, Routledge History of Philosophy, ed. G. H. R. Parkinson and S. G. Shanker, vol. 3 (London and New York: Routledge, 1998). Collaborative work, containing contributions by some of the best contemporary experts on medieval thought. With one exception, all contributors come from the English-speaking world. No coverage of the Byzantine tradition.

Peter Schulthess and Ruedi Imbach, *Die Philosophie im lateinischen Mittelalter. Ein Handbuch mit bio-bibliographischem Repertorium* (Zurich and Düsseldorf: Artemis & Winkler, 1996). Excellent work that focuses upon the Latin tradition, affording ample coverage to the problematic of sources and intellectual practices. Extensive bio-bibliography covering all the major thinkers working or known in the Latin West.

Research Tools

A near-complete survey of new philosophical literature is made available each quarter in the *International Philosophical Bibliography,* which covers the patristic and medieval periods very reliably. Each year, number 4 carries an index of book reviews. In 1998, the *International Philosophical Bibliography* published its forty-ninth volume (printed and distributed by Peeters of Louvain).

The *Bulletin de philosophie médiévale,* which is the journal of the Société internationale pour l'étude de la philosophie médiévale, appears annually (in 1998, volume 40 was published). It provides information about current research in the field, carries news from the most important institutions devoted to the study of medieval thought, announces conferences, lists the addresses of its members, etc. An indispensable research tool (Turnhout, Belgium: Brepols).

The texts of the medieval thinkers are published in a large number of different series. The two most comprehensive ones, however, are Jean-Paul Migne's Patrologia latina, and the Corpus Christianorum. The Patrologia latina was originally printed in 217 volumes that appeared between 1844 and 1855. Four volumes of indexes were added later on, together with, more recently, a five-volume *Supplementum.* (Reprints of all the volumes are still available from Brepols of Turnhout.) Migne intended the PL, as medievalists call it, to cover all the known Christian Latin literature from ca. 200 through the beginning of the Reformation, but later decided to limit his project to texts written up to 1216. Since 1995, the PL is available on CD-ROM (produced by Chadwyck-Healey Inc. of Alexandria, Virginia), with all the advantages in terms of "searchability" that entails. Due to the fact that the PL gives texts in uncritical editions, it has in many cases been superseded by more recent editions. However, as there is still a sizable number of authors and works not available in scholarly editions, the PL remains one of the medievalist's most precious tools.

The Corpus Christianorum is a project that was undertaken jointly by the Benedictine monks of St. Peter's Abbey (Steenbrugge, Belgium), and the publishing house Brepols. Started in 1954, the Latin part of the CC was conceived as a replacement of Migne's Patrologia latina. In two series, a Series Latina and a Continuatio Mediaevalis, it publishes the writings of the Latin authors of the patristic and medieval periods, with the goal of eventually offering a complete library of this literature. (There also exists a Series Graeca.) In 1998, the Series Latina comprised 176 volumes, while the Continuatio Mediaevalis ran up to volume number 170. Like the PL, the CC is available on CD-ROM, under the title, *Cetedoc Library of Christian Latin Texts (CLCLT)*.

Journals

There are a number of fine journals explicitly devoted to the intellectual life of the Middle Ages. Of course, non-medievalist periodicals also occasionally publish material germane to the study of thought in the medieval period.

The *Archives d'histoire doctrinale et littéraire du moyen âge*, often abbreviated *AHDLMA*, were founded in 1926 by Étienne Gilson and Père Gabriel Théry O.P. One of the oldest and most respected reviews of medieval philosophy and theology, the *Archives* have published many articles that have become classics. In 1998, the *Archives* published their sixty-fifth volume (Librairie philosophique J.Vrin, Paris).

The *Recherches de théologie ancienne et médiévale* were founded in 1929 by the Benedictine monks of the Abbaye du Mont-César at Louvain, which was then a great center for the study of medieval thought, apart from playing an important role in the liturgical movement. Like the *AHLDMA,* the *Recherches* have for decades been one of the major periodicals in the field. In 1997 (volume 64), the journal was renamed, *Recherches de théologie et philosophie médiévales/Forschungen zur Theologie und Philosophie des Mittelalters,* and its editorial offices were moved to the Thomas Institute of the University of Cologne (publisher: Peeters of Louvain).

Another old and venerable, yet still very dynamic journal is the *Freiburger Zeitschrift für Philosophie und Theologie*. Founded in 1887 as the *Jahrbuch für Philosophie und spekulative Theologie* and originally published in the small town of Paderborn, Germany, whose Jesuit college contributed to the Neoscholastic renaissance, it appeared as *Divus Thomas* between 1914 and 1953 and assumed its current title in 1954. The *Freiburger Zeitschrift* can be considered the journal of the Fribourg school of medieval studies, although it also prints articles of more general philosophical and theological interest. It regularly carries Ruedi Imbach's *Notabilia,* an overview of "notable" new literature in the field of medieval philosophy. The last *Notabilia* appeared in volume 43 of 1996, pp. 132–153 (the *FZPT* is published by the Paulusverlag in Fribourg, Switzerland).

The *Revue philosophique de Louvain* was created in 1889 by the founder of the Louvain school of philosophy, the later Cardinal Désiré Mercier. It originally appeared under the title, *Revue néo-scolastique,* which aptly summarized its goal and orientation. In the course of its history, the *Revue* has published many studies on medieval thought that have become famous. The great representatives of the Louvain school, such as Maurice De Wulf and Fernand Van Steenberghen, were regular contributors. Although now much broader in scope, the *Revue* continues to publish the occasional piece on medieval thought. The volume for 1998 carries the number 96 (Peeters, Louvain).

Let us move on to some newer journals. Since 1975, the Centro per ricerche di filosofia medievale of the University of Padua has published *Medioevo,* whose subtitle describes the journal as *Revista di storia della filosofia medievale. Medioevo* occasionally prints articles in languages other than Italian, but its principal purpose is to lend a voice to Italian medievalist philosophers (Editrice Antenore, Padua).

Medieval Philosophy & Theology is a new periodical largely (though not exclusively) devoted to the analytic approach to medieval thought. Edited by Norman Kretzmann of Cornell University, it was founded in 1991 and originally published by the University of Notre Dame Press. Since volume 6 of 1997, it is produced by Cambridge University Press.

For some decades, Japanese scholars have shown interest in the study of the thought of the European Middle Ages. *Didascalia: A Journal for Philosophy and Philology from Late Antiquity to the Renaissance* was created in 1995 and is edited by Shimizu Tetsuro of Tohoku University, Sendai. The journal is published for the sake of making Japanese scholars' research known internationally, but it also invites contributions from non-Japanese colleagues. Volume 1 of 1995 (the only one I have seen) contains articles on

Adelard of Bath's doctrine on universals (by Charles Burnett), on Peter Abelard's theory of signification (by Shimizu Tetsuro), and on nominalism (by Iwakuma Yukio). The journal is published by Gakujisha, Tokyo, but seems hard to obtain outside Japan.

The *Bochumer Philosophisches Jahrbuch für Antike und Mittelalter* is the most recent addition to the range of scholarly journals devoted to medieval thought. As the title indicates, the *Bochumer Philosophisches Jahrbuch* covers both the ancient and the medieval periods. It is particularly interested in furthering research on interrelations among various cultural and philosophical traditions, such as Arabic, Judaic, Byzantine, and Latin thought; it publishes discussions and interviews, and—quite unusually—introductory articles that could be of interest to students. The contributions are in English, French, German, and Italian. In 1998, volume 3 appeared. The journal is published by John Benjamins of Amsterdam.

Other journals are devoted, more specifically, to particular medieval thinkers. Especially abundant are periodicals on the thought of St. Thomas Aquinas, such as the *Revue thomiste, The Thomist, Doctor communis,* etc.

Web Sites

The value of the Internet as a research tool for the humanities is beyond doubt, especially in the field of bibliography. The possibility, for instance, of verifying bibliographical data quickly and reliably by consulting the catalogs of the world's major research libraries constitutes a great advantage. With regard to material relating to medieval thought, the Library of Congress is unrivaled for publications in English (http://catalog.loc.gov/). A more international bibliographical research tool is available in the online catalog of the Dutch-speaking branch of the Catholic University of Louvain (http://www.bib.kuleuven.ac.be/bib/).

Numerous other Web sites offer information pertinent to the study of medieval thought. However, due to the ephemeral nature of the medium on which Web pages are published, I shall not provide a long list of digital addresses here. If it is true that the "average life span of a Web page is just 77 days,"[4] most of the information provided would have become obsolete long before the publication of this book. For those keen on "surfing" for Web sites on medieval thought, there are very powerful search engines. Moreover, the Philosophy Documentation Center has recently published the second edition of Dey Alexander, *Philosophy in Cyberspace: A Guide to Philosophy-Related Resources on the Internet,* 2nd ed. (Bowling Green, Ohio: Philosophy Documentation Center, 1998). The best Web site on medieval thought is probably the one maintained by Paul Vincent Spade, of the University of Indiana. Here is the address by which it could be accessed in May, 1999: http://pvspade.com/Logic/. Spade provides many interesting links.[5]

History of the Discipline

Increased reflection upon the history of the discipline is part and parcel of the postmodern turn that medieval studies have taken in recent years. For, if "the truth about history is itself historical," according to Louis Dupré's words quoted in the preface, then we had better make sure we know the historical conditions in which a given approach to history arose. The most comprehensive account (from a traditional perspective) of the origins and development of the Neoscholastic movement is *Christliche Philosophie im katholischen Denken des 19. und 20. Jahrhunderts,* ed. Emerich Coreth S.J., Walter M. Neidl, and Georg Pfligersdorffer, vol. 2: *Rückgriff auf scholastisches Erbe* (Graz, Vienna, and Cologne: Styria, 1988). Another excellent introduction to the history and spirit of the Neoscholastic movement is Fernand Van Steenberghen, *Introduction à l'étude de la philosophie médiévale,* Philosophes médiévaux 18 (Louvain: Publications universitaires; Paris: Béatrice-Nauwelaerts, 1974). A brief characterization of this work has been given in the preface. Somewhat more specific in its scope is Gerald A. McCool S.J., *From Unity to Pluralism: The Internal Evolution of Thomism* (New York: Fordham University Press, 1989). Not limited to the history of the Neoscholastic movement narrowly defined (as a return to St. Thomas in accordance with the program of *Aeterni Patris*), but including the nineteenth- and twentieth-century historiography of medieval science, of the medieval universities, etc., is the following volume: *Gli studi di filosofia medievale fra otto e novecento. Contributo a un bilancio storiografico,* ed. Ruedi Imbach and Alfonso Maierù, Storia e Letteratura 179 (Rome: Edizioni di Storia e Letteratura, 1991). The contributions to this book are in English, French, Italian, and German. A new important study on the origins of the Neoscholastic movement has recently been prepared by John Inglis. In *Spheres of Philosophical Inquiry and the Historiography of Medieval Philosophy,* Brill's Studies in Intellectual History 81 (Leyden: Brill, 1998), Inglis analyzes the approach to the study of medieval philosophy that was developed by the two German medievalists Joseph Kleutgen and Albert Stöckl in the 1850s and 60s. Arguing that this approach constitutes an example of "reverse discourse" created in reaction to the prevailing Kantianism of the time, Inglis insists on its shortcomings, witnessed by the anachronistically clear separation of philosophical and theological concerns, and by the categorization of medieval thought in terms of the modern branches of philosophy (with a primacy accorded to epistemology). A summary of the principal theses of *Spheres of Philosophical Inquiry and the Historiography of Medieval Philosophy* is available in the same author's article, "Philosophical Autonomy and the Historiography of Medieval Philosophy," *British Journal for the History of Philosophy* 5 (1997):21–53.

There are now several books on the lives and works of the great personalities who "invented" the study of the Middle Ages, and of medieval thought, in the nineteenth and twentieth centuries. The most widely publicized of these books is no doubt Norman F. Cantor, *Inventing the Middle Ages. The Lives, Works, and Ideas of the Great Medievalists of the Twentieth Century* (New York: William Morrow, 1991; Cambridge, England: The Lutterworth Press, 1992). For readers interested in medieval thought, the chapters on C. S. Lewis, Dom David Knowles, Étienne Gilson, Sir Richard Southern, and Erwin Panofsky are most relevant. R. Howard Bloch has written a fascinating book on Jean-Paul Migne and his monumental Patrologia project. It is entitled *God's Plagiarist. Being an Account of the Fabulous Industry and Irregular Commerce of the Abbé Migne* (Chicago and London: University of Chicago Press, 1994). The forthcoming volume 3 of *Medieval Scholarship: Biographical Studies on the Formation of a Discipline*, ed. Helen Damico, Garland Reference Library of the Humanities (New York: Garland) will offer intellectual biographies and bibliographies on the scholars who were most influential in shaping the study of medieval thought during the past two centuries, such as Maurice De Wulf, Martin Grabmann, Dom Odon Lottin, Étienne Gilson, etc.

Bilan et perspectives des études médiévales en Europe, ed. Jacqueline Hamesse, Textes et études du moyen âge 3 (Louvain-la-Neuve: Fédération internationale des Instituts d'études médiévales, 1995), is a more general survey of the history and "state of the art" in the various branches of medieval studies. The book contains 32 chapters on all the major aspects of research into the Middle Ages, ranging from paleography and philology to art and archaeology, economic history, Byzantine studies, philosophy, Thomism, and so forth. Indispensable. The American counterpart to this "European" volume is *The Past and Future of Medieval Studies*, ed. John Van Engen, Notre Dame Conferences in Medieval Studies 4 (Notre Dame and London: University of Notre Dame Press, 1994).

The following three volumes are more specifically concerned with postmodern methodological changes in the study of medieval literature, but many of their programmatic essays are also of interest to intellectual history: (1) *The New Medievalism,* ed. Marina S. Brownlee, Kevin Brown-lee, and Stephen G. Nichols, Parallax: Re-visions of Culture and Society (Baltimore and London: Johns Hopkins University Press, 1991); (2) *Medievalism and the Modernist Temper,* ed. R. Howard Bloch and Stephen G. Nichols (Baltimore and London: Johns Hopkins University Press, 1996); (3) *New Medieval Literatures,* ed. Wendy Scase, Rita Copeland, and David Lawton, vol. 1 (Oxford: Oxford University Press, 1997).

Contemporary Approaches to Scholastic Thought

The Neoscholastic movement produced a number of important debates on the nature of Scholastic thought, which I have tried to summarize at the beginning of study 2. Most of the key notions that figured prominently in these debates—"Scholastic synthesis" (De Wulf), Scholastic method (Grabmann), but also "Christian philosophy in the Middle Ages" (Gilson), and the possibility of isolating a "pure" philosophy in the writings of the medieval thinkers (Van Steenberghen)—have lost their paradigmatic character in the "new" approach now practiced by medievalists. Only the formal approach, which locates the specificity of Scholastic thought in its method, has retained some contemporary interest. That Scholasticism is primarily a "form" of thought, rather than being identifiable with any particular "content," has recently been argued by Rolf Schönberger, *Was ist Scholastik?,* Philosophie und Religion 2 (Hildesheim: Bernward-Verlag, 1991). Sir Richard Southern maintains the same thesis in his fine work on *Scholastic Humanism and the Unification of Europe,* 1: *Foundations* (Oxford, England and Cambridge, Massachusetts, 1995). I have attempted to reread Grabmann's *History of Scholastic Method* in a contemporary context in my article, "Histoire et actualité de la méthode scolastique selon M. Grabmann. Appendice: 'Secundum aliquid utrumque est verum': 'Media via' et méthode scolastique chez S. Thomas d'Aquin," in *Actualité de la pensée médiévale,* ed. Jacques Follon and James McEvoy, Philosophes médiévaux 31 (Louvain-la-Neuve: Éditions de l'Institut supérieur de philosophie; Louvain/Paris: Peeters, 1994), pp. 95–118. Study 2 of the present book constitutes a "Foucauldian" development of my earlier attempt to reappropriate Grabmann's approach.

Alain de Libera has endeavored to de-center the study of medieval thought in his book, *Penser au Moyen Âge,* Chemins de pensée (Paris: Éditions du Seuil, 1991). For de Libera, the most worthwhile philosophical movement of the medieval period is the "heterodox Aristotelianism" of the thirteenth century (he speaks, as we know, of a "declericalized Arabism").

In this revival of the Greek ideal of the philosophical life, de Libera sees an answer to the great question concerning the goals of the intellectual life posed by Martin Heidegger—namely, "What is thinking?"

Ruedi Imbach's recent introduction to the study of medieval thought is conceived along similar lines, focusing as it does upon a problem long considered as "marginal": the role played by lay people in the intellectual life of the medieval period. However, in his *Dante, la philosophie et les laïcs. Initiations à la philosophie médiévale 1*, Vestigia 21 (Fribourg: Éditions universitaires; Paris: Éditions du Cerf, 1996), Imbach does not claim that his focus is in any way a privileged one; he only maintains that the problem "has not been accorded all the interest it merits" (p. 6).

A similar emphasis upon the diversity of currents and schools in the medieval period, as well as of legitimate approaches to its history, is to be found in the work of Kurt Flasch. His *Einführung in die Philosophie des Mittelalters,* Die Philosophie (Darmstadt: Wissenschaftliche Buchgesellschaft, 1987) presents medieval thought as a series of "debates," rather than as a homogeneous flow of ideas. Flasch is also one of the few medievalists who have attempted to read the intellectual history of the Middle Ages against a political, economic, and social background. Although this approach is certainly not "Marxist," as some critics were quick to claim, it does not seem sufficiently nuanced sometimes. Nevertheless, this avenue is undoubtedly worth exploring.

In the current Babel of opinions on the meaning and principal interest of the Scholastic tradition, the position advocated by Jan A. Aertsen, of the Thomas Institute in Cologne, is that we need to revive discussion of the "centerpiece of medieval metaphysics," which for Aertsen is the doctrine of the transcendentals. See, for instance, his contribution to the Festschrift for Albert Zimmermann: Jan A. Aertsen, "Gibt es eine mittelalterliche Philosophie?," in *Philosophie und geistiges Erbe des Mittelalters,* ed. Andreas Speer, Kölner Universitätsreden 75 (Winksele, Belgium: Peeters, 1994), pp. 13–30, or the article "What is First and Most Fundamental? The Beginnings of Transcendental Philosophy," in *Was ist Philosophie im Mittelalter? Qu'est-ce que la philosophie au Moyen Âge? What is Philosophy in the Middle Ages? Akten des X. Internationalen Kongresses für mittelalterliche Philosophie der Société Internationale pour l'Étude de la Philosophie Médiévale,* ed. Jan A. Aertsen and Andreas Speer, Miscellanea Mediaevalia 26 (Berlin and New York: de Gruyter, 1998), pp. 177–192. However, it would not seem that this position has found many adherents outside the Cologne school. Aertsen recently presented a detailed study of the transcendentals in the thought of St. Thomas Aquinas: *Medieval Philosophy and the Transcendentals: The Case of*

Thomas Aquinas, Studien und Texte zur Geistesgeschichte des Mittelalters 52 (Leyden, New York, Cologne: Brill, 1996).

The contemporary analytic approach to medieval thought, with its characteristic emphasis upon questions of logic, semiotics, and epistemology, is perhaps best illustrated by John Marenbon's very popular and useful book, *Later Medieval Philosophy (1150–1350): An Introduction* (London and New York: Routledge & Kegan Paul, 1987). Part I of the volume is devoted to the institutional setting of medieval thought, techniques of logic, sources, and so forth. Rumor has it that a new multivolume "analytic" history of medieval thought is currently being prepared under the editorship of Calvin Normore, a medievalist working at the University of California at Los Angeles.

The current debate on the different approaches to the study of medieval thought is reflected in the proceedings of the Tenth World Congress on Medieval Philosophy, held in Erfurt (Germany) in August, 1997 under the auspices of the Société internationale pour l'étude de la philosophie médiévale: *Was ist Philosophie im Mittelalter? Qu'est-ce que la philosophie au Moyen Âge? What is Philosophy in the Middle Ages? Akten des X. Internationalen Kongresses für mittelalterliche Philosophie der Société Internationale pour l'Étude de la Philosophie Médiévale,* ed. Jan A. Aertsen and Andreas Speer, Miscellanea Mediaevalia 26 (Berlin and New York: de Gruyter, 1998).

Foucault and the Middle Ages

While postmodern studies of medieval literature and of such issues as the medieval construction of sexuality abound, explicitly postmodern discussions of medieval philosophy and theology have remained scarce. The piece by Anne Clark Bartlett, "Foucault's 'Medievalism,'" *Mystics Quarterly* 20 (1994):10–18, is excellent, but very short. Bartlett's exploration of the usefulness of Foucault's method for medieval studies, as well as her critique of Foucault's sometimes naively nostalgic vision of the Middle Ages, have been taken up by Carolyn Dinshaw in her essay, "Getting Medieval: *Pulp Fiction,* Gawain, Foucault," in *The Book and the Body,* ed. Dolores Warwick Frese and Katherine O'Brien O'Keeffe, University of Notre Dame Ward-Phillips Lectures in English Language and Literature 14 (Notre Dame and London: University of Notre Dame Press, 1997), pp. 116–163. Attention: the essay is X-rated . . .

As far as I can see, there have so far been no attempts to use Foucault's insights on the structure of the medieval episteme, with the sole exception of Jos Decorte, *De waanzin van het intellect. Twee modellen van de eeuwige strijd tussen goed en kwaad* (Kapellen: DNB/Uitgeverij Pelckmans; Kampen: Uitgeverij Kok Agora, 1989). Starting from Foucault's definition of the pre-sixteenth-century episteme as being centered around the concept of similitude, Decorte argues that the witch-hunt has to be viewed as a transformation of the Scholastic episteme.

Textual Scholarship

Every medievalist should have an idea as to the techniques and problems involved in the study of medieval manuscripts and in the edition of texts from the medieval period. Without this background, he or she will be unable to appreciate an historical dimension that is extremely important for a proper understanding of the intellectual life of the Middle Ages, as well as for the critical reading of medieval texts in contemporary editions. The best general introduction to textual scholarship is D.C. Greetham, *Textual Scholarship: An Introduction,* Garland Reference Library of the Humanities 1417 (New York and London: Garland, 1994). This work provides a reliable overview of the practical and theoretical problems encountered at all the different stages of the process of reconstructing a text from the past. Greetham is also one of the leading experts in the field of postmodern research on textuality. Another stimulating, theory-oriented introduction to contemporary editorial scholarship is furnished by Herbert Kraft in his book, *Editionsphilologie* (Darmstadt: Wissenschaftliche Buchgesellschaft, 1990). The 13 chapters range from a consideration of the historicity of literary works and the "dialectics" of the historico-critical edition, to the problems involved in modernizing punctuation and the use of word processing in establishing editions. Very useful.

As a more specialized handbook of Latin paleography, there is probably nothing better in English than Bernhard Bischoff, *Latin Palaeography: Antiquity and the Middle Ages,* trans. Dáibhí Ó Cróinín and David Ganz (Cambridge, England: Cambridge University Press, 1990). The French equivalent of Bischoff is the fine work by Jacques Stiennon, *Paléographie du Moyen Âge,* 2nd ed., Collection U: Histoire médiévale (Paris: Armand Colin, 1991). The standard bibliographical handbook on the paleography of medieval Latin texts is Leonard E. Boyle O.P., *Medieval Latin Palaeography: A Bibliographical Introduction,* Toronto Medieval Bibliographies 8 (Toronto and Buffalo: Toronto University Press, 1984).

Those of us who do not read medieval manuscripts on a very regular basis will probably need help with the abbreviations. The classic dictionary is Adriano Cappelli, *Lexicon abbreviaturarum. Dizionario di abbreviature latine*

ed italiane, 6th ed., Manuali Hoepli (Milan: Ulrico Hoepli, 1987). Supplement by Auguste Pelzer, *Abréviations latines médiévales. Supplément au
Dizionario di abbreviature latine ed italiane de Adriano Cappelli,* 3rd ed. (Beauvechain, Belgium: Nauwelaerts, 1995). Olaf Pluta has prepared an elec-
tronic dictionary of medieval Latin abbreviations that is constantly being
added to, so that it will eventually be considerably more comprehensive
than Cappelli and Pelzer. Called *Abbreviationes,* it is available from Dr. Olaf
Pluta at the Institut für Philosophie of the University of Bochum, Germany. So far, *Abbreviationes* runs only on Macintosh machines, but an IBM-
compatible version is planned for the near future.

There is no handbook of editorial theory and practice for medievalists.
The classical essay on textual criticism is Paul Maas, *Textual Criticism,* trans.
Barbara Flower (Oxford: Clarendon Press, 1958). Maas's essay is a brilliant
statement of the fundamental assumptions and procedures of the Lachmannian method of textual editing. Of greater practical use, however, is the
work by Martin L. West, *Textual Criticism and Editorial Technique,* Teubner
Studienbücher (Stuttgart: Teubner, 1973). As an introduction to the problems faced by the medievalist in applying Lachmann's method to texts
from the medieval period, one may consult the useful volume entitled, *Les
problèmes posés par l'édition critique des textes anciens et médiévaux,* ed. Jacqueline
Hamesse, Université catholique de Louvain, Publications de l'Institut d'é-
tudes médiévales—Textes, études, congrès 13 (Louvain-la-Neuve: Institut
d'études médiévales, 1992). One of the finest examples of a contemporary
edition of a medieval work is Édouard Jeauneau's recent edition of the *Periphyseon* by John Scottus Eriugena. Jeauneau's preface, too, is excellent:
Iohannis Scotti seu Eriugenae *Periphyseon,* liber 1 and liber 2, ed. Eduardus
Jeauneau, Corpus Christianorum, Continuatio Mediaevalis 161 and 162
(Turnhout: Brepols, 1996 and 1997).

Scholastic Intellectual Practices

Olga Weijers's lectures delivered, in 1993–1994, at the École pratique des
hautes études in Paris offer a state of the art account of what we know
about the intellectual practices that prevailed at the Parisian arts faculty in
the thirteenth and fourteenth centuries: Olga Weijers, *Le maniement du
savoir. Pratiques intellectuelles à l'époque des premières universités (XIIIᵉ-XIVᵉ siècles),* Studia Artistarum, Subsidia (Turnhout: Brepols, 1996). In 14 chapters,
Weijers covers all the issues necessary for a proper understanding of the institutional conditions of intellectual life at the time: curricula and hand-
books, dictionaries and indexes, teaching methods and literary genres,

examinations, and so on. To my knowledge, a similarly comprehensive account does not yet exist for any other medieval university, nor for the Parisian theology faculty. However, there are many studies of a more limited scope, the most important ones of which are listed in Weijers's bibliography. Together with her colleague Louis Holtz, Weijers is the editor of a book series carrying the title, Studia Artistarum (Turnhout: Brepols, 1994–). Being of an orientation similar to *Maniement du savoir*, Studia Artistarum publishes materials relating to the medieval arts faculties. So far, five volumes have appeared, including the first two volumes of a bio-bibliography of the masters teaching at the faculty of arts in Paris between 1200 and 1500, and the proceedings of an important conference: *L'enseignement des disciplines à la Faculté des arts (Paris et Oxford, XIII*ᵉ*-XIV*ᵉ *siècles)*, ed. Olga Weijers and Louis Holtz, Studia Artistarum 4 (Turnhout: Brepols, 1997).

Before embarking upon the question of Scholastic reading techniques and attitudes to the text, one must understand the monastic culture from which the Scholastic one emerged, and to which of course it remained heavily indebted. Fortunately, on this issue there exists the great classic work by the late Dom Jean Leclercq O.S.B., *The Love of Learning and the Desire for God. A Study in Monastic Culture*, trans. Catharine Misrahi, 3rd ed. (New York: Fordham University Press, 1982). Ivan Illich's book, *In the Vineyard of the Text. A Commentary to Hugh's Didascalicon* (Chicago and London: University of Chicago Press, 1993), studies the transition from monastic to Scholastic reading, an issue the author connects in an ingenious way with the current problem of the shift from a book-based to a computer-based culture. Illich not being a medievalist, his book is not free from certain historical inaccuracies. It is strange, for instance, to be apprised that Peter Lombard's *Book of Sentences* is "on Aristotle" (p. 98)! Nonetheless, *In the Vineyard of the Text* makes for very stimulating reading. A more learned and historically reliable, yet also less synthetic account of Scholastic reading is proffered by two essays in Mary A. Rouse and Richard H. Rouse, *Authentic Witnesses: Approaches to Medieval Texts and Manuscripts*, Publications in Medieval Studies 17 (Notre Dame: University of Notre Dame Press, 1991). The essays are: "Statim invenire: Schools, Preachers, and New Attitudes to the Page" (pp. 191–219), and "The Development of Research Tools in the Thirteenth Century" (pp. 221–255). Mary Carruthers argues the fascinating thesis that medieval memory-training resulted in the human body being structured like a book; see her article, "Reading with Attitude, Remembering the Book," in *The Book and the Body*, ed. Dolores Warwick Frese and Katherine O'Brien O'Keeffe, University of Notre Dame Ward-Phillips Lectures in English Language and Literature 14

(Notre Dame and London: University of Notre Dame Press, 1997), pp. 1–33. In the context of reading techniques, another book is worth mentioning for its originality and incisive insights—although it does not deal directly with Scholastic reading, rather being devoted to a famous piece of vernacular Spanish literature: John Dagenais, *The Ethics of Reading in Manuscript Culture. Glossing the "Libro de buen amor"* (Princeton: Princeton University Press, 1994).

Anyone interested in possible connections between Scholastic intellectual practices and Gothic architecture must start by reading Erwin Panofsky's *Gothic Architecture and Scholasticism. An Inquiry into the Analogy of the Arts, Philosophy, and Religion in the Middle Ages* (New York: Meridian, 1957). The criticisms that have been leveled against Panofsky do not, in fact, so much concern this particular book, as his thesis, argued elsewhere, on the influence of Neoplatonic light metaphysics on the design of the cathedral of Saint-Denis. That Panofsky's intuitions regarding analogies between the Scholastic episteme and the architecture of the High Gothic cathedrals were not too wide of the mark is a fact to which a recent book testifies, as it approaches the relationship between learning and building in the Scholastic period from an angle comparable to Panofsky's. In their book *Medieval Architecture, Medieval Learning. Builders and Masters in the Age of Romanesque and Gothic* (New Haven and London: Yale University Press, 1992), Charles M. Radding and William W. Clark focus on the eleventh and twelfth centuries. They maintain that the "cognitive processes" which were utilized by medieval scholars and builders to "impose order on materials, to shape several variables into a whole" (p. 3) bear striking similarities to each other. Finally, Georges Didi-Huberman, *Fra Angelico. Dissemblance and Figuration,* trans. Jane Marie Todd (Chicago and London: University of Chicago Press, 1995) establishes a connection between medieval painting and the structures of negative theology. The theme of possible interrelationships between different aspects of Scholastic culture offers ample potential for future research.

Greek Circularity, Christian Linearity

If it is true, as I have claimed, that we can interpret the clash between Greek wisdom and the "foolishness of the Cross," upon the metaphysical plane, as a tension between the Greek circular worldview and the Christian linear conception of time (and hence, being), then understanding the Scholastic episteme necessitates an appreciation of the theme of circularity in Greek thought. The fundamental work on this underresearched topic is Lynne Ballew, *Straight and Circular: A Study of Imagery in Greek Philosophy* (Assen, The Netherlands: Van Gorcum, 1979). My own book *Omne agens agit sibi simile. A "Repetition" of Scholastic Metaphysics,* Louvain Philosophical Studies 12 (Louvain: Leuven University Press, 1996), contains a chapter on the circularity of being in Plato and Aristotle (pp. 33–62), and another on the transformation of this theme in Neoplatonism (pp. 63–101). Two publications by Klaus Oehler analyze the problem of self-reflexivity in Aristotle in a very stimulating fashion, namely, his booklet, *Ein Mensch zeugt einen Menschen. Über den Mißbrauch der Sprachanalyse in der Aristotelesforschung,* Wissenschaft und Gegenwart 27 (Francfort on the Main: Klostermann, 1963), esp. pp. 37–65, and the essay, "Aristotle on Self-Knowledge," *Proceedings of the American Philosophical Society* 118 (1974):493–506.

That the original Christian conception of time and history was linear was first argued by Oscar Cullmann, in *Christ and Time. The Primitive Christian Conception of Time and History,* revised ed., trans. Floyd V. Filson (Philadelphia: Westminster Press, 1964). *Christ and Time* gave rise to vivid theological discussions, which are documented in Cullmann's preface to the revised edition. Although Cullmann's fundamental thesis on the circular nature of Christian time has come to be accepted as correct, many scholars are not prepared to go along with some of the conclusions the author draws from this insight.

One of the few authors to have investigated the way in which patristic or medieval thinkers attempted to deal with the challenge of the Greek circle is the present Cardinal Joseph Ratzinger, in his early work, *The Theology of History in St. Bonaventure,* trans. Zachary Hayes O.F.M. (Chicago: Franciscan Herald Press, 1971). The only study I know of that shows any awareness of the importance of the circle and the line in the thought of St. Thomas Aquinas is Jan Aertsen, *Nature and Creature. Thomas Aquinas's Way of Thought,* trans. Herbert Donald Morton, Studien und Texte zur Geistesgeschichte des Mittelalters 21 (Leyden, New York, Copenhagen, and Cologne: Brill, 1988). On page 42, Aertsen writes: "The introduction of the motif of circulation is all the more striking since the straight line has at present come to be regarded as the most adequate symbol for the Christian conception of history. Is it perhaps in connection with this tendency that the important place of the idea of circulation in Thomas's thought— and in medieval thought generally—is still insufficiently discerned?" However, Aertsen does not show how Aquinas tried to reconcile the Greek circle with the Christian line.

The Other Aquinas

The interpretation of the thought of Thomas Aquinas that I have outlined
in study 5 is developed in much greater detail in my book, *Omne ens est
aliquid. Introduction à la lecture du "système" philosophique de saint Thomas
d'Aquin* (Louvain and Paris: Peeters, 1996). Some more conservative
Thomists have rejected my interpretation—thus, for instance, É.-H. Wéber
in a review published in the *Revue des sciences philosophiques et théologiques*
82 (1998):302–303. Others, though "perplexed" and critical, have been
more sympathetic, such as Père Serge-Thomas Bonino O.P., the editor of
the *Revue thomiste* (see his review in *Revue thomiste* 97 [1997]:570–574). In
viewing the transcendental *aliquid* as central for an understanding of the
Thomistic project, I am in agreement with Robert E. Wood, who has defended a similar approach in his article, "The Self and the Other: Toward a
Re-Interpretation of the Transcendentals," *Philosophy Today* 10
(1966):48–63. My project of rereading Aquinas in a dialectical perspective
has drawn much inspiration from the brilliant work by Joseph de Finance
S.J., *De l'un et de l'autre. Essai sur l'altérité,* 2nd ed. (Rome: Editrice Ponti-
ficia Università Gregoriana, 1993), which I have discussed in my essay,
"Penser l'Autre: les dimensions de l'altérité selon le P. Joseph de Finance,"
Revue philosophique de Louvain 92 (1994):335–347. For reflections about the
element of negative theology in St. Thomas, the late Josef Pieper's work is
very helpful, especially *The Silence of St. Thomas,* trans. John Murray S.J. and
Daniel O'Connor (New York: Pantheon, 1957). On the general question
of what shape a renewed Thomism could take, one may read with profit
Martin Blais, *L'autre Thomas d'Aquin* (Québec: Éditions du Boréal, 1990).

The Condemnation of 1277

The text of the condemnation of the 219 propositions was originally printed
in *Chartularium Universitatis Parisiensis sub auspiciis Consilii generalis Facultatum
Parisiensium,* ed. Henri Denifle and Henri Chatelain, 1 (Paris: Delalain, 1889;
reprinted, Brussels: Culture et Civilisation, 1964), pp. 543–555. David Piché,
a young medievalist from the Université Laval, has now prepared a long-
awaited new critical edition; it is due to appear shortly: *La condamnation parisienne de 1277. Nouvelle édition, traduction, introduction et notes,* Sic et non (Paris:
Vrin, forthcoming). All contemporary scholarship is based upon the work by
Roland Hissette, *Enquête sur les 219 articles condamnés à Paris le 7 mars 1277,*
Philosophes médiévaux 22 (Louvain: Publications universitaires; Paris: Vander-
Oyez, 1977). This being said, it must be pointed out that the rearrangement

of the 219 propositions according to a modern, more "logical" order is methodologically questionable, as is Hissette's examination of the orthodoxy of the condemned theses upon the basis of a contemporary notion of orthodox Catholicism. On the other hand, Hissette's careful comparison of the condemned theses with the philosophical literature of the time is invaluable. Scholarly discussions of the 219 propositions have received a new impetus since Alain de Libera's claim, advanced in *Penser au Moyen Âge,* Chemins de pensée (Paris: Éditions du Seuil, 1991), that Bishop Tempier deliberately "invented" many of the propositions in order to forestall the creation of a radical alternative to Christian thought, but in the process created that alternative himself. Other notable additions to the literature on the condemnation of 1277 include Luca Bianchi, *Il vescovo e i filosofi: la condanna parigina del 1277 e l'evoluzione dell'aristotelismo scolastico,* Quodlibet 6 (Bergamo: Lubrina, 1990), and Kurt Flasch, *Aufklärung im Mittelalter? Die Verurteilung von 1277,* Excerpta classica 6 (Mainz: Dieterich'sche Verlagsbuchhandlung, 1989).

The Witch-Hunt

The standard introduction to the topic of the witch-hunt is the book by Brian P. Levack, *The Witch-Hunt in Early Modern Europe,* 2nd ed. (London and New York: Longman, 1987). Heinrich Kramer's infamous "summa diabolica" was reprinted in 1992: Heinrich Kramer (Institoris), *Malleus maleficarum 1487. Nachdruck des Erstdruckes von 1487 mit Bulle und Approbatio,* ed. Günter Jerouschek, Rechtsgeschichte, Zivilisationsprozeß, Psychohistorie: Quellen und Studien 1 (Hildesheim, Zurich, and New York: Georg Olms, 1992). There is no English translation of the *Malleus* yet available, but there are French and German versions: Henri Institoris (Kraemer) and Jacques Sprenger, *Le marteau des sorcières,* trad. Amant Danet, Civilisations et mentalités (Paris: Plon, 1973); Jakob Sprenger and Heinrich Institoris, *Der Hexenhammer (Malleus maleficarum),* trans. J. W. R. Schmidt, 13th ed. of the repr. (1906; repr. Munich: Deutscher Taschenbuch-Verlag, 1997). The interpretation of the witch-hunt as resulting from an absolutization of the Scholastic episteme was first proposed by Jos Decorte in his book, *De waanzin van het intellect. Twee modellen van de eeuwige strijd tussen goed en kwaad* (Kapellen: DNB/Uitgeverij Pelckmans; Kampen: Uitgeverij Kok Agora, 1989).

Scholasticism and Modernity

For a long time, the transition from the Middle Ages to the modern age was interpreted as a radical change of paradigm, a complete break with the "darkness" and "superstition" of the Middle Ages, and the dawn of an entirely new age. Before becoming the great medievalist he was to be known as later, Étienne Gilson challenged this myth in his 1913 doctoral dissertation entitled *Index scolastico-cartésien,* 2nd ed., Études de philosophie médiévale 62 (Paris: Vrin, 1979). In 1930, he elaborated upon this study with a second work, *Études sur le rôle de la pensée médiévale dans la formation du système cartésien,* 4th ed., Études de philosophie médiévale 13 (Paris: Vrin, 1975). In 1923, Alexandre Koyré had already published his own study, *Descartes und die Scholastik* (Bonn: F. Cohen, 1923; repr. Bonn: Bouvier, 1971). These researches established that Descartes was steeped in Scholastic terminology and thought—as one might have expected of a quasi contemporary of Suárez! However, Jean-Luc Marion has recently defended a much more precise and radical thesis in his book, *Sur la théologie blanche de Descartes. Analogie, création des vérités éternelles et fondement,* Philosophie d'aujourd'hui (Paris: Presses universitaires de France, 1981). According to Marion, Cartesianism must be interpreted as an attempt to reaffirm the insights of negative theology against late Scholastic thought. Descartes wanted to recapture a more adequate conception of divine transcendence—such as the Thomistic doctrine of analogy—but in challenging late Scholasticism to return to its own truth, created the foundationalist problem of the modern age, the modern subject, and so forth. The whole of modernity thus appears as a failed attempt to be authentically medieval.

NOTES

Preface

1. Tim Weiner, "Think Tank: A Rebellion Against History's Fuzzy Future," *New York Times* (2 May 1998), Arts & Ideas/Cultural Desk section; also see Robert Jütte, "Hinter der Verhüllung. Amerikas Historiker gegen postmoderne Geschichtsschreibung," *Frankfurter Allgemeine Zeitung* 127 (4 June 1998):43.

2. For some short but sagacious remarks on the use of Foucauldian theory in the study of medieval mysticism, see Anne Clark Bartlett, "Foucault's 'Medievalism,'" *Mystics Quarterly* 20:1 (1994):10–18.

3. On the "new medievalism," see the programmatic volume *The New Medievalism,* ed. Marina S. Brownlee, Kevin Brownlee, and Stephen G. Nichols, Parallax: Re-visions of Culture and Society (Baltimore and London: Johns Hopkins University Press, 1991).

4. R. Howard Bloch and Stephen G. Nichols, Introduction to *Medievalism and the Modernist Temper,* ed. R. Howard Bloch and Stephen G. Nichols (Baltimore and London: Johns Hopkins University Press, 1996), pp. 1–22 (at p. 5).

5. The Cambridge medievalist John Marenbon is right, therefore, when he writes in *Later Medieval Philosophy (1150–1350). An Introduction* (London and New York: Routledge & Kegan Paul, 1987), p. 88: "The fact that none of the current approaches to medieval philosophy can be justified on purely historical grounds does not . . . mean that none is justifiable."

6. Louis Dupré, *Passage to Modernity. An Essay in the Hermeneutics of Nature and Culture* (New Haven and London: Yale University Press, 1993), p. 9.

7. Weiner, "Think Tank."

8. Bloch and Nichols, Introduction, p. 1.

9. Marie-Dominique Chenu O.P., *Introduction à l'étude de saint Thomas d'Aquin,* Université de Montréal, Publications de l'Institut d'études médiévales 11, 4th printing (Montreal: Institut d'études médiévales; Paris: Vrin, 1984). English translation, with authorized corrections and bibliographical additions: *Toward Understanding Saint Thomas,* trans. A.-M. Landry and D.

Hughes, The Library of Living Catholic Thought (Chicago: Henry Regnery Co., 1964).

10. On Chenu's work as an historian of medieval thought, see the special issue of the *Revue des sciences philosophiques et théologiques* devoted to "Le Père Marie-Dominique Chenu médiéviste" (volume 81 of 1997, no. 3).

11. Chenu, *Thomas d'Aquin*, p. 6 (my trans. from the French).

12. An approach very similar to Chenu's is to be found in J. Guy Bougerol's excellent introduction to Thomas's Franciscan contemporary, St. Bonaventure: see J. Guy Bougerol O.F.M., *Introduction to the Works of Bonaventure*, trans. José de Vinck (Paterson, New Jersey: St. Anthony Guild Press, 1964). New French edition: *Introduction à saint Bonaventure*, À la recherche de la vérité (Paris: Vrin, 1988).

13. Chenu, *Thomas d'Aquin*, p. 6.

14. Fernand Van Steenberghen, *Introduction à l'étude de la philosophie médiévale*, Philosophes médiévaux 18 (Louvain: Publications universitaires; Paris: Béatrice-Nauwelaerts, 1974).

15. More extensive and up-to-date intellectual biographies of the scholars who have shaped medieval studies in our century are now available in Norman F. Cantor, *Inventing the Middle Ages: The Lives, Works, and Ideas of the Great Medievalists of the Twentieth Century* (New York: W. Morrow, 1991). A still more comprehensive three-volume project on the biographical background of the medievalist discipline is in progress under the editorship of Helen Damico: *Medieval Scholarship: Biographical Studies on the Formation of a Discipline,* ed. Helen Damico, Garland Reference Library of the Humanities, 3 vols. (New York: Garland, 1995–). 2 volumes have appeared so far; volume 3, which will contain biographies of the most influential medievalist philosophers and theologians, is announced for December 1999.

Introduction

1. An earlier, shorter version of this introduction first appeared under the title, "A Change of Paradigm in the Study of Medieval Philosophy: From Rationalism to Postmodernism," *American Catholic Philosophical Quarterly* 72 (1998):59–73. I am grateful to the editor of the *ACPQ*, Professor Robert E. Wood, for permission to reuse parts of this text here. An opportunity to speak to the Dallas Area Medieval Consortium about "What's Going on in the Study of Medieval Philosophy These Days?" (Faculty Club of Southern Methodist University, April 22, 1998) allowed me to continue thinking about the topics discussed here.

2. Ernst Cassirer, *An Essay on Man. An Introduction to a Philosophy of Human Culture* (New Haven and London: Yale University Press, 1944), p. 174. On Cassirer's philosophy of history, see the synthetic account by Steve G. Lofts, "La lecture de l'histoire," in *Éditer, traduire, interpréter: essais de méthodologie*

philosophique, ed. Steve G. Lofts and Philipp W. Rosemann, Philosophes médiévaux 36 (Louvain-la-Neuve: Éditions de l'Institut supérieur de philosophie; Louvain/Paris: Peeters, 1997), pp. 199–216.

3. Lucien Braun, *Histoire de l'histoire de la philosophie,* Association des publications près les universités de Strasbourg 150 (Paris: Ophrys, 1973).

4. See Mark D. Jordan, "Medieval Philosophy of the Future!" in *The Past and Future of Medieval Studies,* ed. John Van Engen, Notre Dame Conferences in Medieval Studies 4 (Notre Dame and London: University of Notre Dame Press, 1994), pp. 148–165.

5. One of the examples of this tendency is the series Les philosophes belges, founded in 1901 by the Louvain medievalist Maurice De Wulf for the publication of texts by medieval thinkers. In the Introduction to volume 1, De Wulf wrote: "De nombreux penseurs, nés sur le sol des provinces belgiques ont illustré les annales de la philosophie. Il a semblé que c'était à la fois servir la science et la patrie que de faire revivre le nom de compatriotes jadis illustres, et de contribuer par la publication et par l'étude de leurs ouvrages à faire connaître leur influence sur la marche des idées" (*Le traité "De unitate formae" de Gilles de Lessines,* ed. Maurice De Wulf, Les philosophes belges 1 (Louvain: Institut supérieur de philosophie, 1901), no pagination). In 1948, Les philosophes belges became Philosophes médiévaux.

6. The most comprehensive history of the Neoscholastic movement is *Christliche Philosophie im katholischen Denken des 19. und 20. Jahrhunders,* 2: *Rückgriff auf scholastisches Erbe,* ed. Emerich Coreth S.J., Walter M. Neidl, and Heinrich M. Schmidinger (Graz and Cologne: Styria, 1988). Also see Gerald A. McCool S.J., *From Unity to Pluralism: The Internal Evolution of Thomism* (New York: Fordham University Press, 1989), and the same author's *The Neo-Thomists,* Marquette Studies in Philosophy 3 (Milwaukee: Marquette University Press, 1994).

7. Fernand Van Steenberghen, *La philosophie au XIIIᵉ siècle,* 2nd ed., Philosophes médiévaux 28 (Louvain-la-Neuve: Éditions de l'Institut supérieur de philosophie; Louvain/Paris: Peeters, 1991).

8. Fernand Van Steenberghen, *Ontology,* trans. Lawrence Moonan (Louvain: Publications universitaires; New York: Wagner, 1970).

9. Étienne Gilson, *Being and Some Philosophers,* 2nd ed. (Toronto: Pontifical Institute of Mediaeval Studies, 1952), p. 154.

10. This thesis has recently been argued in detail by John Inglis, "Philosophical Autonomy and the Historiography of Medieval Philosophy," *British Journal for the History of Philosophy* 5 (1997):21–53. Inglis shows that the approach to the study of medieval philosophy which the two German medievalists Joseph Kleutgen and Albert Stöckl developed in the 1850s and 60s remained influential deep into our own century. The "Kleutgen-Stöckl model of the history of medieval philosophy," as Inglis calls it (p. 35), is characterized by its

"view of philosophy as being autonomous in the Middle Ages" (p. 32); moreover, it attempts to map medieval thought onto the standard branches of modern philosophy. The article just cited is a summary of John Inglis, *Spheres of Philosophical Inquiry and the Historiography of Medieval Philosophy,* Brill's Studies in Intellectual History 81 (Leyden: Brill, 1998).

11. Foucault uses the expression *discours "en retour"* in his *Histoire de la sexualité,* 1: *La volonté de savoir,* Bibliothèque des histoires (Paris: Gallimard, 1976), p. 134. On the concept of "reverse discourse," see David M. Halperin, *Saint Foucault. Towards a Gay Hagiography* (New York and Oxford: Oxford University Press, 1995), pp. 56–62.

12. The whole debate over the possibility of a "Christian philosophy"—which used to be one of the central issues discussed in Neoscholastic circles— uncritically, and unwittingly, presupposed a modern, rationalist notion of philosophy. On this debate, see Fernand Van Steenberghen, "Philosophie et christianisme," in the same author's *Études philosophiques,* Collection Essais, 2nd ed. (Longueuil, Québec: Éditions du Préambule, 1988), pp. 11–59.

13. Even in the English-speaking world, with its traditional leanings toward analytic philosophy, the analytic approach to medieval philosophy never spread beyond the bounds of a limited number of institutions.

14. *The Cambridge History of Later Medieval Philosophy: From the Rediscovery of Aristotle to the Disintegration of Scholasticism, 1100–1600,* ed. Norman Kretzmann, Anthony Kenny, Jan Pinborg, and Eleonore Stump (Cambridge and New York: Cambridge University Press, 1982).

15. On the reductionist tendencies of the analytic approach to medieval philosophy, see Jacques Follon and James McEvoy, "Apologie de la pensée médiévale," in *Actualité de la pensée médiévale,* ed. Jacques Follon and James McEvoy, Philosophes médiévaux 31 (Louvain-la-Neuve: Éditions de l'Institut supérieur de philosophie; Louvain/Paris: Peeters, 1994), pp. 1–16 (at pp. 7f.). It is fair to point out that many analytic philosophers now recognize the shortcomings of the *Cambridge History,* and have come to aim for an approach capable of accounting for a wider range of issues in medieval thought.

16. I cannot help disagreeing with Mark Jordan's claim that, after the demise of the secular and the ecclesiastical motives for the study of medieval thought, no alternatives have yet been found to replace them. See Jordan, "Medieval Philosophy of the Future!," p. 159.

17. Alain de Libera, *Penser au Moyen Âge,* Chemins de pensée (Paris: Éditions du Seuil, 1991). On this book, see the critical study by Jacques Follon, "Le 'néo-médiévisme' d'Alain de Libera," *Revue philosophique de Louvain* 90 (1992):75–81.

18. A. de Libera, *Albert le Grand et la philosophie,* À la recherche de la vérité (Paris: Vrin, 1990), p. 11. I have reviewed this book in *Irish Philosophical Journal* 7 (1990):193–197.

19. A. de Libera, *La philosophie médiévale,* Premier cycle, 2nd ed. (Paris: Presses universitaires de France, 1995).

20. Loris Sturlese, *Die deutsche Philosophie im Mittelalter. Von Bonifatius bis zu Albert dem Großen (748–1280)* (Munich: C. H. Beck, 1993).

21. Corpus philosophorum teutonicorum medii aevi, ed. Kurt Flasch and Loris Sturlese (Hamburg: F. Meiner, 1977–).

22. Dermot Moran, *The Philosophy of John Scottus Eriugena. A Study of Idealism in the Middle Ages* (Cambridge, England: Cambridge University Press, 1989). Moran is professor of philosophy at University College Dublin.

23. The first volume of this project, directed by Professor James McEvoy (formerly professor of medieval philosophy at Louvain, now based at the National University of Ireland, Maynooth), has appeared recently: *Opera Roberti Grosseteste Lincolniensis* 1, Corpus Christianorum, Continuatio Mediaevalis 130 (Turnhout: Brepols, 1995).

24. James J. McEvoy, *The Philosophy of Robert Grosseteste* (Oxford: Clarendon Press, 1982; corrected reprinting, 1986), p. 452.

25. Jos Decorte, *De waanzin van het intellect. Twee modellen van de eeuwige strijd tussen goed en kwaad* (Kapellen: DNB/Uitgeverij Pelckmans; Kampen: Kok Agora, 1989).

26. Ruedi Imbach, *Deus est intelligere. Das Verhältnis von Sein und Denken in seiner Bedeutung für das Gottesverständnis bei Thomas von Aquin und in den Pariser Quaestionen Meister Eckharts,* Studia Friburgensia N.F. 53 (Fribourg: Universitätsverlag, 1976).

27. R. Imbach, *Laien in der Philosophie des Mittelalters: Hinweise und Anregungen zu einem vernachlässigten Thema,* Bochumer Studien zur Philosophie 14 (Amsterdam: B. R. Grüner, 1989) and, by the same author, *Dante, la philosophie et les laïcs. Initiations à la philosophie médiévale I,* Vestigia. Pensée antique et médiévale 21 (Fribourg: Éditions universitaires; Paris: Cerf, 1996).

28. François-Xavier Putallaz, *Insolente liberté: controverses et condamnations au XIIIe siècle,* Vestigia. Pensée antique et médiévale 15 (Fribourg: Éditions universitaires; Paris: Cerf, 1995).

29. Ivan Illich, *In the Vineyard of the Text. A Commentary to Hugh's "Didascalicon"* (Chicago and London: University of Chicago Press, 1993).

30. Studia Artistarum, Études sur la Faculté des arts dans les Universités médiévales, ed. Louis Holtz and Olga Weijers (Turnhout: Brepols, 1994–).

31. Olga Weijers, *Le maniement du savoir. Pratiques intellectuelles à l'époque des premières universités (XIIIe–XIVe siècles),* Studia artistarum, Subsidia (Turnhout: Brepols, 1996).

32. John Marenbon, *Later Medieval Philosophy (1150–1350). An Introduction* (London and New York: Routledge & Kegan Paul, 1987), p. 1.

33. Thomas d'Aquin, *L'unité de l'intellect contre les averroïstes, suivi des textes contre Averroès antérieurs à 1270.* Texte latin. Traduction, introduction, bibliographie,

chronologie, notes et index par Alain de Libera, GF 713 (Paris: GF-Flammarion, 1994).

34. Martin Blais, *L'autre Thomas d'Aquin* (Québec: Éditions du Boréal, 1990).

35. John I. Jenkins C.S.C., *Knowledge and Faith in Thomas Aquinas* (Cambridge, England: Cambridge University Press, 1997). See my review of this book in *Arthuriana* 8:3 (1998):91–93.

36. Géry Prouvost, *Thomas d'Aquin et les thomismes: essai sur l'histoire des thomismes,* Cogitatio fidei 195 (Paris: Cerf, 1996).

37. Philipp W. Rosemann, *Omne ens est aliquid. Introduction à la lecture du "système" philosophique de saint Thomas d'Aquin* (Louvain and Paris: Peeters, 1996).

38. Paul Vignaux, *Philosophie au moyen âge, précédé d'une Introduction nouvelle et suivi de Lire Duns Scot aujourd'hui* (Albeuve: Éd. Castella, 1987), p. 64: "L'historien qui a reçu une formation philosophique doit craindre de trop unifier, de systématiser; il faut qu'il laisse voir la diversité rebelle."

39. See Cornel West, "The New Cultural Politics of Difference," in idem, *Keeping Faith: Philosophy and Race in America* (New York and London: Routledge, 1993), pp. 3–32.

40. Thus, Mark C. Taylor writes: "The works of many of France's most important twentieth-century writers can be understood as extended responses to and critiques of Hegelian philosophy" (Mark C. Taylor, *Altarity* [*sic*] [Chicago and London: University of Chicago Press, 1987], p. xxiv). Also see Alphonse De Waelhens, *La philosophie et les expériences naturelles,* Phaenomenologica 9 (The Hague: Nijhoff, 1961), p. 13: "L'histoire de la philosophie posthégélienne peut être présentée . . . comme une réfutation hégélienne du hégélianisme."

41. In his famous *Differenzschrift,* Hegel writes: "Das Absolute selbst aber ist darum die Identität der Identität und der Nichtidentität; Entgegensetzen und Einsseyn ist zugleich in ihm" (G. W. F. Hegel, "Differenzschrift," in *Jenaer kritische Schriften,* ed. Hartmut Buchner and Otto Pöggeler, Gesammelte Werke 4 [Hamburg: Meiner, 1968], p. 64).

42. It is perhaps interesting to note that the interpretation of Hegel is currently undergoing its own postmodern revision—like the interpretation of so many other authors central to modernity, such as Descartes or Kant. I owe my knowledge of contemporary discussions concerning Hegel to conversations with Olivier Depré, a former colleague of mine at the Université catholique de Louvain. For a concise presentation of recent research especially on the young Hegel, see Olivier Depré, "Hegel, des années des jeunesse à la fondation du premier système. Aperçu de la littérature récente sur le jeune Hegel," *Revue philosophique de Louvain* 91 (1993):111–125 and 260–274.

43. Michel Foucault, *L'archéologie du savoir,* Bibliothèque des sciences humaines (Paris: Gallimard, 1969), p. 21: "Comme si nous avions peur de penser l'*Autre* dans le temps de notre propre pensée."

44. There are a number of excellent introductions to the postmodern philosophical movement. Particularly to be recommended is Mark C. Taylor, *Altarity*. For a more critical, yet sympathetic account, see Wolfgang Welsch, *Unsere postmoderne Moderne,* 4th ed. (Berlin: Akademie-Verlag, 1993).

45. On the history of textual criticism, see Bernard Cerquiglini, *Éloge de la variante: histoire critique de la philologie,* Des travaux (Paris: Éditions du Seuil, 1989). This work has now become available in English translation: *In Praise of the Variant: A Critical History of Philology,* trans. Betsy Wing, Parallax: Revisions of Culture and Society (Baltimore and London: Johns Hopkins University Press, 1999).

46. See Christian Rutten (in collaboration with J.-P. Benzécri), "Analyse comparative des chapitres de la *Métaphysique* d'Aristote fondée sur les fréquences d'emploi des parties du discours; confrontation entre l'ordre du textus receptus, les références internes et l'ordre du premier facteur," *Les cahiers de l'analyse des données* 13:1 (1988):41–68. Also see the same author's "Sur la composition de la *Métaphysique* d'Aristote: de l'utilité de la stylométrie," in *Éditer, traduire, interpréter: essais de méthodologie philosophique* (see note 2 above), pp. 15–23.

47. Werner W. Jaeger, *Studien zur Entstehungsgeschichte der Metaphysik des Aristoteles* (Berlin: Weidmann, 1912). This book was superseded by Jaeger's own *Aristotle. Fundamentals of the History of his Development,* trans. with the author's corrections and additions by Richard Robinson, 2nd ed. (Oxford: Clarendon Press, 1948).

48. For the current debate about editorial technique, it is useful to consult the journal, *Editio: International Yearbook of Scholarly Editing* (Tübingen: Niemeyer, 1987–).

49. Horst Fuhrmann, "Réflexions d'un éditeur," in *Les problèmes posés par l'édition critique des textes anciens et médiévaux,* ed. Jacqueline Hamesse, Université catholique de Louvain, Publications de l'Institut d'études médiévales—Textes, Études, Congrès 13 (Louvain-la-Neuve: Institut d'études médiévales, 1992), pp. 329–359 (at 343f.). The translation is mine.

50. Iohannis Scotti seu Eriugenae *Periphyseon,* liber 1 and liber 2, ed. Eduardus A. Jeauneau, Corpus Christianorum, Continuatio Mediaevalis 161 and 162 (Turnhout: Brepols, 1996 and 1997).

51. Ibid., vol. 1, p. xix.

52. See ibid., vol. 1, p. lxxxi: "Il est impossible, dans les conditions présentes, de fournir au lecteur le film complet et fidèle d'un texte en perpétuel devenir."

53. *L'Altérité. Vivre ensemble différents,* ed. Michel Gourgues and Gilles-D. Mailhiot, Recherches N.S. 7 (Montreal: Bellarmin; Paris: Cerf, 1986).

54. Georg Wilhelm Friedrich Hegel, *Phänomenologie des Geistes,* ed. Wolfang Bonsiepen and R. Heede, Gesammelte Werke 9 (Hamburg: Meiner, 1980), p. 19.

55. "... licet id quod unus homo potest immittere vel apponere ad cognitionem veritatis suo studio et ingenio, sit aliquid parvum per comparationem ad totam considerationem veritatis, tamen illud, quod aggregatur ex omnibus 'coarticulatis,' idest exquisitis et collectis, fit aliquid magnum, ut potest apparere in singulis artibus, quae per diversorum studia et ingenia ad mirable incrementum pervenerunt ... quia, sicut dictum est, dum unusquisque praecedentium aliquid de veritate invenit, simul in unum collectum, posteriores introducit ad magnam veritatis cognitionem ... Est autem iustum ut his, quibus adiuti sumus in tanto bono, scilicet cognitione veritatis, gratias agamus" (Thomas Aquinas, *In duodecim libros Metaphysicorum Aristotelis expositio* 2.1.276, 287, 288, ed. M.-R. Cathala O.P. and R. Spiazzi O.P. [Turin and Rome: Marietti, 1964], my trans.).

56. Ibid., 2.1.275.

57. Thomas Aquinas, *Quaestiones disputatae de veritate* 24.12.c, Opera omnia iussu Leonis XIII P.M. edita 22.3 (Rome: Editori di San Tommaso, 1976), p. 718 ll. 437–439.

58. Josef Pieper, *The Silence of St. Thomas. Three Essays,* trans. John Murray S.J. and Daniel O'Connor (New York: Pantheon, 1957), p. 103.

59. Thomas Aquinas, *Quaestiones disputatae de malo* 5.3.c, Opera omnia iussu Leonis XIII P.M. edita 23 (Rome: Commissio leonina; Paris: Vrin, 1982), p. 136 l. 81.

60. Indeed, older editions of the *Summa* used to contain a *Supplementum tertiae partis* (compiled by St. Thomas's friend and confrère, Reginald of Piperno), in which what is missing in the *Summa* to make it a "complete" theological "system" is added upon the basis of excerpts taken from Aquinas's commentary on the *Book of Sentences.* [P.W.R.]

61. J. Pieper, *The Silence of St. Thomas,* p. 88f. Translation amended in light of the German text, for which see J. Pieper, *Philosophia negativa. Zwei Versuche über Thomas von Aquin,* Hochland-Bücherei (Munich: Kösel, 1953), p. 66.

62. *Fontes vitae S. Thomae Aquinatis, notis historicis et criticis illustrati,* ed. D. Prümmer O.P. and M.-H. Laurent O.P. (Toulouse: Privat, 1911–1937), p. 377.

Study 1

1. The best general introduction to Foucault's life and work is David Macey, *The Lives of Michel Foucault* (London: Hutchinson; New York: Pantheon, 1993).

2. Thomas Flynn, "Foucault's Mapping of History," in *The Cambridge Companion to Foucault,* ed. Gary Gutting (Cambridge, England: Cambridge University Press, 1994), pp. 28–46 (at p. 28).

3. Michel Foucault, *Folie et déraison. Histoire de la folie à l'âge classique,* Civilisations d'hier et d'aujourd'hui (Paris: Plon, 1961), pp. iv and v: "Au centre de ces expériences-limites du monde occidental, éclate, bien entendu, celle

du tragique même,—Nietzsche ayant montré que la structure tragique à partir de laquelle se fait l'histoire du monde occidental n'est pas autre chose que le refus, l'oubli et la retombée silencieuse de la tragédie. Autour de celle-ci, qui est centrale puisqu'elle noue le tragique à la dialectique de l'histoire dans le refus même de la tragédie par l'histoire, bien d'autres expériences gravitent . . . L'étude qu'on va lire ne serait que la première, et la plus facile sans doute, de cette longue enquête, qui, sous le soleil de la grande recherche nietzschéenne, voudrait confronter les dialectiques de l'histoire aux structures immobiles du tragique." This preface to the first French edition of *Madness and Civilization* was omitted in later editions of the work. The English translation by Richard Howard contains only a fragment of it; the present passage is missing altogether (see *Madness and Civilization. A History of Insanity in the Age of Reason,* trans. Richard Howard [1965; New York: Vintage Books, 1988]).

4. *The Birth of Tragedy* is mentioned explicitly by Foucault not in the preface, but in the conclusion of *Madness and Civilization* (p. 288). On Foucault's use of *The Birth of Tragedy,* see Deborah Cook, "Nietzsche, Foucault, Tragedy," *Philosophy and Literature* 13 (1988):140–50.

5. For a useful introduction to *The Birth of Tragedy,* see David Lenson, *The Birth of Tragedy. A Commentary,* Twayne's Masterwork Studies 8 (Boston: Twayne Publishers, 1987). The best English translation is the one by Shaun Whiteside: *The Birth of Tragedy out of the Spirit of Music,* trans. Shaun Whiteside and ed. Michael Tanner (London and New York: Penguin, 1993).

6. See Gary Gutting, "Foucault and the History of Madness," in *The Cambridge Companion to Foucault,* pp. 47–70.

7. *Der Streit um Nietzsches "Geburt der Tragödie." Die Schriften von E. Rohde, R. Wagner, U. v. Wilamowitz-Möllendorff,* ed. Karlfried Gründer (Hildesheim: Olms, 1969), p. 114.

8. What follows is a rapid summary of *The Birth of Tragedy,* chapters 1–14. References are to the German text, for which see: Friedrich Nietzsche, *Die Geburt der Tragödie. Unzeitgemäße Betrachtungen I-III (1872–1874),* in *Nietzsche, Werke,* ed. Giorgio Colli and Mazzino Montinari, 3rd series, 1 (Berlin and New York: de Gruyter, 1972), pp. 3–152.

9. See chapter 1, p. 23, ll. 13–14: " . . . und doch nicht ohne jene flüchtige Empfinding des Scheins . . ."

10. See 2, 26, 18–21: "das Apollonische . . . und das Dionysische, die aus der Natur selbst, ohne Vermittelung des menschlichen Künstlers, hervorbrechen . . ."

11. "Spiegel des Scheines" (5, 41, 5).

12. See 5, 40, 30–31: "aus dem mystischen Selbstentäusserungs- und Einheitszustande."

13. See 1, 25, 18–22.

14. See 2, 27–28.

15. See 4, 35, 29–32.

16. See 7, 48, 12–15.

17. See 7, 52, 23–24: "Vernichtung der gewöhnlichen Schranken und Grenzen des Daseins . . ."

18. See 7, 52, 6: " . . . übermächtigen Einheitsgefühle . . ."

19. See 8, esp. 58–60.

20. See 10, 67, 22–24: " . . . alle die berühmten Figuren der griechischen Bühne Prometheus, Oedipus u.s.w. [sind] nur Masken jenes ursprünglichen Helden Dionysius."

21. See 12, 78, 6–10.

22. See 12, 81, 17: " . . . rationalistischen Methode."

23. See 11, 73, 14–15: "bürgerliche Mittelmässigkeit."

24. This is not a word Nietzsche uses in *The Birth of Tragedy*.

25. See 12, 79, 5–6.

26. See 14, 90, 20–32.

27. See 14, 91, 19–29.

28. See 12, 84, 5–8: " . . . welcher, wie damals, als er vor dem Edonerkönig Lykurg floh, sich in die Tiefen des Meeres rettete, nämlich in die mystischen Fluthen eines die ganze Welt allmählich überziehenden Geheimcultus."

29. See 15, 97, 19–32.

30. See 18, 114.

31. See the preface to the new 1886 edition of the treatise, entitled "Attempt at Self-Criticism": p. 13, ll. 21–28.

32. Foucault, *Folie et déraison,* pp. iii–iv: "On pourrait faire une histoire des *limites,*—de ces gestes obscurs, nécessairement oubliés dès qu'accomplis, par lesquels une culture rejette quelque chose qui sera pour elle l'Extérieur; et tout au long de son histoire, ce vide creusé, cet espace blanc par lequel elle s'isole, la désigne tout autant que ses valeurs. Car ses valeurs, elle les reçoit, et les maintient dans la continuité de l'histoire; mais en cette région dont nous voulons parler, elle exerce ses choix essentiels, elle fait le partage qui lui donne le visage de sa positivité; là se trouve l'épaisseur originaire où elle se forme. Interroger une culture sur ses expériences-limites, c'est la questionner aux confins de l'histoire, sur un déchirement qui est comme la naissance même de son histoire. Alors se trouvent confrontées, dans une tension toujours en voie de se dénouer, la continuité temporelle d'une analyse dialectique et la mise à jour, aux portes du temps, d'une structure tragique."

33. See ibid., p. i.

34. Jonathan Dollimore, *Sexual Dissidence. Augustine to Wilde, Freud to Foucault* (Oxford: Clarendon Press, 1991), p. 182. Also see my comments on this book in *International Journal of Philosophical Studies* 4 (1996):139–153.

35. Foucault, *Folie et déraison,* p. iv: "Au centre de ces expériences-limites du monde occidental, éclate, bien entendu, celle du tragique même."

36. Unfortunately, Foucault himself never undertook the projected study concerning the constitution of the identity of the West through the Orient as its "other." However, a similar study with regard to the relationship between the West and Africa, inspired by Foucault, is available in Valentin Y. Mudimbe, *The Invention of Africa: Gnosis, Philosophy, and the Order of Knowledge*, African Systems of Thought (Bloomington and Indianapolis: Indiana University Press; London: James Currey, 1988); also see Philipp W. Rosemann, *Africa as the "Other" of the West: Problems, Challenges, Chances*, Mtafiti Mwafrika 1 (Nkozi: Uganda Martyrs University—African Research and Documentation Centre, 1999).

37. In fact, Foucault explicitly defines his project as anti-teleological when he writes: "Vers quelle région irions-nous, qui n'est ni l'histoire de la connaissance, ni l'histoire tout court, qui n'est commandée ni par la téléologie de la vérité, ni par l'enchaînement rationnel des causes, lesquels n'ont valeur et sens qu'au delà du partage?" (*Folie et déraison*, p. iii.)

38. See ibid., p. i: "Tâcher de rejoindre, dans l'histoire, ce degré zéro . . ." For the phrase, "charred root of meaning" *(racine calcinée du sens)*, see p. vi.

39. See ibid., p. vii: "Mais sans doute est-ce là tâche doublement impossible . . ." Let us note in passing that Nietzsche distanced himself from his original belief in the imminent return of an authentic sense of the tragic in his "Attempt at Self-Criticism," published in 1886, fourteen years after the first edition of *The Birth of Tragedy.*

40. See ibid., p. v: "L'histoire n'est possible que sur le fond d'une absence d'histoire."

41. See ibid., p. vi: "Le grand œuvre de l'histoire du monde est ineffaçablement accompagné d'une absence d'œuvre."

42. See ibid., p. vi: "Cette structure est constitutive de ce qui est sens et nonsens, ou plutôt de cette réciprocité par laquelle ils sont liés l'un à l'autre."

43. Indeed, the word "archaeology," in its properly Foucauldian sense, already occurs once in the preface. See p. ii: "Je n'ai pas voulu faire l'histoire de ce langage; plutôt l'archéologie de ce silence."

44. See ibid., p. vii: "Faire l'histoire de la folie, voudra donc dire: faire une étude structurale de l'ensemble historique—notions, institutions, mesures juridiques et policières, concepts scientifiques—qui tient captive une folie dont l'état sauvage ne peut jamais être restitué en lui-même."

45. Foucault, *Madness and Civilization. A History of Insanity in the Age of Reason*, trans. Richard Howard, p. 37. For the French text, see the most recent edition: *Histoire de la folie à l'âge classique*, Collection Tel 9 (Paris: Gallimard, 1976), p. 55.

46. This is the only explanation of which I can think that makes sense of the title, *Folie et déraison*. It is true, however, that in the body of the book Foucault seems to be employing the terms "folie" and "déraison" interchangeably.

47. Foucault, *Madness and Civilization*, p. 15/25 (English/French).

48. Ibid., p. 28/37.
49. Ibid., p. 21/31.
50. The passage from which this text is quoted has been omitted in the English translation; for the French see p. 44: "Elle [la folie] est prise dans le cycle indéfini qui l'attache à la raison; elles s'affirment et se nient l'une par l'autre." Note that the French word *folie* combines the meanings of "folly" and "madness," which the English language has come to distinguish.
51. Ibid., p. 49/77.
52. Ibid., p. 41/62.
53. Ibid., pp. 59–60/86.
54. Ibid., p. 63/89; translation amended.
55. See ibid., p. 57/84: "It was in a certain experience of labor that the indissociably economic and moral demand for confinement was formulated."
56. Philippe Pinel, *Traité médico-philosophique sur l'aliénation mentale,* Monumenta medica (An IX; repr. Paris: Cercle du livre précieux, 1965).
57. Foucault, *Madness and Civilization,* p. 259/515.
58. Ibid., p. 262/517; translation amended.
59. Ibid., p. 269/523.
60. Ibid., p. 272/525.
61. Ibid., p. 276/528.
62. Ibid., p. 275/528.
63. Ibid., p. 278/530.
64. Ibid., p. ix/i (1961 ed.).
65. The transformation of sex into discourse is the principal thesis defended by Foucault in volume 1 of his *History of Sexuality,* which appeared in 1976, fifteen years after *Madness and Civilization.* See Michel Foucault, *The History of Sexuality,* 1: *An Introduction,* trans. Robert Hurley (New York: Vintage Books, 1990), esp. chapter 1, entitled "The Incitement to Discourse" (pp. 17–35).
66. See Foucault, *Madness and Civilization,* pp. xi/iii (in the 1961 ed.) and pp. 79/171, 286–289/555–557.
67. Ibid., p. 287/555.
68. This theme has been explored in detail by James Miller, *The Passion of Michel Foucault* (London: HarperCollins, 1993).
69. Foucault, *Madness and Civilization,* p. ix/i (1961 ed.); translation amended.
70. For a discussion of the important concept of the proximate, see Dollimore, *Sexual Dissidence,* esp. p. 33.
71. Foucault, *Madness and Civilization,* p. ix/i (1961 ed.)
72. Michel Foucault, *The Order of Things. An Archaeology of the Human Sciences* (New York: Vintage Books, 1994), p. xxiv. This English version of *Les mots et les choses* does not identify a translator. According to Macey (*The Lives of Michel Foucault,* p. 545, no. 42), the translation is due to Alan Sheridan. For the French text (originally published in 1966), see Michel Foucault, *Les*

mots et les choses. Une archéologie des sciences humaines, Collection Tel 166 (Paris: Gallimard, 1990), p. 14.

73. Ibid., p. xxiv/14.

74. Ibid., p. xxii/13. In *The Order of Things,* Foucault uses the terms "episteme" and "historical a priori" interchangeably. In later works, especially *The Archaeology of Knowledge,* they come to be distinguished as Foucault's technical vocabulary assumes considerable complexity. In the present context, we can dispense with these details, which would be important for a study of the evolution of Foucault's thought.

75. See M. Foucault, "Monstrosities in Criticism," trans. Robert J. Matthews, *Diacritics* 1:1 (1971):57–60. This essay is the funniest reply to a critical review (or rather, to two of them) I have ever come across. Anyone with a sense of humor will thoroughly enjoy it.

76. Ibid., p. 60.

77. See James W. Bernauer S.J., *Michel Foucault's Force of Flight: Toward an Ethics for Thought,* Contemporary Studies in Philosophy and the Human Sciences (Atlantic Highlands, New Jersey and London: Humanities Press, 1990), pp. 45 and 202 n. 113.

78. See *Kant's gesammelte Schriften,* ed. Preußische Akademie der Wissenschaften, 20: *Kant's handschriftlicher Nachlaß,* 7 (1942; repr. Berlin: de Gruyter, 1971), p. 341 ll. 7–11: "Eine philosophische Geschichte der Philosophie ist selber nicht historisch oder empirisch sondern rational d.i. *a priori* möglich. Denn ob sie gleich Fakta der Vernunft aufstellt so entlehnt sie solche nicht von der Geschichtserzählung sondern sie zieht sie aus der Natur der menschlichen Vernunft als philosophische Archäologie."

79. As part of his doctoral dissertation, he translated, and commented upon, Kant's *Anthropology from a Pragmatic Point of View.* The annotated translation (without the introduction) was published as Émmanuel Kant, *Anthropologie du point de vue pragmatique,* trans. Michel Foucault (Paris: Vrin, 1964).

80. See Maurice Florence, "Foucault," in *Dictionnaire des philosophes,* ed. Denis Huisman, 1 (Paris: Presses universitaires de France, 1981), pp. 942–944.

81. Ibid., p. 942. English translation from *Essential Works of Foucault, 1954–1984,* ed. Paul Rabinow, 2: *Aesthetics, Method, and Epistemology,* ed. James D. Faubion (New York: The New Press, 1998), pp. 459–463 (at p. 459). Foucault also reflects on the relationship of his own thought to Kant's in his essay, "What is Enlightenment?," in *The Essential Works of Foucault, 1954–1984,* ed. Paul Rabinow, 1: *Ethics: Subjectivity and Truth,* ed. Paul Rabinow (New York: The New Press, 1997), pp. 303–319.

82. M. Foucault, *The Archaeology of Knowledge and The Discourse and Language,* trans. A.M. Sheridan Smith (New York: Pantheon Books, 1972), p. 127. For the French text, see: M. Foucault, *L'archéologie du savoir,* Bibliothèque des sciences humaines (Paris: Gallimard, 1969), p. 167.

83. Ibid., p. 127/167.

84. Ibid., p. 127/168; translation amended.

85. See Martin Heidegger, "The Question Concerning Technology," in Martin Heidegger, *Basic Writings from "Being and Time" (1927) to "The Task of Thinking" (1964)*, ed. David Farrell Krell, 2nd ed. (San Francisco: HarperSanFrancisco, 1993), pp. 311–341, esp. p. 321.

86. Foucault, *The Order of Things*, pp. xxi–xxii/13.

87. "Episteme" (ἐπιστήμη) in Greek means "knowledge," "science."

88. Foucault, *The Archaeology of Knowledge*, p. 203/265.

89. Foucault, *The Order of Things*, p. 387/398.

90. In one of his many acerbic remarks on this subject, Foucault writes in the conclusion of *The Archaeology of Knowledge:* "But let us leave off our polemics about 'structuralism'; they hardly survive in areas now deserted by serious workers; this particular controversy, which might have been so fruitful, is now acted out only by mimes and tumblers" (p. 201/261).

91. This return beyond Kant's transcendentalism, together with the deconstruction of the subject that is so characteristic of the contemporary Continental philosophical movement has recently been described with great exactitude by Jean-Luc Marion, *Étant donné. Essai d'une phénoménologie de la donation*, Épiméthée (Paris: Presses universitaires de France, 1997).

92. This brief description of structuralism is inspired by Foucault's own in his essays, "Return to History" and "Structuralism and Post-structuralism," in *Essential Works of Foucault, 2: Aesthetics, Method, and Epistemology*, respectively pp. 419–432 and 433–458.

93. Foucault, *The Archaeology of Knowledge*, p. 202/263.

94. Note, in this context, what we said in the introduction about "history-writing in the second power."

95. Note that in the essay, "What is Enlightenment?," Foucault makes a very similar move in defining his attitude toward the heritage of the Enlightenment, which for him is essentially the heritage of Kant. He wholeheartedly embraces (a certain interpretation of) the Enlightenment project, but refuses what he calls the "blackmail" of the Enlightenment: to treat it as sacrosanct, or else to be counted amongst its adversaries. No, Foucault writes, "[w]e must try to proceed with the analysis of ourselves as beings who are historically determined, to a certain extent, by the Enlightenment" ("What is Enlightenment?," in *The Essential Works of Michel Foucault, 1: Ethics: Subjectivity and Truth*, pp. 303–319, at p. 313).

96. Foucault, *The Archaeology of Knowledge*, pp. 206/268 and 208/271.

97. Ibid., p. 209/272.

98. Ibid., p. 208/271.

99. Ibid., p. 210/273. In the context of this study, it would lead us too far astray to follow up the development of Foucault's thought in his later years. For a brief overview, see Flynn, "Foucault's Mapping of History."

100. This section is based upon Part II of *The Archaeology of Knowledge,* entitled "The Discursive Regularities" (pp. 19–76/29–101).

101. Ibid., p. 67/90.

102. Ibid., p. 68/90.

Study 2

1. Maurice De Wulf, "Y eut-il une philosophie scolastique au moyen âge?" *Revue néo-scolastique de philosophie* 29 (1927):5–27.

2. M. De Wulf, *Histoire de la philosophie médiévale,* 1: *Des origines jusqu'à Thomas d'Aquin* (Louvain: Institut supérieur de philosophie, 1924).

3. For the history of the six editions of De Wulf's *Histoire,* see Fernand Van Steenberghen, *Introduction à l'étude de la philosophie médiévale,* Philosophes médiévaux 18 (Louvain: Publications universitaires; Paris: Béatrice-Nauwelaerts, 1974), pp. 297–312.

4. De Wulf, "Y eut-il une philosophie scolastique," p. 12.

5. As quoted in F. Van Steenberghen, *Introduction,* p. 306.

6. Ibid., p. 309.

7. See De Wulf, "Y eut-il une philosophie scolastique," p. 11.

8. This progress will be documented in detail in study 3.

9. For a detailed presentation of Grabmann's life and work as a medievalist, see Philipp W. Rosemann, "Martin Grabmann," in *Medieval Scholarship: Biographical Studies on the Formation of a Discipline,* vol. 3, ed. Helen Damico, Garland Reference Library of the Humanities (New York: Garland, forthcoming).

10. Martin Grabmann, *Die Geschichte der scholastischen Methode,* 2 vols. (1909–1911, repr. Berlin: Akademie-Verlag, 1988).

11. See Philipp W. Rosemann, "Histoire et actualité de la méthode scolastique selon M. Grabmann," in *Actualité de la pensée médiévale,* ed. Jacques Follon and James McEvoy, Philosophes médiévaux 31 (Louvain-la-Neuve: Éditions de l'Institut supérieur de philosophie; Louvain/Paris: Peeters, 1994), pp. 95–118.

12. Grabmann, *Die Geschichte,* 1, p. 37: "In allmählicher Entwicklung hat die scholastische Methode sich eine bestimmte äußere Technik, eine äußere Form geschaffen, sich gleichsam versinnlicht und verleiblicht."

13. See previous note.

14. Richard W. Southern, *Scholastic Humanism and the Unification of Europe,* 1: *Foundations* (Oxford, U.K. and Cambridge, MA: Blackwell, 1995), p. 103. On the current debate about the old question, "What is Scholasticism?" one may read Rolf Schönberger, *Was ist Scholastik?,* Philosophie und Religion 2 (Hildesheim: Bernward, 1991). A good overview of recent research is also provided by Ruedi Imbach, "Notabilia V. Hinweise auf wichtige

Neuerscheinungen aus dem Bereich der mittelalterlichen Philosophie," *Freiburger Zeitschrift für Philosophie und Theologie* 42 (1995):186–212.

15. To what extent is the following approach really "Foucauldian"? Could one not object that Foucault was deeply averse to the grand narratives of the history of ideas? Yes, a certain Foucault no doubt was, namely, the Foucault of the *Archaeology of Knowledge* and the "history of the Same." As was shown in study 1, the Foucault of *Madness and Civilization* and the "history of the Other" did develop strategies for the kind of large scale historical analysis attempted here.

16. Jean-Pierre Vernant, *Myth and Society in Ancient Greece,* trans. Janet Lloyd, European Philosophy and the Human Sciences 5 (Brighton, Sussex: Harvester Press; Atlantic Highlands, New Jersey: Humanities Press, 1980), p. 186. My account of Greek myth is heavily indebted to this book, as well as to the same author's *Myth and Thought among the Greeks* (London: Routledge & Kegan Paul, 1983).

17. This has been a well-established fact for some time now. The first authoritative study of the problem appeared over fifty years ago; see Wilhelm Nestle, *Vom Mythos zum Logos. Die Selbstentfaltung des griechischen Denkens von Homer bis auf die Sophistik und Sokrates,* 2nd ed. (1942, repr. New York: Arno Press, 1978).

18. The best philosophical account of myth in its relationship to language, religion, art, and science is furnished by Ernst Cassirer in his *Philosophy of Symbolic Forms,* esp. vol. 2: *Mythical Thought.* See Ernst Cassirer, *Philosophy of Symbolic Forms,* trans. Ralph Manheim, 3 vols. (New Haven: Yale University Press, 1953–57). On Cassirer's philosophy of myth, which confirms many of the points I am trying to establish in this study, see Steve G. Lofts, *Ernst Cassirer: la vie de l'esprit. Essai sur l'unité systématique de la philosophie des formes symboliques et de la culture,* "Accent" (Louvain: Peeters; Paris:Vrin, 1997), esp. chapter 3 (pp. 53–75).

19. Vernant, *Myth and Society,* p. 190.

20. Ibid., p. 195.

21. Ibid., p. 199.

22. Ibid., p. 195.

23. Ibid., p. 196.

24. See Vernant, *Myth and Thought,* p. 357.

25. See ibid., pp. 360–365.

26. Vernant, *Myth and Society,* p. 193.

27. Nestle, *Vom Mythos zum Logos,* p. 19. Also see Vernant, *Myth and Society,* pp. 202–203.

28. Ibid., p. 204.

29. The first philosopher who, recognizing this tendency, attempted to discover the peculiar structure and, indeed, "logic" of myth was Ernst Cassirer in his *Philosophy of Symbolic Forms.*

30. Nestle, *Vom Mythos zum Logos,* p. 547.

31. For a philological and exegetical commentary on this passage, see Archibald Robertson and Alfred Plummer, *A Critical and Exegetical Commentary on the First Epistle of St. Paul to the Corinthians,* 2nd ed., The International Critical Commentary on the Holy Scriptures of the New and Old Testaments (Edinburgh: T. & T. Clark, 1911, repr. 1978), pp. 16–24.

32. See Porphyry, *On the Life of Plotinus and the Order of His Books,* in *Plotinus,* trans. A. H. Armstrong, 1, The Loeb Classical Library 440 (Cambridge, MA: Harvard University Press; London: Heinemann, 1966), pp. 1–85 (at p. 3).

33. See Aristotle, *Metaphysics,* 12.7 and 12.9, and Klaus Oehler, "Aristotle on Self-Knowledge," *Proceedings of the American Philosophical Society* 118 (1974):493–506. We shall have an occasion to examine this problem at greater length later.

34. See Lofts, *Ernst Cassirer: la vie de l'esprit,* ch. 4, esp. pp. 78–80.

35. On the problem of Rudolf Bultmann's project to "demythologize" Christianity, see Heinrich Fries and Anton Vögtle, "Entmythologisierung," in *Lexikon für Theologie und Kirche,* ed. Josef Höfer and Karl Rahner, 2nd. ed., 3 (Freiburg im Breisgau: Herder, 1959), cols. 898–904.

36. The relationship, both historical and systematic, between the Christian faith and myth is a difficult problem that we cannot discuss in detail here. As an introduction, one may read the excellent article by Günter Lanczkowski, Heinrich Fries and Victor H. Elbern, "Mythos," in *Lexikon für Theologie und Kirche,* ed. Josef Höfer and Karl Rahner, 2nd ed., 7 (Freiburg im Breisgau: Herder, 1962), cols. 746–754. On the historical problem of the relationship between Christianity and Greek myth, see Hugo Rahner S.J., *Greek Myths and Christian Mystery,* trans. Brian Battershaw (New York and Evanston: Harper & Row, 1963).

37. See Nestle, *Vom Mythos zum Logos,* p. 548: "Im Jahr 529 hebt der Kaiser Justinian die platonische Akademie in Athen auf und Benedikt von Nursia gründet im gleichen Jahr das Kloster auf Montecassino. Der christliche Glaube hatte—auf ein Jahrtausend—über den griechischen Logos gesiegt."

38. Tertullianus, *De praescriptione haereticorum,* ed. R.F. Refoulé, Corpus Christianorum, Series latina 1.1 (Turnhout: Brepols, 1954), VII.9–12, p. 193, ll. 32–34 and 36–39: "Quid ergo Athenis et Hierosolymis? quid academiae et ecclesiae? quid haereticis et christianis? . . . Viderint qui Stoicum et Platonicum et dialecticum christianismum protulerunt. Nobis curiositate opus non est post Christum Iesum nec inquisitione post euangelium."

39. The problem as to the extent to which the New Testament itself betrays the influence of Hellenistic thought (as in the prologue to the Gospel of St. John) cannot be dealt with in the present context.

40. The Platonic, Stoic, and Neoplatonic traditions have similarly complex histories, and all of them were to prove influential in the development of Scholasticism.

41. The preceding account is based on the one to be found in *Die Philosophie der Antike, 3: Ältere Akademie—Aristoteles—Peripatos,* ed. Hellmut Flashar, Grundriss der Geschichte der Philosophie, begründet von Friedrich Überweg, völlig neubearbeitete Ausgabe (Basle and Stuttgart: Schwabe, 1983), pp. 191—192.

42. For a magisterial account of the history of Christendom between 250 and 430 A.D., see *Das Entstehen der einen Christenheit (250—430),* ed. Charles and Luce Piétri, Die Geschichte des Christentums 2 (Freiburg im Breisgau/Basle/Vienna: Herder, 1996).

43. Boethius's famous announcement of his project is contained in A. M. S. Boetii *Commentarii in Librum Aristotelis ΠΕΡΙ ΕΡΜΗΝΕΙΑΣ,* ed. Carolus Meiser, 2 (Leipzig: Teubner, 1880; repr. New York and London: Garland, 1987), 2.3, pp. 79—80.

44. Let me emphasize that this historical statement does not represent in any way a disparagement of the intellectual achievements of the patristic thinkers and the early Scholastics. Nonetheless, the fact remains that for a study of the Scholastic tradition from the angle taken in this book, a "leap over the early Middle Ages" is legitimate—which, again, does not mean to deny the intrinsic interest of this period.

45. The Byzantine commentaries on Aristotle are edited in the Commentaria in Aristotelem Graeca, a series launched in the last century under the auspices of the Prussian Academy. The CAG now comprises over fifty volumes. Professor Richard Sorabji, of King's College, London, is the editor of a series of English translations of some of the texts that appeared in the CAG. These translations are published by Duckworth in London. Useful for a first orientation in the field: Klaus Oehler, *Antike Philosophie und byzantinisches Mittelalter. Aufsätze zur Geschichte des griechischen Denkens* (Munich: Beck, 1969); *Aristotle Transformed: The Ancient Commentators and Their Influence,* ed. Richard Sorabji (London: Duckworth, 1990); Alain de Libera, *La philosophie médiévale,* Collection Premier Cycle (Paris: Presses universitaires de France, 1993), pp. 9—51; Georgi Kapriev, "Byzantinische Philosophie," *Bulletin de philosophie médiévale* 39 (1997):49–52.

46. Together with texts in other Eastern languages (such as Armenian, Coptic, Georgian, Ethiopic, etc.), the works of the Christians authors writing in Syriac are being edited in the series Corpus Scriptorum Christianorum Orientalium (Louvain: Peeters, 1903–), which, at the time of writing this text, comprised 571 volumes. A series of English translations now accompanies the CSCO; the first volume has just appeared: Theodore Abū Qurrah, *A Treatise on the Veneration of the Holy Cross,* ed. Sidney H. Griffith, Eastern Christian Texts in Translation 1 (Louvain: Peeters, 1997). Other literature: Sebastian P. Brock, *Syriac Perspectives on Late Antiquity,* Variorum Collected Studies Series 199 (Aldershot, England: Variorum, 1984); idem, *Studies in Syriac Christianity: History, Literature and Theology,* Variorum Collected Studies Series 357

(Aldershot, England: Variorum, 1992); idem, *Syriac Studies: A Classified Bibliography (1960–1990)* (Kaslik, Lebanon: Parole de l'Orient, 1996).

47. Majid Fakhry, *A History of Islamic Philosophy,* 2nd ed. (New York: Columbia University Press; New York: Longman, 1983), p. 12. On these and related issues, one may now read the excellent new study by Dimitri Gutas, *Greek Thought, Arabic Culture: The Graeco-Arabic Translation Movement in Baghdad and Early 'Abbāsid Society (2nd–4th/8th–10th Centuries)* (London and New York: Routledge, 1998).

48. On the history of Jewish philosophy in the Middle Ages, see Colette Sirat, *A History of Jewish Philosophy in the Middle Ages* (Cambridge, England: Cambridge University Press, 1985).

49. For an overview of the translation movement, see Fernand Van Steenberghen, *La philosophie au XIIIᵉ siècle,* 2nd ed., Philosophes médiévaux 28 (Louvain-la-Neuve: Éditions de l'Institut supérieur de philosophie; Louvain/Paris: Peeters, 1991), pp. 67–81 and 101–107.

50. Charles Homer Haskins, *The Renaissance of the Twelfth Century* (1927; repr. New York: Meridian Books, 1957), p. 285.

51. See R. Manselli, "La corte di Frederico II e Michele Scoto," in *L'averroismo in Italia,* Atti dei Convegni Lincei 40 (Rome: Accademia Nazionale dei Lincei, 1979), pp. 63–80.

52. The publication of Averroës's commentaries on Aristotle (Arabic originals, medieval Hebrew and Latin versions, modern English translations) is the object of the Corpus commentariorum Averrois in Aristotelem. For a list of volumes published up to 1988, see Philipp W. Rosemann, "Averroes: A Catalogue of Editions and Scholarly Writings from 1821 Onwards," *Bulletin de philosophie médiévale* 30 (1988):153–221.

53. For the medieval Latin translations of Avicenna, see the volumes of the series Avicenna latinus, ed. Simone Van Riet (Louvain: Peeters; Leyden: Brill, 1968–), 7 vols. to date.

54. The Graeco-Latin translations of the works of Aristotle are being edited in the series Aristoteles latinus, coordinated by the Philosophy Institute of the Katholieke Universiteit Leuven. On the current state of the Aristoteles latinus, see Jozef Brams, "L'*Aristoteles latinus*: bilan d'une édition internationale," in *Actualité de la pensée médiévale,* ed. Jacques Follon and James McEvoy, Philosophes médiévaux 31 (Louvain-la-Neuve: Éditions de l'Institut supérieur de philosophie; Louvain/Paris: Peeters, 1994), pp. 57–68 (includes a list of published and projected volumes) and, by the same author, "The Latin Aristotle and the Medieval Latin Commentaries," *Bulletin de philosophie médiévale* 39 (1997):9–22.

55. See *Guillaume de Moerbeke. Recueil d'études à l'occasion du 700ᵉ anniversaire de sa mort (1286),* ed. Jozef Brams and Willy Vanhamel, De Wulf-Mansion Centre. Ancient and Medieval Philosophy, Series 1, 7 (Louvain: Leuven University Press, 1989).

Study 3

1. Olga Weijers, *Le maniement du savoir. Pratiques intellectuelles à l'époque des premières universités (XIIIe–XIVe siècles)*, Studia Artistarum, Subsidia (Brepols: Turnhout, 1996).
2. Ibid., p. 7.
3. Robert Marichal, "L'écriture latine et la civilisation occidentale du Ier au XVIe siècle," in *L'écriture et la psychologie des peuples. XXIIe Semaine de Synthèse*, ed. Marcel Cohen (Paris: Armand Collin, 1963), pp. 199–247.
4. Ibid., p. 229: "En d'autres termes, il apparaît que, dans l'histoire de l'Occident, tout changement de mentalité est accompagné, et le plus souvent même annoncé, par un changement dans la morphologie et le style de l'écriture."
5. In a similar vein, albeit on a more fundamental level, the German linguist Christian Stetter has recently argued that there exists an intrinsic connection between alphabetic script and the development of a certain kind of formal thought characteristic of Western culture. See Christian Stetter, *Schrift und Sprache* (Francfort on the Main: Suhrkamp, 1997).
6. See Marichal, "L'écriture latine," p. 222.
7. See C. F.R. de Hamel, *Glossed Books of the Bible and the Origins of the Paris Booktrade* (Woodbridge, Suffolk and Dover, New Hampshire: D.S. Brewer, 1984), pp. 35–36. Also see the review by Richard W. Pfaff, "Out of the Cloister," *The Times Literary Supplement,* 16 August 1985:911.
8. A critical edition of the *Glossa ordinaria* is under way in the series Corpus Christianorum, Continuatio Mediaevalis. So far, one volume has appeared. It contains the Latin text of the Gloss on the Song of Songs, together with (most unusually for the CCCM) an English translation: *Glossa ordinaria,* 22: *In Canticum Canticorum,* ed. and trans. Mary Dove, CCCM 170 (Brepols: Turnhout, 1997). On the *Glossa ordinaria,* see Margaret T. Gibson, *The Bible in the Latin West,* The Medieval Book 1 (Notre Dame: University of Notre Dame Press, 1993), and eadem, *"Artes" and Bible in the Medieval West,* Collected Studies CS 399 (Aldershot, Hampshire, and Brookfield, Vermont: Variorum, 1993).
9. De Hamel, *Glossed Books,* p. 24.
10. Ibid., p. 24.
11. See ibid., pp. 35–37.
12. See Marichal, "L'écriture latine," pp. 230 and 240. For a more detailed description, see Bernhard Bischoff, *Latin Palaeography. Antiquity and the Middle Ages,* trans. Dáibhí Ó Cróinín and David Ganz (Cambridge, England: Cambridge University Press, 1990), pp. 127–136.
13. Marichal, "L'écriture latine," p. 241.
14. There is an excellent dictionary that contains many (though by far not all) of the abbreviations employed by the medieval scribes. It is an extremely

useful tool especially for the novice paleographer: Adriano Cappelli, *Dizionario di abbreviature latine ed italiane,* 6th ed. (Milan: Hoepli, 1987). Supplement: Auguste Pelzer, *Abréviations latines médiévales. Supplément au Dizionario di abbreviature latine ed italiane de Adriano Cappelli,* 3rd ed. (Beauvechain, Belgium: Nauwelaerts, 1995).

15. See Marichal, "L'écriture latine," p. 230.
16. See Cappelli, *Dizionario,* pp. xi–lii.
17. See Ludwig Traube, *Nomina sacra. Versuch einer Geschichte der christlichen Kürzung,* Quellen und Untersuchungen zur lateinischen Philologie des Mittelalters 2 (Munich: Beck, 1907).
18. See ibid., pp. 237–266.
19. See ibid., p. 6.
20. "Scribitur autem Jesus *iota,* et *eta,* et *sigma,* et apice desuper apud nos. Nam in Graecorum libris solummodo per *iota,* et *sigma,* et apice desuper invenitur scriptum, et sicut [I read: *sicut et*] alia nomina Dei comprehensive debent scribi, quia nomen Dei non potest litteris explicari" (Christianus Druthmarus, *Expositio in Mattheum,* Patrologia latina 106, col. 1278).
21. " . . . Trinitas litteris non potest nec comprehendi nec explicari, sed ineffabilis est . . ." (ibid., col. 1267).
22. A rapid search of the *Patrologia Latina Database* (published on CD-ROM by Chadwyck-Healey, Inc.) has not allowed me to discover similar discussions anywhere in the texts published in the PL.
23. See Traube, *Nomina sacra,* pp. 131–133.
24. See ibid., pp. 27–33.
25. Ibid., p. 24.
26. See Bischoff, *Latin Palaeography,* p. 152: "This theory cannot, however, be sustained after examination of much more extensive material than was available to Traube; nevertheless an initial motivation by means of the tetragram in Jewish-Christian circles (such as Alexandria) does seem possible."
27. Marichal, "L'écriture latine," devotes pp. 233–243 of his essay to this issue.
28. Charles Rufus Morey, *Mediaeval Art* (New York: Norton, 1942), p. 272. Further down on the same page, Morey adds: "The miniatures of these books not only reflect the Scholastic mingling of philosophy and theology, of Scripture and ethics, but also the respect of the illuminators for the work of their fellow craftsmen who made the Gothic windows."
29. For Foucault's characterization of a "field of concomitance," see Michel Foucault, *The Archaeology of Knowledge and The Discourse on Language,* trans. A. M. Sheridan Smith (New York: Pantheon Books, 1972), p. 58.
30. See Indra Kagis McEwen, *Socrates' Ancestor. An Essay in Architectural Beginnings* (Cambridge, Massachusetts and London: The MIT Press, 1993), for an interesting attempt to link the origins of the Socratic philosophical project to developments in Greek architecture.

31. Erwin Panofsky, *Gothic Architecture and Scholasticism. An Inquiry into the Analogy of the Arts, Philosophy, and Religion in the Middle Ages* (1951; repr. New York: Meridian Books, 1957).

32. Erwin Panofsky, *Abbot Suger on the Abbey Church of St.-Denis and its Art Treasures,* 2nd ed., ed. Gerda Panofsky-Soergel (Princeton: Princeton University Press, 1979).

33. One of the three treatises translated and commented upon by Panosfky in *Abbot Suger on the Abbey Church of St.-Denis* is now available in a new critical edition with extensive explanatory essays: Abt Suger von St.-Denis, *De consecratione. Kommentierte Studienausgabe,* ed. Günther Binding and Andreas Speer, Veröffentlichungen der Abteilung Architekturgeschichte des Kunsthistorischen Instituts der Universität zu Köln 56 (Cologne: Abteilung Architekturgeschichte des Kunsthistorischen Instituts der Universität zu Köln, 1995).

34. See Jean Bony, *French Gothic Architecture of the 12th and 13th Centuries,* California Studies in the History of Art 20 (Berkeley: University of California Press, 1983), p. 494 n. 29. For Bony, Panofsky's *Gothic Architecture and Scholasticism* contains "the deepest analysis ever given of Gothic modes of thought as they manifest themselves in the forms of architecture."

35. The Cologne medievalist Andreas Speer has criticized Panofsky for maintaining the existence of a "genuine cause-and-effect relation" (*Gothic Architecture and Scholasticism,* p. 20) between Scholasticism and Gothic architecture; whether this criticism is justified or not, the validity of Panofsky's overall argument does not depend on this point. See Andreas Speer, "Vom Verstehen mittelalterlicher Kunst," in *Mittelalterliches Kunsterleben nach Quellen des 11. bis 13. Jahrhunderts,* ed. Günther Binding and Andreas Speer (Stuttgart-Bad Cannstatt: Frommann-Holzboog, 1993), pp. 13–52. Similar reflections in idem, "*Kunst* und *Schönheit.* Kritische Überlegungen zur mittelalterlichen Ästhetik," in *"Scientia" und "ars" im Hoch-und Spätmittelalter,* ed. Ingrid Craemer-Ruegenberg and Andreas Speer, Miscellanea Mediaevalia 22 (Berlin and New York: de Gruyter, 1994), 2, pp. 945–966.

36. See Panofsky, *Gothic Architecture,* esp. pp. 30 and 64.

37. See ibid., p. 31.

38. Ibid., p. 43.

39. To be compared with the "breaking" of the shafts in Gothic script!

40. Panofsky, *Gothic Architecture,* p. 48.

41. See ibid., pp. 51–52.

42. Robert Mark, *Experiments in Gothic Structure* (Cambridge, Massachusetts and London: The MIT Press, 1982), pp. 34–49 has demonstrated the structural necessity of the flying buttresses, thus confirming Panofsky's own opinion on the matter (see *Gothic Architecture,* pp. 53–55)—but of course practical value does not exclude meaning! For this reference and a long helpful discussion on Panofsky, I am grateful to my colleague Robert D.

Russell, Jr., Addlestone Professor of Architectural History at the College of Charleston.

43. Morey, *Mediaeval Art,* p. 265.

44. Ibid., p. 265.

45. Panofsky, *Gothic Architecture,* p. 64.

46. See ibid., p. 72.

47. A comparison between medieval architecture and philosophy from a point of view slightly different from Panofsky's, namely that of the creative (cognitive) processes at work in the two disciplines, has recently been undertaken by Charles M. Radding and William W. Clark, *Medieval Architecture, Medieval Learning: Builders and Masters in the Age of Romanesque and Gothic* (New Haven and London: Yale University Press, 1992). In their conclusion (p. 150), the authors formulate a qualified endorsement of Panofsky's theses: "A final perspective on these developments is provided by Panofsky's notion that Gothic architecture and scholasticism shared a common 'mental habit.' We have found a sense in which this is true, although the common elements concern mental process—how problems were conceived of and solved—rather than the characteristics Panofsky believed to be expressed in the works themselves. But the idea that this habit 'spread' from one discipline to another, or to both from the society as a whole, has proven seriously misleading."

48. See de Hamel, *Glossed Books,* pp. 55–56.

49. Ibid., p. 63.

50. The importance of the *pecia* was first discovered by Jean Destrez: see his *La pecia dans les manuscrits universitaires du XIIIᵉ et du XIVᵉ siècle* (Paris: Vautrain, 1935). This pioneering work is now complemented by Graham Pollard, "The *Pecia* System in the Medieval Universities," in *Medieval Scribes, Manuscripts and Libraries. Essays Presented to N. R. Ker,* ed. M. B. Parkes and Andrew G. Watson (London: Scolar Press, 1978), pp. 145–161.

51. See Mary A. Rouse and Richard H. Rouse, "The Book Trade at the University of Paris, ca. 1250–1350," in idem, *Authentic Witnesses: Approaches to Medieval Texts and Manuscripts,* Publications in Medieval Studies 17 (Notre Dame: University of Notre Dame Press, 1991), pp. 259–338.

52. Although Rouse and Rouse caution against too much optimism in this regard: see ibid., pp. 303–305.

53. The various steps at which mistakes can occur in transcribing a text from one support to another have been described by Eugène Vinaver, "Principles of Textual Emendation," in *Studies in French Language and Medieval Literature Presented to Professor Mildred K. Pope* (1939; repr. Freeport, N.Y.: Books for Libraries Press, 1969), pp. 351–369.

54. See David C. Greetham, *Textual Scholarship: An Introduction,* Garland Reference Library of the Humanities 1417 (New York and London: Garland, 1994), pp. 280–283.

55. See de Hamel, *Glossed Books*, p. 36.

56. See Grisham, *Textual Scholarship*, p. 305.

57. Oxford, Bodleian Library, MS Canonici Gr. 97. This manuscript is currently being edited by Professor Candice Taylor Hogan, of Wheaton College, Massachusetts.

58. Titus Lucretius Carus, *De rerum natura libri sex*, ed. Karl Konrad Friedrich Wilhelm Lachmann, 4th ed. (Berlin: Reimer, 1871).

59. See Paul Maas, *Textual Criticism*, trans. Barbara Flower (Oxford: Clarendon Press, 1958).

60. This situation has been somewhat remedied by the volume, *Les problèmes posés par l'édition critique des textes anciens et médiévaux*, ed. Jacqueline Hamesse, Université catholique de Louvain, Publications de l'Institut d'études médiévales—Textes, Études, Congrès 13 (Louvain-la-Neuve: Institut d'études médiévales, 1992). Madame Hamesse lists some less recent literature on the subject on pp. ix–x, n. 7.

61. Maas does not deal with the diplomatic edition, on which see François Masai, "Principes et conventions de l'édition diplomatique," *Scriptorium* 4 (1950):177–193. A recent example of a diplomatic edition is the one I have prepared of Robert Grosseteste's *Tabula*, published in Corpus Christianorum, Continuatio Mediaevalis 130 (Turnhout: Brepols, 1995), pp. 233–320.

62. For the following summary of the Lachmannian method, see Maas, *Textual Criticism*, pp. 1–21.

63. Sometimes, the archetype is the author's copy itself; but in the absence of concrete evidence, we have no right to assume this.

64. Greetham, *Textual Criticism*, p. 315.

65. Maas, *Textual Criticism*, p. 3, § 7.

66. A. E. Housman, "The Application of Thought to Textual Criticism" (1921), in *Collected Poems and Selected Prose*, ed. Christopher Ricks (London: Allen Lane, 1988), pp. 325–339, at pp. 333 and 339.

67. Greetham, *Textual Scholarship*, p. 314.

68. For a summary of these discussions, see ibid., pp. 313–346.

69. Maas, *Textual Criticism*, p. 7, ¶ 10.

70. Martin L. West addresses the problems caused by an "open recension," that is to say, a tradition that, due to contamination, is not susceptible of stemmatization, in his *Textual Criticism and Editorial Technique*, Teubner Studienbücher (Stuttgart: Teubner, 1973), pp. 37–47.

71. Horst Fuhrmann, "Réflexions d'un éditeur," in *Les problèmes posés par l'édition critique* (see note 60), pp. 329–359 (at 343f.).

72. Richard John Tarrant, "L'édition de la littérature latine classique," in *Les problèmes posés par l'édition critique*, pp. 1–56, at p. 4.

73. West, *Textual Criticism*, p. 57.

74. See L. D. Reynolds and N. G. Wilson, *Scribes and Scholars. A Guide to the Transmission of Greek and Latin Literature,* 2nd ed. (Oxford: Oxford University Press, 1974).

75. M. Annaei Lucani, *Belli civilis libri decem,* ed. A. E. Housman, 2nd impression (1927; repr. Oxford: Blackwell, 1950), p. xiii: "I touch with reluctance, as Gibbon might say, and dispatch with impatience an idle yet pretentious game in which Lucan's less serious critics find amusement, and which they call *Ueberlieferungsgeschichte,* because that is a longer and nobler name than fudge."

76. One of the great merits of Van Steenberghen's influential *La philosophie au XIIIᵉ siècle* (a book that, in some other respects, must now be considered obsolete) is the extensive treatment which the author accords to the cultural and institutional background of the philosophical movement in the thirteenth century. See Fernand Van Steenberghen, *La philosophie au XIIIᵉ siècle,* 2nd ed. (1st ed., 1966), Philosophes médiévaux 28 (Louvain-la-Neuve: Éditions de l'Institut supérieur de philosophie; Louvain/Paris: Peeters, 1991).

77. Ibid., p. 48.

78. See ibid., pp. 47–60.

79. Augustine, *De doctrina christiana* 2.144–148, ed. and trans. R. P. H. Green, Oxford Early Christian Texts (Oxford: Clarendon Press, 1995), pp. 124–127.

80. See ibid. 2.37, p. 73: "Obscure passages are often clarified by the inspection of several manuscripts (*plurium codicum . . . inspectio*)."

81. Van Steenberghen, *La philosophie au XIIIᵉ siècle,* p. 47.

82. Grabmann first announced this discovery in a contribution written for a Festschrift dedicated to Maurice De Wulf; see Martin Grabmann, "Eine für Examinazwecke abgefaßte Quaestionensammlung der Pariser Artistenfakultät aus der ersten Hälfte des XIII. Jahrhunderts," *Revue néo-scolastique de philosophie* 36 (1934):211–229 (*Mélanges Maurice De Wulf*). The article was reprinted in Martin Grabmann, *Mittelalterliches Geistesleben. Abhandlungen zur Geschichte der Scholastik und Mystik,* 2 (2nd ed. 1936; repr. Hildesheim/Zurich/New York: Olms, 1984), pp. 183–199.

83. See Claude Lafleur and Joanne Carrier, *Le "Guide de l'étudiant" d'un maître anonyme de la Faculté des arts de Paris au XIIIᵉ siècle. Édition critique provisoire du ms. Barcelona, Arxiu de la Corona d'Aragó, Ripoll 109, ff. 134ra–158va,* Publications du Laboratoire de philosophie ancienne et médiévale de la Faculté de philosophie de l'Université Laval 1 (Québec: Faculté de philosophie, Université Laval, 1992). This edition is a semi-private publication on which it is difficult to lay one's hands. Sincere thanks to Monsieur David Piché, of the Université Laval, for having made a copy available to me. Professor Lafleur is planning to publish his text in the

Corpus Christianorum, Continuatio Mediaevalis (CCCM). The texts of four other introductions to the study of philosophy written by masters of the arts faculty in Paris are available in Claude Lafleur, *Quatre introductions à la philosophie au XIIIe siècle. Textes critiques et étude historique,* Université de Montréal, Publications de l'Institut d'études médiévales 23 (Montreal: Institut d'études médiévales; Paris: Vrin, 1988).

84. See *L'enseignement de la philosophie au XIIIe siècle. Autour du "Guide de l'étudiant" du ms. Ripoll 109,* ed. Claude Lafleur and Joanne Carrier, Studia Artistarum 5 (Turnhout: Brepols, 1997).

85. The state of the art on research concerning the study-guide is summarized in two contributions to the volume cited in the previous note: David Piché, "Compte rendu des exposés de synthèse de Serge Lusignan et Claude Panaccio" (pp. 369–378), Claude Lafleur and Joanne Carrier, "Les *Accessus philosophorum,* le recueil *Primo queritur utrum philosophia* et l'origine parisienne du *'Guide de l'étudiant'* du ms. Ripoll 109" (pp. 589–642, esp. pp. 625–642).

86. See Claude Lafleur, "Introduction," in *L'enseignement de la philosophie au XIIIe siècle,* pp. xi–xvii.

87. To which books of the *Metaphysics* exactly the author of the study-guide is referring by means of the terms *vetus methaphisica* and *methaphisica noua* is a question investigated by Alain de Libera, "Structure du corpus scolaire de la métaphysique dans la première moitié du XIIIe siècle," in *L'enseignement de la philosophie au XIIIe siècle,* pp. 61–88, esp. pp. 68–70.

88. See S. Thomae Aquinatis *In librum De causis expositio,* Prooem. 9, ed. Ceslai Pera O.P., 2nd ed. (Turin and Rome: Marietti, 1972), pp. 4–5: "Et in graeco quidem invenitur sic traditus *liber Procli platonici continens CCXI propositiones,* qui intitulatur *'Elementatio Theologica'.* In arabico vero invenitur hic liber qui apud latinos *'de Causis'* dicitur quem constat de arabico esse translatum et in gaeco penitus non haberi. Unde videtur ab aliquo Philosophorum arabum ex praedicto libro Proculi excerptus, praesertim quia omnia quae in hoc libro continentur, multo plenius et diffusius continentur in illo."

89. On the early history of the University of Paris, see the outlines in Van Steenberghen, *La philosophie au XIIIe siècle,* pp. 72–74 and in John Marenbon, *Later Medieval Philosophy (1150–1350). An Introduction* (London and New York: Routledge & Kegan Paul, 1987), pp. 7–9.

90. For what follows, see Marenbon, *Later Medieval Philosophy,* pp. 20–24.

91. On the character of the university examinations, see Weijers, *Le maniement du savoir,* pp. 119–129.

92. See Magistri Petri Lombardi Parisiensis Episcopi *Sententiae in IV libris distinctae,* 3rd ed., 2 vols. in 3 parts, Spicilegium Bonaventurianum 4 and 5 (Grottaferrata: Editiones Collegii S. Bonaventurae, 1971–1981). There is still no English translation of the *Book of Sentences,* although W. Becket

Soule O.P. (Blackfriars, Cambridge) is currently preparing one for the new Dallas Library of Medieval Latin Texts-Translations (to be published by Peeters of Louvain). Joseph de Ghellinck S.J., *Le mouvement théologique du XIIe siècle. Sa préparation lointaine avant et autour de Pierre Lombard. Ses rapports avec les initiatives des canonistes. Études, recherches et documents*, 2nd ed., Museum Lessianum—Section historique 10 (Bruges: De Tempel; Brussels: L'Édition universelle; Paris: Desclée de Brouwer, 1948), is now superseded by Marcia L. Colish, *Peter Lombard*, 2 vols., Brill's Studies in Intellectual History 41 (Leyden/New York/Cologne: Brill, 1994); also see Nancy Spatz, "Approaches and Attitudes to a New Theology Textbook: the *Sentences* of Peter Lombard," in *The Intellectual Climate of the Early University. Essays in Honor of Otto Gründler*, ed. Nancy Van Deusen, Studies in Medieval Culture 39 (Kalamazoo, Michigan: Medieval Institute Publications, 1997), pp. 27–52.

93. Recent years have seen the publication of a number of important studies on the problem of literary form and philosophy. See, for instance, Berel Lang, *Philosophy and the Art of Writing: Studies in Philosophical and Literary Style* (Lewisburg: Bucknell University Press, 1983), as well as the same author's *The Anatomy of Philosophical Style: Literary Philosophy and the Philosophy of Literature* (Oxford, U.K.; Cambridge, Massachusetts: Blackwell, 1990). Lang is also the editor of an important collective volume on the topic: *Philosophical Style: An Anthology about the Writing and Reading of Philosophy* (Chicago: Nelson-Hall, 1980). Also see *Literarische Formen der Philosophie*, ed. Gottfried Gabriel and Christiane Schildknecht (Stuttgart: J. B. Metzler, 1990), and some of the essays in *Philosophy in History: Essays on the Historiography of Philosophy*, ed. Richard Rorty, J. B. Schneewind, and Quentin Skinner, Ideas in Context (Cambridge and New York: Cambridge University Press, 1984).

94. The following account is based upon Weijers, *Le maniement du savoir*, esp. chapters 3 through 5 (pp. 39–91).

95. There are, therefore, three levels of interpretation to be distinguished in a *lectio*, namely, *littera, sensus*, and *sententia*. From the *lectio*, three kinds of commentary developed: first, the commentary in the form of *lectiones* (the "hybrid" genre); second, the commentary in the form of *quaestiones;* third, the commentary dwelling on the more immediate meaning *(sententia)* of a text.

96. Weijers, *Le maniement du savoir*, p. 103.

97. Weijers's remark (*Le maniement du savoir*, p. 81), that until around 1300, disputations in the faculty of arts dealt exclusively with questions of a logical nature is puzzling, as it contradicts what she says only three pages earlier (p. 78), and also her own findings in Olga Weijers, *La "disputatio" à la Faculté des arts de Paris (1200–1350 environ). Esquisse d'une typologie*, Studia Artistarum 2 (Turnhout: Brepols, 1995), pp. 92–106.

98. See Weijers, *La "disputatio" à la Faculté des arts de Paris*, p. 42.

99. Weijers, *Le maniement du savoir*, p. 87.

100. Ibid., p. 62.

101. M.-D. Chenu O.P., *Introduction à l'étude de saint Thomas d'Aquin*, Université de Montréal, Publications de l'Institut d'études médiévales 11, 4th printing (Montreal: Institut d'études médiévales; Paris:Vrin, 1984), p. 232.

102. ". . . circa hoc contrarie quidam opinati sunt. quidam enim dixerunt, angelos inferiores nunquam essentiam dei videre; sed per illuminationem superiorum, qui eum immediate vident, dei notitiam capere: cui obviat quod dicitur matth. 18, 10: angeli eorum semper vident faciem patris mei; ubi loquitur de angelis inferioris ordinis, hominibus ad custodiam deputatis. alii vero e contrario dicunt, angelos omnes immediate a Deo illuminationem recipere, negantes inferiores a superioribus illuminari, et negantes totum hoc quod dionysius de angelis tradit auctoritatibus sacrae scripturae probatum, et consonum philosophorum doctrinae. unde mediam viam eligentes, dicimus, omnes quidem angelos essentiam divinam immediate videre, ex quo beati sunt; sed non est necessarium quod qui videt causam, videat omnes ejus effectus, nisi ipsam secundum totam potentiam comprehendat; sicut deus seipsum comprehendens, omnia cognoscit; aliorum autem qui ipsum videndo non comprehendunt, unusquisque tanto plura in eo cognoscit, quanto ipsum plenius capit fruitione gloriae; sicut etiam ex principiis speculativis qui melioris intellectus est, plures conclusiones elicere potest. unde in his divinis effectibus pertinentibus ad statum naturae vel gratiae, quae per angelorum officia dispensantur, superiores inferiores illuminant et instruunt, ut expresse habetur in 7 caelest. hier., et in principio 4 de divinis nominibus (Thomas Aquinas, *In IV libros Sententiarum* 2.9.1.2.ad 3, S. Thomae Aquinatis Opera omnia, ed. Roberto Busa S.J., 1 [Stuttgart-Bad Cannstatt: Frommann-Holzboog, 1980], p. 149).

103. "But some men joined him and believed, among them Dionysius the Areopagite and a woman named Damaris and others with them." Pseudo-Dionysius, a Neoplatonic Christian whom we now know to have been a Syrian monk of the fifth century, authored such influential treatises as *The Divine Names, The Mystical Theology, The Celestial Hierarchy,* and *The Ecclesiastical Hierarchy.* From the fact that he gave himself out to be the "Dionysius" mentioned in the Acts of the Apostles, an enormous authority accrued to him in the Christian tradition.

104. On Aquinas's use of the term *via media,* see my article, "Histoire et actualité de la méthode scolastique selon M. Grabmann. Appendice: 'Secundum aliquid utrumque est verum': 'Media via' et méthode scolastique chez S. Thomas d'Aquin," in *Actualité de la pensée médiévale,* ed. Jacques Follon and James McEvoy, Philosophes médiévaux 31 (Louvain-la-Neuve: Éditions de l'Institut supérieur de philosophie; Louvain/Paris: Peeters, 1994), pp. 95–118.

105. S. Thomae Aquinatis *In duodecim libros Metaphysicorum Aristotelis expositio*
2.1.276, ed. M.-R. Cathala O.P. and R. Spiazzi O.P. (Turin and Rome: Marietti, 1964): "[L]icet id quod unus homo potest immittere vel apponere ad
cognitionem veritatis suo studio et ingenio, sit aliquid parvum per comparationem ad totam considerationem veritatis, tamen illud, quod aggregatur
ex omnibus 'coarticulatis,' idest exquisitis et collectis, fit aliquid magnum,'
ut potest apparere in singulis artibus, quae per diversorum studia et ingenia ad mirabile incrementum pervenerunt."

106. Ibid. 2.1.287: " . . . quia, sicut dictum est, dum unusquisque praecedentium
aliquid de veritate invenit, simul in unum collectum, posteriores introducit
ad magnam veritatis cognitionem."

107. See Thomas Aquinas, *Summa theologiae* 1.16.5.c, Opera omnia iussu Leonis
XIII P.M. edita 4 (Rome: Typographia Polyglotta S.C. de Propaganda Fide,
1888), p. 212: "sequitur quod non solum in ipso [scil. Deo] sit veritas, sed
quod ipse sit ipsa summa et prima veritas."

108. " . . . de Deo scire non possumus quid sit, sed quid non sit" (*Summa theologiae* 1.3.prol., Opera omnia iussu Leonis XIII P.M. edita 4, p. 35). This
idea will find its full justification in study 5.

109. On the philosophical significance of the method of the *quaestio,* also see
Thomas Rentsch, "Die Kultur der quaestio. Zur literarischen For-
mgeschichte der Philosophie im Mittelalter," in *Literarische Formen der
Philosophie,* pp. 73–91.

110. Richard W. Southern, *Scholastic Humanism and the Unification of Europe,* 1:
Foundations (Oxford, England and Cambridge, Massachusetts: Blackwell,
1995), p. 38.

111. Bonaventura, *Breviloquium* 2.12, in Doctoris seraphici S. Bonaventurae
Opera omnia 5 (Quaracchi: Collegium S. Bonaventurae, 1891), p. 230:
"creatura mundi est quasi quidam *liber.*"

112. On St. Bonaventure's book metaphysics, see the detailed study by Winthir
Rauch, *Das Buch Gottes. Eine systematische Untersuchung des Buchbegriffes bei
Bonaventura,* Münchener theologische Studien 2.20 (Munich: Hueber,
1961). Also see George H. Tavard A.A., *Transiency and Permanence. The Nature of Theology According to St. Bonaventure,* Franciscan Institute Publica-
tions, Theology Series 4 (St. Bonaventure, New York: The Franciscan
Institute; Louvain: Nauwelaerts; Paderborn: Schöningh, 1954), Part I (pp.
29–118): "The Three Books." The sources of this idea in Hugh of St. Victor are the subject of the article by Grover A. Zinn, Jr., "Book and Word.
The Victorine Background of Bonaventure's Use of Symbols," in *S.
Bonaventura 1274–1974, 2: Studia de vita, mente, fontibus et operibus Sancti
Bonaventurae* (Grottaferrata: Collegio S. Bonaventura, 1974), pp. 143–169.

113. "[C]reatura mundi est quasi quidam *liber,* in quo relucet, repraesentatur et
legitur Trinitas fabricatrix secundum triplicem gradum expressionis, scilicet per modum *vestigii, imaginis* et *similitudinis*" (*Breviloquium* 2.12, p. 230).

114. See Rauch, *Das Buch Gottes,* pp. 115–127.

115. See Bonaventura, *In Hexaëmeron* 13.12, in Opera omnia 5, p. 390.

116. See Jos Decorte, *De waanzin van het intellect. Twee modellen van de eeuwige strijd tussen goed en kwaad* (Kapellen: DNB/Uitgeverij Pelckmans; Kampen: Kok Agora, 1989), pp. 20–29.

117. Rauch, *Das Buch Gottes,* p. 174.

118. See Bonaventura, *Quaestiones disputatae de mysterio Trinitatis* 1.2.c, in Opera omnia 5, pp. 54–55.

119. See Bonaventura, *Breviloquium* 2.11, p. 229.

120. See Bonaventura, *Quaestiones disputatae de mysterio Trinitatis* 1.2.c, p. 55.

121. This is the same point Aquinas makes, using a different terminology, when he says that in the beatific vision, we shall see the essence of God "as a whole, but not totally": "totam essentiam divinam sancti videbunt in patria, sed non totaliter" (Thomas Aquinas, *In IV libros Sententiarum* 4.49.2.3.ad 3, Opera omnia 1, p. 686). Both St. Bonaventure and St. Thomas want to stress that there can be no "pure presence" of God; His transcendence requires that He can never be fully comprehended by any creature.

122. In Foucauldian terms, it is simplistic to say that certain kinds of subjects generate certain kinds of discursive structures; rather, the different historical a prioris characterizing discursive structures give rise to a variety of subject positions. On this point, see Foucault, *The Archaeology of Knowledge,* pp. 54–55.

123. See Jean Leclercq O.S.B., *The Love of Learning and the Desire for God. A Study of Monastic Culture,* 3rd ed., trans. Catharine Misrahi (New York: Fordham University Press, 1982), p. 237.

124. On the history of oral and silent reading, see the synthetic article by Paul Saenger, "Silent Reading: Its Impact on Late Medieval Script and Society," *Viator* 13 (1982):367–414, esp. 376–378.

125. Leclercq, *Love of Learning,* p. 73.

126. Ibid.

127. See ibid., pp. 73–74.

128. Ibid., p. 74.

129. John Dagenais, *The Ethics of Reading in Manuscript Culture. Glossing the "Libro de buen amor"* (Princeton: Princeton University Press, 1994), p. 22.

130. On this point, see Marichal, "L'écriture latine," pp. 207–208 and 215.

131. The shift from monastic to Scholastic reading techniques is the subject of the book by Ivan Illich, *In the Vineyard of the Text. A Commentary to Hugh's "Didascalicon"* (Chicago and London: University of Chicago Press, 1993). The book can be criticized for some historical inaccuracies (Illich is in fact not a medievalist), but its general thrust seems sound to me.

132. See Saenger, "Silent Reading," p. 396.

133. On this topic, the research of Mary and Richard Rouse, of the University of California at Los Angeles, has broken new ground. See Mary A. Rouse and

Richard H. Rouse, "*Statim invenire:* Schools, Preachers, and New Attitudes to the Page," in idem, *Authentic Witnesses* (see note 51), pp. 191–219; "The Development of Research Tools in the Thirteenth Century," in *Authentic Witnesses,* pp. 221–255; "Concordances et index," in *Du livre manuscrit. Mise en page et mise en texte,* ed. Henri-Jean Martin and Jean Vezin (Paris: Éditions du Cercle de la Librairie/Promodis, 1990), pp. 219–228; "La naissance des index," in *Histoire de l'édition française,* ed. Henri-Jean Martin and Roger Chartier, 1: *Le livre conquérant. Du Moyen Âge au milieu du XVIIe siècle* (Paris: Promodis, 1982), pp. 77–85. Also see Weijers, *Le maniement du savoir,* pp. 157–180.

134. I edited this text a few years ago in Robert Grosseteste, *Tabula,* ed. Philipp W. Rosemann, Corpus Christianorum, Continuatio Mediaevalis 130 (Turnhout: Brepols, 1995), pp. 233–320. Also see my study, "Robert Grosseteste's *Tabula,*" in *Robert Grosseteste: New Perspectives on His Thought and Scholarship,* ed. James McEvoy, Instrumenta Patristica 27 (Steenbrugge: in Abbatia S. Petri; Turnhout: Brepols, 1995), pp. 321–355. The Rouses claim (*Authentic Witnesses,* p. 196 n. 13) to have identified another copy of Grosseteste's index, namely, in Paris, Bibliothèque nationale, MS nouv. acq. lat. 540. However, in the article just cited, I have shown the text in the Paris manuscript to be fundamentally different from Grosseteste's index.

135. Illich, *In the Vineyard of the Text,* p. 103.

136. See ibid., p. 82.

137. See Saenger, "Silent Reading," pp. 399–400.

138. See ibid., 396–397.

139. See A. J. Minnis, *Medieval Theory of Authorship. Scholastic Literary Attitudes in the Later Middle Ages,* 2nd ed. (1984; repr. Aldershot: Wildwood House, 1988), esp. pp. 33–39.

Study 4

1. Foucault's unpublished papers are kept at the Centre Michel Foucault of the Dominican Bibliothèque du Saulchoir in Paris, which he used for his research during the last five years of his life, from 1979 to 1984.

2. David Macey, *The Lives of Michel Foucault* (London: Hutchinson; New York: Pantheon, 1993), p. 466.

3. See Michel Foucault, "Le combat de la chasteté," *Communications* 35 (May 1982):15–25. An English translation is published as: "The Battle for Chastity," in *The Essential Works of Michel Foucault, 1954–1984,* ed. Paul Rabinow, 1: *Ethics: Subjectivity and Truth,* ed. Paul Rabinow (New York: The Free Press, 1997), pp. 185–197.

4. Anne Clark Bartlett, "Foucault's 'Medievalism,'" *Mystics Quarterly* 20 (1994):10–18 (at 15).

5. Michel Foucault, "Préface à la transgression," *Critique* 195–196 (August/September 1963):751–769 (at 751). English translation: "A Preface to

Transgression," in *Essential Works of Foucault, 1954–1984,* ed. Paul Rabinow, 2: *Aesthetics, Method, and Epistemology,* ed. James D. Faubion (New York: The Free Press, 1998), pp. 69–87 (at p. 69). In my quotation, I have significantly altered this translation, which glosses over the difficulties of Foucault's language by departing wildly from the original text.

6. Michel Foucault, "On the Genealogy of Ethics: An Overview of Work in Progress," in *The Essential Works of Michel Foucault, 1954–1984,* 1: *Ethics,* pp. 253–280 (at p. 256).

7. See Foucault, "Preface to Transgression," p. 71: "Perhaps the importance of sexuality in our culture . . . derives from nothing else than this correspondence which connects it to the death of God."

8. Michel Foucault, *The Order of Things. An Archaeology of the Human Sciences,* trans. not identified [Alan Sheridan] (1971; repr. New York: Vintage Books, 1994), p. 44.

9. Ibid., p. 17. For the French text, see Michel Foucault, *Les mots et les choses. Une archéologie des sciences humaines,* Collection Tel 166 (1966; repr. Paris: Gallimard, 1992), p. 32.

10. Ibid., p. 30/45.

11. See ibid., p. 21/36.

12. The Louvain medievalist Jos Decorte was the first scholar to use the categories elaborated in "The Prose of the World" in the context of a study on medieval thought; the results of his work vindicate this strategy. See Jos Decorte, *De waanzin van het intellect. Twee modellen van de eeuwige strijd tussen goed en kwaad* (Kapellen: DNB/Uitgeverij Pelckmans; Kampen: Kok Agora, 1989), pp. 29–38.

13. Foucault, *The Order of Things,* p. 18/33.

14. Ibid., p. 18/33.

15. Ibid., p. 21/36.

16. See Sancti Aurelii Augustini, *De trinitate libri XV,* ed. W. J. Mountain and Fr. Glorie, 2 vols., Corpus Christianorum, Series latina 50/50A (Turnhout: Brepols, 1968).

17. Foucault, *The Order of Things,* p. 23/38; trans. amended.

18. Ibid., p. 25/40.

19. Ibid., pp. 23–24/39.

20. Ibid., p. 24/39.

21. Ibid., p. 24/39; trans. amended.

22. Ibid., p. 26/41.

23. Ibid., p. 27/41.

24. "Classical" is used here in the French sense of the term, where *l'époque classique* designates both the classical age and its revival in the seventeenth century.

25. Foucault, *The Order of Things,* p. 27/42.

26. Ibid., p. 28/43.

27. Ibid., p. 43/58.

28. Ibid., pp. 33–34/48–49; trans. amended.

29. The conception of the world as text will also be familiar to anyone acquainted with postmodern thought. This fascinating parallel between the Scholastic and the postmodern episteme is a question I hope to address in a future study. For a first orientation, see Thomas J. Wilson, *Sein als Text. Vom Textmodell als Martin Heideggers Denkmodell. Eine funktionalistische Interpretation,* Symposion 63 (Freiburg and Munich: Alber, 1981).

30. Foucault, *The Order of Things,* p. 40/55; trans. amended.

31. Ibid., p. 41/56.

32. Ibid., p. 36/51.

33. Ibid., pp. 41/55–56; trans. amended.

34. Ibid., p. 30/45; trans. amended.

35. See, for instance, Thomas Aquinas, *Summa theologiae* 1.4.3.c, Opera omnia iussu Leonis XIII P.M. edita 4 (Rome: Typographia Polyglotta S.C. de Propaganda Fide, 1888), p. 53.

36. See Philipp W. Rosemann, *Omne agens agit sibi simile. A "Repetition" of Scholastic Metaphysics,* Louvain Philosophical Studies 12 (Louvain: Leuven University Press, 1996), esp. pp. 33–101.

37. See Lynne Ballew, *Straight and Circular: A Study of Imagery in Greek Philosophy* (Assen: Van Gorcum, 1979), pp. 4–6.

38. See idem, pp. 45–50. These pages are also printed in the author's essay, "Straight and Circular in Parmenides and the 'Timaeus,'" *Phronesis* 19 (1974):189–209.

39. References are to the text and translation of David Gallop, *Parmenides of Elea: Fragments. A Text and Translation with an Introduction,* Phoenix Supplementary Volume 18/*Phoenix* Pre-Socratics 1 (Toronto: University of Toronto Press, 1984).

40. Ballew, *Straight and Circular,* p. 6.

41. The reading ἀληθείης εὐκυκλέος is not uncontroversial. Diels defended it vigorously in his edition of the fragments; for although it is attested by only Simplicius (against the combined testimony of Plutarch, Clemens Alexandrinus, Sextus Empiricus, and Diogenes Laërtius, who all give εὐπειθέος, 'persuasive'), Diels was convinced that it corresponded to "the inner core of Parmenedian speculation" (see Hermann Diels, *Parmenides: Lehrgedicht* [Berlin: Reimer, 1897], p. 55). G. Jameson, "'Well-Rounded Truth' and Circular Thought in Parmenides," *Phronesis* 3 (1958):15–30, has argued against Diels, but many modern editors (though not Gallop) still prefer the Simplician version: see, for instance, Leonardo Tarán, *Parmenides. A Text with Translation, Commentary, and Critical Essays* (Princeton, N.J.: Princeton University Press, 1965), p. 7. It should be noted, however, that while ἀλήθεια εὐκυκλής is certainly the most striking formulation of the circularity of truth in the *Poem,* it is not the only one; fragment 5,

for instance, expresses very much the same idea: "And it is all one to me | Where I am to begin; for I shall return there again."

42. See Ballew, *Straight and Circular,* p. 49.

43. This is the interpretation suggested by Ballew, *Straight and Circular,* pp. 48–49.

44. Ballew, "Straight and Circular," p. 202.

45. A. E. Taylor, *A Commentary on Plato's Timaeus* (Oxford: Clarendon Press, 1928), p. 102.

46. Diels, *Parmenides: Lehrgedicht,* p. 88.

47. Plato, 9: *Timaeus, Critias, Cleitophon, Menexenus, Epistles,* trans. R. G. Bury, The Loeb Classical Library 234 (Cambridge, Massachusetts: Harvard University Press; London: Heinemann, 1929), pp. 60–63.

48. See ibid., 28A–30A, pp. 48–55.

49. Ibid., 29A, p. 50.

50. Ibid., 28A, 29A (twice), pp. 48/50.

51. See ibid., 28A, p. 48: "νοήσει μετὰ λόγου περιληπτόν"; 29A, p. 52: "λόγῳ καὶ φρονήσει περιληπτόν."

52. Ballew, *Straight and Circular,* p. 79.

53. Plato, 3: *Lysis, Symposium, Gorgias,* trans. W. R.M. Lamb, Loeb Classical Library 166 (Cambridge, Massachusetts: Harvard University Press; London: Heinemann, 1925), pp. 194–197.

54. See Hans Meyer, *Natur und Kunst bei Aristoteles. Ableitung und Bestimmung der Ursächlichkeitsfaktoren,* Studien zur Geschichte und Kultur des Altertums 10.2 (Paderborn: Schöningh, 1919), p. 121 n. 3: "Das von Aristoteles scharf formulierte und stark betonte Gesetz der Synonymie ist sachlich schon platonisch."

55. The following interpretation is guided by the excellent commentary of Gerhard Krüger, *Einsicht und Leidenschaft. Das Wesen des platonischen Denkens,* 5th ed. (Francfort on the Main: Klostermann, 1983).

56. Plato, *Symposium,* 206C, p. 191.

57. Ibid., 206C, p. 190.

58. Ibid., 210D, pp. 204–205.

59. Plato, 1: *Euthyphro, Apology, Crito, Phaedo, Phaedrus,* trans. Harold North Fowler, The Loeb Classical Library 36 (Cambridge, Massachusetts: Harvard University Press; London: Heinemann, 1914), 83A-B, pp. 288–289.

60. Foucault's concluding remark in *The Archaeology of Knowledge* is a critique of the Platonism that underpins much of the Western intellectual tradition, linking rational discourse to a quest for eternal life: "Discourse is not life: its time is not your time; in it, you will not be reconciled to death; you may have killed God beneath the weight of all that you have said; but don't imagine that, with all that you are saying, you will make a man that will live longer than he" (Michel Foucault, *The Archaeology of Knowledge and The Discourse on Language,* trans. A. M. Sheridan Smith [New York: Pantheon, 1972], p. 211).

61. See Ballew, *Straight and Circular,* pp. 123–128.

62. Klaus Oehler, *Ein Mensch zeugt einen Menschen. Über den Mißbrauch der Sprachanalyse in der Aristotelesforschung,* Wissenschaft und Gegenwart 27 (Francfort on the Main: Klostermann, 1963), p. 40.

63. Aristotle, *De anima* 2.4, 415a26–b7, ed. William David Ross (Oxford: Clarendon Press, 1961). The translation I shall be using throughout this section for the quotation of Aristotle is: *The Complete Works of Aristotle. The Revised Oxford Translation,* 2 vols., ed. Jonathan Barnes, Bollingen Series 71 (Princeton: Princeton University Press, 1984). This passage: p. 661.

64. Aristotle, *On Coming-to-be and Passing-away* 2.11, 338b6–18, ed. Harold H. Joachim (1922; repr. Hildesheim and New York: Olms, 1970); rev. Oxford trans.: p. 554.

65. Ἀνακάμπτω: "to bend back, make return, return."

66. See *Aristotelis Meteorologicorum libri quattuor* 1.9, ed. F. H. Fobes (Cambridge, Massachusetts: Harvard University Press, 1919).

67. Ibid. 1.3, 339b27–30 (trans. p. 556); also see *On the Heavens* 1.3, 270b19–20, *Metaphysics* 12.8, 1074b10–13.

68. On Aristotle's interest in proverbs, see Klaus Oehler, "Der Consensus omnium als Kriterium der Wahrheit in der antiken Philosophie und der Patristik. Eine Studie zur Geschichte des Begriffs der Allgemeinen Meinung," in idem, *Antike Philosophie und byzantinisches Mittelalter. Aufsätze zur Geschichte des griechischen Denkens* (Munich: Beck, 1969), pp. 234–271, at pp. 238–239.

69. A good résumé of the main issues and arguments aired in recent research concerning the νόησις νοήσεως is to be found in Thomas De Koninck, "La 'Pensée de la Pensée' chez Aristote," in *La question de Dieu selon Aristote et Hegel,* ed. Thomas De Koninck and Guy Planty-Bonjour (Paris: Presses universitaires de France, 1991), pp. 69–151.

70. Aristotle, *Metaphysics* 12.9, 1074b34–35, ed. William David Ross, 2 vols. (Oxford: Clarendon Press, 1924). For an excellent interpretation of *Metaphysics* 12.7 and 12.9, see Klaus Oehler, "Aristotle on Self-Knowledge," *Proceedings of the American Philosophical Society* 118 (1974):493–506. On the significance of the ancient conception of self-reflexivity for the history of philosophy, see the same author's *Subjektivität und Selbstbewußtsein in der Antike* (Würzburg: Königshausen und Neumann, 1997).

71. Oehler, "Aristotle on Self-Knowledge," p. 506.

72. Aristotle, *Metaphysics,* 12.9, 1974b36.

73. On the self-reference of the human νοῦς, see Klaus Oehler, *Die Lehre vom noetischen und dianoetischen Denken bei Platon und Aristoteles,* 2nd ed. (Hamburg: Meiner, 1985), pp. 186–212.

74. For a list of the occurrences of this phrase in the Aristotelian corpus, see Hermann Bonitz, *Index Aristotelicus* (1870; repr. Graz: Akademische Druck- und Verlagsanstalt, 1955), p. 59, col. b, ll. 40–45. Aristotle's use of the

ἄνθρωπος ἄνθρωπον γεννᾷ example has most comprehensively been treated by Oehler, *Ein Mensch zeugt einen Menschen,* esp. pp. 37–65.

75. Aristotle, *Physics* 2.1, 193b8–9, ed. William David Ross (Oxford: Clarendon Press, 1936); rev. Oxford trans: p. 330.

76. The context of this sentence is Antiphon's argument that the nature of a thing cannot be its form because "if you planted a bed and the rotting wood acquired the power of sending up a shoot, it would not be a bed that would come up, but *wood*" (*Physics* 2.1, 193a12–14; trans. p. 329)—nature being understood as the principle of reproduction. Although Aristotle does not accept Antiphon's argument, he seems to be accepting the exclusion of artifacts from the law of similarity; or at least he does not pursue the matter further in the present context.

77. Aristotle, *Metaphysics* 7.7, 1032a25.; rev. Oxford trans.: p. 1630.

78. Ibid., 1032b11–12; trans.: p. 1630.

79. Ibid., 1032b5–6; trans: p. 1630.

80. The vague "something other" is in fact the soul.

81. Aristotle, *Metaphysics* 12.3, 1070a4–9; rev. Oxford trans.: p. 1690.

82. It is not entirely clear who coined the term, but one of the first to use it must have been Franz Brentano, *Aristoteles und seine Weltanschauung* (Leipzig: Quelle & Meyer, 1911), pp. 62–66: "Das Gesetz der Synonymie"; also see Hans Meyer, *Geschichte der Lehre von den Keimkräften von der Stoa bis zum Ausgang der Patristik* (Bonn: P. Hanstein, 1914), p. 21: "Satz der Synonymie," p. 198: "Gesetz der Synonymie."

83. Aristotle, *Categories,* 1, 1a5–6, ed. Lorenzo Minio-Paluello, Scriptorum Classicorum Bibliotheca Oxoniensis (Oxford: Clarendon Press, 1949); rev. Oxford trans.: p. 3.

84. Aristotle, *Metaphysics* 7.9, 1034a21–22.

85. Aristotle, *Categories* 1, 1a1–2; trans.: p. 3.

86. Alexander of Aphrodisias employs them indifferently in his commentary upon the passage; see Alexander Aphrodisiensis *In Aristotelis Metaphysica Commentaria,* ed. Michael Hayduck, Commentaria in Aristotelem Graeca 1 (Berlin: G. Reimer, 1881), pp. 498–499. Also see Aristotle, *Metaphysics,* ed. Ross, 2, p. 192.

87. See Richard Sorabji, "The Ancient Commentators on Aristotle," in *Aristotle Transformed. The Ancient Commentators and Their Influence,* ed. Richard Sorabji (London: Duckworth, 1990), pp. 1–30, esp. pp. 3–5: "The Harmony of Plato, Aristotle and Other Greek Philosophers."

88. Plotinus's works, the *Enneads,* are available in an excellent English translation by the British classicist Arthur Hilary Armstrong: Plotinus, trans. A. H. Armstrong, 7 vols., The Loeb Classical Library 440–445 and 468 (Cambridge, Massachusetts: Harvard University Press; London: Heinemann, 1966–1988). The *Enneads* are cited in the way in which they were arranged

by Plotinus's pupil Porphyry. For instance, II.3.12, 3–11 is a reference to *Ennead* II.3, paragraph 12, lines 3 through 11.

89. Ibid.,V.3.15, 26–31 = vol. 5 of the Armstrong trans., pp. 124–125.

90. See ibid.,V.1.9, 7–9; vol. 5, pp. 42–43: "Later, Aristotle makes the first principle (τὸ πρῶτον) separate and intelligible, but when he says that it knows itself (νοεῖν δὲ αὐτὸ ἑαυτό), he goes back again and does not make it the first principle."

91. See ibid.V.3.10, 23.

92. Ibid.,V.6.5, 10–12; vol. 5, pp. 212–213.

93. Ibid.,V.4.2, 15–19; vol. 5, pp. 144–147.

94. Ibid., vol. 5, p. 146 n. 1.

95. Ibid., VI.8.17, 25–27; vol. 7, pp. 284–285: "αὐτὸς ἄρα αὑτῷ ὅ ἐστι πρὸς αὑτόν καὶ εἰς αὑτόν, ἵνα μηδὲ ταύτῃ πρὸς ἔξω ἢ πρὸς ἄλλον, ἀλλὰ πρὸς αὑτὸν πᾶς."

96. V.1.6, 18, vol. 5, pp. 30–31, describes the One as "ἐπιστραφέντος ἀεὶ ἐκείνου πρὸς αὑτό," "always turned toward itself."

97. Ibid.,V.5.6, 26; vol. 5, pp. 174–175.

98. Ibid.,VI.7.40, 42 (vol. 7, pp. 212–213) andVI.8.12, 1 (vol. 7, pp. 264–265).

99. Ibid.,V.3.10, 37; vol. 5, pp. 106–107.

100. E. F. Bales, "Plotinus's Theory of the One," in *The Structure of Being. A Neoplatonic Approach,* ed. R. Baine Harris, Studies in Neoplatonism 4 (Norfolk, Virginia: International Society for Neoplatonic Studies, 1982), pp. 40–50, at p. 49.

101. Plotinus, trans. A. H. Armstrong,VI.9.3, 54; vol. 7, pp. 314–315.

102. Kevin Corrigan and P. O'Cleirigh, "The Course of Plotinian Scholarship from 1971 to 1986," in *Aufstieg und Niedergang der römischen Welt,* II: *Principat,* 36: *Philosophie, Wissenschaften, Technik,* 1, ed. Wolfgang Haase (Berlin and New York: de Gruyter, 1987), pp. 571–623, at p. 592.

103. Armstrong: "to it."

104. Plotinus, trans. A. H. Armstrong,V.1.7, 1–6; vol. 5, pp. 32–35.

105. V.1.7, 5–6 ("πῶς οὖν . . . ὅρασις αὕτη νοῦς") is one of the most hotly debated passages in the *Enneads.* For the history of the scholarly discussion, see *Plotini Opera,* 3, ed. Paul Henry and Hans-Rudolf Schwyzer, Museum Lessianum, Series Philosophica 35 (Paris and Brussels: Desclée de Brouwer; Leyden: E. J. Brill, 1973), p. 397; Michael Atkinson, *Plotinus: Ennead V.1. On the Three Principal Hypostases. A Commentary with Translation,* Oxford Classical and Philosophical Monographs (Oxford: Clarendon Press, 1983), pp. 157–160; the most recent treatment of the passage is John Bussanich's detailed commentary in his *The One and its Relation to Intellect in Plotinus. A Commentary on Selected Texts,* Philosophia antiqua 49 (Leyden: Brill, 1988), pp. 37–43. On its most basic level, the question raised by the sentence, "ἢ ὅτι τῇ ἐπιστροφῇ πρὸς αὐτὸ ἑώρα" is one of accentuation: are we to read

πρὸς αὐτό, taking the entire sentence to mean, "by its return *to it* [i.e., to the One] it [i.e., the Intellect] sees"? Or is it preferable to follow the lection πρὸς αὐτό, with a rough breathing (= "by its return *to itself* it [i.e., the One] sees")? Manuscript evidence militates in favor of αὐτό, but then, αὐτό itself can be either reflexive or nonreflexive, so that we are left with a genuine philosophical problem, which is twofold: (1) is self-reversion compatible with the nature of the One; (2) can we view this self-reversion as being productive of Intellect? Concerning question (1), many passages can be adduced to show that Plotinus frequently described the One in terms of self-reference: some of the most pertinent texts have already been discussed earlier on. As for question (2), are there other texts in the *Enneads* where the generation of νοῦς is identified with the self-reflexivity of the One? It would not seem so. But this is no reason to reject the evidence of the one text we have, since the doctrine contained in it can be demonstrated to be in line with a particular side of Plotinus's thought.

106. Plotinus, trans. A. H. Armstrong, V.2.1, 7–13; vol. 5, pp. 58–59.
107. See Klaus Kremer, *Die neuplatonische Seinsphilosophie und ihre Wirkung auf Thomas von Aquin,* Studien zur Problemgeschichte der antiken und mittelalterlichen Philosophie 1 (Leyden: Brill, 1966), p. 156.
108. Plotinus, trans. Armstrong, V.4.2, 7–8; vol. 5, pp. 144–145.
109. Karl-Heinz Volkmann-Schluck, *Plotin als Interpret der Ontologie Platos,* 2nd ed., Philosophische Abhandlungen 10 (Francfort on the Main: Klostermann, 1957), p. 125.
110. Plotinus, trans. Armstrong, III.8.5, 24–25; vol. 3, pp. 376–377.
111. Plotinus studied in Alexandria for over ten years.
112. Plotinus, trans. Armstrong, V.8.6, 1–12; vol. 5, pp. 256–257. On Plotinus's comparison between the nondiscursive thought of Intellect and the comprehension of hieroglyphic inscriptions, see Werner Beierwaltes, *Plotin, Über Ewigkeit und Zeit,* Klostermann Texte Philosophie (Francfort on the Main: Klostermann, 1967), p. 58; and Eugénie De Keyser, *La signification de l'art dans les Ennéades de Plotin,* Université de Louvain, Recueil de travaux d'histoire et de philologie 4.7 (Louvain: Bibliothèque de l'université/Publications universitaires de Louvain, 1955), pp. 60–62.
113. Oscar Cullmann, *Christus und die Zeit. Die urchristliche Zeit- und Geschichtsauffassung* (Zollikon and Zurich: Evangelischer Verlag, 1946). English translation: *Christ and Time. The Primitive Christian Conception of Time and History,* revised ed., trans. Floyd V. Filson (Philadelphia: Westminster Press, 1964).
114. See ibid. (English trans.), p. 146.
115. Ibid., p. 54.
116. See, for instance, the remarks in Joseph Ratzinger, *The Theology of History in St. Bonaventure,* trans. Zachary Hayes O.F.M. (Chicago: Franciscan Herald Press, 1971), p. 173 n. 8.

117. Cullmann, *Christ and Time,* p. 51. Ratzinger agrees: see *The Theology of History in St. Bonaventure,* p. 143.
118. See ibid., pp. 51–60.
119. See Richard C. Dales, *Medieval Discussions of the Eternity of the World,* Brill's Studies in Intellectual History 18 (Leyden: Brill, 1990); Richard C. Dales and Omar Argerami, *Medieval Latin Texts on the Eternity of the World,* Brill's Studies in Intellectual History 23 (Leyden: Brill, 1991).
120. See Thomas Aquinas, *De aeternitate mundi,* Opera omnia iussu Leonis XIII P.M. edita 43 (Rome: Editori di San Tommaso, 1976), pp. 49–89.
121. See Ratzinger, *The Theology of History in St. Bonaventure.*
122. "Medium enim, cum amissum est in circulo, inveniri non potest nisi per duas lineas se orthogonaliter insecantes" (Bonaventure, *In Hexaemeron* 1.24, in Doctoris seraphici S. Bonaventurae Opera omnia 5 [Quaracchi: Collegium S. Bonaventurae, 1891], p. 333; my trans.).
123. Delorme's edition has "C" here, which does not make sense.
124. S. Bonaventurae, *Collationes in Hexaëmeron* 1.24, ed. Ferdinandus Delorme O.F.M., Bibliotheca Franciscana Scholastica Medii Aevi 8 (Quaracchi: Typographia Collegii S. Bonaventurae, 1934), p. 11; my trans. Bonaventure's explanation becomes somewhat elliptical toward the end. Through the center of line AB, another line is drawn that intersects with AB at right angles, leading to two opposite points on the circumference. If this new line, designated as EF, is divided into two equal parts, the point of division will be the center of the circle. (I should like to thank Dr. Charles Burnett, of the Warburg Institute in London, for discussing this passage with me.)
125. Ratzinger, *The Theology of History in St. Bonaventure,* p. 146.

Study 5

1. This attitude is typified in Father Frederick Copleston's popular *History of Philosophy,* where we read that "apart from his devotion to experimental science, St. Albert's thought is of interest to us primarily because of its influence on St. Thomas Aquinas" (Frederick Copleston S.J., *A History of Philosophy,* 2: *Augustine to Scotus* [1950; repr. London: Search Press, 1976], p. 300).
2. See Fernand Van Steenberghen, "Un incident révélateur au Congrès thomiste de 1950," *Revue d'histoire ecclésiastique* 84 (1989):379–390.
3. See Jan A. Aertsen, *Nature and Creature. Thomas Aquinas's Way of Thought,* Studien und Texte zur Geistesgeschichte des Mittelalters 21 (Leyden/New York/Copenhagen/Cologne: Brill, 1988), p. 391: "The torrent of publications about Thomas Aquinas that was started by the commemoration of the seven hundredth anniversary of his death (1974) continues unabated. Yet one who surveys the flood of literature is soon overcome by doubt that it represents any genuine renewal. Is Thomas still a vital, formative force in

philosophical thought? The *élan* with which people turned to Thomas for decades after the encyclical *Aeterni Patris* (1879) seems to have ebbed away."

4. "Nulle lecture n'est parfaitement vraie (au sens où la vérité est l'adéquation parfaite de la lecture et de l'œuvre, ou, pour employer des termes modernes, l'objectivité parfaite de la lecture), mais nulle lecture n'est parfaitement fausse; elle est une lecture humaine, partielle et finie" (Michel Corbin S. J., *Le chemin de la théologie chez Thomas d'Aquin,* Bibliothèque des Archives de philosophie N.S. 16 [Paris: Beauchesne, 1974], p. 48).

5. Martin Blais, *L'autre Thomas d'Aquin* (Québec: Éditions du Boréal, 1990).

6. André Léonard, *Le fondement de la morale. Essai d'éthique philosophique générale,* Recherches morales, Synthèses 15 (Paris: Éditions du Cerf, 1991). I have discussed this remarkable book in "Nova et vetera: 'Le fondement de la morale' de Mgr. A. Léonard," *Revue philosophique de Louvain* 91 (1993):126–136.

7. Pamela M. Hall, *Narrative and the Natural Law. An Interpretation of Thomistic Ethics* (Notre Dame and London: University of Notre Dame Press, 1994).

8. I have developed the interpretation outlined in this study more fully in my book, *Omne ens est aliquid. Introduction à la lecture du "système" philosophique de saint Thomas d'Aquin* (Louvain and Paris: Peeters, 1996).

9. Thomas Aquinas, *Quaestiones disputatae de veritate* 1.1.c, Opera omnia iussu Leonis XIII P.M. edita 22.1 (Rome: Editori di San Tommaso, 1975), p. 5. All translations from Aquinas are my own, and references are to the Leonine edition for all texts available in it.

10. "Si autem modus entis accipiatur secundo modo, scilicet secundum ordinem unius ad alterum, hoc potest esse dupliciter. Uno modo secundum divisionem unius ab altero et hoc exprimit hoc nomen aliquid: dicitur enim aliquid sicut aliud quid, unde sicut ens dicitur unum, in quantum est indivisum in se ita dicitur aliquid, in quantum est ab aliis divisum" (ibid.).

11. In the following article, I have provided some examples of the way in which *aliquid* has been misunderstood: "*Aliquid:* ein vergessenes Transzendentale," in *Was ist Philosophie im Mittelalter? Qu'est-ce que la philosophie au Moyen Âge? What is Philosophy in the Middle Ages? Akten des X. Internationalen Kongresses für mittelalterliche Philosophie der Société Internationale pour l'Étude de la Philosophie Médiévale,* ed. Jan A. Aertsen and Andreas Speer, Miscellanea Mediaevalia 26 (Berlin and New York: de Gruyter, 1998), pp. 529–537. One of the few Thomists who have interpreted *aliquid* correctly is, not surprisingly, a philosopher known for his dialectical bent of mind; see Robert E. Wood, "The Self and the Other: Toward a Re-Interpretation of the Transcendentals," *Philosophy Today* 10 (1966):48–63.

12. As pointed out by Jan A. Aertsen, *Medieval Philosophy and the Transcendentals. The Case of Thomas Aquinas,* Studien und Texte zur Geistesgeschichte des Mittelalters 52 (Leyden/New York/Cologne: Brill, 1996), p. 110.

13. On this point, see Alphonse De Waelhens, *La philosophie et les expériences naturelles,* Phaenomenologica 9 (The Hague: Nijhoff, 1961), p. 109.

14. See, for instance, Thomas Aquinas, *In IV libros Sententiarum* 1.23.1.1.c, Opera Omnia, ed. Roberto Busa S. J., 1 (Stuttgart-Bad Cannstatt: Frommann-Holzboog, 1980), p. 63: "subsistere autem dicit determinatum modum essendi, prout scilicet aliquid est ens per se, non in alio, sicut accidens . . . inde patet quod esse dicit id quod est commune omnibus generibus; sed subsistere et substare id quod est proprium primo praedicamento."

15. *"[R]edire ad essentiam suam* nihil aliud est quam rem subsistere in seipsa" (Thomas Aquinas, *Summa theologiae* 1.14.2.ad 1, Opera omnia iussu Leonis XIII P.M. edita 4 [Rome: Typographia Polyglotta S.C. de Propaganda Fide, 1888], p. 168).

16. "Sed tamen sciendum quod reditio ad essentiam suam in libro De causis nihil aliud dicitur nisi subsistentia rei in se ipsa" (Thomas Aquinas, *Quaestiones disputatae de veritate* 2.2.ad 2, Opera omnia iussu Leonis XIII P.M. edita 22.1, pp. 45–46). Also see *In Librum de causis expositio* 15.15.304, ed. Ceslai Pera O.P., 2nd ed. (Turin and Rome: Marietti, 1972), p. 88.

17. *Summa theologiae* 1–2.3.2.c, Opera omnia iussu Leonis XIII P.M. edita 6 (Rome: Typographia Polyglotta S.C. de Propaganda Fide, 1891), p. 27; ibid. 3.9.1.c, Opera omnia iussu Leonis XIII P.M. edita 11 (Rome: Typographia Polyglotta S.C. de Propaganda Fide, 1903), p. 138.

18. See Robert Spaemann and Reinhard Löw, *Die Frage Wozu? Geschichte und Wiederentdeckung des teleologischen Denkens* (Munich and Zurich: Piper, 1981).

19. *Summa theologiae* 1.5.2.ad 1, Opera omnia iussu Leonis XIII P.M. edita 4, p. 58.

20. *In IV libros Sententiarum* 1.prol., Opera omnia, ed. Busa, 1, p. 1.

21. I borrow this terminology from Stanislas Breton, "La déduction thomiste des catégories," *Revue philosophique de Louvain* 60 (1962):5–32 (at 15).

22. Thomas Aquinas, *Quaestiones disputatae de potentia* 2.1.c, ed. Paul M. Pession, in S. Thomae Aquinatis *Quaestiones disputatae,* 2, 10th ed. (Turin and Rome: Marietti, 1965), p. 25.

23. Thomas Aquinas, *Summa theologiae* 1.4.3.c, Opera omnia iussu Leonis XIII P.M. edita 4, p. 54.

24. The different kinds of causal similarity are most concisely summarized in *Quaestiones disputatae de veritate* 27.7.c, Opera omnia iussu Leonis XIII P.M. edita 22.3 (Rome: Editori di San Tommaso, 1976), p. 815; also see Philipp W. Rosemann, *Omne agens agit sibi simile. A "Repetition" of Scholastic Metaphysics,* Louvain Philosophical Studies 12 (Louvain: Leuven University Press, 1996), pp. 281–288.

25. See, for instance, *Summa theologiae* 1.4.2.c, Opera omnia iussu Leonis XIII P.M. edita 4, p. 51; *Quaestiones disputatae de potentia* 7.5.c, p. 198.

26. There are still other forms of *reditio,* such as the reflexivity of the human mind. Aquinas draws a map of the different kinds of *reditio* in the *Summa contra gentiles* 4.11, Opera omnia iussu Leonis XIII P.M. edita 15 (Rome: apud Sedem Commissionis Leoninae, 1930), p. 32. This well-known chapter is analyzed in detail in Philipp W. Rosemann, *Omne agens agit sibi simile,* pp. 262–270; idem, *Omne ens est aliquid,* pp. 116–139; Reto Luzius Fetz, *Ontologie der Innerlichkeit. "Reditio completa" und "processio interior" bei Thomas von Aquin,* Studia friburgensia 52 (Fribourg: Universitätsverlag, 1975); *Vruchtbaar woord. Weijsgerige beschouwingen bij een theologische tekst van Thomas van Aquino,* ed. Rudi A. te Velde, Wijsgerige Verkenningen 9 (Louvain: Universitaire Pers Leuven, 1990).

27. As we remember, according to Nietzsche, in the earliest days of Greek tragedy, the actor was conceived as the Apollonian incarnation of the god Dionysius.

28. See William Smith, *A Smaller Latin-English Dictionary* (London: John Murray, 1865), s.v. "persona," p. 424.

29. I intend to pursue this problem further in a future study.

30. This etymology of πρόσωπον is not quite correct: πρόσωπον = πρός + ὤψ, ὠπός ('eye, face').

31. Thomas Aquinas, *In IV libros Sententiarum* 1.23.1.1.c, Opera omnia, ed. Busa, 1, p. 63; also see *Quaestiones disputatae de potentia* 9.3.ad 1 and *Summa theologiae* 1.29.3.ad 2.

32. Thomas Aquinas, *Quaestiones disputatae de veritate* 4.6.c, Opera omnia iussu Leonis XIII P.M. edita 22.1, p. 134. In his review of my book *Omne ens est aliquid,* Père Serge-Thomas Bonino O.P. has questioned my use of this text, arguing that it belongs to an early period in St. Thomas's intellectual career (see *Revue thomiste* 97 [1997]:570–574, at 572). There is, however, a perfectly parallel text to be found in the *Summa theologiae,* namely 1.18.4.ad 3.

33. Thomas Aquinas, *Summa theologiae* 1.18.4.ad 3, Omnia opera iussu Leonis XIII P.M. edita 4, p. 230.

34. For the preceding interpretation of the text from the *Quaestiones disputatae de veritate,* see Jean-Luc Marion, *Sur la théologie blanche de Descartes. Analogie, création des vérités éternelles et fondement,* Philosophie d'aujourd'hui (Paris: Presses universitaires de France, 1981), p. 37.

35. Thomas Aquinas, *In IV libros Sententiarum* 1.14.2.2.c, Opera omnia, ed. Busa, 1, p. 36. Also see ibid. 1.2.div. textus, p. 6 and ibid. 4.49.1.3.resp. ad 1^{am} quaest., p. 681.

36. This interpretation is inspired by a remark of Joseph de Finance S.J., *Être et agir dans la philosophie de saint Thomas,* 3rd ed. (Rome: Presses de l'Université Grégorienne, 1965), p. 152: "Toute créature reste en quelque manière extérieure à soi, puisqu'elle ne coïncide pas avec ce qu'elle a de plus central, mais Dieu, en personne, occupe ce centre. Il est plus intérieur aux êtres que ces êtres mêmes."

37. Thomas Aquinas, *Summa contra gentiles* 3.21, Opera Omnia iussu Leonis XIII P.M. edita 14 (Rome: Typis Riccardi Garroni, 1926), p. 50.

38. Thomas Aquinas, *Summa contra gentiles* 2.18, Opera omnia iussu Leonis XIII P.M. edita 13 (Rome: Typis Riccardi Garroni, 1918), p. 305.

39. Thomas Aquinas, *Quaestiones disputatae de potentia* 3.3.c, p. 43.

40. In what follows, references to God by means of the masculine personal pronoun are made in accordance with traditional usage; I do not intend to make any statement about God's "gender."

41. Thomas Aquinas, *Super evangelium S. Ioannis lectura* 1.11.213, ed. Raphael Cai O.P., 5th ed. (Turin and Rome: Marietti, 1952), p. 43; also see *In IV libros Sententiarum* 4.49.2.3.ad 3 and *Summa theologiae* 1.12.7.c.

42. Thomas Aquinas, *Quaestiones disputatae de veritate* 8.2.c, Opera omnia iussu Leonis XIII P.M. edita 22.2 (Rome: ad Sanctae Sabinae, 1972), p. 221.

43. For this interpretation of the beatific vision, see Antoine Vergote, "Psychanalyse et religion," in *Psychanalyse. L'homme et ses destins,* ed. Jean Florence et al. (Louvain and Paris: Peeters, 1993), pp. 311–338, esp. p. 322.

44. See Thomas Aquinas, *In IV libros Sententiarum* 2.1.1.4.c, Opera omnia, ed. Busa, 1, pp. 124–125 and *Summa theologiae* 1.105.5.c.

45. Thomas Aquinas, *Quaestiones disputatae de veritate* 12.6.c, Opera omnia iussu Leonis XIII P.M. edita 22.2, p. 388.

46. See Thomas Aquinas, *Summa theologiae* 1.2.3.c.

47. Thomas Aquinas, *Quaestiones disputatae de veritate* 11.1.ad 13, Opera omnia iussu Leonis XIII P.M. edita 22.2, p. 353.

48. Thomas Aquinas, *Summa theologiae* 1.3.prol., Opera omnia iussu Leonis XIII P.M. edita 4, p. 35.

49. Thomas Aquinas, *Quaestiones disputatae de veritate* 2.1.ad 9, Opera omnia iussu Leonis XIII P.M. edita 22.1, p. 42.

50. For an introduction to the history of negative theology, see Deirdre Carabine, *The Unknown God. Negative Theology in the Platonic Tradition: Plato to Eriugena,* Louvain Theological & Pastoral Monographs 19 (Louvain: Peeters; Grand Rapids, Michigan: Eerdmans, 1995). Jean-Luc Marion offers a contemporary reappraisal of the tradition of negative theology in his influential *God Without Being,* trans. Thomas A. Carlson, Religion and Postmodernism (Chicago and London: University of Chicago Press, 1995). For a contemporary negative theology from a Derridian perspective, see Mark C. Taylor, *ERRING. A Postmodern A /theology* (Chicago and London: University of Chicago Press, 1984).

51. Hall, *Narrative and the Natural Law,* p. 105.

52. Mark D. Jordan, *The Invention of Sodomy in Christian Theology,* The Chicago Series on Sexuality, History, and Society (Chicago and London: University of Chicago Press, 1997), pp. 165 and 158, respectively. In two previous publications, I have tried to sketch out some implications of the attempt to bring negative theology to bear upon the ethical field: *Omne ens est aliquid,*

pp. 163–190 and "Penser l'Autre: l'éthique de la théologie négative," *Revue philosophique de Louvain* 93 (1995):408–427.

53. Ernst Cassirer, *An Essay on Man* (New Haven and London:Yale University Press, 1944), p. 12; also see the useful essay by John Saward, "Towards an Apophatic Anthropology," *Irish Theological Quarterly* 41 (1974):222–234.

54. André Léonard, "Compte rendu de Martin Rhonheimer, *Natur als Grundlage der Moral,*" *Studia moralia* 26 (1988):291–300, at 293.

55. "[M]ateria moralis est varia et deformis, non habens omnimodam certitudinem" (Thomas Aquinas, *Sententia libri Ethicorum* 1.3, Opera omnia iussu Leonis XIII P.M. edita 47.1 [Rome: ad Sanctae Sabinae, 1969], p. 11).

56. Thomas Aquinas, *Summa theologiae* 1–2.94.2.c, Opera omnia iussu Leonis XIII P.M. edita 7 (Rome:Typographia Polyglotta S.C. de Propaganda Fide, 1892), p. 170.

57. See Thomas Aquinas, *In IV libros Sententiarum* 2.24.2.4.c, Opera omnia, ed. Busa, 1, p. 195.

58. See Thomas Aquinas, *Summa theologiae* 1–2.5.8.c, Opera omnia iussu Leonis XIII P.M. edita 6, p. 54.

59. A quotation from the Roman jurist Ulpian (170–228).

60. Thomas Aquinas, *Summa theologiae* 1–2.94.2.c, Opera omnia iussu Leonis XIII P.M. edita 7, p. 170.

61. Ibid. 1–2.34.1.c, Opera omnia iussu Leonis XIII P.M. edita 6, p. 235.

62. Ibid. 1–2.94.4.ad 3, Opera omnia iussu Leonis XIII P.M. edita 7, p. 172.

63. See Thomas Aquinas, *In IV libros Sententiarum* 2.24.2.4.c, Opera omnia, ed. Busa, 1, p. 195; *Summa theologiae* 1–2.94.4.c, Opera omnia iussu Leonis XIII P.M. edita 7, pp. 171–172.

64. Thomas Aquinas, *Summa theologiae* 2–2.64.2.c, Opera omnia iussu Leonis XIII P.M. edita 9 (Rome:Typographia Ployglotta S.C. de Propaganda Fide, 1897), p. 68.

65. Léonard, *Le fondement de la morale,* p. 257.

66. Thomas Aquinas, *In IV libros Sententiarum* 4.33.1.2.c and ad 1, Opera omnia, ed. Busa, 1, p. 598. I am not aware of the existence of such a radical text in Aquinas's later work. In the *Summa,* Aquinas no longer speaks of the variability of human nature, and exceptions to the natural law seem to be identified as clearly being due to deficiencies. See, for instance, *Summa theologiae* 1–2.94.4.c and 1–2.31.7.c—although even these texts leave room for interpretation.

67. Thomas Aquinas, *Summa theologiae* 1–2.91.4.c, Opera omnina iussu Leonis XIII P.M. edita 7, p. 156.

68. Thomas Aquinas, *In IV libros Sententiarum* 2.24.2.4.c, Opera omnia, ed. Busa, 1, p. 195.

69. Thomas Aquinas, *Quaestiones disputatae de veritate* 17.1.ad 1 in contr., Opera omnia iussu Leonis XIII P.M. edita 22.2, p. 518.

70. Ibid. 17.3.ad 4, p. 523.

71. Léonard, *Le fondement de la morale,* p. 311.

72. See Thomas Aquinas, *Summa theologiae* 1–2.19.5.c, Opera omnia iussu Leonis XIII P.M. edita 6, p. 145.

73. On these questions, see ibid. 17.1–5, with Léonard's commentary in *Le fondement de la morale,* pp. 308–317.

Study 6

1. The Condemnation of 1277 was first published in *Chartularium Universitatis Parisiensis sub auspiciis Consilii generalis Facultatum Parisiensium,* ed. Henri Denifle and Émile Chatelain, 1 (Paris: Delalain, 1889; repr. Brussels: Culture et Civilisation, 1964), pp. 543–555. Roland Hissette, in his fundamental study, *Enquête sur les 219 articles condamnés à Paris le 7 mars 1277,* Philosophes médiévaux 22 (Louvain: Publications universitaires; Paris: Vander-Oyez, 1977), rearranges the propositions in a more "logical" order, which he adopts from Pierre Mandonnet, *Siger de Brabant et l'averroïsme latin au XIIIe siècle,* 2 vols., 2nd ed., Les Philosophes Belges 6–7 (Louvain: Publications universitaires, 1908–1911). As this order corresponds to no historical reality, I have chosen to use the text provided in Kurt Flasch, *Aufklärung im Mittelalter? Die Verurteilung von 1277,* Excerpta classica 6 (Mainz: Dieterich'sche Verlagsbuchhandlung, 1989). I do not, however, follow Flasch in his interpretation of the condemnation, on which see Roland Hissette, "Note sur le syllabus 'antirationaliste' du 7 mars 1277," *Revue philosophique de Louvain* 88 (1990):404–416. The new critical edition of the Condemnation for which medievalists have long been waiting has now been prepared by David Piché, of the Université Laval in Québec, and should appear shortly: *La condamnation parisienne de 1277. Nouvelle édition, traduction, introduction et commentaire,* Sic et non (Paris: Vrin, forthcoming).

2. See Hissette, *Enquête sur les 219 articles,* p. 8: "les 219 propositions se suivent dans un désordre étonnant." Also see John F. Wippel, "The Condemnations of 1270 and 1277 at Paris," *Journal of Medieval and Renaissance Studies* 7 (1977):169–201, at 171: "evidently haphazard nature of the prohibited doctrines."

3. Flasch, *Aufklärung im Mittelalter?,* p. 89.

4. Ibid., p. 112.

5. Ibid., p. 137.

6. Ibid., p. 89.

7. See Fernand Van Steenberghen, *La philosophie au XIIIe siècle,* 2nd ed., Philosophes médiévaux 28 (Louvain-la-Neuve: Éditions de l'Institut supérieur de philosophie; Louvain and Paris: Peeters, 1991), pp. 321–370.

8. On Siger, the standard work of reference is Fernand Van Steenberghen, *Maître Siger de Brabant,* Philosophes médiévaux 21 (Louvain: Publications universitaires; Paris: Vander-Oyez, 1977).

9. See Van Steenberghen, *La philosophie au XIIIe siècle*, pp. 361–370.
10. See Mandonnet, *Siger de Brabant*, 1, pp. 148–153.
11. Van Steenberghen, *Maître Siger de Brabant*, p. 243.
12. See Hissette, *Enquête sur les 219 articles condamnés.*
13. See ibid., pp. 276–277.
14. Ibid., p. 293.
15. See ibid., pp. 274–275.
16. See ibid., p. 294.
17. See Martin Grabmann, "Das Werk *De amore* des Andreas Capellanus und das Verurteilungsdekret des Bischofs Stephan Tempier von Paris vom 7. März 1277," *Speculum* 7 (1932):75–79.
18. See Hissette, *Enquête sur les 219 articles condamnés*, pp. 294–300.
19. See ibid., p. 315.
20. Van Steenberghen, *Maître Siger de Brabant*, p. 74.
21. Ibid., p. 146.
22. See Hissette, *Enquête sur les 219 articles condamnés*, p. 318.
23. The "state of the art" in research on the condemnation of 1277 in reflected in several contributions to the Tenth International Congress on Medieval Philosophy: see especially the contributions by Alain de Libera, Luca Bianchi, John E. Murdoch, Silvia Donati, and Claude Lafleur in *Was ist Philosophie im Mittelalter? Qu'est-ce que la philosophie au Moyen Âge? What is Philosophy in the Middle Ages? Akten des X. Internationalen Kongresses für mittelalterliche Philosophie der Société Internationale pour l'Étude de la Philosophie Médiévale*, ed. Jan A. Aertsen and Andreas Speer, Miscellanea Mediaevalia 26 (Berlin and New York: de Gruyter, 1998).
24. See, for instance, Wippel, "The Condemnations of 1270 and 1277," p. 186.
25. See Alain de Libera, *Penser au Moyen Âge*, Chemins de pensée (Paris: Éditions du Seuil, 1991); also see Luca Bianchi, *Il vescovo e i filosofi: la condanna parigina del 1277 e l'evoluzione dell'aristotelismo scolastico*, Quodlibet 6 (Bergamo: Lubrina, 1990).
26. De Libera, *Penser au Moyen Âge*, pp. 123–124.
27. Ibid., p. 194.
28. Ibid., p. 194.
29. See ibid., p. 204.
30. See Pierre Hadot, *Philosophy as a Way of Life: Spiritual Exercises from Socrates to Foucault*, ed. Arnold I. Davidson, trans. Michael Chase (Oxford, England and Cambridge, Massachusetts: Blackwell, 1995); and Juliusz Domański, *La philosophie, théorie ou manière de vivre? Les controverses de l'Antiquité à la Renaissance*, Vestigia 18 (Fribourg: Éditions universitaires; Paris: Éditions du Cerf, 1996).
31. Aristotle, *Metaphysics* 12.7, 1072b26–27, ed. William David Ross, 2 vols. (Oxford: Clarendon Press, 1924).

32. The Latin *reflecto* means "to turn back," designating a circular kind of movement.
33. De Libera, *Penser au Moyen Âge*, p. 203.
34. Ibid., p. 15.
35. Ibid., p. 204.
36. A reprint of the first edition of the *Malleus* has recently been made available: see Heinrich Kramer (Institoris), *Malleus Maleficarum 1487,* ed. Günter Jerouschek, Rechtsgeschichte, Zivilisationsprozeß, Psychohistorie, Quellen und Studien 1 (Hildesheim, Zurich, New York: Olms, 1992). There are modern translations of the *Malleus maleficarum* into German and French, but not into English. See Henri Institoris (Kraemer) and Jacques Sprenger, *Le marteau des sorcières,* trad. Amant Danet, Civilisations et mentalités (Paris: Plon, 1973); Jakob Sprenger and Heinrich Institoris, *Der Hexenhammer (Malleus maleficarum),* trans. J. W. R. Schmidt, 13th ed. of the repr. (1906; repr. Munich: Deutscher Taschenbuch-Verlag, 1997).
37. Günter Jerouschek, "Einführung: 500 Jahre Hexenhammer," in Kramer, *Malleus Maleficarum,* pp. v–xxix, at p. v. The volume also contains an English translation of Jerouschek's introduction (pp. xxxi–lv); however, as the translation is often unidiomatic, my references are to the original German text.
38. Ibid., p. v.
39. This is not to say the witch-hunt was not part of a larger movement toward persecution and the enforcement of orthodoxy that started as early as the eleventh century. Without my being able to do justice to the full complexity of the problem, it is significant to note that "considerable ambiguity in attitudes towards persecution" persisted "throughout Latin Christendom in the period from 1000 to 1350" (Peter D. Diehl, "Overcoming Reluctance to prosecute Heresy in Thirteenth-Century Italy," in *Christendom and Its Discontents. Exclusion, Persecution, and Rebellion, 1000–1500,* ed. Scott L. Waugh and Peter D. Diehl [Cambridge: Cambridge University Press, 1996], pp. 47–66, at p. 48).
40. Jerouschek, "Einführung," p. vi.
41. For the table of contents of the *Malleus maleficarum,* see fols. 2r–3v.
42. Ibid., fol. 4r.
43. See ibid. 2.1.2, fol. 48v.
44. See ibid. The historian Brian P. Levack has identified a number of core characteristics that make up what he calls the "cumulative concept of witchcraft"; see Brian P. Levack, *The Witch-Hunt in Early Modern Europe,* 2nd ed. (London and New York: Longman, 1995), pp. 29–50.
45. See Kramer, *Malleus maleficarum* 2.1, fol. 43v.
46. Ibid. 2.2.1, fol. 79v.
47. Ibid. 2.2, fol. 77v.

48. Jos Decorte, *De waanzin van het intellect. Twee modellen van de eeuwige strijd tussen goed en kwaad* (Kapellen: DNB/Uitgeverij Pelckmans; Kampen: Uitgeverij Kok Agora, 1989), p. 15; also see p. 42.

49. Decorte's analysis of the Scholastic episteme follows the one suggested by Foucault in *The Order of Things. An Archaeology of the Human Sciences* (New York: Vintage Books, 1994).

50. See Decorte, *De waanzin van het intellect,* pp. 44–45.

51. See Kramer, *Malleus maleficarum* 2.2, fol. 48v.

52. See Decorte, *De waanzin van het intellect,* p. 46.

53. See Kramer, *Malleus maleficarum* 3.14, fol. 105v.

54. Levack, *The Witch-Hunt in Early Modern Europe,* p. 20.

55. See Kramer, *Malleus maleficarum* 3.14, fol. 105v.

56. See ibid. 3.13–17, fols. 105v–110r.

57. See Levack, *The Witch-Hunt in Early Modern Europe,* p. 25.

58. Kramer, *Malleus maleficarum* 3.13, fol. 106r.

59. Ibid. 2.1, fol. 43v.

60. Ibid. 1.6, fol. 20v.

61. See Levack, *The Witch-Hunt in Early Modern Europe,* p. 133.

62. See Jerouschek, "Einführung," p. vi.

63. See Decorte, *De waanzin van het intellect,* p. 50.

64. See Kramer, *Malleus maleficarum* 3.14 and 15, fols. 106r and 107v.

65. Levack, *The Witch-Hunt in Early Modern Europe,* p. 156.

66. Using the explanatory model developed in this section, one could try to examine whether there are similar connections between the Enlightenment project and colonialism/slavery, or between the culture of the Weimar republic and Nazism.

67. The following book is useful to give the contemporary reader a taste of Suárez's *Disputations:* Jorge J. E. Gracia and Douglas Davis, *The Metaphysics of Good and Evil According to Suárez. Metaphysical Disputations X and XI and Selected Passages from Disputation XXIII and other Works. Translation, with Introduction, Notes, and Glossary,* Analytica (Munich, Hamden, and Vienna: Philosophia, 1989).

68. See Christiane Schildknecht, "Erleuchtung und Tarnung. Überlegungen zur literarischen Form bei René Descartes," in *Literarische Formen der Philosophie,* ed. Gottfried Gabriel and Christiane Schildknecht (Stuttgart: Metzler, 1990), pp. 92–120.

69. Ibid., p. 102.

70. In this context, and in light of our remarks concerning changing attitudes toward textuality in study 3, it is interesting to note that the Reformation was prepared by, and in turn contributed to, changed attitudes toward the text of Scripture; see Jaroslav Pelikan, *The Reformation of the Bible—The Bible of the Reformation.* Catalog of the Exhibition by Valerie R. Hotchkiss and David Price (New Haven and London: Yale University Press; Dallas: Southern Methodist University—Bridwell Library, 1996).

71. Thomas Aquinas, *In IV libros Sententiarum* 1.8.1.2.c, S. Thomae Aquinatis Opera omnia, ed. Roberto Busa S.J., 1 (Stuttgart-Bad Cannstatt: Frommann-Holzboog, 1980), p. 22.

72. See Jean-Luc Marion, *Sur la théologie blanche de Descartes. Analogie, création des vérités éternelles et fondement,* Philosophie d'aujourd'hui (Paris: Presses universitaires de France, 1981), pp. 43–139.

73. Ibid., p. 96.

74. On this text, see Marion, *Sur la théologie blanche,* pp. 102–103 with note 9.

75. In the sense of "aim" or "goal," but also in the sense of "point where something stops, or beyond which it does not exist."

76. The standard work on indulgences, considered in light of the history of the sacrament of penance, is still Bernhard Poschmann, *Der Ablass im Licht der Bussgeschichte,* Theophaneia 4 (Bonn: Hanstein, 1948); also see Herbert Vorgrimler, *Buße und Krankensalbung,* Handbuch der Dogmengeschichte 4.3, 2nd ed. (Freiburg, Basle, and Vienna: Herder, 1978).

77. See Poschmann, *Der Ablass,* pp. 1–14.

78. See ibid., p. 25.

79. See ibid., pp. 45 and 103.

80. See ibid., pp. 44–46.

81. See ibid., p. 56. Poschmann seems to be contradicting himself when, on page 87, he remarks that it is "historically untenable" to say that the indulgences came to be applied only gradually to possible punishments in the hereafter.

82. See ibid., pp. 82–99.

83. Vorgrimler, *Buße und Krankensalbung,* p. 208.

84. See Poschmann, *Der Ablass,* pp. 63–68.

85. Vorgrimler, *Buße und Krankensalbung,* p. 209.

86. Bernhard Lohse, *Martin Luther: An Introduction to His Life and Work,* trans. Robert C. Schultz (Philadelphia: Fortress Press, 1986), p. 44.

87. See Martin Luther, *Psalm 26,* trans. Jaroslav Pelikan, in *Luther's Works,* 12, ed. Jaroslav Pelikan (Saint Louis: Concordia, 1955), pp. 181–194, at p. 187: "I can say, 'Thus my teaching stands, and so it is correct.' It is a good teaching. This is evident from the fact that it builds upon the Lord Christ, it lets God be our Lord God, and it gives God the glory."

88. On the theme of the hidden God in Luther, see Otto Hermann Pesch, *Hinführung zu Luther,* 2nd ed. (Mainz: Matthias-Grünewald-Verlag, 1983), pp. 244–263.

89. *Œuvres de Descartes,* ed. Charles Adam and Paul Tannery, new ed., 5 (Paris: Vrin, 1974), p. 9, ll. 16 and 7 (Paris:Vrin, 1973), p. 549, ll. 20–21.

90. See Martin Luther, *Disputation against Scholastic Theology,* trans. Harold J. Grimm, in *Luther's Works,* 31, ed. Harold J. Grimm, 3rd printing (Philadelphia: Fortress Press, 1971), pp. 3–16.

91. I have discussed this important book in "Der maskierte Philosoph. Die verborgene Theologie des Cartesianismus," *Frankfurter Allgemeine Zeitung,* 11 March 1992: N5.

92. See, for instance, *Œuvres de Descartes,* ed. Charles Adam and Paul Tannery, new ed., 1 (Paris: Vrin, 1974), p. 151, l. 1–p. 152, l. 9; and Marion, *Sur la théologie blanche,* pp. 27–42.

93. See Marion, *Sur la théologie blanche,* p. 296.

94. See ibid., pp. 135–139.

95. See René Descartes, *Meditation* 3, in *Œuvres de Descartes* 7, p. 51, ll. 18–20: "Sed ex hoc uno quod Deus me creavit, valde credibile est me quodammodo ad imaginem et similitudinem ejus factum esse."

96. See Marion, *Sur la théologie blanche,* pp. 427–454.

Appendix

1. See Fernand Van Steenberghen, *La bibliothèque du philosophe médiéviste,* Philosophes médiévaux 19 (Louvain: Publications universitaires; Paris: Béatrice-Nauwelaerts, 1974).

2. See Étienne Gilson, *History of Christian Philosophy in the Middle Ages,* The Random House Lifetime Library (New York: Random House, 1955).

3. See David Knowles, *The Evolution of Medieval Thought,* 2nd ed., ed. D. E. Luscombe and C. N. L. Brooke (London and New York: Longman, 1988).

4. David Plotnikoff, "Don't Be Surprised If a Web Site That's Here Today Vanishes Tomorrow," *The Dallas Morning News,* vol. 149, no. 329, 25 August 1998:2F.

5. For a comprehensive list of Web sites devoted to medieval thought, see Jacob Schmutz, "La philosophie médiévale sur l'Internet," *Bulletin de philosophie médiévale* 40 (1998): 117–28.

SUBJECT INDEX

Only the main text of this book has been indexed (not the notes).

abbreviations, *see* handwriting
Aeterni Patris (encyclical), 2–3, 133
aliquid (transcendental), 135–7, 185
ἀνακάμπτειν (returning upon oneself), 118
  compare reditio
analogy, 174–5, 180–1
Apollonian (and Dionysian), 20–4, 49
archaeological method (in Foucault)
  categories, 40–3
  definition, 39
  as "history of the Same," 36
  Kantian roots, 38
  non-reductionist character, 28, 31
  political implications, 40
  no "science," 39
architecture (Gothic), 66–8, 202
Aristotelian tradition, 54–8
auctoritas (and *ratio*), 47, 90–1, 100–01, 184

beatific vision, 146–7
book metaphysics, 94–5, 101, 157

Cambridge History of Later Medieval Philosophy, 4–5
Carolingian renaissance, 60, 63, 68, 71
cathedrals, *see* architecture (Gothic)

circularity, *see* self-reflexivity, *compare* linearity
concordantia, 68
Condemnation of 1277, 81, 159–65, 185–6, 204–5
creation, 144–6
curricula, 76–82, 200

degré zéro, see zero degree
dialectics
  of Apollonian and Dionysian forces (Nietzsche), 20–3
  in Gothic architecture, 67, 100
  in Gothic handwriting, 63, 66, 100
  of history (Foucault), 24–6, 33–5
  of madness and reason (Foucault), 28–35
  of the One and the many (Plotinus), 123–7
  in Thomas Aquinas, 136, 139, 147–49, 156
Dionysian, *see* Apollonian
discours "en retour," see reverse discourse
double truth, 160, 162

editorial techniques, *see* textual criticism
episteme, 36, 38, 159
eternal truths (in Descartes), 180–1
etymology, 135, 141
evil, 170–2, 186

five ways, 48, 133, 148

Gloss, 61–3, 69, 166, plate 2

handwriting
  abbreviations, 63–6, 199–200
  Caroline minuscule, 60–1, plate 1
  Gothic, 61–3, plates 2 and 3
  as historical a priori, 60–6
  literature on, 199
heterodox Aristotelianism, 161–4,
  196–7
historical a priori, 36–8
"human begets human" (ἄνθρωπος
  ἄνθρωπον γεννᾷ), 120–21, 140,
  160

Iliad, 49
indexes, 98–100, 200, plates 5 and 6
indulgences, 176–9
intellectual practices, 7, 59, 100, 183,
  200–2

Lachmannian method, see textual
  criticism
lectio divina, see reading techniques
liberal arts, 76, 78–80
limit-experiences, 24–6
linearity
  in Aristotle, 116, 117–18, 130
  in biblical Christianity, 129–30,
    164, 185, 203
  in Bonaventure, 131–2, fig. 4.1
  in Homer, 111
  in Plato, 113–14
  in Plotinus, 126
  in Thomas Aquinas, 142–4
  compare self-reflexivity
literary forms, 200
  commentary, 86–7, 109–10, 184
  philosophical relevance, 85–6
  quaestio, 15–16, 88–93, 166–7,
    173–4, 184

λόγος (and μῦθος), 48–50, 183

madness
  Christian folly and Greek wisdom,
    50–4, 183
  and reason according to Foucault,
    28–35
  and reason in the witch-hunt,
    168–72, 198–9
manifestatio, 66–7
media via, 101
modernity (origins of), 165–81, 186,
  205–6
monastic culture, 68–9, 96–7, 201
μῦθος (see λόγος)

natural law, 149–53
negative theology, 63–6, 147–8,
  179–80, 202
Neoscholasticism, 2–5, 134, 189, 194–5
new medievalism
  avant la lettre, xii
  definition, ix–x
  in philosophical literature, 5–9,
    196–8
  and postmodern culture, 9–10,
    13–17
  programmatic essays on, 195–6
  roots in Kantianism, 1
  and textual criticism, 10–13
νόησις νοήσεως (self-thinking
  thought), 119–20, 123

pecia, see transmission (of texts)
person (persona, πρόσωπον), 141
post-structuralism, 39
Presocratics, 49
psychoanalysis, 32

quaestio, see literary forms
quidam, 90

ratio (see auctoritas)

reading techniques, 7, 96–100, 101, 201–2
reditio, 137–8, 140
   compare ἀνακάμπτειν
Reformation, 179
resemblance, 105–7, 168–9
   see also similarity
return (of the repressed), 22, 23, 25–7, 30, 32–3, 35, 170, 186
reverse discourse, 4

Scholasticism
   defined doctrinally, 45–6
   defined formally, 46–8
   Foucauldian approach to definition, 48–54
   transformation, 166–79
script, *see* handwriting
scriptorium, see transmission (of texts)
self-reflexivity
   in Aristotle, 115–22
   in Bonaventure, 131–2, fig. 4.1
   in Homer, 111
   literature on, 203
   in Parmenides, 111–12
   in Plato, 112–15
   in Plotinus, 124–8
   in Thomas Aquinas, 136–8, 142–7, 203, fig. 5.1
   in the witch-hunt, 169–70
   compare linearity
similarity (between cause and effect), 110–11, 114, 117, 120–22, 139–40, 144, 184–5
   see also self-reflexivity
stationarius, see transmission (of texts)
structuralism, 39

"study-guide" (codex Ripoll 109), 79–82, 86, 100
sub-ject, 38–9, 97, 99

teaching methods, 200
   disputations, 87–8
   lectures, 86, 109–10
text (world as), 94–5, 97, 101, 108–10, 128–9, 201
textual criticism
   diplomatic edition, 72
   history of, 71
   Lachmannian method, 11–13, 72–6
   literature on, 199–200
   philosophical presuppositions, 10–13, 75
tragedy/tragic, 20–4
transcendentals, 134–7
transmission (of texts)
   pecia, 69–70
   scriptorium, 69
   stationarius, 69
   types of scribal errors, 70–1

University of Paris
   career of a student, 83–5
   foundation, 82–3
   see also teaching methods, "study-guide"
univocity, 175–6, 179–80

way of life (philosophy as), 163–5, 185–6
witch-hunt, 165–72, 186, 205
Word (Second Person of the Trinity), 95–7, 142–5, 149, 184

zero degree, 25–27, 33

NAME INDEX

Only the main text of this book has been indexed (not the notes).

Abelard, P., 179
Aertsen, J.A., 197–8, 203
Aischylos, 21, 49
Albert the Great, Saint, 5–6, 83, 133, 178
Albrecht of Brandenburg, 179
Alexander II, Pope, 178
Alexander, D., 193
Andronikos of Rhodes, 56
Anselm of Canterbury, Saint, 47
Aristotle, 10–11, 50, 52, 54–8, 81–2, 115–22, 137, 140, 157, 160–1, 164–5, 166, 203
Augustine, Saint, 77–8, 106, 122, 166

Baeumker, C., xii
Ballew, L., 111, 113, 116, 203
Bartlett, A.C., 103–4, 198
Benedict of Nursia, Saint, 53, 71, 96
Bernauer, J., 36
Bianchi, L., 205
Bischoff, B., 199
Blais, M., 8, 134, 204
Bloch, R.H., ix, 195–6
Boethius, A.M.S. (Roman philosopher), 56, 76, 79, 81, 141
Boethius of Dacia (medieval Aristotelian), 162, 164–5
Bonaventure, Saint, 83, 94–5, 101, 109, 131–2, 203
Bonino, S.-T., 204

Boyle, L.E., 199
Braun, L., 2
Brownlee, K., 196
Brownlee, M.S., 196

Cantor, N.F., 195
Capellanus, A., 162
Cappelli, A., 64, 199
Carruthers, M., 201
Cassirer, E., 1, 149
Charlemagne, 60, 71
Chatelain, H., 204
Chenu, M.-D., xi-xii, 45, 76, 88
Christian of Stablo, 64–5
Clark, W.W., 202
Copeland, R., 196
Corbin, M., 134
Coreth, E., 194
Cullmann, O., 129–30, 185, 203

Dagenais, J., 97, 202
Damico, H., 195
Danet, A., 205
Decorte, J., 6, 167–8, 170, 198–9, 205
de Finance, J., 204
de Hamel, C., 61, 69
de Libera, A., 5–6, 8, 133, 163–4, 185, 190, 196–7, 205
Denifle, H., 204
de Saussure, F., 39, 94
Descartes, R., 173–4, 180–1, 206
De Wulf, M., xii, 45–6, 192, 195–6
Didi-Huberman, G., 202
Dinshaw, C., 198

Dionysius the Areopagite, Pseudo-, 71, 90, 91, 122, 166
Dupré, L., ix, 194

Eriugena, John Scottus, 6, 12–13, 46, 200
Euripides, 22, 23

Flasch, K., 6, 160–1, 197, 205
Follon, J., 196
Foucault, M., 4, 10, 19–44, 59, 183–7
    Archaeology of Knowledge, 35–43, 104
    Madness and Civilization, 19, 24–35, 104, 159
    and the Middle Ages, 103–4, 198–9
    and Nietzsche, 27–8, 33
    Order of Things, 38–9, 105–10, 128
    "A Preface to Transgression," 103–5
Frederick II, the Great, 58
Fuhrmann, H., 12, 75

Gilson, É., 3, 45, 189, 195–6, 206
Grabmann, M., xii, 47, 54, 76, 79, 195–6
Greetham, D.C., 70–1, 74, 199
Grosseteste, Robert, 6, 71, 81, 98–9

Hall, P., 134, 149
Hamesse, J., 195, 200
Haskins, C.H., 58
Hegel, G.W.F., 9–10, 14–16, 23–4
Heidegger, M., 10, 66, 197
Hesiod, 49
Hissette, R., 162–3, 204–5
Holtz, L., 7, 201
Homer, 49, 111
Houseman, A.E., 74
Ḥunain b. Isḥaq, 57

Ibn Rushd (Averroës), 58, 81, 160–3
Ibn Sīnā (Avicenna), 58, 81, 166
Illich, I., 7, 99, 201

Imbach, R., 7, 190, 192, 194, 197
Inglis, J., 194–5

Jaeger, W., 11
Jeauneau, É., 12–13, 76, 200
Jenkins, J.I., 8
Jerouschek, G., 166–7, 172, 205
Jordan, M.D., 149
Justinian I, the Great, 53

Kant, I., 1, 23–4, 36–7, 38, 40, 85, 194
Kleutgen, A., 194
Knowles, D., 189, 195
Koyré, A., 206
Kraft, H., 199
Kramer, H., 165–72, 205
Kretzmann, N., 192

Lachmann, K., 11, 72
Lafleur, C., 79
Lawton, D., 196
Leclercq, J., 96–7, 201
Leo XIII, Pope, 2–3
Léonard, A., 134, 149–50, 152
Levack, B.P., 169, 172, 205
Lewis, C.S., 195
Lohse, B., 179
Lombard, Peter, 61–2, 84–5, 88
Lottin, O., xii, 195
Lupus of Ferrières, 71
Luther, M., 85, 179–80

al-Ma'mūn, 57
Maas, P., 72, 74–5, 200
Macey, D., 103
Maierù, A., 194
Maimonides, Moses, 58
Mandonnet, P., 162–3
Marenbon, J., 7–8, 190, 198
Marichal, R., 60–3, 66
Marion, J.-L., 175–6, 180–1, 206
McCool, G.A., 194
McEvoy, J., 6, 196

Mercier, D., 192
Mersenne, M., 180
Michael Scotus, 58, 81
Migne, J.-P., 190–1, 195
Minnis, A.J., 100
Moran, D., 6
Morey, C.R., 66, 67

Nardi, B., xii
Neidl, W.M., 194
Nestle, W., 53
Nichols, S.G., ix, 196
Nietzsche, F., 19–24, 183, 186
Normore, C., 198

O'Brien O'Keeffe, K., 198, 201
Oehler, K., 120, 203

Panofsky, E., 66–8, 195, 202
Parmenides, 49, 111–12
Paul, Saint (Apostle), 51–2, 171, 183
Pelzer, A., xii, 200
Pfligersdorffer, G., 194
Piché, D., 204
Pieper, J., 204
Pindar, 49
Pinel, P., 31
Plato, 22–3, 40, 50, 52, 81, 112–15, 157, 203
Plotinus, 52, 122–28, 203
Pluta, O., 200
Porphyry, 52
Poschmann, B., 178
Proclus, 138, 203
Prouvost, G., 8–9
Putallaz, F.-X., 7

Radding, C.M., 202
Ratzinger, J., 131, 203
Rauch, W., 95
Rosemann, P.W., 9, 196, 203–4
Rouse, M., 98, 201
Rouse, R., 98, 201

Rutten, C., 10–11

Scase, W., 196
Schildknecht, C., 174
Schmidt, J.W.R., 205
Schönberger, R., 196
Schopenhauer, A., 23–4
Schulthess, P., 190
Siger of Brabant, 162, 164–5
Socrates, 20, 22–3
Sophocles, 21, 49
Southern, R.W., 47, 93, 195–6
Spade, P.V., 194
Speer, A., 197
Sprenger, J., 205
Stiennon, J., 199
Stöckl, A., 194
Sturlese, L., 6
Suárez, F., 173–4, 175–6, 179–80, 206

Tempier, É., 159–65, 185, 205
Tertullian, 53, 77
Tetsuro, S., 192
Thomas Aquinas, Saint, 110, 133–58, 165–6, 184
    on analogy, 174–5
    on the beatific vision, 146–7
    contemporary relevance, 14–17
    on creation, 144–6
    on eternity of the world, 131
    on ethics, 149–56
    on final causality, 138
    five ways, 48, 133, 148
    on indulgences, 178
    on negative theology, 147–9
    new approaches to his thought, 8–9, 204
    on operation, 138–42
    on the transcendentals, 134–7
    use of the *quaestio,* 88–93
Traube, L., 64–5

Van Engen, J., 195

Van Steenberghen, F., xii, 3, 46, 76, 79, 161–3, 189, 192, 194, 196

Vernant, J.-P., 48–50

Vignaux, P., 9

Vorgrimler, H., 178

Warwick Frese, D., 198, 201

Wéber, É.-H., 204

Weijers, O., 7, 59–60, 86–8, 183, 200–1

West, M.L., 75, 200

Wilamowitz-Möllendorff, U. von, 20

William of Moerbeke, 58

Wood, R.E., 204

Zimmermann, A., 197